WORK AND POWER

WORK AND POWER

The Liberation of Work and the Control of Political Power

Edited by

Tom R. Burns
Universities of Oslo and Stockholm

Lars Erik Karlsson
University of Luleå

Veljko Rus
University of Ljubljana

 SAGE Studies in International Sociology **18**
sponsored by the International Sociological Association/ISA

For information address

SAGE Publications Ltd
28 Banner Street
London EC1Y 8QE

SAGE Publications Inc
275 South Beverly Drive
Beverly Hills, California 90212

British Library Cataloguing in Publication Data
Work and power. — (Sage studies in international sociology; 18).
1. Employees' representation in management
2. Power (Social sciences)
I. Burns, Tom R.   II. Karlsson, Lars Erik
III. Rus, Veljko   IV. International Sociological Association
658.31'52   HD5650   78-63143

ISBN 0-8039-9846-5
ISBN 0-8039-9847-3 Pbk

Library of Congress Catalog Card Number
78-63143

First Printing

CONTENTS

III STRATEGY AND CRITIQUE OF STRATEGY

INTRODUCTION AND OVERVIEW

Tom R. Burns
Universities of Oslo, Norway and Stockholm, Sweden/Scandinavian Institutes of Administrative Research, Sweden
Veljko Rus
University of Ljubljana, Yugoslavia

The general theme with which the papers collected in this volume are concerned is the liberation of work and the control of political power. Particular attention is given to the interplay between the shop-floor level and the macro-political context of work and work life. The liberation of work is viewed here as the process of extending workers' control over the means of production, production processes, their products, the organizational structure, and, above all, the institutional context of work. This definition necessarily relates the liberation of work to the macro-socio-political context. The liberation and democratic control of political power is viewed, similarly, in terms of processes and conditions whereby workers exercise control over political processes, policy-formation, and planning.

The study of work life has been an important area of research in the social sciences, particularly sociology. Much of this work has been focused on the shop-floor level, and to a lesser extent on the

The papers collected here were presented or developed out of an International Conference on The Liberation of Work and Political Power, arranged at the Inter-University Centre, Dubrovnik, Yugoslavia, in February 1977. We are grateful to Professors Rudi Supek and Eugene Pusic and the Inter-University Centre for their assistance in arranging the conference. We also want to express thanks to Walter Buckley, Steven Deutsch, Jozef Figa, David Held, Gerry Hunnius, and Carlos Johnson for their helpful comments and criticism concerning the introduction to, and organization of, the papers collected in this volume.

enterprise level. This may, in part, reflect the social psychological perspective prevailing in sociology. It also reflects the interests of workers — and many of those committed to serving the cause of workers — in improving their work situation at the shop-floor level, a context in which they face day to day problems.[1] In addition, it reflects the interests of management in solving particular contemporary problems of worker motivation, productivity and absenteeism, among others, which have become increasingly serious in advanced capitalist societies.

Most of the research on work life has neglected matters of political power, and vice versa. In practical affairs, similarly, strategies to democratize work life are formulated and carried out separately from strategies to democratize political life. On the one hand, efforts are directed toward 'improving the quality of work life', 'enriching job content', 'rotating jobs', or pushing for even more radical measures such as 'co-determination' and 'self-management'. On the other hand, initiatives are taken in the political sphere to achieve 'decentralization', 'new forms of citizen participation', 'development of new information and social auditing schemes for public services'.

Such part descriptions, analyses and treatments of work life, political, or other societal problems are widely believed to make up a rational and practical approach to comprehending and solving such problems. This is partly because more global approaches entail particularly difficult and complex methodological and practical problems, which in most instances remain unsolved (see later discussion). Also, the well-developed specialized and reductionist character of most social science research supports and legitimizes this tendency. It is widely believed that specialized (and, therefore, on the aggregate level, piecemeal) analysis and problem-solving strategies result in cumulative improvements. Along such lines, for example, many social democratic leaders and theorists suggest that a set of piecemeal reforms make up, cumulatively, an overall strategy which is more constructive than global, often totalitarian strategies to achieve socialist transformation.[2]

In our view, piecemeal approaches fail, in general, at the task of comprehending[3] and solving basic societal problems. For one thing, they do not address underlying structures and processes in a society which cut across institutional areas, shaping problems in different spheres of social life. At the same time, piecemeal problem-solving efforts generate their own problems. Efforts on different levels or in different areas of social life, such as work life and politics, interact and aggregate to produce unintended and unregulated problems. These evoke, in turn, further problem-solving efforts. If the same basic problem-solving approach continues to be used, the result is a vicious spiral of problem-solving attempts generating problems. The approach itself becomes more and more the problem.

The notion of the interrelatedness or unity of social phenomena underlies our critical view of piecemeal approaches and our advocacy of a more holistic approach. The various aspects of social life do not consist of a chance aggregation of elements but make up an interconnected system. Such a system, to a substantial degree, develops — and to some extent is developed by human agents with certain interests and purposes — as a social totality. However, this totality is characterized by inconsistencies and tensions, which are sources of conflict, restructuring efforts and social change.

A major task for both social theory and practice, we are suggesting, is to explore and to try to develop more holistic approaches toward work and work life. This would entail, above all, giving consideration to economic, technological, socio-political, and cultural factors and their dynamic interrelationships, which shape and reshape work conditions and work experiences. Questions such as the following could be posed and, possibly, answered eventually:

— In what ways do technological changes at the shop-floor level affect the division of labor and change macro- and micro-organizational work structures as well as social stratification in society as a whole?

— What are the social and political effects of more autonomy and more participative workers' behavior at the level of everyday shop-floor activity? How do they affect labor union activity and structure, or the power distribution between management and labor, and societal power structures?

— What are the effects of democratization of work on work attitudes, status relationships within work organization, global orientation of working classes, and the social stratification of society?

Similar questions may be posed relating to political developments and their ramifications, particularly with respect to work life:

— What are the effects of changes of political power on everyday work relationships and work conditions at the shopfloor level?

— What are the effects of state, public, or cooperative ownership on disalienation and the liberation of work?

— To what extent does the abolishment of market and the establishment of social planning change traditional hierarchical structures within work organizations?

— To what extent does the political power of workers' parties increase workers' control at the shop-floor level and influence the distribution of power within work organizations? Or the organizational and technological developments of work organizations?

Although such questions are seldom raised in the social sciences, they are theoretically and practically urgent questions. They are urgent, at least to the extent that we wish to increase our understanding of the global properties and dynamics of modern societies and to increase the usefulness of social science in societal problem-solving and development.

A more holistic approach to work and to the interplay between work life and political life has theoretical, methodological and practical implications:[4]

— On the theoretical plane, this entails distinguishing levels of analysis and examining them simultaneously, along with their interplay and mutual effects.

— It also entails considering new methods of study and analysis which can be used in such research.

— In practical terms, one attempts to explore and develop a critical perspective and strategies with respect to the dialectic between the liberation of work and the control of macro-political power. If institutions in different spheres of social action are interdependent, the liberation of work cannot be achieved without corresponding and coordinated changes in political and sociocultural spheres.

Traditional socialist theory, as a more holistic approach to social reality, attempts to describe and analyze the contradictions of capitalism, such as those between the relations of production and the forces of production or between the private nature of property and the increasingly social character of production. Socialism is presumed to overcome these contradictions through the abolishment of private ownership and the substitution of a planned economy for a market economy. The 'liberation of work' is assumed to be an automatic outcome of such macro-societal changes.

In the 'socialist countries' with public ownership and planned economies, the prevalence of totalitarian theories and practices which ignore or even deny the possibility of alienation in work and social relations is, therefore, not perhaps surprising. The character of all parts of the social system is considered to be pre-determined by the nature of the total system; hence, empirical exploration of actual work conditions and relations does not have a meaningful and legitimate status. That is, investigations and analyses of everyday work life — which are contrary to the assumption that the liberation of work and the solution of basic social contradictions have been achieved through socialist revolution and 'dictatorship of the proletariat' — are a priori denied value and validity. As Mucha (1978) points out, in spite of open adherence to Marxism, that is, the materialist dialectic of society, and despite the general criticism of functionalism, 'the analysis of phenomena and problems in socialist societies has been based mainly on the model of integration and harmony — stable change and equilibrium . . .' This indicates a type of approach to social phenomena in which 'the system' or the whole is assumed to dominate its parts.[5]

We shall not discuss further here the validity of piecemeal and holistic approaches to the description and analysis of societal problems and to problem-solving efforts. Our purpose here has been, rather, to suggest the limited character of such viewpoints, prevalent in contemporary capitalist and socialist societies, respectively:

— in the first case, parts of social reality are treated as independent of one another; social reality is fragmented; there is no sense of the totality of society. The stress is on limited programs and reforms which can be readily justified, no matter how temporary or how much determined by immediate political opportunities or interests.

— in the second case, the sense of systemness or totality prevails; but there is a lack of the sense of the parts, of the concrete experiences and problems which human actors interpret and try to solve in everyday life. The stress is on taking and holding total power at the macro-level.

We are not proposing here that an integrated theory of the liberation of work and the control of political power be developed. The formulation of such a theory is probably not feasible at this point.

But it would be useful, in our view, to identify and analyze knot points at different levels and in different spheres of society where work and political structures and processes are interconnected and interact dialectically.

Several such points and related theses, some of which motivated the Dubrovnik Conference, others of which emerged out of the papers presented and the discussion at the Conference, are indicated below:

(i) Work, work processes, and work organization can be most effectively investigated and analyzed in relation to their complex settings, that is economic, technological, political, and sociocultural contexts.

(ii) Work activity, its organization, and products are shaped by these contexts. On the other hand, they contribute to shaping such contexts.

(iii) From an economic perspective — a perspective which is also influential in sociology — work, or more precisely labor, is a factor of production. It is a means to produce consumption goods and capital.[6] A major thesis here is that work is more than a factor of production. It also contributes to or is a factor in the following:

> — the self-production of workers (their knowledge, competence, and degree of confidence as well as motivation);
> — the production and reproduction of social relationships, including status and authority relationships in the work sphere as well as in political and sociocultural spheres;[7]
> — the production and reproduction of relationships between human society and nature, and, according to Marx, an even more complex possibility, 'the production of the humanization of nature and the naturalization of the human being'.

(iv) The liberation of work is necessarily linked to the control of political power. A strategic question here is the extent to which workers can liberate work and also exercise political power on their own.[8] The possibility that control over work and over political power can be exercised to a substantial degree by the working class, as a self-developing, self-transforming subject of history,[9] implies that an elite taking the role of avant-garde is not necessary. If this viewpoint is correct — and not merely an idealistic construction — then 'dictatorship of the proletariat' can be realized through self-organization and self-management of this class.[10]

Not all of the aspects of work life, and its relationship to political

life, are taken up in the papers collected here. The focus in this collection is on the relationship of work to political power. The book
is divided into three parts. Part One addresses itself to historical
struggles and developments relating to industrial democracy. Horvat's paper deals with general trends in democratic countries, while
the Dahlström and the Baumgartner *et al* papers are concerned with
linkages between work life reforms and political power in Sweden
and Yugoslavia respectively.

The papers in Part Two address themselves to theoretical questions and formulations. Abell outlines systematically rules for non-
hierarchical systems and stresses that the democratic basis for
structuring and legitimizing social organization is increasingly
replacing the rational-legal basis.[11] The paper of Baumgartner,
Burns and DeVille presents an holistic framework for the description, modeling and critique of industrial democracy reforms, including self-management. This is applied in preliminary
assessments of contemporary developments in Western capitalist
societies. The paper by Rus examines several concrete hypotheses
about factors limiting workers' influence in Yugoslav self-
management institutions. On a more general level, Batstone draws
on Weber's concept of social organization, and in particular
bureaucratic rules and procedures, to point out some of the constraints and limitations on the possibilities of democratic practice in
work organizations, under present institutional and organizational
arrangements.

The papers in Part Three are concerned with critique and
strategy. A variety of considerations and viewpoints are presented.
Valentin, Hunnius and Clayre raise a number of critical questions
about the possibilities and limitations of democratization of work
life, particularly in the context of capitalist institutions. Hunnius
and Valentin stress particularly the system maintaining consequences of such reforms. Gustavsen advocates the role of research,
and particular sorts of research strategies, in the democratization
of work.[12] At the same time, Gustavsen argues that 'grand theory'
has been misused.[13] Vanek, in the final article, attempts to link self-
management to the larger international political economy, and in
this larger context, makes proposals for macro- and micro-
restructuring of economic life and their interrelationships.

Contemporary social science requires new perspectives with
which to analyze society globally and which can link different areas

of social activity and experience that have been usually treated separately. Hence, our ambition here has not been so much to improve on the description and analysis of work processes per se, nor has it been to deepen theories oriented to political structure and movement. The principal aim has been to stimulate theoretical and strategic initiatives oriented to the interrelated changes and developments occurring in work life and in political life. Hopefully, these efforts will contribute to the identification and analysis of critical knot-points where changes in work and power interact with each other, and which may prove to be of strategic importance. Out of such efforts, both in research and in practice, new approaches to the liberation of work and political power will emerge.

NOTES

1. As Hobsbawn has pointed out, workers typically do not perceive the workings of the 'capitalist system', monopoly capital, contradictions within the capitalist system as such. Rather, they experience their concrete manifestations: the factory, assembly line, foremen, technological change, dequalification tendencies, and job insecurity. These concrete experiences do not lead automatically to an abstract, general characterization of the capitalist context in which work and the work place operate. A challenge for both theory and practice is to identify specific grievances with respect to specific targets, at the same time that these are linked to macro-aspects of the capitalist system.

Batstone et al. (1976), on the other hand, argue that workers are typically aware of the larger structures of power within which they have to act, but that they tend to accommodate to these by accepting and conforming to the dominant norms and forms of conduct. Nevertheless, he suggests that their behavior is based on am-bivalent attitudes. They are not committed fully to the structures or to the norms and forms of conduct. This ambivalence means that their attitudes and demands can change dramatically. That is, quiescent workers may in certain situations suddenly articulate radical demands. Thus, the confinement of their interest to 'local, low-level issues' reflects a particular structural context. Changes in this context may well lead to different attitudes and patterns of behavior. Therefore, industrial democracy reforms such as co-determination and *mitbestimmung* may become politically and structurally important once they have been introduced (even if workers initially do not show much interest in them).

2. For instance, it is supposed that stepwise reforms on the micro-level of work organization and stepwise reforms on the macro-level of the state system will result in the more or less progressive socialization of contemporary capitalist societies. This perspective presumes either that these changes do not interact with one another, producing unintended consequences, or that spontaneous mutual (and presumably positive) adaptation occurs between different spheres of social action and between the macro- and micro-levels of society.

3. Managerial and labor union approaches to 'worker participation' suggest fragmentation and incoherence in societal perspectives and problem-solving. In management versions, labor should play an advisory role; in some union versions, workers' control or, at least, co-determination should be established. Neither approach takes into account contradictions of the viewpoints as well as contradictions between piecemeal changes at the micro-level of work organization and those at the macro-level of political and social organization of society.

Consequently, numerous experiments in work life have had minimal impact since they did not, and most probably could not, spread over the entire society as an integrated movement and eventually become a characteristic feature of the wider social context — for such a development depends on political processes and movement. Reports of 'non-supportive social environments' and 'encapsulation' associated with such experiments are indications of the limitations of piecemeal approaches to social practice and social theory.

4. Of course, it is possible that these phenomena are not directly connected at all. One could hypothesize that the segmentation of these two areas is a necessary condition for the relative stability of Western as well as Eastern European societies. For such segmentation of society permits changes to be absorbed by stepwise accommodation of the whole system, through separating conflicts from one another. In this way conflict resolution and societal management are made less difficult. Thus, increasing conflict need not necessarily lead to the destruction of society, but to further segmentation, more sophisticated and complicated public management and regulation of conflict.

5. Since social structure and the institutional set-up are taken for granted or remain in the background, such an approach is inherently static and conservative.

6. This view of work is also prevalent in socialist societies. Work is a means to industrialize, to achieve national and individual wealth, and to accumulate surplus. This is not to say that work has the same significance in capitalist and socialist societies — two social contexts, obviously differing in a number of important respects. The legitimate function of labor under capitalism is to produce commodities for exchange which are profitable to the owners of the means of production.

7. Workers as employees, or wage-laborers, contribute to the production and reproduction of the power of the enterprises in which they work. As members of workers' collectives, they also produce and reproduce social relationships characteristic of these collectives.

8. Some, e.g. Serge Mallet and Bogdan Denitch, suggest that workers' skills, knowledge and training make traditional hierarchical (bureaucratic) structures irrational since workers possess knowledge required for effective social action (see Denitch, 1977).

9.   We define working class in the broadest terms to encompass all employees, including white collar, service and professional workers.

Of course, basic problems remain in developing a theory and the practice of democratic socialism as self-management and self-planning of the working class. Does work as a human activity have potential for humanization and self-liberation of the human species? Some would argue that work activity does not have such capacity. Marx, like Hegel, believed that all of history is nothing but the self-creation of human beings through their own work. Others are doubtful about this basic hypothesis: they argue that the liberation of work is a contradiction, since work is nothing more than oppressive activity. Accordingly, the prospects of socialism are not in the liberation *of* work, but in liberation *from* work, through automation and efficient technology which will reduce 'necessary work' to a minimum. These prognoses are found in some of Marcuse's work.

10.   One possible implication of this is that no special social organizations, such as party, state apparatus and the like, are necessary for such a class to pursue and to develop its interests. Obviously, this structural position is oversimplified, since it fails to take into account time, the fact that states and political parties already exist and that they have played a major role in developing the new working classes in socialist countries. These institutions do not necessarily represent the future, but part of the present reality. With the continual development in the course of industrialization of new working class segments, including technicians, state and party have tended to come more and more into conflict with important segments of the working class.

11.   In general, private property, ownership institutions, and forms of rational-legal organization are being increasingly questioned and constrained in new ways. As Denitch (1977) points out, this development probably has more radical implications than 'nationalization' of the means of production.

12.   The Demos group in Sweden (J. Carlson, Pelle Ehn, Barbro Erlander, Maja-Lisa Perby and Åke Sandberg) has developed strategies along similar lines. See 'Planning and Control from the Perspective of Labour: A Short Presentation of the Demos Project', *Accounting, Organizations, and Society*, 1979, in press.

13.   On the other hand, our earlier discussion suggests the limitations of narrow theoretical or empiricist approaches where the global or systemic implications of social action or multiple programs and activities fail to be recognized and interpreted.

REFERENCES

Batstone, E. V., I. Boraston and S. Frenke (1976), *Shop Stewards in Action*. Oxford: Blackwell.

Denitch, B. (1977), 'Western Europe's New Left Socialism', *Working Papers for a New Society,* Winter, pp. 68-76.

Mucha, J. (1978), 'The Role of Contradictions and Conflicts in the Development of Socialist Society'. Paper presented at the IX World Congress of Sociology, Uppsala, Sweden, August 1978.

I
HISTORICAL AND BACKGROUND STUDIES

1

EFFICIENCY, SATISFACTION AND DEMOCRACY IN WORK: IDEAS OF INDUSTRIAL RELATIONS IN POST-WAR SWEDEN

Edmund Dahlström
University of Gothenburg, Sweden

I INDUSTRIAL AND PRODUCTION RELATIONS

This paper intends to shed some light on the post-war changes in industrial relations with a focus on efficiency, satisfaction and democracy in Swedish industry. It presents a national case of industrial relations. Many of the patterns analyzed here are part of an international post-war history. No systematic attempt will be made to spell out what is specific for Sweden and what is common for

This paper is a revised and shortened version of a mimeographed report presented at two seminars in Warsaw, October 1976 and Dubrovnik, February 1977. A shortened version of the original report, leaving out the historical background, has been published in *Acta Sociologica* 1977 (No. 1). The present paper focuses on the post-war development up to 1975 and leaves out certain aspects of industrial relations and the relation of welfare in work to that outside work.

European countries. This will have to be determined through further comparative studies. However, some comparative suggestions are made. Ideas of industry will be related to broader ideas of the production system and societal relations. The term 'industrial relations' is used in a limited sense referring mainly to social relations on the plant and enterprise level. Ideas of industrial relations concern notions of who decides what and when in the enterprise (the local power and control issue), how the work and production system is organized to attain efficiency and job satisfaction (the socio-technical question), the relations between management and unions on the local level, the leadership-relations between superiors and subordinates and forms of personnel management. Ideas of the production system and production relations cover notions of industrializing elites and ownership, of centralized or decentralized patterns of economic organization, of the place and role of markets of different types, of economic development and economic growth and its determinants, of business cycles and the control of employment, price stability and balance of trade, of economic welfare and welfare policy, of labor market relations and bargaining systems and governmental policy in this area, etc.

Labor efficiency-productivity has always been the main interest of economists, employers, managers and specialists on rationalization. Its value to labor has been rather ambiguous: workers and employers have a common interest in increased efficiency and productivity in relation to competitors within the country or outside. The more efficiency the greater the surplus and the more to bargain over for wages. But it is the capitalist who appropriates the surplus, and increased efficiency may imply increased efforts, greater safety risks, more risk of lay-offs and unemployment or reduced level of piece-rates.

Efficiency is generally defined in relation to goal attainment and resource utilization. Increased efficiency implies more goal attainment and less resource consumption. The delimitation of goals has been a controversial issue in the post-war period. To what extent do enterprises have goals other than profit maximization and to what extent should they have? The changing environment of enterprise has partly forced it to work with a broader set of goals, including, for example, the consolidation of enterprise and employment of employees. But profit maximization is still the dominating goal for enterprise.

The determinants of labor efficiency have been a crucial problem for organizational theory and a permanent preoccupation of employers and managers. Organizational theories have had different views on the optimal incentives and motivators and these ideas have been important for the organization of industrial enterprises. The effect of job-satisfaction and participation on productivity has been one of the most controversial issues.

The post-war period has seen an increased interest in the role of satisfaction of the employee. The high level of employment and the rising aspirations for increased education and a higher standard of living have forced management to engage in issues of personnel management; how to get, keep, develop, stimulate and discharge or pension employees. Personnel management has become increasingly interested in problems of job-satisfaction and job-efficiency. The degree of job-satisfaction is a function of the degree of the aspiration-level and perceived exchange of the job. Rising expectations may result in increased dissatisfaction if the amount of positive exchange and perceived exchange are not also raised.

The issue of democracy in production and work is the most controversial of the three values (efficiency, satisfaction and democracy).[1] Both employers and employees are inclined to agree on the theoretical legitimacy of efficiency and satisfaction, though with reversed priorities, but their views on industrial democracy seem to be incompatible in principle. Employers and management have not been prepared to accept the notion of democracy in production, while labor has been in favor of the general notion. Workers have been split by differing views as to what kind of democracy is required in production, and by what means it can be obtained. Syndicalistic, Social Democratic, Liberal and Communist workers have all had different ideas of employee power.

Disagreements about democracy in production concern how democracy is defined and how democracy is related to efficiency and satisfaction with the job. Democracy may refer to the democratic transformation of the whole economy (economic democracy), the power of employees over their own company through representatives (representative industrial democracy), or the influence of single employees or work groups over their work and working conditions (industrial democracy as self-determination). The efficiency concept may apply to the total economy, the industrial sector, the enterprise or the contribution of the employee. Theories of how different types of democracy relate to different types of efficiency are many. In general, those in favor of more democracy in work tend to stress its favorable effect on efficiency and vice versa. The same applies to assumptions of how democracy relates to job-satisfaction.

The issue of industrial democracy is part of the broader issue of socialism and the question of what constitutes a socialist society as distinguished from capitalistic society, and what succession of steps are sufficient to accomplish socialism. Here we find divergent views among schools of socialism. Generally, it is assumed that socialism is characterized by a collective steering of production transcending private ownership of the means of production, thus implying both economic and industrial democracy. However, there has been considerable disagreement about the role of industrial democracy, for example, over the form of workers' control.

It is obvious that measures towards increasing industrial democracy are dependent upon measures for increasing economic democracy. The control of the people over the whole economy that is stated in the Social-Democratic program not only concerns the power of the employees over their own factory but also the control of consumers, local authorities, regional authorities and central state authorities over the production system as a whole. The discussion on this issue in the Social-Democratic Party has often emphasized the legitimate influence of the consumers and the dangers of limiting economic democracy to employee power.[2]

II THE POST-WAR PERIOD

Sweden today demonstrates the typical social composition of post-industrial society or late capitalism.[3] In the 1970s more than half of the employed work in the service sector and only 5 percent in agriculture. The class structure follows the pattern of 'mature capitalism': the manual workers comprise about 50-55 percent with a declining share the last decade, the employers are a declining part together with farmers including about 10-15 percent, and then the middle strata (the white collar employees) are a rapidly expanding strata with 30-35 percent. The class compositions are reflected in the size of the unions. Today the blue collar unions include 1,800,000 members and the white collar unions about 900,000 members. The class composition is also indirectly reflected in support for the political labor movement. Since the democratization of suffrage in 1920, the Social Democrats have mobilized about 35-40 percent of the votes; and the Communists about 5-10 percent.

The post-war program of the labor movement (1944) emphasized full employment, a higher standard of living, economic efficiency, rationalization of branches, governmental economic planning and control.[4] Economic democracy meant governmental influence over the economy through economic planning. The unions were to play an important role in planning and governmental steering through central bodies. Nationalization was a question of convenience and efficiency, not of principle. To the extent that private industry did not function efficiently, collective industrial organization would be considered.

Full employment has been the leading endeavor of the labor movement.[5] LO has strongly influenced the shaping of post-war labor market policy. The resources and tasks of the Central Labor Market Board, County Employment Boards and Local Employment Service agencies have expanded widely. The measures of labor market policy have consisted of services for labor exchange, creation of employment through public works, investment reserves, subsidies for stockpiles, regional development grants and loans, moving allowances, unemployment cash allowances, etc. The new labor market policy has strongly emphasized labor mobility and different grants for compensating costs of moving have been used (travel grants, separation allowances, starting grants and equipment allowances). This mobility conception has been tied to a general macro-economic efficiency philosophy of labor economists that has received strong support from management and bourgeois parties. These ideas are closely related to ideas of industrial rationalization to be dealt with later on.

The questions of industrial democracy and of industrial relations were left to management and unions to settle according to the line of self-regulation in the labor market. The central agreement on joint consultation bodies had been concluded in 1946 and was seen as an explorative experiment in industrial democracy, following ideas that had been presented by a governmental committe in 1923. Enterprises with more than 50 employees were to establish enter-

prise boards (*företagsnämnder*) for information and joint consultation. Their task was to discuss issues of productivity, job satisfaction, safety and personal policy.

The endeavor of the labor movement as it was manifested in the
post-war program became the dominating political issue of the
1940s and the early 1950s. The struggle is usually labeled the
'debate of planned economy' (*planhushållningsdebatten*).[6] The
Social Democrats were accused of wanting to nationalize the
economy and as a consequence suppress democracy. The discussion
should be seen with the Cold War as background and compared
with the struggle in many countries, for example England, between
reformist labor and bourgeois parties.

The Social Democratic Government had expected a post-war
depression. Instead there occurred an intensive inflationary expansion with its peak in the Korean War boom. This gave fewer
reasons for structural transformation of the production system and
engaged the government in efforts of stabilization with freezing of
wages as a culmination.

The reaction of employers towards the planned economy drive of
the Social Democrats was divided. There was at first a majority for
a more aggressive and uncompromising line, attacking the ideas of
economic planning.[7] However, another group of employers with a
more positive view towards state economic planning gradually
became influential. This more 'modern' and 'progressive' group of
often younger employers and managers saw limited governmental
planning and legislation strengthening capitalism, and they could
point to similar policies in other countries run by bourgeois
parties.[8] These more progressive managers also supported new
ideas as to how enterprises should be run, implying more employee
participation and job-satisfaction.

During the post-war period there has been a cyclical variation of
cooperation and conflict between the Social Democratic Government and labor movement on the one side and employers and their
powerful organizations on the other.[9] Periods of strong tension between employers' groups and the labor movement included the
'planned economy debate' (1945-48), the conflict over the pension
reform (1956-59) and the disagreement over the claims for industrial democracy and collective capital control (1965-75). The
cooperative periods (1949-56 and 1960-65) have been characterized
by the establishment of central bodies for joint consultation be-

tween business and government. The employers' more cooperative attitude to government has been favored by external threats to the economy which showed industry's need of specific governmental supporting action and/or legislation, and by the parliamentary strength of the Social Democrats. The majority of employers have always preferred bourgeois party government and have been prepared to favor a governmental change when possible. Employer-managers have granted money from enterprise surplus to bourgeois parties while blue collar trade unions have channeled money to the Social Democrats.

These changes in the political field are interactively related to changes in the economic structure and production relations and together they have influenced the industrial relations which will be discussed in the following sections. The above-mentioned acceptance of public economic planning and governmental regulation and intervention in the economic field should be seen in the perspective of the changing structure of productive forces and market structure. Changes in industrial relations are strongly influenced by both transformation of industrial macro-structures and by changes in the political frame, for example, changes of market structures, central agreements between employers and union organizations, and labor legislation. New ideas of rational organization reflect external changes and consequent demand for adjustment to new situations. The challenge of high employment and rising employee aspirations to job environment and job satisfaction is such a case. The same goal of profit maximization may require other solutions in new situations, and this may, for instance, explain the development of personnel management policies in the post-war period. But personnel policy also reflects new ideas about man and his social nature and motivation and the necessity of offering opportunities for communication and self-determination as incentives. These ideas may reflect other structural trends, for instance the higher level of education and the democratization of civic culture in general.

The more conspicuous structural trends in the production system in post-war Sweden shall be briefly mentioned.[10] The extended markets, with increasing international competition, accumulation of capital, capital-demanding technology and rising level of wages and salaries have stimulated concentration in industry. There has always been a high degree of concentration of ownership in certain

branches of Swedish industry due partly to its international orientation, for example in manufacturing, iron, mining and the pulp industry. There are big differences between the more export-oriented
sector and the more protected sector, for example the consumption
industry. There has been an increase in the number of mergers each
year. The 25 largest enterprises have increased their share of the
total employment in manufacturing industry during the last decade
from 28 to 34 percent. The largest enterprises with more than 500
employees today comprise more than 60 percent of the employment
in manufacturing industry, 63 percent of the production value and
70 percent of registered capital.

The owner concentration varies in different industrial branches
and does not exclude the existence of a large number of production
units (work places) spread around the country. There has been a
decrease in the number of production units in the construction industry: there were 21,000 production units with more than 4
employees each in 1945 and 13,000 in 1972 while the average
number of employees in each unit increased from 35 to 69 in the
same period.

Private ownership dominates Swedish industry, though there has
been a considerable expansion of the public sector since 1945,
mainly in the service sector. The private sector, including the co-
operatively organized, comprises 95 percent of employment in
manufacturing, 93 percent in agriculture and forestry, 85 percent in
construction, 100 percent in commerce, 51 percent in communications and 36 percent in services. There has been an increased
tendency for the state to intervene in industry and establish different types of joint ventures or state-owned enterprises. The growing requirement for capital investment and increased difficulties in
certain sectors with the intensified international competition have
been the main reasons for these interventions, but they have up to
now not changed the basic structure of dominant private ownership
of industry. The organizational patterns prevailing in state-owned
industry and in the cooperatively-owned enterprises are in general
similar to those of private industry. The same policy of profitability
and rationalization has been dominant, and ownership has only
marginally affected the organizational structure. The changes of
enterprise environment in Sweden are mostly the same as may be
found in other European capitalist countries:

    1. The accelerated rate of technological change, demand for in-

creasing capital investment per worker, accelerated rate of capital conversion, enhanced advantages of size of enterprise and production unit, and increased demand for long-range planning with careful calculation of profitability.

2. An expansion of technological knowledge and applied research. Enhanced importance of marketing with advertising and increased dependence on publicity and public relations. Expansion of public regulations, planning and support.

3. Increased importance of economic interest organizations of different types.

4. Increased pressure for inter-enterprise cooperation, partly counteracted by legislation against monopolies and cartels.

5. Increased international competition with an accelerated growth of multinational enterprises (foreign and Swedish).

6. The changing structure of business cycles with stagflationary traits.

7. The expansion of unions and unionization in all employment areas with the development of bargaining and negotiation relationships.

8. A raised standard of living with shorter working hours and an expansion of social services.

9. A rapid expansion of the educational system with increased standard of education in the labor force.

10. Full employment with periodical labor shortage and labor turnover.

These trends have obvious effects on industrial relations but they are partly counteracting each other. Some of the trends favor mainly efforts towards efficiency and rationalization and intensive utilization of employees, for example, international competition, increased capital demands and concentration tendencies. Other trends demand more consideration for employee welfare, for example, the increase in union size and strength, the higher standard of living, of social services and of educational standard and labor shortage.

Concentration and centralization are the dominating trends of the post-war period and they have penetrated all institutional areas, including industry (as mentioned), private, cooperative and public economic organizations, interest organizations such as unions, other types of organizations of 'peoples movement' character, political institutions such as communes (the local units for municipal authority), parties and mass media producing units (e.g. daily papers). The concentration of the blue collar trade union movement is a good example.[11] The number of national blue collar unions decreased from 46 in 1940 to 29 in 1970, with an increase of the average size of national unions from 21,000 members to 58,000 members. During the period 1940-70 the number of members associated with LO increased from 971,000 to 1,680,000, the number of local branches decreased from 7,930 to 2,448 and the average number of members in each branch increased from 125 to 686 members. Efficiency and increasing competition have been the main reasons given for concentration.

Tensions and unrest arose in Swedish society in the latter part of the 1960s as in other advanced capitalist countries.[12] The intensified criticism may be related to the many structural changes during the post-war period. Increased welfare and full employment gave wage earners more power. This was reinforced by the expansion of unions and their more influential position. The more rapid increase of welfare outside work compared with the standard of working environment generated higher aspirations for work improvement. The discrepancy between political ambitions for equalization and alleged distribution of welfare on the one hand and the actual unequal distribution of welfare on the other induced discontent and firm demands. The rapid centralization, concentration, bureaucratization and technocratization put more people in a powerless and alienated position and induced discontent. The general spread and acknowledgement of democratic values detrimental to the prevailing authoritarian patterns of industry called for organizational changes. The decline of the Cold War made people less inclined to tolerate frustrations and injustice for national reasons. The rising educational standard and explosion of mass media stimulated new ideas and aspirations. There emerged a post-war generation grown up under relative abundance without experience of unemployment and war, and indoctrinated in the hopes and promises of democratic welfare ideology that was much more prepared for outspoken criticism and actions against injustice.

A change in outlook in the political field occurred in the middle of the 1960s. There seemed to be a general widespread mood of satisfaction with social conditions in Sweden in the beginning of the 1960s. Sweden was a welfare society offering its citizens benefits and opportunities, and with the prospects of increased economic growth, some needed reforms were introduced. Several studies and reports appeared in the latter half of the 1960s to revise this picture, showing that there existed another and poorer Sweden, that the welfare distribution was unequal, that the economic growth perspective did not consider environmental destruction and pollution, that work environment included serious health risks and exploitation, that the international scene was dominated by a threatening exploitation.[13]

Students of modern literature in Sweden have dated new ideas from 1965.[14] From that time there appeared an increased criticism of social structure and policy in Sweden. Most established institutions received their share of this. The critical theme very much concerned industrial relations and the exploitation of the rank and file. Employers, unions and bureaucrats were held responsible for the unsatisfactory conditions. Several novels were published showing the damaging effects of a bad working environment, piecework, long hours, and inhumane supervision. Journalists, film producers and theatrical groups tried to elucidate the exploitive relations. Through the mass media they spread to a large proportion of the people. Even popular culture in its different manifestations transmitted some of the ideas.

There is an indication of increasing tensions on the labor market from 1968 on. There were more illegal (wildcat) strikes from that year. In a comparative perspective, however, Sweden still stands out as one of the more 'peaceful' capitalist societies, judged by the number of work-days lost through strikes or lock-outs. The strikes that occurred received an unusual, positive response in the mass media and from different associations and groups. This was particularly true of the strike in LKAB-mines in the north of Sweden in 1969. There was positive support of the miners and money was collected for the strikers and attacks on the establishment made.

Studies of industrial relations indicate a set of conditions that can be related to the increasing tension in industry.[15]

1. There has been a stronger variation in the employment level since 1965, with recessive tendencies and structural unemployment. The stagflationary character with combined inflation and stagnation tendencies has aroused irritation.

2. The gap between what the solidaric wage policy offered workers in the high profit industries and what they 'reasonably'

might expect to earn with respect to the profits caused serious irritation in many enterprises.

3. The bargaining system included tension-generating structures.
The restrictive peace obligations prohibited workers from using the
strike weapon from the moment central agreements were made.
This meant that local negotiations that followed central negotiations were carried out in 'peace' conditions. The employers' priority of interpretation made it difficult for the worker to negotiate
about existing agreements. This gave the employer a tremendous
advantage in piece-rate negotiations. 'Paragraph 32' excluded important questions from negotiations, for example replacement,
work organization, work environment, lay-offs (with certain exceptions according to agreements of 1938 and 1964), etc.

4. The relation between management and unions may partly be
described as centrally symmetric and locally asymmetric. It was difficult for local union representatives to put enough pressure on
management to take care of local interests that because of the rising
expectations were seen as legitimate. This applied, for instance, to
the physical work environment and safety, setting of piece rates,
authoritarian patterns of supervision, harsh and partly inhumane
working rules, etc. To the asymmetrical factors may also be added
the access to information and experts that management always
could command.

5. The large number of immigrants may have contributed to the
higher strike tendency. The immigrant workers were frustrated
with difficult working and housing conditions and their knowledge
of institutionalized patterns of industrial relations was limited.

III IDEAS OF INDUSTRIAL
ORGANIZATION

Exploring ideas of industrial organization requires an awareness of
different levels of thinking and reality:

Level 1:   The most abstract ideas of organizational structures and
           forms covering different types of organizations. These
           ideas are generated by successful managers, influential
           consultants and/or social scientists.

Level 2:   The more practically oriented recommendations from policymakers on different levels, covering parts of the economy or an industrial branch.

Level 3:   The stated policy, blueprints, recommendations, etc. of each single enterprise or plant.

Level 4:   The objective social structure of each enterprise. We often know less about the objective structure than about the normative cognitions of policymakers.

When trying to explore post-war ideas of organization on the first of the above-mentioned levels, there are some difficulties having to do with the lack of consensus between different scholars as to organizational schools and their theories' meaning and importance. There is little agreement between different theoreticians on how to classify organizational theories. To my mind, this is due to the fact that organizational theory implies a considerable number of political-ethical presumptions. As long as these are not made explicit, it is difficult to understand the theories and relate them to each other. Different organizational theories seem to emphasize different aspects.[16] Rationality models bring out the means-end thinking of organizations and emphasize the cognitive side, disregarding certain informal and integrative patterns. System models are inclined to stress integrative aspects of organizations and certain simple regulating mechanisms.

There have been some interesting changes in organizational theory since the Second World War which seem to indicate changes in practical thinking and organizational structure, but the relationships among theory, practical thinking and organizational structure are complicated. Leading consultative experts have discerned the following schools in the international community of organizational experts, mainly in the capitalist west, which also apply to Sweden:[17]

The bureaucratic model (Max Weber, A. Etzioni, etc.).
Scientific management (Frederick W. Taylor, L. Bilbreth, etc.).
The administration school (Henry Fayol, Gulick, Urwick, etc.).
The human relations school (F. Rothlisberger, W. Dickson, Elton Mayo, Chris Argerys, etc.).
Decision and communication theory (Chester Bernard, Herbert Simon, J. March, J. Cyert, etc.).

Managerial system theory and cybernetics (for Sweden, Eric Rhenman, Dick Ramström, etc.).
The socio-technical school (F. Emery, E. Trist, E. Thorsrud, etc.).

The consultative experts are themselves part of the process they are
trying to describe and their analysis of other schools is not always
fair or adequate. Max Weber's thoughts, for example, are generally
misunderstood. However, a bureaucratic school of traditional
bureaucracy may be discerned without involving Max Weber and
his followers.

The older models of organizational thinking tend to conceive a
rather mechanical relation between decision and execution,
superiors and subordinates, and decision making and performance,
with some kind of direct steering of the rank and file (operators)
either in the form of strict supervision, mechanical control or pay
after result (for instance, in the form of piecework). The older
models also implied a static conception, assuming a rather permanent environment and goal-structure. The later models are more
open: there is less of structured and rigid, permanent hierarchies
and central regulations and more of participation, autonomy of
local echelons and rank and file and also of mutual communication, cooperation and participation.[18] The human relations school
reflects clearly the changing labor market structure with higher
employment, higher labor turnover, rising expectations, more
demands from stronger unions and general changes in values and
conceptions.

However, the schools do not only reflect a succession of structural states but also a differentiation of industrial strata and groups
with different ways of thinking. The ideas of the bureaucratic and
administrative school are still found among administrative executives'[19] scientific management, in rationalization and work
study departments, human relations, among personnel experts,
system theory and communication and decision theory, among
younger executives from business schools and technical schools,
especially in process industries, etc. The latter schools have a more
abstract and vague character, and it is difficult to judge how the
ideas take form in concrete organizational structures.

The fact that system theory tends to emphasize the integrative
and cooperative side of organizations may give this way of thinking
a specific legitimating function for employers in conflict with

unions. Some system thinkers have strongly emphasized the integrative structure of organizations and have seen the manager as a balance master in a sort of equilibrium situation with different 'interest parties', such as capital owners, wage earners, consumers and local authorities. This model was used as an argument against union claims for more power, indicating the conclusion that more union power would induce disequilibrium and thus threaten the survival of the enterprise.[20] This use or misuse of system theory indicates the political content and presumptions of organizational theory.

The Second World War was fought against Fascism with its authoritarian and anti-intellectual ideas, and after the war there was a general optimism for the establishment a more democratic society, with science as a means for solving social problems. These ideas were strongly prevalent in the United States, and because of the strong position of the United States after the war, they spread to Sweden. Rationalization was given the broader meaning of application of science and of science solving social problems, a kind of technological optimism. The behavioral sciences seemed to give promising prospects for the development of democratic relationships and human relations in industry.

It has been mentioned previously that the decade after the First World War saw the appearance and gradual diffusion of a 'modern outlook' among employers, accepting governmental responsibility, intervention and economic planning. The same group tended to emphasize a more human-relations-oriented outlook towards management and industrial organizations, implying a rational personnel management, better information and communication with employees, encouragement to participation, salaries/wages for results in the form of bonus of profit-sharing. These ideas were parly accepted by labor (see below, section 4).

Management became increasingly interested in job satisfaction, employee communication and participation. This trend was significant in the US, where ideas of human relations had attracted much interest, and great expectations were attached to cooperation between management and employees. Institutions for research and consultation concerning better management and personnel policy arose. The managers' interest was stimulated by labor market condition with high employment and high labor turnover. Research was called for and studies on job satisfaction and incentives for productivity were made partly after American models.

However, there existed clear limits to what employers were prepared to offer; management prerogatives, as they were defined in central agreements, for instance, the right to hire, replace and discharge employees and to direct and organize work (Paragraph 32). Laws regulated the power of the capital owners and their managers and did not give employees any right to participate in decision-making bodies. It was up to the manager-employer to decide what might be delegated and what participation be allowed. 'Organization' thus implied employer-manager organization, and this is reflected in the organizational modification that occurred in theory and practice. Organizational openness and employee-participation have always been limited by the fundamental power conditions. The new managerial ideas of the 1940s and 1950s included notions of a more rational personnel management, more 'considerate' and 'socially skillful' leadership, better employee information and communication and, in general 'human relations' with more psychological insight and social skill.[21] The 1960s brought out some new ideas of enterprise organization that were oriented towards 'socio-technical' structure of the production process. The socio-technical school saw the industrial organization as a totality of social and technological factors that needed to be integrated in total planning: socio-technical planning. This required that the organization meet the basic human needs of security, variation, participation and opportunities to learn and develop. Concrete solutions were suggested, realized and evaluated, for example job enlargement and self-steering groups. These ideas were tried out in Norway within a joint mangement-union arrangement.[22] The socio-technical school offered a serious criticism of prevailing ideas among experts on rationalization and work studies. These experts emphasized specialization and direct steering through piece-rate systems, tight supervision and machine control. The ideas of the socio-technical school may be seen as an extension of some of the basic assumptions of the human relations school.

Today, both managers-employers and the union movement seem to accept many of the basic ideas of human relations and the socio-technical school, but the parties seem to conceive these improvements in different cognitive frames. The employers perceive them as part of 'good management' and technological planning. Blue collar unions tend to see them as part of industrial democracy and as being tied to changes of power structure. I shall deal with the latter view in the next section and limit this section to the ideas of employers and managers. The new ideas of management have recently been given a systematic presentation in a report from the Employer Associations' technical section. This outfit has been involved in extensive explorative activity under the theme, 'new work forms' (*nya arbetsformer*).[23]

The report recommends enterprises to work towards broader goals, and it is suggested that satisfaction in work should be included as an explicit goal and always taken into account in the organization of jobs and in personnel management. The employees should be offered more influence concerning their own working relations and more 'everyday democracy'. Jobs should be so designed that they give the incumbent meaningful and stimulating work, thus building into the job a natural incentive for productivity. There is a general criticism of making jobs too specialized with too short cycles. Job enlargement is seen as promising in many situations. Organizational planning should be worked out with more cooperation between chief and co-workers. The term 'co-worker' (*medarbetare*) is significant for the new outlook. There is also criticism of using individual piece-rates for many jobs and other forms of pay for result are recommended, for instance time pay with bonus.

The recommendations of the SAF group have clear political references and imply tactical advice. Organization plans should be generated within the management-controlled 'line-system'. Politicians and scientists and other experts not immediately under control of the employer are said to be 'unrealistic' and 'impractical'. The cases referred to as successful have followed this pattern and the evaluation of them has been done in close cooperation with SAF's technical department. The fact that these ideas have for decades been explored and recommended by social scientists and other specialists is partly concealed. It is the 'practical men' of private industry that should be given the credit.

IV IDEAS OF INDUSTRIAL
   DEMOCRACY

1. The Priority of Economy and Efficiency

The post-war program of the Swedish labor movement enhanced
the notion of increased control of people over the production
system.[24] This control implied mainly a more extensive governmental steering of the whole economy by various types of economic
policy. It was generally assumed that this type of economic control
was compatible with private ownership. Many goals were common
for management and wage earners: increased economic growth,
economic efficiency, branch rationalization and economic stability.
The labor movement gave a clear priority to problems of full
employment and solidaric wage policy. The issue of nationalization
was seen pragmatically in the light of efficiency; nationalization
was motivated in areas where private-owned industry could not
function even with support by government. The 'economic
socialism' of reformism thus meant the accomplishment of different macro-economic welfare goals such as full employment,
economic growth, higher standard of living, equal income distribution. 'Economic democracy' was seen as a secondary question and
as a problem of finding suitable means for welfare goals.

The question of industrial democracy was also seen as something
secondary and given little attention in programs and discussions.
The union movement had supported the idea of establishing works
councils (*företagsnämnder*), confirmed in the 1946 agreement with
the employers. The idea of works councils agreed with suggestions
that had been presented in a governmental report of 1923 and with
Anglo-Saxon models tried out during the war in the effort to defeat
the Nazis. The same type of agreements were made in other Scandinavian countries. It was hoped that these boards would promote
efficiency, work satisfaction and mutual understanding. Studies
that were made of these boards and their effects indicated that the
results were mainly concerned with 'mutual-understanding' between management and union leaders. They had marginal effects,
if any, on industrial relations in general, and most employees had
little information and little knowledge of their functions and consequences.[25] The central agreement was revised in 1958 and 1966 with

little effect.

The labor movement in the 1940s gave priority to central economic issues such as questions of efficiency and employment. Questions concerning job satisfaction and industrial democracy were left to the unions to tackle on a day-to-day basis. Job satisfaction was seen as something very subjective and difficult to grasp. It called for scientific research for exploration and elucidation. Ideas and experiences from America, for instance those of Western Electric, were mentioned and referred to in a positive manner. Conferences around these themes resulted in very vague conclusions about the necessity of 'placing the human being in the centre'.[26]

In general, questions of economic and industrial democracy have been given little consideration in the Social Democratic movement up to the end of the 1960s. The main reports of the trade union labor movement presented at the LO-congresses of 1951 and 1961 were devoted to problems of the rational organization of the economy, how to accomplish macro-economic goals such as full employment, economic growth, price stability, foreign payments balance, more even income distribution and the creation of a solidary wage policy.[27]

The Swedish Social Democrats believed that there was plenty of room for cooperation between the parties of the labor market to promote efficiency in industry. This philosophy was stated as early as the 1920s in the government report on industrial democracy, and it re-occurred in the post-war program of the labor movement, where it was suggested that the unions should be given more influence in the planning of industry.[28] In several governmental investigations in the 1940s and 1950s, it was suggested that branch bodies should be established for purposes of joint consultation in industrial planning. In 1947 the LO proposed an organization for branch planning. The employers' organization resisted such proposals and refused to participate in such arrangements. The desire to achieve high productivity and rapid economic growth was one of the driving forces behind the wage policy of solidarity by the side of solidarity and equality goals.[29] Large profits remained in the sector of the economy with the greatest competitive power, thereby helping this sector to consolidate and expand more rapidly. The disadvantage was that the wage earners who had helped to generate the earnings of the most profitable complanies did not receive a 'reasonable' share of these profits. There was an inherent conflict between the wage-solidaric policy and the desire to achieve a 'fair' income in relation to capital distribution. This generated another reason for establishing branch organizations; to create wage-earners' funds, a part of the profit should be placed in wage-earner investment funds.

Proposals for branch funds were presented at the 1951, 1961 and 1966 LO congresses without succeeding in getting majority support. There were other means of correcting the 'excessive' profit surplus of the more profitable enterprises, for instance through taxation. The 1961 proposals for branch councils included goals both of rationalization and wage earners' funds.[30] In a highly industrialized democratic welfare society, economic growth should take new forms and the private sector should gradually lose its importance as the basis of economic advance. However, it was emphasized that these councils should cover broad societal interests and not only include employers' and union representatives but also representatives of consumer and public interests.

The main objective of the councils should be rationalization, and they were named branch rationalization funds. The funds would be generated through fees linked either to wage costs or to the turnover of the enterprise. The funds were to be established through negotiations and collective agreements between unions and employers' associations. The endeavor was to find new ways for capital formation that did not imply a continuous growth of capitalist property.

The idea of establishing wage funds did receive majority support at the LO congress in 1971 but with rather limited enthusiasm. However, there were proposals that the wage earners' funds should also aim to give more influence to wage earners on production and investment issues. A leading labor economist who had been a supporter of branch funds for many years received the task of preparing the issue for the next congress in 1976.

The congress's instruction to the committee indicated the following goals:[31]

1. To solve the problem of excess profits as a consequence of the solidary wage policy.

2. To counteract the concentration of property that followed with the autonomic enterprise capital formation (*självfinansiering*).

3. To increase the influence of the wage earners over economic processes.

The report preparation did not attract much interest until 1974, when the whole issue of wage earners' funds came into the focus of interest. This was partly due to an increased interest in employee influence and industrial democracy. The leading labor economist worked out a proposal for internal discussion in the union movement. A first proposal for a wage earners' fund was prepared in 1975 for discussion in the trade union movement.[32] The same year the government appointed a committee to examine questions of employee influence on company wealth. To the LO congress of 1976 an elaborate proposal for wage earners' funds was presented. This proposal received strong support. The idea is that private companies with a minimum number of employees should contribute to wage earners' investment funds as a share of enterprise profit. The shared profits are not removed from the company but issued in the form of new shares of corresponding value. The shift of ownership of the company in favor of employees depends upon the size of profits and how large a percentage of profits are set aside for the fund. The funds are centrally organized. The dividends of the funds shall be used for the benefit of the wage earners, for example for training, research in the field of working environment, experts or information. With the increase of the funds' ownership, the representation of wage earners in decision-making boards will increase. Representatives are elected by the local unions.

The salaried employees also discussed the question of the wage earners' fund in their unions and at the TCO congress in 1976.[33] They did not decide on any solution and are considering several alternatives: whether or not there should be individual shares or if the fund should be centrally or locally organized.

The issue of wage earners' funds became one of the hottest political issues in 1976.[34] The employers worked out alternatives with individual profit sharing.[35] The Employers' Federation (SAF) gave up its principal resistance against profit-sharing schemes. A few companies introduced new forms of profit-sharing.[36] LO's proposal was heavily criticized, not only from the Communists on the left. The employer critics mean that LO's solution does not accomplish the original aims. There will be a concentration of property and power in the central unions. The trade union movement will face difficulties in the role both of owner and of employee representatives. The ownership will mainly concern profitable enterprises, and the non-profitable will remain outside, etc. The case of wage earners' funds gives an interesting illustration of how the issue of economic and industrial democracy has been dominated by the questions of the solidary wage policy, and income and property distribution, and not discussed from its own premises. It shows how important principal problems are brought in from the perspectives of a dominating problem-definition. However, the increasing interest that the wage earners' funds attracted in 1974 had to do with the increasing interest in industrial and economic democracy. This trend in the middle of the 1960s needs some further comment.

2. Changing Attitudes Towards Industrial Democracy

The reformist blue collar union movement in the 1940s and 1950s saw the prevailing bargaining system with its basic agreements as the legitimate frame of reference for industrial democracy. Joint consultation was seen as an appendage of the main bargaining system where negotiating strength was regarded as the basis for success. There existed a skeptical attitude towards joint-consultation arrangements where the outcome was dependent upon the employers' benevolence. There was also an explicit notion that unions and union representatives should not take any responsibility for management affairs. This was clearly stated in the program of 1961 for industrial democracy (*Fackföreningsrörelsen och företagsdemokrati*).[37]

The existing bargaining system with its collective agreements was the foundation of union-management relations. Through bargaining and collective agreements the unions could influence wages, employment, work environment and other relations. Through joint consultation the workers could obtain information and try to influence management in favor of better solutions on issues of common interest relating to job-satisfaction, efficiency and personnel management. But unions should not through any kind of arrangement take responsibility for management decisions concerning profits, investments and general economic issues. This might bring local representatives into conflict with central representatives and threaten the existing bargaining system. The union movement should support the line of non-interference of government and the regulation of industrial relations through central agreements. The 1966 LO-congress confirmed the general policy of the labor union movement with some critical reservations.[38] Dissatisfaction with the effects of the labor market policy was expressed and political measures called for to give more support and service to those who had difficulties in getting jobs in the labor market. There was also a criticism of the existing way of organizing production, and claims were raised for more consideration of job satisfaction in the planning of production organization and jobs. It was also claimed that the employees should have possibilities of influencing the construction of jobs and work processes and that more research should be devoted to the task of finding forms that were more satisfactory from the human point of view. The ideas of more stimulating and less specialized jobs and more self determination in work were presented. It was generally argued that work and production should be reorganized in such a way that tendencies toward alienation could be reduced, and the idea that wage earners could be offered compensations outside work for unsatisfactory working conditions was criticized. No specific resolutions were taken at the 1966 conference.

The increasing interest and demands for industrial democracy in the political field and mass media at the end of the 1960s produced certain results. In 1968 the government established a delegation for enterprise democracy in the Department of Industrial Affairs to support and initiate experiments in industrial democracy in government-owned enterprises. In 1970 a corresponding delegation was established for state administration and in the municipal field. The agreement of 1966 between SAF, LO and TCO on enterprise councils also included the establishment of a committee for research, and initiatives in the field of management-union coopera-tion, and some experiments in enterprise democracy got started in the end of the 1960s. Several publications eludicated the issue of in-dustrial democracy and suggested more or less radical solutions for increased employee participation and power.[39]

There was a clear sharpening of claims among union leaders be-tween 1966 and 1969.[40] In 1966 a new agreement, with few small revisions, was made between SAF, LO and TCO on enterprise councils. The main new point was that issues of personnel manage-ment should be handled by a joint committee that could work with a budget of its own. The extent of the committee's influence was, however, dependent upon the employer's benevolence. The LO-congress appointed a committee to prepare the issue of industrial democracy for the next congress in 1971. This committee found that there was a strong dissatisfaction with the new agreement among railway and metal workers and typographers. Several national unions expressed claims for participation in decision-making (*medbestämmande*) at their conferences. The workers wanted to participate in decisions concerning personnel management, production management, production organization, leadership and employment. This required abolition of Paragraph 32. The employers' priority of interpretation was another source of asymmetry that needed to be eliminated. There was little hope for negotiating such results. The experience of previous difficulties of negotiating an agreement with management in 1966 inclined the committee to suggest a legislative line, not central negotiations.

The 1970 TCO congress approved the principle that the question of industrial democracy must be given equal status with wage and employment conditions in the work of union organizations.[41] It also claimed more participation in decision-making and minority representation for employees on the boards of companies. The question of industrial democracy was also raised in several party statements during the election campaign of 1970. Some of the bourgeois parties saw solutions along the lines of increased individual ownership of shares and profit sharing. Ideas of increased self determination in work also appeared in party programs. The change of program and policy in the Communist Party (*Vänsterpartiet kommunisterna*) during the last decade has placed more emphasis on industrial democracy as part of socialist transformation.

In 1971 the LO congress gave explicit support to the report on industrial democracy containing the following claims:[42]

1. That existing labor laws should be revised and amended to the benefit of the union movement, partly replacing the existing regulations of Paragraph 32 with a new labor law that would generate more symmetrical relations between capital and labor.

2. The right to bargain should be extended to include such matters as personnel management, organization, project development and supervision.

3. Employment should be protected by new laws restricting managers' powers to dismiss and lay-off employees.

4. Laws of work safety should be amended, giving more power to safety stewards and more resources for public safety control, and safety research should be expanded.
5. Employees should be granted representation on company boards.
6. The precedence of the employer in interpreting agreements should be exchanged for a corresponding precedence for unions.
7. The shaping and design of work-process and jobs should allow more freedom and autonomy (self-determination) and offer more variation and stimulation.
8. Supervisory authority should be replaced by cooperation and employee self-determination.

The pressure from the trade union movement led to the appointment of governmental investigation committees on different labor acts. The proposals of these investigations, the revisions of these proposals by government and the final proposals that were decided by parliament followed mainly the lines promoted by the union congresses. The following acts have been passed:

Laws on representation of employees in certain companies on an experimental basis (1972, 1977).
Security of Employment Act (1974).
Promotion of Employment Act (1974).
The Act Concerning the STatus of Shop Stewards (1974).
The Worker Protection Act (1974).
Act of Participation in Decision-Making (1977).

These laws have been supplemented by central agreements between labor market organizations:

Agreement on Rationalization (1972).
Agreement of Economic Committees and Employment Consultants (1975).
Agreement of Work Environment and Guide Lines for Enterprise Health (1976).

According to the Act of Security of Employment, an employee can only be dismissed on 'reasonable' grounds.[43] The law specifies priority rules in cases of grounded dismissals, and the seniority principle is one of them. The law requires a minimum of a month's notice from employer or employee. The obligatory period of notice increases with age to a maximum of 6 months.

The Act of Participation in Decision-Making[44] extends the right of unions to collective agreements on decision-making in many areas such as organization, project development, personnel management, supervision, etc. By means of residual right to industrial action, the parties may resort to industrial action if actualized questions concerning participation are not regulated in collective agreement. The local trade union enjoys precedence of interpretation in disputes about collective agreement. The employers' primary obligation to negotiate requires that management initiate negotiations with trade unions before making any change in management or supervision of work.

The employer is required to provide employees with information on company production plans, economic situation, personnel policy, etc. Labor peace obligations are required and employees may be sued for damages in cases of violation of the rules. However, in cases of wild-cat strikes, the local union is required to start negotiations to settle the issue. Damages for breaking peace obligations have been sharpened.

There has also been rising interest and expectation in the other area of industrial democracy: the employees' control and self-determination of the work process and work environment. The thinking here was stimulated by some practical experiments carried out by the socio-technical school in Norway, sponsored by a joint committee of labor market organizations.[45] The experiments concerned increased participation of employees and the development of self-steering groups. Other social scientific studies confirmed the thesis that a higher degree of participation, autonomy and self-steering on the job created more job satisfaction and a higher degree of engagement and stimulation on the job and also outside it.[46] These ideas had been presented and supported in the report to the 1966 LO-congress as mentioned above. They were taken up by the report on industrial democracy in 1971, and decisions were taken to claim employees' participation in decision-making concerning the organization of jobs and work processes and the shaping of more meaningful, stimulating and self-determing jobs.[47]

TCO congresses and experts had also discussed parallel issues and had come to similar conclusions in 1970 and 1973. The expert group on democracy in industry had discerned a special aspect of industrial democracy called self-determination, and it argued for more self-determination in work.[48]

In 1976 both the LO-congress and the TCO-congress gave strong support to claims for increased self-determination and other claims related to increased job satisfaction and more meaningful and stimulating jobs. A survey of social psychological research was presented in a report showing the importance of freedom and autonomy in work for mental health and for an active orientation to society in general.[49] Employee participation in decision-making concerning organization of job environment, work process and jobs should, according to the report, be aware of standards of self-determination, variation, stimulation and meaningfulness of jobs and raise the standard of job satisfaction. The LO report, 'Solidaric Participation in Decisions', raised the following claims: self-determination concerning forms of payment, forms of group organization, daily work, supervision and influence on administration and planning.

Notions of job environment and safety and health in work have gone through an interesting transformation during the last decade in relation to the ideas of work process and job design.[50] These changes have also been influenced by social and psychological research and both the human-relations and socio-technical schools have contributed. A manifestation of this is found in the recent report of the governmental investigation committee on work environment:

> The essential aim of the new Act is to afford protection against health hazards and accident risks. But the Act also sets out to do more than protect workers against certain negative phenomena endangering health and security. In keeping with the broader view which is now taken of the working environment the proposal is also founded on the establishment of working conditions in which the individual can experience his work as a meaningful and rewarding part of his life.

> An important section of the Act concerns cooperation between employer and employee. Considerable emphasis is placed on the participation of employees in the shaping of the work environment, but attention is also drawn to the role of public authorities in furnishing guidance and intervening when necessary to ensure that the legislation serves its purpose.

The importance of working with a broader environment concept and considering self-determining job requirements have been supported at the LO-congress and TCO-congress in 1976.[51] The old claim for medical care in places of work has been emphasized during the last decade with increasing strength. An agreement on health care has been made between the labor market organizations.[52] Health care in the place of work is oriented mainly towards prevention and accident aid, while the ordinary medical service is supposed to be taken care of by the public health service. The work health care should be seen as part of the extended safety functions and the safety committee of the enterprise will be responsible for health on the job.

The concept of rationalization has been elaborated and related to broader goals than was the case in the beginning of the post-war period. LO and SAF agreement on time and motion studies has been symptomatically substituted by an agreement on rationalization.[53] This agreement states that the goals of rationalization should not only be related to traditional technical development but should also consider demands for better work environment. A holistic view on rationalization is proposed. It is generally agreed that new work conditions should satisfy requirements of health and safety. The danger of too much specialization is mentioned. Rationalization is directed towards goals of good job environment. Studies of work should be carried out in an open manner with information accessible to workers. Rationalization should be based on an intimate cooperation between management and employees. The rank and file worker should be engaged in rationalization and shop stewards should be given training in rationalization techniques.

These reforms for improving conditions of work and industrial relations are still on the program and legislative level and we do not know what objective changes in industrial relations will occur. There are many counteracting forces, for example, the resistance of capitalistic market structure, trends of concentration and centralization, the pressure of international competition and economic recession, the restrictions of multinational enterprises, the inertia in existing buildings, machines and production systems, the prevailing ideas of employers and managers and their organizations, barriers to mobilization among employees for participation in union work, etc. The change in government in 1976 to a coalition of Centre, Liberal and Conservative parties will probably give a legislative stalemate, and plans for collective capital participation of unions will not be realized. They will possibly be transformed to a private capital participation of employees.

There has been a general consensus that these reforms require resources for research to follow up and evaluate consequences. A governmental sponsored centre for research on working life has been established with the task to study the reforms and their consequences.

NOTES

1. Dahlström, E., *Fördjupad företagsdemokrati.* Stockholm: Prisma, 1969; E. Dahlström, 'Produktion och jämlikhet' in G. Nordenstam (ed.), *Värde, välfärd och jämlikhet.* Lund: Studentlitteratur, 1972.

2. Svening, O., *Socialdemokratin och näringslivet.* Stockholm: Tidens förlag, 1972; S. Johansson, *När är tiden mogen? En fråga för programkommissionén.* Stockholm: Tidens förlag, 1972; N. R. Andersson, K. Blomqvist and L. Eliasson, *Kan Sverige styras kooperativt?* Stockholm: Tidens förlag, 1976.

3. Data on the composition of the labor market, social strata and social classes are analyzed in the following publications: S. Carlsson, *Yrken och samhällsgrupper.* Stockholm: Almqvist & Wiksell, 1968; L. Lewin, B. Jenssen and D. Sörbom, *The Swedish Electorate 1887-1968.* Stockholm: Almqvist & Wiksell, 1972; H. Berglind and B. Rundblad, *Arbetsmarknaden i Sverige. Ett sociologiskt perspektiv.* Stockholm: Esselte Studium AB, 1975; H. Berglind, 'From Industrial to Service Society', paper given at the Polish-Swedish Symposium on Sociology of Work and Social Policy in Warsaw, 1976.

4. *Arbetarrörelsens efterkrigsprogram. De 27 punkterna med motivering.* Stockholm: Wictor Pettersons Bokindustriaktiebolag, 1945.

5. Meidner, R. and H. Niklasson, *Arbetsmarknad och arbetsmarknadspolitik.* Malmö: Studentlitteratur, 1970; B. Öhman, 'LO och arbetsmarknadspolitiken efter andra världskriget i Tvärsnitt'. *Sju forskningsrapporter utgivna till LO:s 75-årsjubileum 1973.* Stockholm: Prisma; Berglind and Rundblad, op. cit.; B. Furåker, *Stat och arbetsmarknad. Studier i svensk rörlighetspolitik.* Stockholm: Arkiv, 1976.

6. Lewin, L., *Planhushållningsdebatten.* Stockholm: Almqvist & Wiksell, 1967, pp. 263-347.

7. Ibid., pp. 263-347, 'The harvest policy', pp. 348-422, 'Progressive managers';
S. A. Söderpalm, *Direktörsklubben. Storindustrin i svensk politik under 1930- och
1940-talen.* Stockholm: Zenit, 1976, pp. 139-153; M. Dahlqvist, *Staten,
socialdemokratin och socialismen. En inledande idéanalys.* Lund: Prisma, 1975, pp.
165 ff.

8. Browald, T., *Företagen i en förändrad värld i Näringsliv och samhälle*, 1953,
p. 71; *Företagen och framåtskridandet. Diskussionsunderlag för SNS lokalgrupper*,
1956.

9. Elvander, N., *Näringslivet och första statsmakten — relationer under
efterkrigstiden i näringslivets 900 organisationer*, 1974.

10. Systematic analyses of the development of the Swedish economy in the post-
war period are found in the following books: E. Lindbeck, *Blandekonomi i om-
vandling*, 1973; B. Södersten (ed.), *Svensk ekonomi*, 1974; E. Westerlind and R.
Beckman, *Sveriges ekonomi; Struktur och utvecklingstendenser*, 1974; D. Tarschys,
et al., *Offentlig sektor i tillväxt*, 1976; On concentration and fusionprocesses, see for
example, R. Rydén, *Fusioner i svensk industri*, 1971; B. Nygren, *Studier av fusioner
inom svensk industri 1968-1971*, 1973; *Industri. Sveriges officiella statistik* (yearly
publication).

11. Eriksson, K., 'Facklig demokrati. Begrepp och utvecklingstendenser',
Gothenburg University, Sociological Department (mimeographed), 1973.

12. Several interesting attempts have been made to explain and understand the
cultural changes of the 1960s, e.g., P. Berger, B. Berger and H. Kellner, *The
Homeless Mind. Modernization and Consciousness*, 1973; R. Ingelhart, *The Silent
Revolution in Europe. Changing Values and Political Styles Among Western
Publics*; G. Statera, *Death of a Utopia, The Development and Decline of Student
Movements in Europe.* New York: Oxford University Press, 1975. The most
penetrating work on Swedish post-war development is presented in Walter Korpis's
work, *The Working Class in the Welfare Society. Work, Unions and Politics in
Sweden.* London: Routledge & Kegan Paul, 1977.

13. Inge, G. and M. B. Inge, *Den ofärdiga välfärden.* Stockholm: Tidens förlag,
1967. A special governmental investigation was appointed to study low incomes in
1965. There was an increasing awareness of serious obstacles for income leveling.
With the appointment of Rudolf Meidner, the leading LO economist, as chairman,
this committee became more active and generated a set of reports that elucidated the
unequal income distribution and attracted a tremendous interest. See 'Kompendium
om låginkomstutredningen' (mimeographed report, Stockholm, 1971).

14. Björck, S., H. Sillnäs and B. Palmqvist, *Litteraturhistoria if fackformat.
Svensk diktning från 80-tal till 70-tal.* Stockholm: Tema, 1971; T. Broström,
Modern svensk litteratur. Stockholm: Aldus, 1974, pp. 172 ff.

15. Korpi, W., *Varför strejkar arbetarna?* Stockholm: Tidens förlag, 1970; H.
Hart, and C. v. Otter, *Lönebildning på arbetsplatsen. En sociologisk studie.*
Stockholm: Prisma, 1973; *Hamnarbetarstrejken i Göteborg november 1969.*
Stockholm: Zenit, 1970; *Stuvarstrejken i Ådalen 1970.* Stockholm: Prisma, 1971; E.
Dahlström, et. al., *LKAB och demokratin. Rapport om en strejk och ett forskn-
ingsprojekt.* Stockholm: Wahlström & Widstrand, 1971.

16. Abrahamssom, B., *Organisationsteori. Om byrakrati, administration och
självstyre.* Stockholm: AWE Gebers, pp. 77-148.

17. Ramström, D., *Administrativa processer. Organisationslära och företagsledning*, Stockholm: Bonniers, 1963; E. Rhenman and B. Stymne, *Företagsledning i en förändrad värld*, Stockholm: Bokförlaget Aldus/Bonniers, 1965; H. Mabon, *Organisationslärans utveckling*, Vällingby: M & B fackboksförlag, 1971.

18. Some organizational scientists have observed similar underlying dimensions of different schools, e.g., T. Burns and G. M. Stalker, *Mechanistic and Organic Systems in Industrial Man*, Harmondsworth: Penguin Books Ltd, 1969; G. H. Rice, and D. W. Bishoprid, *Conceptual Models of Organization*, New York: Appleton-Century-Crofts, 1971; Abrahamsson, op. cit., pp. 81 ff. and 110 ff.

19. See, for instance, *Samspelet i en organisation och principer för ledarskap*. En rapport fran administrativt projekt i LKAB. Published by LKAB, 1969.

20. Eric Rhenman's system analysis of the enterprise in *Företagsdemokrati och företagsorganisation* (Stockholm: Företagsekonomiska forskningsinstitutet, 1964) is used as an argument against increased representative industrial democracy by employers' association in *Samarbete i framtidens företag. (Betänkande utgivet av SAF:s referensgrupp)*, Stockholm, 1965. See comments by Edmund Dahlström in LO Journal, *Fackföreningsrörelsen* (1965:24).

21. Davis, K., *Human Relations at Work*, New York: McGraw-Hill, 1957; A. Lundquist, *Personalledningens grunder*, Uppsala: Appelbergs Boktryckeri AB, 1968.

22. Thorsrud, E. and F. E. Emery, *Medinflytande och engagemang i arbetet. Norska försök med självstyrande grupper*, Stockholm: Utvecklingsrådet för samarbetsfrågor, 1969.

23. *Nya arbetsformer. Rapport från 500 försök 1975*, Stockholm: SAF:s tekniska avdelning.

24. *Arbetarrörelsens efterkrigsprogram*, op. cit., pp. 190-218.

25. See, for example, E. Dahlström, *Industri och arbetsorganisationer i Svensk samhällsstruktur i sociologisk belysning*, Stockholm: Svenska Bokförlaget, 1965, pp. 135 ff.

26. Karlbom, T., *Blodprov på arbetsglädje*, Stockholm: Kooperativa förbundets bokförlag, 1949; G. Vestlund, *Arbetsglädjens problem*. Stockholm: Brevskolan, 1949; Konferensen människan och arbetet, 'Föredrag och diskussioner vid Sveriges socialdemokratiska ungdomsförbunds konferens i Stockholm den 5-6 december 1949', Stockholm: Frihets förlag.

27. *Fackföreningsrörelsen och den fulla sysselsättningen*. Stockholm: LO, 1951; *Samornad näringspolitik*. Stockholm: LO, 1969.

28. Wigfors, E., *Materialistisk historieuppfattning. Industriell demokrati*. Stockholm: Tidens förlag, 1970, pp. 99-166.

29. The history of branch rationalization bodies and wage-earner funds is not written and is scattered round in many works, e.g., Lewin, op. cit., pp. 263-409; Öhman, op. cit.; A. Wredén, *Kapital till de anställda. En studie av vinstdelning och löntagarfonder*. Stockholm: SNS, 1976; Kollektiv kapitalbildning genom löntagarfonder, *Rapport till LO-kongressen*. Stockholm: LO, 1976.

30. *Samordnad näringspolitik*, op. cit., pp. 188 ff.

31. Kollektiv kapitalbildning genom löntagarfonder, op. cit., pp. 16 ff.

32. Meidner, R., A. Hedberg and G. Fond, *Löntagarfonder*. Stockholm: Tidens förlag, 1975.

46 *Work and Power*

33. *Löntagarkapital. TCO:s arbetsgrupp för samhällsekonomiska frågor.* Stockholm: TCO, 1976.

34. Wredén, op. cit., pp. 95 ff.

35. *Företagsvinster, Kapitalförsörjning, Löntagarfonder. Rapport från en arbetsgrupp inom näringslivet.* Stockholm: Näringslivets förlagsdistribution, 1976.

36. Wallander, J., *I huvudet på en kapitalist.* Stockholm: Askild & Kärnekull, 1974, pp. 147 ff.

37. *Fackföreningsrörelsen och företagsdemokrati.* Stockholm: LO, 1961.

38. *Fackföreningsrörelsen och den tekniska utvecklingen. Rapport från en arbetsgrupp till 1966 års LO-kongress.* Stockholm: Prisma, 1966; E. Dahlström, B. Gardell, B. Rundblad, et. al., *Teknisk förändring och arbetsanpassning. Ett sociologiskt bidrag.* Stockholm: Prisma, 1966; E. Bolinder, *Individen och den industriella miljön. Medicinska synpunkter.* Stockholm: Prisma, 1966.

39. Karlsson, L.-E., *Demokrati på arbetsplatsen.* Stockholm: Prisma, 1969; Dahlström, *Fördjupad företagsdemokrati,* op. cit., An insightful account of the enterprise experiments is given in L.-E. Karlsson, 'Ny facklig strategi — Från samråd till medbestämmande'. Mimeographed report, 1977.

40. Schiller, B., 'LO, paragraf 32 och företagsdemokratin i Tvärsnitt'. *Sju forskningsrapporter utgivna till LO:s 75-årsjubileum 1973,* op. cit., pp. 288-398.

41. *Rapporter från SAMKO. TCO. Demokratisering av arbetslivet. 1970, 1971 och 1972.* Stockholm: TCO.

42. *Demokrati i företagen. Rapport till LO-kongressen.* Stockholm: LO, 1971.

43. Gustavsson, S., *Trygghet i anställning. Lagen om anställningsskydd mm.* Stockholm: Rabén och Sjögren, 1974, pp. 21 ff.

44. Bergqvist, O. and L. Lunning, *Medbestämmande i arbetslivet.* Stockholm: Liber förlag, 1976.

45. Thorsrud, E. and F. E. Emery, *Mot en ny bedriftsorganisasjon. Experimenter i industrielt demokrati fra samarbeidsprosjektet. LO/NAF 1969.* Oslo: Johan Grundt Tanum Förlag.

46. Gardell, B., *Produktionsteknik och arbete. En socialpsykologisk studie av industriellt arbete.* Stockholm: Personaladministrativa rådet, 1971.

47. *Demokrati i företagen,* op. cit., pp. 81ff. Act of Representation on Company Boards in Bergqvist and Lunning, op. cit., pp. 324 ff.

48. *Rapporter från SAMKO,* op. cit.

49. Gardell, B: *Arbetsinnehall och livskvalitet.* op cit.; *Solidariskt medbestämmande. LO-kongressen 1976.* Stockholm: LO; *Villkor i arbetet — en skrift om personalpolitik. TCO-kongressen 1976.* Stockholm: TCO.

50. *Arbetsmiljölag, Slutbetänkande avgivet av arbetsmiljöutredningen.* Stockholm: SOU 1976:1. Specially English text, pp. 451-68; *Bakgrund till förslag om arbetsmiljölag,* Stockholm: SOU 1976:2; *Rapporter i psykosociala frågor,* Stockholm: SOU 1976:3.

51. *Arbetsmiljön, Rapport till LO-kongressen 1976.* Stockholm: LO, 1976; Tjänstemännens arbetsmiljöer, *Arbete, Hälsa, Välbefinnande,* Stockholm: TCO, 1976.

52. *Arbetsmiljöavtalet, Avtal om allmänna regler för arbetsmiljöverksamheten i företagen samt rekommendationer för partssamarbete i företagshälsovårdscentraler (arbetsmiljöavtalet) och överenskommelse om riktlinjer för företagshälsovården.* SAF, LO, PTK, 1976.

53. *Avtal mellan Svenska Arbetsgivarföreningen och Landsorganisationen i Sverige angående rationalisering träffat i juni 1972.*

2

PATHS OF TRANSITION TO WORKERS' SELF-MANAGEMENT IN THE DEVELOPED CAPITALIST COUNTRIES

Branko Horvat
University of Zagreb, Yugoslavia

'The carrying of Universal suffrage in England', wrote Marx in 1852, 'would...be a far more socialistic measure than anything which has been honoured with that name on the Continent. Its inevitable result, here [in England], is *the* political supremacy of the working class'.[1] Exactly forty years later his friend and collaborator, Friedrich Engels, remarked in a letter: 'During forty years Marx and myself have been tirelessly repeating that the democratic republic for us is the only political form in which the struggle between the working class and the class of capitalists may first become universal and then be completed together with the decisive victory of the proletariat.'[2]

Today, i.e., a century later, all developed capitalist countries have long ago established universal suffrage. Most of them are republics, and those which are not are occasionally more democratic than those which are. In England and Germany, the two countries referred to by our authors, workers represent the majority of population. In both countries Labor parties are in power and have been so several times in the past. In some other countries Social Democratic parties have held political power for many years. And yet, in none of them has socialism been established. Neither can that be expected to happen very soon. Both violent revolution and peaceful — and piecemeal — reforms have failed to produce socialism so far.

Our analysis has uncovered some of the reasons for that. Capitalist development has been fast enough so as to enable all classes to share — albeit unequally — in the benefits. The ruling class was able to grant substantial political and economic concessions and yet to retain the reins of political and economic power. The workers were concerned with the lower levels of need satisfaction and failed to develop effective socialist consciousness. Workers' organizations, trade unions and parties, have to a large extent been integrated into the system and failed to produce a viable radical alternative. In the struggle for survival, unions and Labor parties were forced to build bureaucratic structures which enhanced their power but greatly reduced their socialist potential. To put it succinctly, the society was not ripe for socialism.

Yet, Marx and Engels were undoubtedly right when they asserted that under political democracy the conditions for a socialist transformation are most favorable. We have now to investigate how to exploit these conditions effectively. We may proceed in five stages, first studying the two fundamental preconditions for a social change, next considering the available instruments and, finally, designing two institutional changes.

I THE SATISFACTION OF NEEDS
CRISIS

Whenever a discrepancy develops between the forces of production and production relations, sooner or later the latter will have to be adjusted. In late capitalist society this discrepancy is reflected in the failure of the system to satisfy certain fundamental needs. Observing the prolonged misery of the working class, the nineteenth century socialists believed that the system's failure to improve the material level of living would generate an increasing discontent which would eventually result in a revolutionary explosion. This belief proved to be unjustified. It was replaced by another belief, connected with the obvious contradiction between the social nature of production and private appropriation. Observing periodic slumps, many socialists came to believe that capitalism would become increasingly unable to harmonize supply and demand, that business cycles would become more violent, that unemployment would increase, that further accumulation would become impossible, and at some point the system would break down (Z. Boudin, F. Sternberg and though with a different explanation, H. Grossman). This did not happen either. The theory of *Zusammenbruch* proved false. The system managed to increase the level of living substantially, and even to reduce the inequality in income distribution. Unemployment and business cycles, though not eliminated, were brought under certain control. The rate of growth and accumulation, if anything, increased.

The third widespread belief concerned the colonies. The colonies, it was argued, were indispensable for a normal functioning of capitalism, because they provided outlets for capital and commodity exports (Rosa Luxembourg). Imperialism, as it were, resulted from this necessity to secure ever expanding markets. Without them capitalism could not survive. After the Second World War colonial empires disintegrated, former colonies won their independence and capitalism survived, with trade expanding faster than ever before. In general, it was not consumption or the barriers to accumulation or the structure of the markets where the system failed to satisfy the needs; it was the work process itself.

In 1969 the Survey Research Center at the University of Michigan conducted a revealing survey of more than 1,500 American workers. The population of the United States at that time enjoyed the highest standard of living in the world. It was found that one out of every four workers under thirty felt dissatisfied with his work. This percentage was identical for both blue-collar and white-collar workers under thirty. The percentage of discontented workers was the same for all levels of education. Of the eight top-ranked aspects of work, six were related to the content of the worker's job. Good pay ranked only fifth, after interesting work, enough help and equipment to get the job done, enough information to get the job done and enough authority to do the job.[3] This survey was undertaken after it became apparent that work discontent resulted in serious production disruptions such as

wildcat strikes, high labor turnover, absenteeism, poor quality of
output, slow-downs and outright sabotage. 'The younger
worker...says he hates the job, particularly the monotonous factory job. At times he hates it so much that he deliberately will
throw a monkey wrench in the machinery, or turn to drugs to
escape boredom. To him, whether the job is better than it used to
be or pays more and gives benefits is beside the point.'[4] Obviously
the affluent, educated worker is no longer prepared to consider his
work as purely instrumental for something else. He wants to engage
in *meaningful* work. 'The prospect of tightening up belts every two
minutes for eight hours for thirty years doesn't lift the human
spirit'. The young worker feels 'he's not master of his own destiny.
He's going to run away from it every time he gets a chance. That is
why there's an absence problem.'[5] The worker is no longer satisfied
with the collective bargaining which treats him as a 'pay category'.
Neither will he tolerate being 'moved' from one job to another or
being 'put to work' on a machine like a piece of a tool without participating in the respective decisions. The system encounters an
unresolvable contradiction. Unemployment does not discipline
workers any longer; it creates dangerous political ferment. Secure
employment, on the other hand, generates the will to control one's
own destiny.

Better education and further increases in the standard of living
will strengthen these attitudes. And so will changes in family life
brought about by the equalization of the status of women. When a
man is the only bread-winner, he will endure all hardships only to
support his family. He will seek his personal fulfilment through his
family. 'As long as the money comes in, and as long as the family
provider is not threatened, most men will go along...with the work
routine, however arduous it is. If, however, the man's role as
breadwinner grows less vital, the whole fragile bargain threatens to
break down'.[6] In this respect the employment of women and the
free education of children cause a profound change. The marital
partners share the financial responsibilities while social insurance
and public education make savings for old age, medical treatment
and tuition fees unnecessary. The social relations and the conditions of work, the quality of life, emerge as the most important life
concern.

While workers are becoming more sensitive to how they are
treated, the employers are becoming more vulnerable. Work

discontent is for them a serious danger. Slaves and serfs can operate but the simplest and crudest machines. More sophisticated machinery, invented during the industrial revolution, required free wage labor. Similarly, the highly capital-intensive plants and automated lines of late capitalist society require a new kind of labor force. The entire assembly line comes to a standstill if one member of the crew is missing. Great damage, out of any proportion to the wage cost, can be caused by poor work in a continuous process plant. Major savings in production costs are no longer to be found in cutting the workers' wages. They come from improved yields, reduced waste and avoidance of shut-downs. If the modern forces of production are to function properly, workers must be responsible and reliable. For that, they must be content with their jobs. That is why the employers — regardless of their individual or class preferences — must find remedies for work discontent. And they, in fact, are rather busy experimenting with all sorts of solutions suggested by the hired experts. In the United States special legislation was introduced providing for 'research for solutions to the problem of alienation among American workers and to provide for pilot projects and provide technical assistance to find ways to deal with that problem...'.[7]

If work is to become less monotonous and boring, the jobs ought to be rotated, enriched and enlarged; jobs must be upgraded so as to promise workers a way of transcending dead-end jobs, isolated subordinates ought to be replaced by autonomous work groups, automatic management by participatory management. The 'scientific' Taylorist organization of work, whereby complex operations are broken down into elementary motions and workers asked to perform these motions like trained cattle, is abandoned and the trend is reversed. Fragments are reintegrated. The assembly line in a car factory is broken into separate teams. Billing clerks in a telephone company are given complete responsibility for certain accounts, rather than a single operation on each account. Piecework is replaced by team work, and work teams are given a certain measure of autonomy in work design. Workers are given the authority to control the product assembly and the assignment of jobs along the assembly lines. Hourly wages are replaced by weekly salaries. Insulting status differences are eliminated. The amenities for blue-collar workers are equalized with those of white-collar workers.

All these measures have generated certain productivity gains; work discipline has improved, supervisory and management costs have been reduced. They have also contributed to an improvement of the work conditions and to a certain humanization of work.

It is good to see capitalists competing in improving the work conditions — in contrast to what happened during Marx's time when the sweating system, long working day and low wages were the sources of high profit. But current improvements do not even touch the main source of trouble, the autocratic hierarchy within the productive establishment. The work remains alienating, the worker discontented and the production system in constant jeopardy.

Since work is existentially important, discontent with work leads to a discontent with life. The Michigan Survey shows that very neatly. Those who have negative attitudes towards work have also negative attitudes towards life. In both respects the self-employed report least dissatisfaction. This is clearly due to the independence they enjoy, to the possibility, however small, of self-determination. But the percentage of self-employed is constantly dwindling. Work and life dissatisfactions are increasing. Society is becoming ripe for a change. The change will not be caused by material poverty, but by the failure of the system to satisfy the higher, historically determined needs. 'That is, the chief accusation against capitalism is no longer that it cannot produce the goods necessary for a decent standard of living, but that it fails to create the fundamental conditions for human freedom and self-expression. It does not permit, at any level, individual self-determination...'.[8]

II THE LEGITIMACY CRISIS

In the first turbulent post-war year, 1919, William Straker, the Northumberland miners' agent, expressed the following views to the Sankey Commission on the Nationalization of the Mines:

> In the past workmen have thought that if they could secure higher wages and conditions they would be content. Employers have thought that if they granted these things workers ought to be contented. Wages and conditions have improved; but the discontent and unrest have not disappeared. Many good people have come to the conclusion that working people are so unreasonable that it is useless

trying to satisfy them. The fact is that the unrest is deeper than pounds, shillings, and pence, necessary as they are. The root of the matter is the striving of the spirit of man to be free.[9]

Yet, there could be no producer freedom for the miners in Britain, the most liberal of all capitalist states. Strikers were defeated, mines remained in private hands, employers' autocracy was re-established. It is only now, half a century later, that this freedom has come to be generally considered as a fundamental human need. That, of course, must have far reaching consequences concerning the legitimacy of the existing order.

If an order fails to satisfy certain fundamental needs, its legitimacy will be questioned. The legitimacy 'involves the capacity of the system to engender and maintain the belief that the existing institutions are the most appropriate ones for society.'[10] If an increasing number of people are dissatisfied with work and life, the institutions cannot be the most appropriate. And if the institutions fail to function properly, the value configuration of the community must have changed. This, in fact, is the crucial point. For an increasing number of individuals, the existing social arrangements cease to be justified. They feel that a change is possible. And if possible, it ought to be undertaken.

Some fundamental values such as freedom, democracy, equality of opportunity may not change, but they gradually acquire a new content and a different interpretation. Consider the concept of democracy. Can a society be democratic if the democracy applies only to political life and stops at the factory gate? Behind the gate democratic rights are suspended and a repressive autocracy is established. Why should such a duality be justified, i.e., tolerated? In 1965 the organ of the German business interests, *Industriekurier*, wrote: 'The democratization of economy is as meaningless as the democratization of barracks or prisons'.[11] A century ago such a pronouncement would not have caused much disagreement. Today it does not indicate that economic democracy is impossible, but rather that corporations are organized like barracks or prisons. And that is simply not acceptable any longer.

Similar reasoning applies to other values mentioned above. Taking a job with a firm does not appear as a mere free contract any longer. If the firm is organized like a barracks or a prison, then the wage contract implies surrendering one's own personal freedom.

Closely related is the treatment of property. It may remain sacrosanct and yet one may refuse to justify the use of property for appropriation and disposal of the labour of others. The latter resembles slavery and so wage slavery becomes a socially meaningful concept. Democracy and wage slavery are obviously not compatible. As for the equality of opportunity between rich and poor, or between weak and powerful, it sounds like a coarse joke, not like a serious proposition.

The erosion of legitimacy is always accompanied by an erosion of moral standards in public life. A new term, the 'credibility gap', has come to be used to describe one aspect of this phenomenon. Atrocities of the French military machine in Algeria and American genocide in Vietnam produced deep moral crises in these two countries. The Watergate affair, the ITT subversion in Chile and the worldwide Lockheed corruption affair are some instances of the credibility gap.

It is not difficult to indicate the inherent contradictions of the system. Business authoritarianism tends to be extended into political authoritarianism, which, of course, means the death of democracy. The cost of armaments and repression destroys the rationality of economic calculus. Free business initiative destroys ecological balance and, on the world scale, prevents development of poor countries. The list can be extended at will.

No social order can be changed if it succeeds in preserving its legitimacy. That is why the erosion of capitalist legitimacy is of fundamental importance for a socialist transformation. It proceeds spontaneously, as in the cases described above. It can also be speeded up. To do that is the revolutionary mission of the intellectuals. On that point also Lenin and Kautsky would agree. A study of the revolutions would reveal that desertions of intellectuals precede successful revolutions.[12] The intellectuals question the legitimacy of the old order, reinterpret the values and create new consciousness. They explore the alternatives and work out possible solutions. 'There is no revolutionary movement without revolutionary theory' (Lenin).

Not every attack on the established values will undermine the system's legitimacy. Some may even strengthen it. Consider the following set of conservative bourgeois values as juxtaposed to the values of the hippy counterculture:

Bourgeois	Hippy
Conservative	Rebel

Hard work	Leisure
Achieving	No purpose
Decent, straight	Shocking
Growth	Stagnation

Although the hippy has also a case, the naive negation of the established values can only generate strong resistance. The old values will be defended and the pseudo-radical critique will be dismissed as silly. For hard work may mean 'Puritan ethic', and also work for the community. Work, being existential activity, has been valued by all societies and leisure is certainly not a substitute but a complement to it. What one would like to do is to increase spontaneity and creativity of work, not to abolish it. Achieving may be alienating, as when oriented to money and power accumulation, but it may also mean perfection in arts and good craftsmanship. 'No purpose' is certainly not a humanizing alternative. Stupid and hypocritical conventions of the 'straight' bourgeois society cannot be fought by frivolity and obscenity but by genuine decency. Finally, the damaging effects of growth cannot be eliminated by stagnation but by a socially controlled growth.

This brief exercise into pseudo-radicalism suggests the following simple rule. There is no need to deny historical continuity in cultural development. Socialism does not represent a mere negation but rather a new — if you wish, dialectical — synthesis. Thus free initiative, responsibility, individual freedom, competition, democracy and other old values ought to be included in the list of radical political slogans and be appropriately reinterpreted. For instance:

— Free initiative of associated producers, not a monopoly control of corporate oligarchy.

— Free men in free society, not wage slavery and the rule of plutocracy and bureaucracy.

— Genuine democracy of full participation, not a fake democracy for bosses.

— Self-management, not managerial authoritarianism.

— Equality of opportunity, not class stratification.

— Self-government, not party machinery.

— Competition in good life, not in exploitation or killing.

— Respect for individual personality, not for the possession of property or power.

— Culture of fully developed individuals, not primitivism of crippled money makers or office holders.

— Production for better living, not for destruction.

— Expansion of useful output, not of waste and pollution.

— Greater efficiency, not unemployment and waste of resources.

In the 1976 German elections the Conservative opposition fought against the ruling Social Democrats under the slogan: *Freiheit oder Sozialismus* (Freedom or Socialism). This *Freiheit* was not meant to be exactly the same as freedom in the present paper. But the mere fact that Conservatives could mobilize voters under such a slogan — and amost win — indicates that something was wrong with traditional socialism. Both its main variants, Social Democracy and Communism, failed to destroy the legitimacy of the bourgeois order. Bourgeois revolutions produced certain essential individual liberties. The socialist revolution needs neither deny them nor oppose them; it should transcend bourgeois freedom. If freedom is to be really meaningful, it will imply a control of existential conditions of one's own life. In this essential sense, freedom can be attained better in socialism than in any alternative system. Thus the strongest ideological weapon of bourgeois society can be turned against it and used for powerful attacks on its legitimacy. The twenty-ninth thesis, announced at the Paris Sorbonne on the turbulent 13-14 June 1968, proclaimed: "The bourgeois revolution was legal, the proletarian revolution was economic. Ours will be social and cultural so that the man can become that what he is'.[13]

III TRADE UNIONS AND SOCIALIST PARTIES AND THEIR POLICIES

During the long years of class struggle the working class created two organizations to protect its interests, the unions and the political parties. These organizations can be used as instruments of socialist transformation. One must not forget the limitations of the two organizations. Both of them have certain stakes in the old system. Their leaderships will not suddenly burst with a revolutionary enthusiasm for a genuine socialism. But the need satisfaction and the legitimacy crisis will generate mounting grass roots pressure. Besides, the logic of the struggle is such that each of the combatants must exploit the disadvantages of the adversary in order to establish his own domination. In fighting for their domination, unions and pro-socialist parties will give support to socialist transformation. Let us see how this can be done.

The traditional dilemma between violent revolution and peaceful reform has by now been resolved.[14] Violence is neither possible nor desirable. Socialism progresses fastest by using means appropriate to its own nature. Hatred today cannot produce love tomorrow. Attitudes and consciousness cannot be changed overnight. The change is gradual and brought about as the transformation progresses. One may perhaps speak of peaceful revolution as the most efficient vehicle of social transformation in late capitalist societies.

There is, however, a more subtle form of the old dilemma. Violence — no, but neither cooperation. Things must be made as difficult as possible for the class enemy. The worse, the better — is an appropriate strategy. Permanent fighting keeps the fighting spirit alive and prevents capitalists from corrupting the workers. The gap between the two classes must be kept as wide as possible; no bridges. Non-cooperation and vigorous opposition will force the ruling class to make concessions and eventually to surrender.

History has not vindicated this strategy. The straining of social relations produces autocracy, not the revolution; the preservation of class differences prolongs the life of capitalism and does not promote the development of socialism. Like all negative strategies, this approach reflects a position of weakness, not one of strength; it reveals the lack of a constructive alternative rather than the presence of a well elaborated program of social transformation. If we really know what we want to do, why not make capitalists collaborate with us, in order to achieve the task? On the other hand, if non-cooperation and conflict maintenance is proclaimed to be the guiding principle, then (a) potential allies will be alienated; (b) disruptive activities will give the employers excuses for coordinated repression and the intervention of the state; (c) by not assuming the responsibility for participating in management, workers will lose a golden opportunity to learn how to run the firms, and (d) as a result of all this the duration of capitalism is likely to be unnecessarily prolonged. A much better strategy seems to be to insist on a positive program of socialist construction and to let the opposing forces take the blame for obstruction, conflicts and damage to the economy and the society. This is also a much more difficult task than merely opposing anything that the ruling class does. Yet if the unions include the majority of the working population — as they should — and the pro-socialist party or parties win the elections — as they certainly can — this is a realistic task. The limits of cooperation and the speed of reform are then determined by the attitudes of the opponents. The more rigidly they stick to their privileges and the more they refuse to cooperate, the less will they be able to claim legitimacy for their activities and the less will they be able to claim legitimacy for their activities and the faster will public opinion swing in favor of socialist construction.

Suppose the two conditions — majority unionization and the control of government — are fulfilled. What are the strategic policies that a Labor/Social-Democratic/Communist government is best advised to adhere to? There seem to be six such policies:

1. High rate of growth which enhances the affluence of the community is, at least nominally, in the interest of everybody. Fast growth eliminates unemployment and increases the bargaining position of workers. Job security and affluence orient them towards self-management. The same is the effect of reduced work time as a result of increased productivity. If profits also increase, there is nothing wrong in that. On the one hand, the bourgeoisie needs an inducement to cooperate, while on the other, a different policy will make sure that these profits are used for socialist purposes. High rate of growth presupposes a certain degree of social planning and this also is a socialist measure.

2. The redistribution of income so as to eliminate publicly recognized poverty. Besides, public expenditure on social services ought to contribute to a general reduction in standard of living differences. The rest is left to direct collective bargaining between labor and capital. In this area interests are clearly opposed. But the clash of interests has been successfully institutionalized. The gains of the workers and the poor from income redistribution are rather obvious. The employers gain if they avoid strikes. What the reasonable limits are depends partly on the relative strengths and partly on the public opinion. In spite of opposed interests, common ground exists. Social services contribute to an effective equality of

men and women (making productive employment of women possible), eliminate fear of existential risks and cause the emergence of higher needs.

3. Free education at all levels so as to enable every individual to develop his faculties depending only on his own efforts. It has been established through empirical research that education enhances democratic attitudes and increases interest in self-management. It also increases productivity. If the task of redistribution is taken by policy No. 2, and the burden of education is shared by all, then policy No. 3 is difficult to oppose. Party and union schools ought to provide education in political self-government and participation in business management.

4. Substantial subsidies for culture. High pressure advertising habits, lack of alternative experience, and 'keeping up with the Joneses' in a competitive bourgeois environment where accumulation of things is a sign of progress and prestige, creates what is known as consumerism. i.e. an enormously inflated need for material objects. As a result, income, time and energy are diverted to the satisfaction of the lowest needs, at the expense of the highest. Man is reduced to only one of his dimensions, and behaves as homo consumens. As such, he is well suited for late capitalism and completely unsuited for socialism. In order to develop higher needs, man must cultivate his mind. Education is one, but a quite insufficient, move in this direction. It must be complemented by an effective access to the culture of the community. Since the taste for things little known must first be developed, 'heavy advertising', 'competitive pricing' and subsidies are necessary. High quality fiction must be made so cheap that a taxi driver will be induced to buy it and read it while waiting for the customers — as the proverbial Moscow taxi driver does. If workers' homes are filled with books, workers' heads will be filled with socialist ideas. Museums, art galleries and public libraries ought to be planted all over the country with entrance fees abolished. Tickets for drama and ballet performances and for musical recitals ought to be priced so as to fill theatres and concert halls. Amateur drama, musical and arts groups ought to be encouraged and 'houses of culture' built as often as schools and town halls. That this can be done is shown by the experience of some etatist countries. Once mass participation in culture is achieved, yet another precondition for a socialist society

will be fulfilled. People who enjoy music, buy paintings and frequent museums are not likely to be persuaded that an accumulation of gadgets is the prime purpose in life. Neither will they consider wage labor and business autocracy as obvious and unavoidable.

These policies, however important, are designed to create only the preconditions for transition. The actual transition is the task of the two remaining policies. One of them is concerned with industrial democracy, the other with the expropriation of capital, and both of them with the gradual destruction of the basis for class exploitation.

IV INDUSTRIAL DEMOCRACY

A study of the history of employer-worker relations reveals three development stages. At first, employers were absolute bosses and workers were treated as servants. The employers had unrestricted power to hire, dismiss and fine the workers. The exploitation was brutal, the relations between the two classes savage. The attempts by workers to set up protective organizations were crushed. Unions were outlawed. When in the second half of the last century unions were gradually legalized, they emerged as the fighting organizations of the working class. They often combined trade and political activities and fought over both industrial and political issues. The First International was created by the unions, not the parties. Strikes were used to improve work conditions and to extend political liberties. The general strike was considered as a suitable means for an eventual radical social transformation. An open and ruthless class war raged throughout the entire period. This period is known as that of liberal capitalism. It ended with the First World War.

Around the turn of the century, political and industrial organizations of the working class were separated and were relatively well institutionalized as parties and unions. After the war the first workers' parties — in Germany, England, Scandinavia and elsewhere — came to power. The class war was institutionalized. Employers and workers created national bargaining organizations. This was — and still is — the period of organized capitalism.

Unions were integrated into the system. From the point of view of the worker, the function of the unions was to secure higher wages and supply social security. From the point of view of the employers, their function was to keep order on the labor market. Employers came to realize that it pays to collaborate with unions rather than insist on an arbitrary power. Two general principles of collaboration were established: (a) unions will restrict their activities to industrial conflicts and avoid political confrontations; (b) management prerogatives cannot be subject to collective bargaining. The latter meant that the formerly unrestricted power was replaced by what was considered to be strategic power denoted as 'management prerogatives'. These included the right to hire, replace, transfer and dismiss the employees and to direct and organize work, as was neatly — to give an example — formulated in the famous paragraph 23 of the Swedish central labor-capital agreement in 1906, which was made an obligatory clause for collective bargaining contracts by the Swedish Employers' Confederation. Joint consultation was compatible with the two principles. The spheres of competence seemed clearly and unambiguously demarcated.

Yet workers have never ceased to consider unions as primarily weapons against exploitation rather than merely instruments for improvements in the standard of living. A new development was inaugurated after the Second World War with the first step towards co-determination in Germany. An *Arbeitsdirektor* (Personnel Director) was introduced into top management, and labor representatives into the Supervisory Council. The minority labor representation in the Supervisory Council develops towards parity. The Works Councils' powers are strengthened. Scandinavian countries are following the German example. The multinational European companies, to be incorporated by the European Economic Community, will have labor participation in the boards of directors. A Swedish government bill of 1976 — exactly 70 years after the appearance of paragraph 23 — makes the management of a company, its structure, supervision of work, equipment, working hours, working environment, etc. negotiable. The erosion of management prerogatives is in the full swing. This third stage of employer-worker relations marks the beginning of the transition period.

In 1865 John Stuart Mill wrote 'that the relation of masters and workpeople will be gradually superseded by partnership in one of two forms: in some cases, associations of the labourers with the capitalist; in others, and perhaps finally in all, associations of labourers among themselves'.[15] In this respect Mill, of course, was not taken seriously by his bourgeois colleagues. A century passed before the first of his two categories of cases began to materialize. Instead of being called and treated as a servant — the English Master and Servant Act was replaced in 1867 — or hired hand, the worker is becoming a partner, a *medarbetare* (co-worker). When the Norwegian law on employee representation on company boards was debated in 1973, even the Conservatives voted for it. The old order is losing its legitimacy; it cannot be defended any longer.

Co-determination implies participation at the shop floor and at the company level. The workers are directly involved in the former, the unions in the latter. Workers are winning the right to participate in the measurement and evaluation of work; in making the time schedule of work and breaks; in planning the vacations; in job design and the determination of safety measures; in deciding on transfers to other jobs; they insist of being informed in advance on intended measures of rationalization and to have the right to check management decisions. Participation and autonomy at the workplace will not mean too much if the workers are excluded from strategic decisions on new organization or technology, investment ventures or mergers. That is why labor participation in the boards of directors is required. And here the unions, spanning entire industries, have great scope for new and completely unorthodox activities.

The institutionalized initiative of the unions is occasionally supplemented — often against the will of the union management — by wildcat strikes and occupation of factories. The latter happens when a firm is about to go bankrupt and workers take over the management in order to save the firm (i.e. to keep their jobs). This is an evidence sui generis on the comparative efficiency of contemporary private management. Outside industry, the participation issue is most present at the university. In the European tradition the university is in fact the oldest self-governing institution, but the encroachment on its autonomy by the state power and the development of professorial autoritarianism have reduced the scope of university self-government. The well known student revolt of the 1960s reversed this trend. Finally, with the growing unionization of public servants, participation is becoming an issue in public services as well.

Co-determination has been extensively criticized. Some of the critiques are justified, others are simply mistaken. It is said that co-determination serves the purpose of disciplining the workers, of avoiding strikes[16] and so increasing profits. Self-steering groups, works councils and parity representation induce the workers to identify themselves with the shop or with the firm; this sort of local patriotism for the firm destroys workers' solidarity and is nothing but an extended egoism. Members of the supervisory boards become corrupted by their new privileges. They forget whom they represent and behave like bosses, particularly if — as union nominees — they serve on a number of boards. Workers' representatives are torn by double loyalties at the bargaining table: they must press for better conditions for workers and at the same time defend the interests of the company. Unions must refuse to accept any responsibility for production, sales and profits. Otherwise, they will put in jeopardy their fundamental role as agents of workers' interests. Co-determination is either real, and lures the workers away from the unions and weakens union power, or is a swindle. In either case it is a highly dubious affair.

Co-determination is, obviously, a very contradictory institution. Yet, every transition is full of contradictions. Attempts to avoid contradictions by preserving organizational purity amount to a conservative defense of the status quo. Corrupting influences of directorial posts may be reduced by rotation, democratic control by the rank and file and a prohibition of multiple mandates. Unions will best serve workers' interests if they promote change. Today, change implies participation. Every participation implies responsibility. Egoism cannot be eliminated by alienation. And if the work alienation is to be reduced, the worker must become interested in his shop and his firm in order to develop a meaningful interest in his own work. If it is really true that participation increases profits and reduces the number of strikes, it is a highly commendable institution, for it demonstrates that economic efficiency can be improved only by destroying capitalist production relationships.

The trends seem certain. What the unions have to do is to press for an extension of participation towards parity — and beyond. In order to make that possible, the ownership relations must be changed as well.

V SOCIALIZATION OF PRODUCTIVE CAPITAL

Capitalism is a social system based on the ownership of capital. This, of course, is a banal observation. But it directs attention to one important fact: the ideological justification for the familiar organizational-distributional formula: workers receive wages for their labor and obey commands of the owners; owners receive profits (interest) on their capital and exercise control. To individuals reared in a capitalist environment, this formula belongs to the category of natural rights and self-evident truths. However, if the ideological backing is removed, if the legitimacy of the system is questioned, the formula suddenly appears quite arbitrary. Why should not workers also participate in profits and in decision making? The nineteenth century argument was that the owner waited and abstained from consumption and, therefore, must be compensated by profits (interest). A mere comparison of consumption levels of owners and workers makes this argument rather dubious. The current standard argument is that the owner bears risk and has to be compensated for that.[17]

Yet the worker bears risk as well, he can lose his job. In fact, his risk is comparatively greater. The owner can spread the risks by acquiring a diversified portfolio of shares, while the worker has just one labor power and one job.[18] Regarding the control over labor, that was a matter of a 'free' wage contract. As long as the other party was weak, the management prerogatives could not be touched. When the power relations changed, they became negotiable as well and so command and control ceased to be the natural rights of capitalists.

Thus the issue will not be resolved by theoretical means: it is the changes in social relations which matter in such cases. Two ideological changes can be observed. The worker is becoming a partner in the production process, a co-entrepreneur. Consequently, it is right and proper for the worker to participate in profits and decision making. On the other hand, the system generates automatically a concentration of wealth[19] and power which is at odds with the proposed ideals of democracy. Democratic control can be established by means of participation in management and deconcentration of productive wealth. The latter implies some sort of profit sharing. We thus reach again the same conclusion. As co-determination has already been discussed in the preceding section, we shall now turn our attention to profit sharing.

The discussion and experimenting with profit sharing are as old as capitalism. Profit sharing has been recommended as a device which will make workers loyal to the firm, provide work incentives and keep out trade unions. What is new in the current developments is an insistence on the right to share in profits, a replacement of cash payments by a distribution of shares and, finally, the establishment of collective trust funds rather than individual appropriation of shares. If a part of profits is paid out in cash, it represents an addition to wages and this is the end of the story. If it is paid out in shares to individual workers, these shares are likely to be sold and, in any case, an increase in the number of miniscule shareholders does not change anything in the control of industry. Collective ownership, however, makes for a radical change.

France was a pioneer in the field. In 1917 a law was passed establishing *Sociétés anonymes à participation ouvrière:* collective funds were to be created by a distribution of shares free of charge to the employees in order to strengthen their position. The situation was not ripe for this innovation and the law remained a dead letter. Half a century later, in 1967, France became the first country in which profit sharing was made compulsory in firms with more than 100 employees. The money received could be placed in various funds, given as loans to the firm or used to buy shares in the firm. Only small percentages of the total amount were used for the last purpose. Though this law contributed to the development of participation, it did not cross the threshold which separates reforms preserving capitalism from reforms destroying capitalism. That crucial step was made and the pattern was set a few years later on another continent. In Peru in 1970 a decree was passed making compulsory the distribution of a certain percentage of profits — 15 percent in the manufacturing firms — in the form of shares into indivisible workers' funds. As the percentage of stock ownership increases, the works' participation in the running of the firm increases as well. Thus by means of collective ownership the capitalist market itself is used to effect an expropriation of capital. The capitalist rules of the game are used to replace capitalists by workers.

Apart from outright state intervention, which until recently seemed the only method available, the socialization of private productive capital can be achieved by three different methods or their combinations. The Peruvian method, as we have just seen, uses profits to acquire shares. [20] The amount distributed is, therefore, proportional to the profits earned by the firm. The other method, which we may denote as Danish,[21] adds a certain markup to the standard wage bill. This sum is then converted into equity capital in the firm. In this case the profits which are distributed are not proportional to capital invested but to 'labor invested' as measured by wages. It may be argued that workers and capitalists are owners of two risk-bearing factors of production and therefore profits should be distributed in proportion to their inputs to the production process, i.e. in proportion to wages and capital.[22] This theory is equally arbitrary as the theory mentioned before, but is better suited to the changing mood of the time. In practice, however, consequences are different, as we shall see in a moment. Finally, it is possible to invest accumulated pension funds into the risk bearing capital. Since these funds are made up of contributions from the workers' wages, the voting shares acquired ought to be used for establishing working-class control over the industry. This method, which is likely to be only supplementary, may be denoted as Swedish. In Sweden, Common Pension Funds (*Allmäna Pension Fonderna*) have more money than the value of the entire existing corporate stock and a certain percentage — as yet rather small — may, according to a parliamentary decision, be used for investment in the risk bearing capital.

The main advantage of the Danish method is that it is simpler to administer. Next, the employers will find it more difficult to evade the obligations. On both scores the Peruvian method is less efficient. In Peru, employers managed to sabotage the law by showing low profits or even losses; by increasing the wages in order to both corrupt workers and reduce profits. Private investments were reduced. Manufacturing firms were combined with service or selling firms to which profits were transferred. Multinational firms represented an especially awkward problem since they could easily remove profits from the books in any particular country. Wages, however, must be paid out and so markups on wages cannot be avoided. But the Danish method has its drawbacks also. It taxes labor intensive industries more than capital intensive ones, which means that the former will first come under labor control. Since the former are usually not the technologically most advanced or efficient industries, it may happen that an image be created of workers' management associated with lower efficiency. Besides, since wages do not represent a residual like profits, an unprofitable industry may be hit (the value of shares declining toward zero) while in a highly profitable industry profits may be used for private enrichment. A possible remedy is to differentiate markups according to profitability and/or labor intensity, but this would complicate administration. Next, the initial markup must be small and can only gradually be increased. Even in that case, the employers may use it as an excuse for inflationary pricing.

In general, our preliminary analysis indicates that wage bill markup is probably preferable in a less developed country where the government administration is not very efficient and the market is far from being delicately balanced. Also, in such a country investment resources — profits available for investment — are generally scarce and can suitably be enlarged by a markup on wage bills. In fact, that was the motivation behind the Danish trade unions' proposal: unions were willing to support larger profits, in order to speed up economic growth, provided that the workers shared in the control of the new capital. In an economically advanced country the situation is generally likely to be reversed and the profit sharing method might appear more desirable. It is an interesting historical paradox that the pioneers, Peruvians and Danes, acted the other way round.

Let us now have a closer look at the profit sharing method. Since profits represent a residual, this method is neutral with respect to costs, wages and prices. The only change occurs exactly where it is desired, in the distribution of ownership. If the contribution to the

fund is 20 percent of profits before tax, dividends and tax amount
to 40 percent and gross profitability is 5, 10 and 20 percent respectively, it will take 75, 35 and 25 years before the fund acquires one-
half of the firm's stock.[23] Due to dispersed stock ownership, it is
often sufficient to own a small percentage of stock in order to be
able to control the firm. If this percentage is 20, and other conditions remain the same, workers will acquire control of the firm in
23, 12 and 6 years. A number of consequences follow. Dispersed
stock ownership makes possible a rather fast establishment of effective workers' control. The higher the rate of profit (and, of
course, the higher the share of contributions to the fund) the sooner
the control will be established. If, as is generally believed, capitalist
management favors high profits, workers can now agree and
wholeheartedly collaborate. The solidarity wage policy of the
unions becomes easier and more effective. Since for technological
and demand reasons profitability varies among industries, solidarity wages, i.e., approximately equal wages in various industries, will
result in substantially different rates of profit. But extra profits will
now not be pocketed by private capitalists (though they will share
too); extra profits will be used to speed up the socialization of the
profitable industry. The new issues of shares may lengthen the transition period. But this effect will be neutralized if the proceeds of
the fund (workers' dividends) are used to buy new shares. The pension funds may be used for the same purpose. Since the fund cannot be appropriated, it represents social property. For that reason
contributions to the fund are not taxed. Since they remain in the
firm as equity capital, saving in tax means an increased net profitability and additional investment resources. The capitalist
management ought to welcome that. It is only the absentee owners
(shareholders) who will protest because the value of the shares will
decline. It may be added, however, that an increase in tax or in the
interest rate — which happens all the time — also reduces the value
of shares.[24] What reduces the value of the stock increases the relation between the contribution and the stock, i.e., speeds up the
relative growth of the fund. The development of self-management
often improves business ethics. An effect of this kind can be expected here as well. For tax purposes the stock held is evaluated below
its market value. An undervalued stock would mean that more
shares are to be distributed to the fund, with the consequences just

enumerated. Thus it may pay to be honest.

Workers' participation in management is a request to be judged on its own merit and is not necessarily associated with the ownership titles. But in a capitalist environment, the acquisition of ownership may help and may speed up the process considerably. The simplest solution would be to make participation of workers in management and on the board of directors of a particular firm dependent on the stock ownership accumulated in the fund. Once the relative size of the fund makes an effective control of the firm possible, the Workers' Council takes over the running of the firm. However, the simplest solution is not always the most efficient one. What one wants to achieve is not simply a redistribution of wealth and power, but an orderly transition to a new socio-economic system. Two institutions can be instrumental in that process: the unions and the state. Since it is desirable to minimize the use of the state power, the formidable task of a radical restructuring of production relations will have to be assumed by the unions. This is surely the most important, the most difficult, and the most challenging task in the entire history of the unions. To the extent they succeed, they will render themselves unnecessary. For, that will imply nothing less than an emancipation of the working class.

Unions will operate two categories of funds. In one of them — a single one — the equity stock acquired by labor will be accumulated. This is the Social Property Fund. The second category will consist of several funds disposing of the dividends accruing to the stock owned by labor. These are the Labor Funds.

The Social Property Fund, one for the entire country, is more of symbolic importance and is in fact a bookkeeping institution. All shares acquired by labor are deposited here, but the proceeds flow to the Labor Funds according to an agreed-upon scheme. Regarding the state corporations and the firms not incorporated as joint stock companies, the shares may be replaced by ownership certificates. The certificates are issued annually to the same relative amount of gross profit as in the joint stock companies. This amount is expressed as a percentage share of the firm's capital. These percentages are accumulated in the SPF and the corresponding dividends (calculated as some average proportion of net profits) are sent to Labor Funds. According to the capitalist rules of the game, the shares and certificates held by the SPF generate proportional voting rights which are also administered by the Labor Funds.

There can be at least three types of territorial (central, regional and local) and two types of industrial (for the firm and for the industry branch) Labor Funds. What is the proper function of each of these funds? Since the new task of the unions consists in participating in production decisions, the crucial role will be played by the Branch Funds. Modern unions, unlike the older craft unions, are also organized on the 'branch' basis and this will facilitate the task of operating the funds. The funds are managed by elected boards on which government representatives sit as well. The main task of the Branch Funds is simply to prepare a fully-fledged workers' self-management. Workers themselves are familiar with shop floor operations and so they can participate directly at that level. In order to extend the participation to the level of the firm, help is needed from the outside. If this help is not forthcoming, the workers may be manipulated by the old management, or they may take wrong decisions which would discredit self-management. The Branch Funds, like the branch unions, are familiar with the work conditions of a particular industry. They know its products, the market problems. Thus they can directly help with advice to Works Councils. The funds will select candidates for the boards of directors and top management in collaboration with the Works Councils. These officials are nominated if and when elected by the councils. The BFs help to work out statutes for the councils and render organizational help. They organize courses in self-management. They use the dividend money to buy new shares, to buy out firms about to become bankrupt — if the workers request that — and to set up fully labor managed firms in their branches. The Branch Funds may, for the time being, reserve the right to make some strategic decisions such as those regarding the merger or the dissolution of a firm or a heavy investment and modernization program, while on all other matters Works Councils vote independently at shareholder meetings.

Participation at the firm level consists initially of three different components. Workers elect their Works Council, which consists exclusively of workers (blue as well as white-collar) and is primarily concerned with the problems on the shop floor. The Branch Funds are concerned primarily with the problems at the firm level. The work community, which consists of all persons employed in the firm, i.e., of workers and managers, operates the firm's Labor Fund which represents the results of the work of all. The fund sends an agreed-upon part of the annual dividends of the labor owned stock — say one-half — to the Branch and Central Funds. The other half is used according to the preferences of the work community. The work community may use the available resources to buy additional shares in the firm, to give a loan to the firm, to make contributions to a local Labor Fund, to finance educational, cultural or recreational activities or institutions, to provide for social welfare purposes and to increase wages. The decisions on these matters will provide practical experience for collective decision making and will also help to integrate the three components of participation into, eventually, one single self-management.

The Central Labor Fund is concerned with ironing out regional differences. It intervenes when a massive buying of shares or other investment proves necessary. It finances research, education, and information dissemination concerning labor management. It may fund chairs in labor management and finance graduate courses for managers. It is not sufficient that workers get educated, managers must be educated as well. If left to themselves, the universities will continue to educate managers for capitalist firms. Consequently, the unions must intervene, and the money of the CLF is best suited for the purpose. The CLF may also establish an auditing agency which will provide services to Works Councils and a management bureau which will serve as a consulting agency, give technical and managerial aid to labor managed firms and provide the labor-appointed managers in the private firms.

After a certain number of years the voting rights generated by the increasing stock ownership will begin to matter. Labor Funds will have at their disposal substantial amounts of money and labor managed firms will cease to be rare exceptions. At that stage the coordination of institutions at the regional level may become necessary. This may require setting up Regional Labor Funds. Once the transitional period is more or less completed, labor funds will envolve into institutions of the labor managed economy. The Central, Regional and Local Labor Funds will be transformed into Federal, State and Communal Investment Funds. The dividends will become the price for the use of social property. The Firm

Fund will merge with the business funds of the firm. Only the Branch Funds — of central importance during the transition period — will lose their function. They may give birth to branch banks and various research, educational and other institutions serving the branch. In the meantime they will have established a practice of branch planning.

VI TWO ISSUES LIKELY
TO BE RAISED

It may be asked: why would employers accept a profit sharing policy which will eventually lead to an expropriation of private productive capital? The answer is that they would not. They will oppose and sabotage the policy as much as they can, but they will realize that the other two alternatives are even worse. These alternatives are: labor unrest and/or government intervention (assuming that the government is controlled by the socialist parties). From the point of view of employers, a gradual change at least partly under their control and which will become substantial only after a number of years — when they will have retired — is vastly preferable to a sudden, unexpected change. In the meantime, the government may be defeated, the conditions may change and there is a chance that the policy be reversed. From the point of view of labor, the transition time is not necessarily fixed, the developments may be speeded up by concerted union and government action. The time that will elapse before full control is established will not be lost. Workers will learn how to run the firms. Both parties have a chance to be right. It is exactly the uncertainty in human affairs that makes the policy tolerably acceptable. The outcome is not necessarily predetermined. It depends on the involvement of the parties, on human action. In the process, repetition and custom render initially shocking and irritating relations usual and customary. In the end even employers — like Norwegian Conservatives — will vote for workers' management. After all, professional managers, as far as they are genuinely professional, ought to be able to manage the firms under the Workers' Councils at least as efficiently as under the Board of Directors and, very likely, more efficiently.

At this point we encounter another possible question: if the labor managed firms are really more efficient than their capitalist and etatist counterparts, why do not they outcompete the latter firms in the market? Is not the whole discussion about the transition policy misplaced? If the labor managed firms are more efficient, they will expand and socialism will be established in any case. If they are less efficient, the policy aimed at reduced efficiency must be self-defeating. The answer to this question is that a labor managed firm cannot survive in a capitalist environment regardless of its potential efficiency. Let me quote an historical analogy.

A capitalist firm, characterized by management hiring legally free workers for money wages, is clearly more efficient than a feudal estate or an ancient slave factory. After all, that is why capitalism has replaced previous social orders and has become a dominant socio-economic system. Yet these potentially very efficient capitalist enterprises — together with commodity and money markets — have existed in previous societies and have not prospered. The three main ingredients of capitalist entrepreneurship — mobility of factors, contract law and property rights — were also present and yet to little avail. Commenting on this fact, Max Weber wrote:

> . . . The specific features of modern capitalism, in contrast to these ancient forms of capitalist acquisition, the strictly rational organization of work embedded in rational technology, nowhere developed in such irrationally constructed states, and could never have arisen within them, because these modern organizations, with their fixed capital and precise calculations, are much too vulnerable to irrationalities of law and administration.[25]

It remains to find out what are the irrationalities of capitalism which make workers' management difficult to install.

A labor managed firm is similar to a producer cooperative. Most producer cooperatives eventually fail. There are at least three reasons for this:

(a) Cooperatives find it difficult to obtain bank and trade credit. They are also discriminated against by private firms in terms of supply of necessary raw materials and of marketing of their finished products. Capitalist economy behaves like an organism with an organ transplanted from another organism: it spontaneously rejects the alien tissue.

(b) Cooperative self-management implies a radical reduction of salary spans for managers. Thus, capitalist firms have no difficulty in bribing away the most capable business administrators. Particularly because it is easier to issue commands than to treat the workers as fellow equals.

(c) Once a cooperative begins to expand, new workers must be employed. In a capitalist environment that causes social differentiation. The founding members tend to treat the newcomers as hired labor. Very soon the cooperative degenerates into an ordinary capitalist enterprise.

The last observation implies that self-management is behaviorally incompatible with private or collective ownership. It requires social ownership. Thus we now part with the producer cooperatives and consider genuine labor managed firms.

(d) Social ownership means that the right to participate in decision making is derived from employment and not from ownership. That, in turn, implies a thorough overhaul of the entire legal system. Yugoslavia changed three constitutions in the first twenty-five years of the development of workers' management. An inappropriate legal and institutional setting renders most trival problems, otherwise solved automatically, extremely complicated; it takes a lot of time, energy and ingenuity to sort them out. An alien system generates unnecessary costs.

(e) Ideology and vested interests complete our list. In a capitalist setting, a worker managed firm is a deviant. Even well intended business producers and authorities do not know how to treat it. Does it represent a business or a political risk? What criteria should one apply? Trades unions find its position utterly ambiguous. Who is here the employer and who the worker? What about working-class solidarity? What is the role of a trade union in a worker managed enterprise? Is there any? Thus all well intended members of the establishment are bound to be highly suspicious. But not everybody is well intended. Those who are not will be openly hostile. Efficiency improvements, even within existing firms, will be opposed if they conflict with the ruling ideology and the vested interests. 'As long as the authoritarian firm makes a normal or reasonable profit, the people in power prefer to maintain the established order rather than create a more efficient but democratic organization. The goals of preserving the existing differences in power, status and incomes are by far more important values than the overall efficiency of the firm'.[26] It is a simple fact that the efficiency potential in a microeconomic organization can be exploited only if macroeconomic, indeed social, environment is changed appropriately.

Changes in social environment require persistent political struggle. The fundamental strategy of this struggle is, as our analyses indicate, to do whatever helps human development. For socialism is the other word for humanism.

NOTES

1. K. Marx: 'The Chartists', *New York Daily Tribune*, 25 August 1852.

2. The letter to Turati, 6 February 1892.

3. N. Q. Herrick, 'Who's unhappy at Work and Why', *Manpower*, January 1972, pp. 3-7. Similar were the findings of a Canadian study a few years later. It turned out 'that the single most important consideration in the minds of Canadians proved to be interesting work' and 'that intrinsic aspects of work such as having sufficient information and authority outweight the importance of extrinsic features such as salary or comfortable surroundings'. M. Burstein et al., *Canadian Work Values: Findings of a Work Ethic Survey and a Job Satisfaction Survey*, Ottawa, Information Canada, 1975, pp. 29-30.

4. The report by H. Johnson and N. Kotez in the *Washington Post*, 10 April 1972.

5. Walter Reuter, president of the United Automobile Workers Union, a few weeks before his death, in a television interview. Quoted from R. Edwards, M. Reich, T. Weisskop, *The Capitalist System*, Englewood Cliffs, NJ, Prentice Hall, 1972, p. 259.

6. D. Yankelovich, 'Changing Attitudes toward Work', *Dialogue*, No. 4, 1974, 3-12, p. 12.

7. Cf. H. Wachtel, 'Class Consciousness and Stratification in the Labor Process', in R. Edwards et al., *Labor Market Segmentation*, Lexington, Mass., D.C., Heath & Co., 1977, 95-122, p. 112.

8. R. Aronson and J. C. Cowley, 'The New Left in the United States', in R. Miliband and I. Saville, eds., *Socialist Register*, London, Merlin, 1967, p. 84.

9. Evidence to the Sankey Commission on the Nationalisation of the Mines, 1919.

10.   S. M. Lipset, *Political Man*, New York, Doubleday, 1963, p. 64.

11.   7 October 1965; once again on 6 November 1968. Quoted from F. Deppe et al., *Kritika saodlučivanja*, Beograd, Komunist, 1974, p. 183.

12.   Something of the kind seems to have happened in Sweden after 1965. 'From that time' — reports Edmund Dahlström — 'there appeared an increased criticism of social structure and policy in Sweden. Most established institutions received their share of this. The critical theme very much concerned industrial relations and the exploitation of the rank and file. Employers, unions and bureaucrats were held responsible for the unsatisfactory conditions. Several novels were published showing the damaging effect of working conditions, piece-work, long hours and inhumane supervision. Journalists, film producers and theatrical groups tried to elucidate the exploitive relations. Through the mass media they spread to a large proportion of the people. Even popular culture in its different manifestations transmitted some of the ideas. It is hard to deny the effect of these ideas'. ('Efficiency, Satisfaction and Democracy in Work' mimeographed paper for the Dubrovnik Conference in Self-Management, January 1977, p. 18.) In 1975 Meidner's Report, to be mentioned later, appeared. A year later a trade union congress gave strong support to requests for self-management. In the same year the Social Democrats were defeated after having held power for almost half a century. That can be taken as a sign of too little, rather than too much, genuine socialism.

13.   Quoted according to M. Marković, 'Nova ljevica i kulturna revolucija', *Praxis*, 1970, 927-44, p. 943.

14.   'We are no longer divided', writes Italian socialist Lelio Basso in 'Prospects of European Left', 'into supporters of revolution and supporters of gradual conquest of power; instead we are divided into those willing to be integrated into capitalist society and those who consider that the present society, the conditions and chances are ripe for a socialist reconstruction of the society'. (In M. Pečujlić et al., eds., *Marksizam*, Beograd, Sl. List, 1976, p. 919.)

15.   J. S. Mill, *Principles of Political Economy*, W. J. Ashley edition reprinted by A. M. Keley, New York, 1961, p. 764.

16.   The following table provides some information on the point made:

Number of working days per 1,000 employees lost due to industrial actions

	1964-73 average
Sweden	43
West Germany	43
Japan	217
France	277
Britain	633
United States	1,247

L. Forsebäck, *Industrial Relations and Employment in Sweden*, Stockholm, Swedish Institute, 1976, p. 67. Of the countries quoted, various forms of co-determination existed only in West Germany and Sweden.

17.   The more sophisticated version of the agreement is the widely accepted theory of the American economist Frank Knight, who argued that an entrepreneur bears uninsurable risks called uncertainty.

18.   As was argued by the Swedish trade union economist Rudolf Meidner, in the debate on the Wage Earner Funds (*Ekonomisk debatt*, 1/1976, p. 78).

19.   In the United Kingdom 6 percent of population own 75 percent of total personal wealth and represent 92 percent of tax payers who own shares. (J. E. Meade, *Efficiency and the Ownership of Property*, London, Allen and Unwin, 1964, p. 27). In the United States 1.6 percent of the total adult population in 1953, who had $60,000, or more each in total assets, owned 82 percent of all corporate stock, all state and local government bonds, and from 10 to 33 percent of each other type of personal property; 1 percent of adult population received 40 percent of the total property income; 2.3 percent of households owned about 80 percent of the national productive capital. (R. J. Lampman, *The Share of Top Wealth-Holders in National Wealth: 1922-1956*, Nat. Bureau of Econ Research, Princeton, Princeton Univ. Press, 1962, pp. 23, 195, 108). In Sweden one percent of tax payers own three-quarters of equity capital and 5 percent of taxpayers own one half of personal wealth (R. Meidner et al., *Löntagarfonderna*, Stockholm, Tiden, 1976, pp. 38, 43).

20.   Rudolf Meidner and his colleagues wrote a book showing how this method may most advantageously be applied to the Swedish economy, and then wrote a report to the 1976 Trade Unions Congress. The congress accepted it. Cf. *Löntagar fonder*, Stockholm, Tidens, 1975; *Kollektiv kapital bildning genom löntagar fonder*, Stockholm, Prisma, 1976.

21.   The Danish Federation of Trade Unions presented a plan, which in its first stage was defeated in parliament, whereby employers would be obliged to gradually increase contributions to an 'Employees' Investment and Dividend Fund' from initial 1/2 percent to final 5 percent of the total wage bill. Two-thirds of the contribution to the fund may be claimed back by the employer for investment in the firm. It has been estimated that the fund's share in the corporate stock will amount to 14 percent after 10 years and to 26 percent after 20 years.

22.   H. Ch. Cars, 'Meidners modell — kritik och alternativ', *Frihetlig Socialistisk Tidskrift*, 6/1975, pp. 15-21. In an attempt to show that Marx's labour theory of value was wrong, Paul Sammnelson, a Nobel Prize laureate, unwittingly provided a 'proof' for the two-factor theory: 'If labor grows at exponential rate $1 + g$ and goods are priced at their synchronized labor costs; then the bourgeois pricing formula $A_0 (g) = a_0 (1 + g) [1-a (1 + g)]^{-1}$ must be charged by national planners' ('Understanding the Marxian Notion of Exploitation', *Journal of Economic Literature*, 1971, 399-431, p. 429). Here a_0 stands for unit labour inputs, a for unit capital imputs, and g is the rate of profit, the same for both inputs.

23.   The general formula for this sort of calculations is

$$\frac{F_{\underline{t}}}{S_{\underline{t}}} = 1 - \left[\frac{1 + \pi \ (1 - \lambda - u\ )}{1 + \pi \ (1 - u\ )} \right]^t$$

where F = fund, S = stock, π = gross rate of profit, λ = the share of contributions in gross profit, u = dividends + taxes, t = year.
Cf. Meidner, op. cit., p. 129.

24.	Without fund con-tribution Tax 40% Interest 5%	With fund contribution		
		Tax 40% Interest 5%	Tax 50% Interest 5%	Tax 40% Interest 10%
Profit before tax	100	100	100	100
Contribution to the fund (20%)	—	-20	-20	-20
Tax	-40	-32	-40	-32
Profit after contri-bution and tax	60	48	48	48
Dividends	60	48	40	48
Value of stock $\left[\dfrac{\text{dividends}}{\text{interest rate}}\right]$	1,200	960	800	480
$\dfrac{\text{Contribution}}{\text{value of stock}}$	—	2.1%	2.5%	4.2%

25. M. Weber, *Economy and Society,* New York, Bedminster Press, 1968, p. 1395.

26. L. E. Karlsson, 'Experiences in Employee Participation in Sweden: 1969-74', in *Economic Analysis and Workers' Management,* 1975, 296-330, p. 316.

3

SELF-MANAGEMENT, MARKET, AND POLITICAL INSTITUTIONS IN CONFLICT:
Yugoslav Development Patterns and Dialectics

Tom Baumgartner
Université de Louvain, Belgium

Tom R. Burns
*Universities of Oslo, Norway and Stockholm,
Sweden/Scandinavian Institutes of
Administrative Research, Sweden*

Dusko Sekulić
University of Zagreb, Yugoslavia

I INTRODUCTION

Self-managed work organizations are, in general, those where
workers (shop-floor workers, technicians, and administrators) have
the right to control the means of production, the resources of the
organization in which they work, its organizational structure and
processes, and its products, without undue interference from state,
party, or other interests. Workers — either directly, as in small

Authors' note: We are grateful to Vesna Pusić, Veljko Rus, and Stane Saksida for
their criticisms and suggestions on an earlier version of the paper. The arguments
and conclusions, however, are the sole responsibility of the authors.

enterprises, or through their delegates, as in larger enterprises — decide on economic plans, determine salaries (above a government set minimum), make investment and development decisions, distribute the organization's income and other benefits such as apartments and vacation time, select their top administrators, and resolve internal dilemmas and conflicts.

In our view, self-management enterprises with a maximum degree of egalitarian relations are an emergent form of production or work organization and will replace the hierarchical corporate forms now dominant. This development corresponds to the emergence of the capitalist corporate enterprise from 1800. Among the arguments, both explaining and supporting today's development, three of the most prominent are:

— *Rationality argument*: By fostering conscientious, responsible attitudes toward work and social ownership, self-management enterprises provide for maximum development and utilization of human resources and creative potentialities available in a work force.

— *Legitimation argument:* Organizational structures, processes and planning in self-management organizations are legitimized through their greater consistency with democratic norms and ideology than hierarchical corporate forms and thus enable more effective decision-making, planning and implementation. That is, democratic participation in collective decisions and democratic legitimation is extended to the enterprise itself, thus advancing the formation of democratic social institutions, a development which began in full earnest around 1800 in the Western world.

— *Development argument:* Through participation in self-management organs and processes, workers have opportunities to acquire competence and confidence which are likely to be carried over into other spheres of social action, e.g. child socialization and political activities. Political experience, for instance, will in turn reinforce participation and competent performance within enterprises.

The emergence and development of self-management values and institutions must be examined in their specific historical and social structural context. This paper attempts to do this in the case of Yugoslavia. It focuses on the establishment and functioning of self-management in Yugoslavia in the context of Yugoslavia's international relationships, market institutions and participation in the international division of labor, and a communist political movement determined to build socialism as well as to maintain the dominant leadership of the party.

In the following section we describe briefly the background and development of Yugoslav self-management institutions. This provides a basis for the discussion in sections 3 and 4 concerning socioeconomic developments in Yugoslavia following the establishment of self-management. The limitations of self-management institutions operating under market allocation rules and the technical division of labor are pointed up. In particular, we indicate several of the ways in which economic and technical conditions and forces constrain and distort the actual practice of self-management as well as interfere with the realization of socialist values such as equality and solidarity: by inducing an emphasis on technical and economic values rather than on social and political ones, by fostering unequal accumulation and uneven development rather than equalization, and by failing to provide social integrating values and institutions. Section 3 focuses on micro-organizational features of self-managed enterprises; due to the technical division of labor and differential involvement in work processes, different categories of participants develop differential capabilities and knowledge. Section 4 takes up macro-level aspects: uneven accumulation and development patterns by region, sector and enterprise in Yugoslavia. These processes of social differentiation lead to corresponding as well as opposing developments within the political and socio-cultural spheres. Opposition is manifested in conflict and struggle between those seeking to maintain (and reproduce) — and those struggling to change — existing institutions, the 'rules of the game', and patterns of development. Such processes are related to qualitatively different phases and dialectical shifts in societal development, discussed in section 5. These developments and shifts are generally not controllable or subject to planning through self-managed enterprises.[1]

II THE DEVELOPMENT OF SELF-MANAGEMENT IN YUGOSLAVIA: A BRIEF OVERVIEW[2]

The triumph over the German Occupation by the Popular Liberation Movement under the leadership of the Communist Party (later
renamed the League of Yugoslav Communists [LYC]) set the stage
for the development of contemporary Yugoslavia. The movement
supporting the liberation was very heterogeneous (made up of different social groups with different motives and interests). The party
was the only major actor which dominated and integrated these different groups. Other forces participating in the liberation movement lacked the power and legitimation to overcome the suspicion
and opposition of others and to integrate the whole. Organized
social actors outside of the liberation movement, who might have
been capable of playing a key role, had either lost in the internal
struggle (e.g. royalists or Chetniks led by General Draza Mihailovic
and various 'home guards')[3] or had associated themselves with the
Germans. With the victory of the movement, they disappeared
from the scene. This left the Communist Party, which at the outbreak of the war had been an illegal group, insignificant in number
but with growing influence, in charge.[4]

In addition to the fact that all serious internal rivals for power
had disappeared or been removed from the scene, the party had a
number of other advantages in consolidating and developing its
power (Dubey, 1975:26):

— The prestige and legitimation it had acquired from its
courageous and successful leadership of the partisan resistance
against internal and external enemies during the second world war.

— The fact that it could represent and draw support from all
sections of the country, and had no special bias or commitment
toward any particular linguistic, regional or religious group.

— The active support of the Soviet Union, together with the
tolerance (following what had eventually become close military collaboration in the war years) of England and the US.

In sum, the party was the only well-organized social actor enjoy-
ing both widespread internal as well as external legitimation. It
alone was capable of acting in all spheres of Yugoslav social life,

political/military, economic, and socio-cultural. Efforts at organizing new forces within the liberation movement (and after the war within the new political system) were successfully prevented by the party. The monopoly of power in the post-war period was consistent with the ideological principles of the 'ruling party' and 'dictatorship of the proletariat.'

Thus, the party was prepared, both organizationally and ideologically to initiate institution building and transformation, a type of structural power which we refer to as meta-power (Baumgartner et al., 1976). Such power is based on control over key institutional spheres and processes which can be used to mobilize resources and to maintain or change societal institutions (e.g., private property relations).

The dynamics of post-war Yugoslav society can be described and analyzed in terms of the interests and capability of the Communist Party to structure and restructure institutions in response to:

— changes in the environment of the country (e.g., international political and economic developments);

— intended changes within the society;

— unintended consequences of changes introduced within the system.

The development of Yugoslav self-management and related social institutions can be divided into four periods (see, for example, Gorupić and Paj, 1970; Bošnjak et al., 1978).

— 1947-52: planned economy managed by the state administration;

— 1953-64: construction of the system of worker and social self-management and its institutional definition in the Constitutions of 1953 and 1963.

— 1965-71: self-management with full-fledged market allocation and the emergence of challenges to the top political leadership, the so-called laissez-faire period.

— 1972-present: attempts to re-establish political and ideological constraints on the functioning of self-managed enterprises and autonomous economic and political processes.

The system institutionalized immediately after the second world war was characterized by a Soviet model of socialist development with substantial centralization and bureaucratization.[5] The first two years of the five year plan beginning in 1947 showed an im-

pressive increase in output. Then, disagreements with the Soviet
Union broke out, culminating in the break in mid-1948 and the
1948 Cominform resolution expelling Yugoslavia from the 'community of socialist nations.'[6]

This international event marked a dramatic external change in
the economic, political and even military condition of Yugoslavia.
In particular, the break with, and economic boycott by, the Soviet
Union and other Cominform countries made fulfillment of the
1947-52 plan impossible for at least three reasons (Dubey, 1975:28):

— There was a rapid reduction, literally to zero, in exports to
and imports from what had previously been — and had been expected to remain — the principal trading partners. Imports from
the socialist countries, which had been 56 percent of the total in
1947, had ceased altogether by 1950.

— Both 1950 and 1952 were years of drought and exceptionally
poor harvests.

— The new external threat motivated the Yugoslav Government
to increase its defense expenditures substantially (approximately by
a factor of 3 during the period 1947-52), so that by 1952 it reached
as high as 20 percent of national product).[7]

Between 1948 and 1952 there was virtually no growth.[8] At the
same time, the political-military situation for Yugoslavia was extremely tense.[9] The weakness of imperative central planning, particularly in the face of enormous problems of adjustment created
by the break with the Cominform countries, became increasingly
apparent. Longer term planning was given less and less attention,
and the actual practice became to formulate annual plans only.

The economic and political difficulties led to pragmatic efforts at
institution restructuring and innovation. At the enterprise level,
changes were made in December 1949 with the introduction of the
first workers' councils as consultative bodies in a number of enterprises. Dedijer (1971) writes that the political leadership recognized
that the economy could only be rescued if the workers were
mobilized and granted broader rights, and if rigid bureaucratic
forms were broken down.

Although the initial response of the Yugoslav leadership was a
defensive one — 'they had not committed wrong' — gradually they
took the initiative. The defects and limitations of the Soviet System
became matters for extensive discussion and analysis. There arose a

debate in Yugoslavia concerning the nature and problems of the transition to a fully socialist society, matters which for many communists had been settled by the 'successful' example of the Soviet Union. New concepts and principles were developed which were essential to the task of mobilizing socialists and legitimizing the Yugoslav position.[10]

The political elite introduced self-management institutions into Yugoslavia, to a large extent in response to inter-system competition and threat. This institutional innovation was intended to provide a source of legitimation and an institutional basis on which to oppose the Soviet Union (1953 Program of the League of Yugoslav Communists).[11] The innovation was initiated with economic units and was only later extended to socio-political and territorial units, in particular, communes. All of this led, through experimentation, reformulation of concepts and further innovation to an alternative strategy and model for socio-economic development and construction of a socialist society. The strategy combined normative and socio-political features along with purely economic ones.

The system of participatory socialism with market allocation was worked out and tested between 1953 and 1971. Already in 1950 elected workers' councils emerged as advisory or consultative bodies (520 enterprises by late 1950). These councils had no formal decision-making power. However, they had the right to propose measures on any matter concerning the management of the enterprise and the director was obliged to take their views into account. With the introduction of such bodies, the direct external influence of state agencies began to be challenged and the director's powers, instead of being exclusively controlled by the state, became subject to the influence of workers' collectives through the councils. Yet, the director, with his direct command over the technical staff and the hierarchical management pyramid and his role in representing the enterprise to the outside world, had an effective monopoly on the knowledge and information possessed by the enterprise. As central administrative planning of the economy was gradually done away with, greater knowledge and greater initiative was demanded of the technical and management staff of the enterprise in order to operate successfully in a competitive market. Thus, there emerged duality of influence (or competing organizational principles) — a duality which continues to exist and to

generate conflicts (see later discussion):
— the new democratic self-management bodies and processes;
— the traditional, hierarchical management organization with
the existing enterprise-internal structure of management unaltered.
In 1952 the control of all state enterprises was formally vested in
the workers' councils. These were regarded as the trustees of the
fixed capital which was provided to the enterprises by the state. At
the same time all production decisions became the responsibility of
the enterprises themselves. Although initially the director of each
enterprise was still appointed centrally, by late 1952 the appointment was vested in the local authority (the commune) and in the
following year this was replaced by a system of appointment by a
committee representing the workers' council and commune
(municipality). (Gorupić and Paj [1970] describe the shifts of
authority and the main conflicts of interest.) The federal ministries
which had devised and administered the plan were abolished, and
replaced by secretariats with much smaller staff and greatly
restricted functions. In December 1951 a law on 'Planned Management of the National Economy' established as of 1952 a system of
annual plans (a second five-year plan was not initiated until 1956).
It introduced the practice of what was known as planning of 'basic
proportions' in which the amount and broad allocation of investment was determined, while the decisions regarding quantity and
quality of output and, to some extent, its price were left to enterprises. Before 1952 the investment allocations of the plan were implemented through the budget. This arrangement was abolished
with the Law on Planned Management.
The development of the system after the 1953 Constitution —
which gave self-management a legal and constitutional basis and
thus greater legitimation than simply a major government policy,
as in the preceding phase — followed the general principles and
patterns of development already initiated in the previous phase:
self-management, decentralization, liberalization, and increased
reliance on market mechanisms.[12] The increasing reliance on such
mechanisms was not the result of a conversion to a capitalist model
of development, but reflected reasoning about effective conditions
in which self-management might best be realized. In general, the
Yugoslav leadership tried to work out the practical implications of
the management strategy that it had adopted (Dubey, 1975).
As central administrative planning was weakened or done away

with altogether, enterprises were given increased autonomy at the same time that their responsibility for business performance was increased. They were expected to operate successfully in a competitive market. In particular, they gained increased control over the distribution of income. This is indicated by the increase in the proportion of enterprise income at their disposal in the form of net personal incomes, depreciation and enterprise funds. This proportion increased from 43 percent in 1959 to 55 percent in 1964 and 62 percent in 1966. (Also, the proportion of depreciation and enterprise funds to total net income increased from 17 percent in 1959 to 27 percent in 1964 [Dubey, 1975:34].) Other developments indicating increased self-management took place as well. For example, until 1958 the directors of enterprises were appointed by a committee on which the enterprise had one-third representation. After 1958, half the members of the committee were from the enterprise. Eventually, the workers' councils were given the power to appoint directors from lists approved by the selection committee.

Parallel with the development of enterprise autonomy, there was progressive decentralization of the powers of the federation to republics and local governments. The basic idea was that self-management of enterprises should entail increasing self-government by communities. At the same time republic and local governments were to play a role in the 'supervision' of enterprises in their territory, at least in the initial stages. That is, instead of centralized state control at the federal level, enterprises were to face decentralized government regulation at the commune level.

Corresponding to this development there occurred a redefinition of the party role, to make it more an ideological and educational weapon than a decision-making or administrative body. This entailed movement away from total regulation to a separation of party and state, and the ongoing separation of state and economy. The renaming of the party as the League of Yugoslav Communists in 1952 was indicative of this change. This was not meant to imply that the importance of the party should decline. As its program stated in 1958: 'the working class cannot give up the weapon of its class struggle, the dictatorship of the proletariat and the leading role of the League of Yugoslav Communists,' because of the existence of 'antagonistic forces' which endanger the existence of socialism (Dubey, 1975:50). The process of decentralization, however, was implemented also within the party organization. The report of the Eighth Congress of the LYC (1964) commented that the independence and initiative of the organizations within the LYC had increased, so that instead of being 'agents for passing on views and executors of tasks assigned, they were becoming participants in the adoption of conclusions and decisions' (Dubey, 1975:51). The process of decentralization in Yugoslavia was marked by internal debate and struggle within the party. A struggle within the party in the early 1960s between those in favor of greater self-management and those for greater centralization resulted in the success of the former. This set the stage for the very substantial reforms from 1965 until 1969.[13] Dubey points out (1975:36):

> While significant progress toward decentralization and self-management had been made by 1964, it was much less than would appear at first sight. There continued to be a large degree of central control of the economy, and particularly of investment, in the interests of coordination and stabilization or ensuring what was termed the 'basic proportions' of development. The emphasis placed on achieving greater regional equality was another reason for central intervention in investment allocation. There was also a large degree of control of prices and wages. The state continued to control the prices of 70% of the products and thus exercised a strong influence on the pattern of decentralized resource use.
>
> . . . there was also some resistance to the ideas of the new economic system and its implications, which slowed the process of decentralization and self-management. Such views were increasingly voiced in 1961 and 1962 when there was a reduction in the rate of growth. This was attributed to the significant increase in enterprise autonomy that occurred in 1961, and a return to the old system of income distribution in enterprises and greater state influence in investment allocation was demanded. The ideological opposition was defeated. The Constitution of 1963 and the Eighth Congress of the League of Communists of Yugoslavia in 1964 reaffirmed the basic principles of Yugoslav development.

The economic reform of 1965 consisted of a number of measures adopted during 1964-67 which were designed to achieve three major objectives: (a) to give greater autonomy to enterprises and limit the role of the state in the economy by reducing taxation on enterprises and leaving investment decision to them; (b) to correct, by major price adjustments, the long-standing distortions in relative prices, and thus improve the pattern of output and investment; (c) by devaluing the dinar, approximately halving customs tariff rates, and liberalizing imports and the foreign exchange regime to integrate the economy more closely with the world economy and exert pressure on Yugoslav enterprises to increase efficiency (Dubey, 1975). The measures were adopted over a number of years. The reduction in taxation of enterprises occurred in 1964, the devaluation and principal price adjustments in July 1965 and the liberalization of the foreign exchange regime in January 1967.

In the period following 1965 steps were taken strengthening the autonomy of enterprises and self-management structures as a whole. The basic law of 1965 on enterprises formally established the concept of organizations as free associations of responsible work partners (as opposed to wage earners) managing the organization directly or through delegated bodies. The primary autonomous organization for this purpose is the 'work unit' (or, after 1974, 'basic organization of associated labor') — such as a production unit or professional service section. The share of industrial commodities under price controls also descreased from 1965 to 1970 from more than 70 percent to 43 percent. A law of 1968 on the assets of enterprises provided wider scope for inter-enterprise cooperation. Amendment XV to the Constitution, passed in 1969, gave enterprises freedom in creating and designing their own inner self-management structures (for example in the authority, number and interrelationships of different self-managing bodies). With the passage of Amendment XV, the only structural legal requirement was the establishment of a workers' council. Other and additional self-management bodies were to be regulated by the statutes of each enterprise (Hunnius, 1973:277). Thus, enterprises were given the right to define for themselves the role of individual as well as collective executive bodies. The practical result was to enhance and to legitimize the existing powers of managers and technicians within enterprises. In general, there was decreasing interference in enterprise affairs from political authorities, e.g. communal bodies. For instance, the influence over the choice of enterprise director shifted completely in 1968 to the enterprise's workers' council.

A major change instituted in this period related to the role of the banks and financial institutions in Yugoslavia. The classical concept of statist socialism insisted on state monopoly over investment. Self-management (developed in the theoretical works of Yugoslav economists and politicians, not necessarily consistently) implied self-financing of enterprises.

The Law of Banking and Credit of 1964 gave state investment funds to the banks, thus making them more or less autonomous systems providing services to enterprises rather than acting as agents for the central or other government bodies. From this time

dates the process of strengthening the banks, although the banks
were still partially connected with centers of political power, and
partially with managerial elites. But eventually they became independent centers of power. The growing importance of banks can
be seen from data about the source of financial investment.

TABLE 1
Investment in fixed assets by source of finance
(in percent)

	1952	1955	1962	1964	1966	1971	1975	1978[1]
State	98	64	59	36	15	16	16	7
Work organizations	2	35	38	32	46	33	47	48
Banks		1	3	32	39	51	37	45
Total	100	100	100	100	100	100	100	100

Sources: 1952 and 1955 from Dubey (1975), other years from Statistical Bulletin
SDK (Service of Social Accounting) No. 1/1975, 12/1977 and 5/1978.

1. For January-May only.

In 1961 (before the economic reform), 61.7 percent of investment
was in the hands of political organizations, 29.5 percent in the
hands of enterprises and 0.9 percent in the hands of banks. By 1970
50.6 percent of investment was controlled by banks, 27.4 percent
by enterprises, and only 15.7 percent by political-territorial
organizations.[14] (A detailed discussion of investment policy in this
period is found in Bendekovic, 1975.)

This development of the banking system was regarded as a
crucial factor in the mobilization of savings and their allocation to
the most efficient use. The shift from public to bank financing,
where banks are typically more oriented uni-dimensionally to profitability considerations, is one indicator of the depolitization of
the economy during this period. This translated into more clear-cut
pressures on enterprises from their managements to be profitable.
In general, economic accountability and stress became more pronounced, and the mandate to take action to deal with 'unprofitable' enterprises more securely established.[15]

Although economic concerns were important from the beginning, there were also strong ideological aspects of giving self-managed enterprises greater autonomy and control over their resources. Over time, economic considerations came to dominate: enhancement of productivity, exploiting the advantages of modern technology, and participating in the international division of labor (see section 5). Self-managed enterprises operating under market allocation were to provide institutional conditions to facilitate innovation and productivity, to reward individual and collective (enterprise) efforts and skill, and to produce goods and services at higher quality and lower prices (Zukin, 1975:23).[16]

The establishment of a system of self-managed enterprises operating under market allocation of resources is the identifying feature of Yugoslav institutional development. By the end of the 1960s the self-managed enterprise was an autonomous body with the status of a legal person, with freedom to contract for capital goods, raw materials, and workers. The assets of the enterprise were social property,[17] but it could mortgage or dispose of them. The enterprise was free to determine what to produce, how to produce it, how much of it to produce, and in principle, the price of its products.

The management of self-managed enterprises was carried out by a workers' council elected by all the workers (the work collective), a managing board, and a director, who was appointed by the workers' council. The workers' council elected its executive body, the managing board. This was actually — but not necessarily — from its own membership. The board had from 3 to 17 members (the director ex officio) elected for one-year periods; if a member was elected twice in succession, he or she was then ineligible for the next two years.[18] The board had important functions including the supervision of the director's work, ensuring the fulfillment of the plans of the enterprise, and the drawing up of the annual plan (Gorupić and Paj, 1970; Pateman, 1970).

The director, together with the 'collegium' of department heads, was responsible for the administration of the enterprise and the execution of the workers' council's decisions. He also had other powers legally defined, such as the power to sign contracts in the name of the enterprise, to represent it in dealings with external bodies and to ensure that the enterprise operated within the law.

The management of the enterprise, including decisions on basic policy, was formally the responsibility of the workers' council and the managing board, while the responsibility for implementing decisions and for organizing production was given to the director alone.

The workers' council met collectively. Each member served for two years (but members were subject to recall by the electorate). Half of the council members were elected annually. To ensure wide participation, no person could serve more than two terms consecutively. The workers' council decided on the internal relationships in the enterprise, adopted economic plans and annual financial reports, decided on the utilization of funds and the distribution of the enterprise earnings between personal income and investment. The workers' council also decided matters concerning employment and dismissal of personnel.

When an enterprise failed to operate successfully and was unable to meet the income payments to its members, it was usual to appoint assignee management, normally chosen by the commune. Such assignee management is limited in the first instance to one year, though this can be continued where necessary.

From 1950 until the present time, Yugoslavia has undergone dramatic transformations: the decentralization of the state apparatus from the federal level to republics, communes, and enterprises, the development of a new type of work organization, self-management,[19] the introduction of market institutions, the transformation of imperative planning into indicative planning and then, more recently, the attempt to establish new types of planning and coordinating institutions, the incorporation of the Yugoslav economy into the international division of labor, the partial separation of the party from the state apparatus, and the renaming of the party as the League of Communists with a stress on its educational, ideological, and persuasive role and a de-emphasis (until recently) of an administrative/decision-making role in societal regulation and development.

All of the most important decisions about the development of Yugoslav institutions have been taken initially by a small group of party leaders. Moreover, the introduction of self-management institutions and values into Yugoslavia can be viewed to a substantial degree as more of a discontinuity than a continuity with earlier institutional development. The concept and ideology of self-management was not a factor in the thinking and experience of the party leadership. The self-management concept cannot be found in any document of the Communist Party before or during the war or during the first years after the war. The party's concept of socialism was based on the model of the Soviet Union: a 'people's democracy' with substantial central planning and government control of all important societal activities and developments.

Moreover, the concept of self-management was not present in the ideology or thinking of any other group which participated in the liberation movement. In sum, one can say that the introduction of self-management was discontinuous, 'an imposition on societal development', since (i) until 1948 the party leadership with the power to shape and reshape institutions nevertheless oriented Yugoslav society toward a Soviet Union type of model; this was completely consistent with the guiding ideology of this group; and (ii) other groups, which might offer any opposition to this development, had no concept of self-management.

This implies that self-management as an ideology and way of organizing society was not the result of a movement (and groups supporting this movement). On the other hand, one should bear in mind that the liberation movement was necessarily a decentralized movement, and stressed active participation and local initiative. The experience and success of this movement was a part of the ideology and cultural heritage of post-war Yugoslavia.[20] It provided a potentiality, both in structural forms and ideology. These could be activated to deal with societal problems, such as the crisis facing Yugoslavia after the 1948 break with the Soviet Union. That this potentiality of Yugoslav society was activated and managed by the political leadership is not disputed. But they did not create the potentiality, they simply used and transformed it.[21]

The very institutions established or restructured by the political elite may produce effects and lead to developments which they did not intend, and which compel them to take further action. At the same time, decisions and values institutionalized early in the process constrain to some extent their possible institutional responses in later phases. Due to a lack of knowledge, competence, or because of preoccupations with other spheres of action, the political elite may fail to regulate certain institutional areas which permit actors within these areas to establish and develop social power. Such power, e.g., in the case of Yugoslavia, the power of the managerial-technical elite in the economic sphere may, under certain conditions, be translated into power in other spheres of social action and into meta-power and the capability of not only shaping social institutions to its advantage, but challenging or competing with, and even undermining the legitimation of the initial holders of societal meta-power, the political elite. Typically, however, emerging power groups lack linkages throughout — or possibilities to penetrate — all major institutional areas. In the Yugoslav context, nationalist movements provide a quick and ready way to establish such linkages, and for this reason, they appear in the Yugoslav context as a potentially serious threat to the existing social order (see section 5).

III MANAGEMENT/LABOR RELATIONSHIPS AND OTHER MICRO-ORGANIZATIONAL FEATURES OF SELF-MANAGED ENTERPRISES

The reproduction of inequality in capitalist enterprises and in the capitalist system as a whole depends, in part, on the unequal distribution of managerial/technical skills, organizational capabilities and knowledge (see Chapter 5). The investigation of such distributions is also crucial to our knowledge of the extent to which self-managed enterprises tend to maintain or develop social hierarchy, which limits or undermines the realization of self-management values and institutions.

Productive activity has multiple consequences (products), entailing benefits and costs. These tend to be distributed unequally even in self-managed enterprises because of the technical division of labor (hierarchy and segmentation) and the differential involvement of enterprise members in planning and work processes. That is, even if 'all of the workers' in self-managed enterprises control some products of their labor, e.g., the distribution of net income, they do not control all of the socially important or strategic products of productive activity.[22] The technical division of labor, and economic structures and processes generally, structure a variety of socio-cultural as well as political consequences.

Through the functions they perform in the social division of labor, managerial and technical groups (top and middle management, accountants, engineers, economists, and shop-floor supervisors) acquire and develop valuable knowledge, skills, social linkages and status. Those in operative and laboring functions cannot acquire such resources or acquire them only with the greatest of difficulty. For instance, information acquired through management and technical processes serves as a basis for many self-management decisions. Managers can filter and decide on the distribution, the way of presenting and timing information. This control — in many instances monopolistic control — over information enables them to play a dominating role in self-management processes, and to determine or heavily influence self-management decisions and plans (Obradović, 1972, 1976). As Županov has pointed out, 'a skillful manipulation of information can limit collective decision-making to the mere voting for the decisions made in advance by management' (cited in Obradović, 1976:27).[23] Also, the knowledge, skills, and contacts which managers and technicians acquire in the performance of their functions are resources often transferable to political and socio-cultural spheres of social action. Such transference can then feedback to reinforce the division of labor (however, there may be opposing movements, see section 5). In general, Yugoslav self-management during the 1960s consistently showed oligarchic patterns of power and influence, often to an increasing degree — and therefore, conditions and developments incompatible with the self-management norm of a democratic distribution of power within work organizations (Obradović, 1976).

Of course, the actual situation is more complex. The intensity of participation tends to vary with level and area of decision-making. It is most intensive in areas of immediate concern to workers, such as matters of income and social welfare. Managerial and technocratic influence is greatest at the level of the whole enterprise and the problem areas of enterprise organization and planning, selection of technology, solution of technical and economic problems, marketing considerations, etc.[24]

The influence of managers and technicians tends to be reinforced if workers select leaders and authorize decision-making powers to those who have technocratic credentials and orientations because they believe this will ensure the viability and success of their enterprise in a dynamic market system. In this way they may satisfy short-term income goals on the basis of good economic results of the enterprise. But this achievement may be at the expense of the development of their own managerial and technical knowledge and capability. Stephen's study (cited in Pateman, 1970) of a shipyard in Split found that although the proportion of manual workers on the workers' council rose from 61.3 to 72.4 percent from 1955 to 1967, in 1967 only 2.7 percent of the representatives were semi-skilled and 2.9 percent unskilled. Split workers explained the low representation of the least skilled as due to generally low educational levels and the desire for the 'best men to hold office'.[25] In general, market institutions and competition contribute to reinforcing the power and prestige of the managerial and technical elite because they are expected to make the enterprise succeed and grow.

In sum, the technical division of labor is not only an organization of production. It entails social differentiation and power/dependence relationships, both within enterprises as well as, to a certain extent, outside of them. It tends to keep many workers relatively ignorant and only peripherally involved (or able to be involved) in the major technical and economic decisions of the enterprise. It also contributes to differentiation in orientations and values.

Yugoslav studies on self-management not only found that managers and professional personnel enjoyed greater initiative in enterprise decision-making and planning but that they were more prepared than workers to take risks regarding the consequences of decisions (e.g., trying new productions, production processes or organizational forms). Županov, in a study of ten Croatian factories in 1966, found that the majority of workers favored the continuation of price controls.[26] Only the managerial group was in favor of the elimination of price controls, and even in this group one-third wanted controls to continue. In response to the question of whether an unprofitable enterprise should be kept going with government support in an attempt to improve it or be closed down, the majority of workers opposed shut-down. White-collar employees and supervisors were approximately evenly divided in their opinion while the majority of managers and staff were in favor of closing down unprofitable enterprises (Županov, 1969).

The high level of influence of managers and technicians in enterprise decision-making and planning is certainly welcomed from the viewpoint of the maximization of production (and thus also income) growth (Drulović, 1973).[27] But the loss of relative influence in self-management institutions, especially on the part of unskilled and semi-skilled production workers, has at least two negative consequences.

First, those who already have above average education, knowledge, and experience in crucial power areas are structurally and functionally favored to acquire even more of these valuable capabilities. Second, to the extent that the better educated and trained personnel are also those who occupy administrative and managerial positions in the enterprise, managerial control over the enterprise increases at the expense of control by the total work force of the enterprise. This development will be reinforced if the language of the specialists and their shared understandings dominate in the meetings of the various councils and committees, thus reducing the effective participation of those workers who lack access to this language and models of shared understandings and interpretations.

In this way, a dynamic process of (re-) institutionalization of managerial and technical control may take place and be reproduced in self-managed enterprises. The active participation of unskilled and uneducated workers decreases, and their influence in the councils and committees declines, as indicated by Table 4. Between 1956 and 1968 there was a marked increase in the proportion of chairmen of workers' councils elected from among white collar workers (from 24.6 to 44.5 percent), without an increase in the proportion of such workers in the labor force. The share of skilled, semi-skilled and unskilled workers' decreased (especially the latter two categories).[28]

In sum, studies of self-managed enterprises conducted in the 1960s showed that the enterprise director, management generally, and technicians exerted a substantial degree of discretionary control over enterprises, despite the fact that the workers' councils were legally the legislative bodies of the enterprises and chose the director and other organs of management. This pattern is only in part the result of the differential possession and acquisition of managerial skills, the unequal access to and control of information, and the dependence of common production workers on managers and technicians for enterprise viability and success. Equally as important has been management's necessary and often automatic access to and close links to influential social actors in other spheres (local politicians, party leaders, etc.) and higher-level institutions

TABLE 4
Membership of workers' councils and boards of management in enterprises (percent)

Qualifications	Labor force of the economy		Membership of workers' councils					Membership of managing boards				
	1955	1970	1956	1960	1965	1970	1972	1956	1960	1965	1970	1972
Manual workers												
Highly skilled[1]	6.2	7.6	14.3	15.1	16.7	17.2	17.4	17.9	19.3	19.7	18.2	17.8
Skilled	29.2	29.9	38.0	40.5	37.8	33.7	32.3	33.1	34.9	31.0	20.4	22.6
Semi-skilled	19.5	14.9	13.7	13.4	10.8	9.1	8.9	9.5	8.9	6.8	3.4	4.0
Unskilled	24.3	27.1	10.5	7.8	8.0	7.4	6.7	5.6	4.5	4.3	2.2	2.5
Non-Manual Workers												
Higher education	3.2	4.3	3.5	4.1	5.9	10.1	11.6	8.1	11.0	13.8	27.2	25.3
Secondary education	8.3	9.9	11.8	12.0	13.0	16.0	17.0	15.7	15.0	17.4	22.9	22.3
Lower grade education	9.3	6.3	9.2	7.0	7.3	6.4	5.9	10.7	6.4	6.9	5.6	5.5

Sources: Statistički godišnjaci Jugoslavije, 1971, 1972, 1973. This data concerns the economy and therefore excludes 'non-economic' activities classified in Yugoslav statistics as culture, health, schools, government and social agencies (the level of education of the labor force is higher in these areas). The enterprises covered here are those which have elections for workers' councils. Enterprises with less than 50 employees do not have elections; everyone is automatically a member of self-management organs. Approximately 25 percent of the labor force is engaged in such small enterprises.

1. While the percentage of manual workers participating in worker councils and managing boards has declined over time (76 percent to 65 percent, 66 percent to 47 percent, respectively) the proportion of highly skilled workers participating has increased in the workers' councils and held its own in managing boards. One might conclude that there is a tendency for representative and management functions to be carried out by an elite group of 'workers' consisting of managers, technicians and other non-manual workers with higher and secondary education, and highly skilled workers.

2. One cannot directly infer differentials in influence or control among different categories of workers from this data. 'Control' is a complex-matter relating to social processes in different spheres and at different levels.

(federal and republic planners and inspectors, bankers). This provides managers and technicians with informational advantages as well as external persons and arguments which they can refer to in legitimizing their choices and decisions. They have also the possibility of calling on these persons and organizations, through party, trade union and government channels, to influence the opinions and judgments of enterprise workers. The problem is not only one of external contacts. Many of the roles in different social spheres, at least at the local level during the 1960s, were occupied by one and the same person (Hunnius, 1973:287). The cumulation of decision-making positions in socio-political organizations, commune assemblies, and self-management bodies in enterprises was often complemented with the rotation of single-office holders in such a way that the same group of cadres exchanged the different positions (Hunnius, 1973:272).[29]

Actors occupying these cumulated positions and participating in office rotation are typically the better educated and higher skilled as well as the more active persons.[30] They will be able to absorb, assess, and act upon the information which usually comes to their attention in their functions within the different spheres.[31] Both position in the structure of relationships and access to important information provide these actors with strategic power resources. Situated at the interlinkages of the different spheres, they are in a position to use their knowledge in such a way as to have a predominant influence within and between spheres. In this way, social power tends to accumulate in their hands. The widespread acquisition and development of decision-making abilities and knowledge in organizational and managerial matters is inhibited.

In addition to the substantial power and initiative of managers and technicians in self-management processes within enterprises, the economic elite gained increased freedom from interference from their socio-political environment.[32a] One indicator of this relative autonomization from political and ideological regulation has been the tendency to professionalize management concepts and roles (Županov, 1969). (This is not to imply, however, that the economic elite did not also play strategic roles in political and ideological processes [see section 5].) In one survey Županov found that the actual role of general manager was perceived by half of the respondents as a 'professional role' and by the other half as a 'political role'.[32b] But almost all respondents agreed that ideally the role of the manager should be professional and not political. Consequently, a majority of respondents were against the principle of rotation of personnel in enterprise positions, since they felt that this principle should be applied only to political functionaries. The general opinion was that the manager should behave in accordance with the role of professional businessman, if the different roles which the general manager must play at one and the same time (professional businessman, keeper of legacy, political functionary, leader of the collective, and executive organ of self-management bodies) come into conflict.[33]

This section has addressed itself to the nature of relations of production under Yugoslav self-management operating under market allocation of resources. The means of production are not privately owned and sanctions based on property concepts are not available to managers. Nevertheless, the social division of labor (hierarchy and segmentation) and the technologies utilized (e.g. assembly lines, scale, and corporate structure) operate to develop and reproduce unequal power and control relationships and uneven accumulation of knowledge, capabilities, and social linkages among actors engaged in production.[34]

IV SELF-MANAGED ENTERPRISES AND MARKET PROCESSES OF UNEQUAL ACCUMULATION AND DEVELOPMENT

Capitalist enterprises operating in market systems accumulate and develop unequally (see Chapter 5). Self-managed enterprises — acting as collective entrepreneurs, transacting with one another under market rules — tend also toward the differential accumulation of resources, capabilities and social power.[35] In the absence of institutional limits on such accumulation, enterprises develop unequal capabilities to shape or take advantage of action opportunities '(e.g., the development of new products and production processes and movement into new markets) or to avoid or overcome negative conditions (e.g., a recession, loss of a market, major technological changes requiring reorientation of production, etc.). Especially noteworthy are differential accumulation and development of capital, management knowledge and skills, technology and overall development capabilities (e.g., to conduct research and development), different standards of living for workers, and different levels of legitimation and capability of influencing political conditions.

Such uneven development capabilities support further differential accumulation and vice versa. The outcome is the emergence of advanced and backward enterprises, sectors, and regions. The former are inclined to use their powers to assure the persistence of market conditions and rules advantageous to their interest. In this way, differential accumulation and uneven development may be maintained and reproduced.

The differential accumulation and uneven developments occur at different societal levels:

— Between regions (see Tables 5 and 6).

— Between sectors, e.g., between agricultural and industrial production and in industrial production between advanced and traditional sectors. (These differences are, of course, associated with those between regions, because of the different production profiles of various regions.)

— Between enterprises, e.g., monopolistic or oligopolistic enterprises versus small enterprises in highly competitive markets; or enterprises expanding versus those stagnating or declining (the latter variation is often associated with the sectors or branches in which enterprises operate).

There have been and continue to be substantial disparities in the levels of economic development and standards of living between different republics and autonomous regions. These have been recognized as a major political, economic and social issue throughout the postwar period (Dubey, 1975:12).[36] Although there are less developed areas within even the wealthier republics, the differentials between the republics (and autonomous regions) have been the center of attention, both because of their magnitude and because they are associated with political units with differences in language, nationalities, religion, and culture.[37]

The per-capita income of the underdeveloped regions (Bosnia-Herzegovina, Kosovo, Macedonia, Montenegro) remains substantially lower than the national average (see Table 5). They also continue to be relatively backward according to social indicators used in any assessment of standard of living and socio-economic welfare (percentage of illiterates, population per hospital bed, infant mortality). Moreover, although they have shown significant progress in the quality of life as indicated by the proportion of illiterates in the population aged 10 or more (reduction from 2/5 to 1/5) and infant mortality (halved), the per-capita income differences with the more developed regions have continued to grow (see Tables 5 and 6).

Similarly, personal incomes for labor with similar skills differ by a factor of 3 to 4, both across economic sectors or branches and across enterprises within sectors. These differences are a function of differences in efficiency, in capital endowments, and market structure. Capital intensive — and rapidly expanding sectors and enterprises — can afford to pay much higher wages (personal incomes) by distributing part of the return to capital and favorable market situation as wages.[38] (But this also creates pressures for increasing personal income in other sectors or in other enterprises.) High income levels are also found in branches where one or a few firms dominate. And, of course, personal income levels tend to vary between enterprises which do well and those which do not. The largest firms have been growing more rapidly than others, and consequently, their share of the aggregate economic activity of the economy has increased steadily.

Sacks reports (1976: 383-84):[39]

> In every year the largest firms' share of total assets is greater than their share of total employment, indicating that they are more capital-intensive than the average industrial firm. This fact explains why their share of sales is greater than their share of employment. It also means that each worker in these firms 'controls', through his workers' council, a disproportionate share of the real wealth of the sector (and an even larger share of the real wealth of the entire economy).

As Tables 4 and 5 indicate, strong tendencies toward a 'dual economy' and uneven development generally occur in the Yugoslav system. This is particularly likely in the case of Yugoslavia since it launched its self-management system in the context of already substantial social differences and uneven development. These conditions have been a principal source of social movement and opposition to institutional conditions within Yugoslavia (section 5).

TABLE 5
Index of per capita incomes

Regional Differentiation	1953 Actual	1971 (1966 Prices)		
		Actual	Same population growth[1]	Same GMP growth[2]
Developed regions	100	100	100	100
Underdeveloped regions	65	50[3]	57	56
Bosnia-Herzegovina	74	53	60	65
Kosovo	42	28	37	29
Macedonia	60	56	62	55
Montenegro	60	58	64	53

Source: Dubey (1975).

1. Population growth assumed to be the same as for Yugoslavia as a whole (17.4) in developed and underdeveloped regions. The column indicates the impact of differences in economic growth on relative per capita income. (GMP = Gross Material Product which excludes public services.)

2. GMP assumed to be the same for Yugoslavia (240.9) in developed and underdeveloped regions. The column indicates the impact of differences in growth of population on relative per capita incomes.

3. Even though there has been a rapid improvement in the standard of living in the less developed regions since the second world war (that is, the regions of Bosnia-Herzegovina, Kosovo, Macedonia, and Montenegro), they have been losing ground relative to the developed regions.

TABLE 6
Selected development indicators

	Bosnia-Herzegovina	Kosovo	Macedonia	Montenegro	Underdeveloped regions	Developed regions	SFRY (Yugoslavia)
Per capita GMP, 1971	441.0	196.0	424.0	430.0	394.0	807.0	663.0
Growth rate of GMP 1953-71 (1966 prices)							
Total	6.3%	6.6%	7.6%	7.6%	6.7%	7.4%	7.3%
Per capita	4.9%	4.2%	6.3%	5.3%	5.2%	6.8%	6.3%
Gross fixed investment as % of GMP (1953-1969) (1966 prices)	29.9%	29.1%	43.8%	52.6%	35.0%	24.2%	26.6%
Share of industrial production							
1953	11.6%	2.6%	3.1%	0.6%	17.9%	82.1%	100.0%
1970	12.1%	2.0%	5.0%	1.5%	20.6%	79.4%	100.0%
Share of agriculture in GMP (1966 prices)							
1953	39.6%	51.8%	46.5%	38.5%	42.3%	39.2%	39.9%
1970	19.5%	26.2%	26.3%	15.1%	21.5%	19.5%	19.9%
Fixed assets per worker in industry (thousands of 1966 dollars)							
1952	43.6	52.4	44.2	71.3	45.7	51.4	50.2
1970	109.8	124.1	84.2	152.5	108.2	85.9	91.3

TABLE 6 (continued)

Share of fixed assets in industry							
1962	12.80%	1.89%	2.88%	1.29%	18.86%	81.14%	100.0%
1970	17.14%	3.25%	4.86%	2.74%	27.99%	72.01%	100.0%
Percentage of illiteracy (10 years or older)							
1953	40.2%	54.8%	35.7%	30.1%	40.4%	19.1%	25.4%
1971	22.7%	32.2%	18.0%	17.2%	22.7%	11.7%	15.2%
Population per hospital bed							
1950	503.0	820.0	467.0	264.0	484.0	261.0	304.0
1970	253.0	364.0	185.0	165.0	236.0	153.0	174.0
Infant mortality per 1000 live births							
Average 1950-54	134.0	154.6	138.8	88.6	135.7	101.1	115.7
1971	53.6	89.6	81.9	34.6	68.2	31.6	48.9

Source: Dubey (1975:191).

V PHASES AND DIALECTICAL SHIFTS
IN YUGOSLAV DEVELOPMENT

Yugoslavia has experienced several phases of socio-economic development in the post-war period (see page 85). The period of Yugoslav development up until the early 1950s stressed ideological and political features of development, although, of course, there was considerable attention given to economic and technical matters. Beginning in the early 1950s a phase of economic/technical preoccupation emerged and reached its height in the period 1964-71. In the earliest phase the party, and the party's top leadership dominated. After 1964, the economic-technical elite and professional politicians with local and regional constituencies predominated. The top leadership of the LYC appeared to be fragmented and on the defensive. The current phase (1972-present) has entailed the re-emphasis of political and ideological criteria and a reassertion of political institutions and objectives, particularly at the national level, over economic-technical aspects.

The phases are differentiated by the emphasis given to particular dimensions, goals, norms and standards of evaluation, and support or opposition to particular patterns of social action and structural developments. Each phase exhibits particular institution structuring, restructuring and innovation tendencies, for instance:

— An ideological-political phase where political institutions and values are given priority, that is, there is an emphasis on socialist norms and values (especially those opposed to wage and other economic inequalities and uneven development), solidarity, societal integration, and political and ideological control of economic institutions (and therefore with less stress on productivity, economic-technical expertise, specialization, and differentiated incentive systems).

— A technical-economic phase where economic institutions and values are given priority, with an emphasis on economic productivity, capital accumulation, efficiency, technocratic expertise, professional qualifications and performance, (differentiated) material incentive systems, and economic objectives and standards generally.

Shifts from one phase to another are typically associated with conflicts among groups associated or identified more with one set of goals, norms, and institutionalized patterns of social action than others (see discussion Chapter 5, pp. 188-198).[40] There is a struggle over societal development, for instance, with respect to maintaining or changing characteristic structures and processes. A given phase generates certain consequences, intended and unintended. Different socio-political groups react, either opposing or supporting and reinforcing existing trends. Overall effective support reinforces the characteristic pattern of that phase. Effective opposition tends to bring about a phase characterized by a set of goals, norms, standards of evaluation, and patterns of social action which were secondary or neglected in the preceding phase.

What is of particular interest here are assessments and initiatives of the dominant political leadership in Yugoslavia, and their use of meta-power in restructuring institutional arrangements, rules of the game, and other features which identify a phase of development. The most recent phase (1972-present) was initially characterized by a shift away from an economic/technical emphasis to a more ideological/political one — this has involved the LYC leadership in substantial restructuring and innovations in institutions. This development was related to both problems of socio-economic performance and its social consequences and to matters of power in the society. We discuss these two interrelated aspects separately.

Socio-economic Aspects

The period 1965-71 of increasing autonomy of enterprises and of the economic sphere from political control led to both desirable and undesirable consequences:

— relative rapid growth, the increase in production averaging 7 percent per year during 1964-72;[41]

— the fixed assets per worker have risen sharply since 1964, having been fairly stable until 1964; the capital output ratio, declining until 1965, has tended to increase particuarly in industry;

— exports' share of GNP continued to grow;[42]

— substantial increases in personal income;[43]

— relatively large and increasing unemployment;[44]

— substantial emigration abroad to West European countries (approximately 700,000 Yugoslav workers abroad, 45 percent of them of peasant origin);

— during 1968-70 there emerged serious inflationary pressures and increasing balance of payments deficits;[45]

— increased differences in income levels and in the accessibility to collective goods and services by various social groups and communities;

— uneven development and growing inequality generally between enterprises, sectors of the economy, and regions of Yugoslavia;

— increasing pluralism, above all nationalistic tendencies.

Although some of the economic indicators were positive, several key ones, such as rates of inflation and unemployment and increased socio-economic differentiation, were substantially negative. Self-management institutions, particularly enterprises operating relatively autonomously under market allocation, generated socio-economic consequences which were inconsistent with some of the leading norms and values of self-management socialism (as discussed in sections 3 and 4). The oligarchic tendencies (section 3) and uneven accumulation and development patterns (section 4) indicated that economic objectives, activities, and institutional arrangements to increase productivity and income, profitability, and growth operated to some extent in opposition to values and institutions relating to democratic participation, equality, and solidarity. Moreover, serious social and political problems emerged during 1970-71.

Socio-political aspects

The power and legitimation of the political leadership, which had established the institutional set-up in the first place, appeared to be threatened by the emergence of intra-societal competing groups and social movements opposed to the particular development tendencies and features of the institutional set-up in Yugoslavia. This situation was one aspect of the emergence of pluralistic centers of power in Yugoslavia, associated with economic and political decentralization. These various developments, summarized below, were interrelated and in this sense should be viewed as part of a system development, a dynamic totality (see Chapter 5).[46]

— Decentralization of the economy and development of the open market facilitated the increased autonomy of enterprises from political and ideological regulation. The managerial and technical elite came to increasingly dominate self-managed enterprises. At the same time, this elite penetrated political (as well as socio-cultural) circles. The emergent elites of managers and technicians in the different republics stressed economic growth and rationality, professionalism and meritocracy, and institutional arrangements to advance these and related values. These new elites could also challenge the top political elite in the context of economic policy-making, as well as in a variety of settings which could be seen to be relevant to the maintenance of their own creative dominance.

— Non-egalitarian developments were increasingly apparent in the economic sphere and had, of course, socio-cultural and political implications: (i) personal accumulation and enrichment, increasing variation in standards of living, life styles and life chances; (ii) the economic power and conglomeration of some enterprises and sectors increased while others lagged behind; (iii) regions and republics accumulated and developed unequally.

— General problems of coordination and societal integration became increasingly prominent. This was manifested either in im-mobilization in the face of serious problems such as inflation or balance of payments difficulties or in the vigorous pursuit of self-interest. Decentralization of the political system brought into play pluralistic factions of the republican and local level politicians (e.g. much greater *informal* autonomy, than previously, of the republics and republican parties and more orientation of professional politi-cians to particular interests of their republics, regions, and special groups). This development was reinforced by uneven development of republics and regions, the enormous socio-economic gaps be-tween the wealthiest and poorest regions, and their competition for economic resources and economic advantages.

— There emerged social movements, for example, students reac-ting to economic inequality and the apparent lack of democracy,[47] nationalistically oriented circles[48] strove to enhance or protect their national interests vis à vis other national interests in Yugoslavia. In some instances, ties developed between the emerging managerial and technical elite and nationalistic/cultural elites. Such developments are especially dangerous since nationalistic tenden-cies could prevail over other tendencies and loyalties such as Yugoslav Party orientation.

Because the concept of self-management is a legitimizing feature of Yugoslav socialist ideology and the value system of the society (Denitch, 1977:153-57), every group appeals for its proposals to, or grounds its arguments on, self-management and the development of self-management institutions and values. Of course, operationalization of the concept of self-management — its concrete interpretation and application — differs for different groups.[49] During the period of liberal development, the economic technocrats interpreted self-management in terms of increasing enterprise autonomy. This autonomy combined with an oligarchic distribution of power within enterprises meant freedom of the oligarchy from external political and ideological regulation. It was also this group which argued for and sought to legitimize economic rationality connected with economic growth and qualitative restructuring of the economy in accordance with the demands of a dynamic market.

The 'self-management faction' within the political leadership initiated the Constitutional Amendment XV (1969), which gave enterprises freedom in creating and designing their own inner self-management structures (see page 91). In many enterprises this meant a strengthening of the managerial bodies including that of the director (Hunnius, 1973:277). New executive bodies, such as directors' boards and business boards, were created where managers and technicians played a clearly dominant role. In such ways the power and status of the technostructure within enterprises was not only enhanced but increasingly legitimized.

These developments were paralleled by changes in the economic system especially concerning the bearer of investment. The growing power of banks and financial institutions is indicated by the data in Table 1. Of course, this development was compatible with the stress on economic values and norms (as opposed to more socio-political and solidarity values).

On the broader socio-political scene, the increasing influence of managers and technicians was observable in the 'House of Producers' (which was one of the important houses within the parliamentary structure preceding the 1974 Constitution). In matters of economic policy, programs, and institution formation and adaptation, expertise was a decisive factor. On all levels (federal, republic, and commune parliaments) economic managers and technicians penetrated and played a dominating role in legislative bodies.[50]

The Yugoslav economy and political system became increasingly pluralistic — later referred to as laissez faire. This was also characteristic of cultural and intellectual life during this period. Moreover, the increasing pluralism within the polity was linked to the growing power of the economic technocracy. In the beginning this pluralism was limited to the different factions of the political elite, but later it broadened. Some factions of the political elite connected themselves to new groups striving for power, in particular the managerial/technical elite (see footnote 50).[51]

Decentralization of the economy, self-management institutions operating under market conditions, economic competition and inequality, and political decentralization resulted then in the emergence of pluralistic centers of power in Yugoslavia — where initially, there were no autonomous centers of power to speak of. The increasing pluralist tendencies and conflicts characteristic of the late 1960s and early 1970s threatened the existing distribution of meta- or structural power. Meta-power relationships themselves could have been restructured in terms of the emergence of legalized or legitimized pluralism within the political sphere in combination with the ever-growing influence of the managerial/technocratic elites. The influence of the latter rested not only on the autonomization of the economic sphere but on their penetration of, and alliances with actors in, the political and socio-cultural spheres. Although such interpenetration existed earlier, it was then primarily based on political criteria and objectives. The growing influence of the technocratic groups rested, above all, on their claims of assuring economic efficiency and potentialities for socio-economic development.

The dominant political leadership took action to halt the growing pluralism and the apparent threat to its domination over the system (and possibly, threat to the system itself).[52] These steps were taken ostensibly to deal with other problems, for instance the increasing inequality within enterprises and between sectors and regions of Yugoslavia, uneven development generally, the dominance of market institutions and economic considerations over self-management and political institutions and values, and the particularistic, above all nationalistic, interests and distortions incompatible with Yugoslav socialist ideology and the viability of Yugoslavia as a society. The most significant actions of the political elite were to restructure institutions as well as to introduce new institutions.[53] This was accompanied by the removal of persons, or shifts in personnel, from key positions (which often commanded the most attention in newspaper accounts).[54] Key instances of such restructuring were:

— Dehierarchization of enterprises, increased power to basic organizations of associated labor (BOAL), with the enterprise consisting of a contractually integrated cluster of BOALs to deal in external relationships and to appear in the market.

— Attempts, through increased involvement and influence of political actors and communes as well as through contractual institutions, to control self-managed enterprises and their development in accordance with broader societal interests and to constrain some of the economic and related imbalances and distortions discussed earlier. This meant, of course, reduction in the autonomy of enterprises, above all their politicalization.

— Introduction of institutional devices in the 1974 Constitution to increase coordinating, planning and integrating capabilities: social compacts, self-management agreements, delegation system, integrated economic, social, and physical planning.[55] Also, self-managed interest communities were established in the spheres of health, education, culture, research, and sport. Transport and electric power 'networks' were set-up. A central planning office charged with revitalizing planning, which had been neglected at the federal level from the 1960s on, was created.

— Steps were taken to enhance differences in power between political and economic/technical elites, that is, to re-establish and maintain the domination of the political over the economic sphere, above all through party and labor union activity.[56]

— Purges of 'nationalistic elements' at the same time that republics and autonomous provinces were given more economic autonomy.

The concept of self-management was redefined or reinterpreted in the process. The intent was to increase the influence of workers, particularly the less skilled workers, and to decrease or limit the influence of managers and technocrats. In particular, the power of workers' councils was formally increased at the same time that the new institution of the 'assembly of all workers' (of a BOAL) was introduced and given special rights. Also, to increase the competence of workers in management processes, they were given access to specialized units providing accounting, financial analysis, and other services. At the macro-level, the new institution of legal defender of self-management, and the new parliamentary system based on the principle of delegation was established. Directors were not to be elected to self-management bodies. Simiarly, they could not be elected to the new Chambers of Associated Labor, corresponding to the former 'House of Producers'.

Enterprise autonomy has been de-emphasized. Mechanisms to promote political and ideological influence and regulation over enterprise decision-making and development have been re-activated or established (e.g. concerning income distribution). However, this de-autonomization is not to be accomplished through state regulation but through new institutions which are considered compatible with self-management, such as self-management agreements and social compacts.[57] The contractual nature of these institutions is designed to compel different actors to coordinate their actions and interests as well as to regulate one another's development. That is, they should protect the global interests of the larger collectivity or society from narrow 'enterprise egotism'. Compacts and self-management agreements are the tools and expression of the new planning system (Kalogjera, 1977). This planning system is unique in its attempt to protect the independence of the different basic social units of the economic, political and socio-cultural spheres from interference and pressure by the state (especially the federal and even republican state administrations). In a word, it is an institutionalized form of planning designed to be compatible with self-management institutions (Bošnjak et al., 1978).[58]

The LYC and labor unions have been formally given more prominent roles in socio-economic and government processes. The increasing role of the party does not automatically mean greater influence of workers. The party functions as an integrator of the interests and demands of many groups, not only those in whose name it claims to speak. Moreover, the social composition of the party indicates that every second manager is a member of the party, every fourth professional, but only every eleventh worker and sixteenth peasant.

Not all the results of the period of pluralistic development were undone. The autonomy of the republics and autonomous provinces has been increased to a certain extent and justified in terms of the right to self-management at the republic or province level. However, this autonomy and pluralism is purged of any nationalistic trait and, in practice, is very much limited to economic matters. The political elites in the republics (and provinces) can advocate the economic interests of their respective regions and they retain enlarged economic independence from the federal leadership. The integration on the federal level is henceforth to be based on common economic interests and the political/ideological motivation of solidarity. But political democratization is limited. The LYC is the only societal actor able to influence decision-making at all levels and in all spheres.

The success of the LYC's multi-faceted strategy of institution restructuring and innovation was helped by its judicious use of the widespread unease about increasing income inequalities, uneven development, and the difficulty or inability to solve collective action problems and to check nationalistic tendencies. The consistency of the reforms with these criticisms helped them assure widespread support. The justification of the reforms was helped by its consistency with one of the basic ideological tenets shaped during the post-liberation period, decentralization and self-management.[59]

Although the structural changes which have been introduced are supposed to increase the power of workers inside as well as outside enterprises, workers do not appear to make up a relatively autonomous movement on the global level, which could assert itself via à vis other societal groups, above all the party. The characteristic feature of worker action is its local nature. Thus, strikes tend to be limited to small numbers within factories. They do not occur in a branch or in a territory — this would require a broader organization or societal movement than presently exists. On the other hand, democratization appears to have been strengthened at the enterprise level by increasing the power of basic organizations of associated labor (BOALs) and workers' assemblies as opposed to enterprise level self-management organs and management bodies. At the same time, these changes are likely to weaken the social power of the managerial and technical elites (and their values, standards, patterns of activity and leadership, etc.) in relation to the political elite, in that they are constrained in the use of their expertise and of economic power materialized in social capital and property (Rusinow, 1977:328). Thus, 'democracy' at the macro-level — and understood here as increased participation, at least of different elite groups in political processes — would appear to be weakened.[60] The principle is a well-known one: atomization of social units, in this case production units, contributes to maintaining the power of a political elite.

VI CONCLUDING REMARKS

The arrangement of multiple institutions in a society — in the case of Yugoslavia, self-management, social ownership of the means of production, market allocation, and a decentralized polity with a single revolutionary party — makes up a dynamic totality. Conflicting social values and patterns of social activity are pursued through multiple and partially incompatible institutions. The operation of one institution limits or undermines the intended operation and development of another. For instance, institutional activities and development (or pressures for development) relating to the market economy interfere with or undermine the activities and development of other institutions, such as those associated with democratic participation and self-management. The result may be that the latter devolve or are encapsulated and remain underdeveloped. In this sense one may speak of contradictions and opposing tendencies among societal institutions.

Societal development entails institutional innovation, the shaping and reshaping of social institutions. The outcomes of such processes cannot be fully predicted. Invariably, there will be unintended consequences and unanticipated developments. Therefore, institutional change — whether motivated by system maintaining or system transforming interests — involves some degree of social experimentation. This is particularly so in the case of Yugoslavia since, as Dubey (1975) suggests, the Yugoslavs have had no clear-cut societal model to follow. Rather, they have been engaged in the process of developing and testing such a model. The workability and compatibility of concepts and institutions have had to be tested and judged through praxis, and alterations made on the basis of performance results and experience. Basic laws and even the constitution have been changed frequently. Periods of rapid and qualitatively distinctive changes (e.g., 1953, 1961, 1965 and 1971-72) have been followed by periods of consolidation.

The analysis in this paper (and in Chapter 5) suggests that a system of self-managed enterprises does not entail in itself the full liberation of work. Nor does it imply the liberation of political power (or workers' control over political power). Such a system fails to provide workers with the structural power to shape the institutional environment and rules governing self-managed enterprises, above all the regulation of political power.

A more complete or extensive liberation of work would entail extending workers' control beyond the enterprise to cover the environments within which the enterprise functions — that is, the economic and market institutions as well as the political and sociocultural spheres. Such control is a necessary but not a sufficient condition. It must also be exercised in such a way as to produce conditions and processes compatible with the further development and reproduction of self-management institutions.

The description and analysis presented in this chapter does not, however, conclude with a blueprint for final solutions.[61] It is unlikely that even the best of societal models would tell us what the emerging institutional arrangement will or even should entail, at least not in any detail. But the process of development can be understood as a continuing process of social learning, institutional innovation and experimentation, critical assessment in terms of socialist values and ideology, and further restructuring and experimentation.[62] And in the meta-process of shaping new institutions, it is essential that the broadest possible participation is achieved. For this is also production and its work calls for liberation.

NOTES

1. It is our hope that the following description and analysis, even in the highly tentative form presented here, will contribute to the discussion and clarification of the creative potentialities in, as well as constraints on the development of self-management institutions in Yugoslavia.

2. This section draws very substantially on the following sources: Dubey (1975), The International Institute for Labour Studies (hereafter, IILS) (1972), and Rus (1977). Other materials used are Bošnjak et al (1978), Hunnius (1973), Zukin (1975), and Rusinow (1977).

3. That is, each of the two main political causes which had existed before 1945 — the maintenance of a regime dominated by old Serbia and its ruling group before the war and the establishment of a fully independent Croatian State during the war — had been not merely defeated but totally discredited.

4. At the outbreak of the war, the party was an illegal organization with 6,455 members and 17,800 members in SKOJ (the party youth organization) (Bilandžić, 1973).

5. Up until 1948 the Communist Party of Yugoslavia was recognized as highly 'bolshevized' (Deutscher 1972:577-78; Stojanovic, 1973).

6. The break with the Soviet Union and Cominform must be viewed in its international context, the growing tensions between the Soviet Union and the USA, and the emerging Cold War. 'Deviationism' not only threatened to undermine Soviet domination over other Communist countries in Eastern Europe, but to weaken Eastern Europe as a buffer area which the Soviet Union sought to establish. There were also disagreements between the Soviet Union and Yugoslavia about questions of socio-economic development, about a suitable rate of Yugoslav industrialization, Yugoslavia's place in the international socialist division of labor, and the economic (and ultimately political) relations with the Soviet Union. Boris Kidrić, one of the leading postwar economists, recalls (cited in Bon, 1975:42-43):

> Their purpose was to keep Yugoslavia as an agricultural and raw-material producing appendage, which is why they opposed our setting up basic industries that would help us become independent. We were offended by their opposition to our economic plan and our industrialization program...They called us megalomaniacs and said that our industrialization program was an Utopian dream.

7. For three years, from 1949 through 1951, the combined percentage of G.M.P. (Gross Material Product) committed to investment and defence expenditures exceeded 40 percent (Dubey, 1975:28).

8. Even if the harvest fluctuations are averaged out over the periods 1947-49 and 1951-53, the average rate of growth in national product was only about 4 percent. Dubey (1975:28) points out that this was low in relation both to later achievements and to the rate of growth in the immediate postwar years (although higher than the interwar average).

9. Yugoslavia feared an invasion. Border incidents with Hungary, Bulgaria, and Romania increased. Besides the external threat, there was the threat of the Soviet Union exploiting national divisions within Yugoslavia. Also, there were factions within the Yugoslav Communist Party sympathetic to the Soviet Union ('Stalinists') who might have gained widespread support within the party (these elements were particularly strong in some units, for example, the Montenegran Communist Party). Eastern European countries sent radio broadcasts to 'loyal communists' to replace the 'Tito group'. Propaganda was also directed at officers in the army.

At the same time, trials were conducted in Eastern Europe during this period, in which 'Titoist plots' of the most unlikely sorts were revealed. Dedijer (1971:212, 130-31, 140-45) describes various forms of pressure in addition to the economic ones. (The most systematic description of the conflict is given in Randonjić, 1975.)

10. As Zukin stresses (1975:53), the Yugoslav communists were compelled to find a way to define their continuing revolution as socialist, and also as totally divorced from the leading exemplar of socialism at that time, that is the Soviet Union. This called for finding criteria to define their revolution and development strategy as distinct and genuinely socialist as well as opposed to the Soviet Union as a model. Official Yugoslav arguments after 1948 held the Soviet Union to be etatist or state capitalist and *not* socialist. Early articles questioning the socialist character of the Soviet system are Baće (1949) and Pijade (1949).

11. In any description and analysis of Yugoslav post-war institutional development, it is essential to stress that the Yugoslav Communist Party had a popular base — and a military capability of its own — in contrast to parties in other Eastern European countries (the partisans had liberated Yugoslavia without the Red Army). This enabled the Tito leadership to develop a type of national communism (as in the case of China, also) with opportunities and motivation for self-reliant innovation and experimentation, which has been possible only to a very limited degree in other Eastern European countries (with the exception of Albania and to a much lesser extent Romania). That is, the high level of innovation in developing and changing social institutions has to a large extent been a function of national independence and self-reliance of the leadership as well as of its internal support and legitimation (Ionescu, 1976:31):

> This kind of leader is trusted by the people to be able to take on another power that might threaten national integrity — both Tito and Mao turned easily against the Soviet Union with the support of their people...They could change their policies without relinquishing their leadership.

12. In 1953, in the course of rewriting the 1946 Federal Constitution, the government tried to clarify the semi-autonomous status of enterprises as well as the rights and duties of the workers: Zukin (1975:59-60) writes:

> A federal government proclamation of that time stated officially that enterprise autonomy — as far as plans, profits, and wages are concerned — was an essential component of workers' self-management. However, the state maintained certain controls to ensure that the enterprise would fulfill its financial obligations to the government, to its workers, and to its own continued functioning. The 1953 proclamation also upheld the right of work collectives to manage economic organizations directly and through workers' councils, assemblies of agricultural cooperatives and other representative organs which they themselves elect and recall.

13. In 1966, A. Randović who was vice-president of Yugoslavia and head of the secret police and who had supported centralization tendencies was ousted from the party leadership. Zimmerman (1976:68-69) writes:

If we are to believe the accounts of the victors, Ranković was opposed to the whole proposed direction of Yugoslav policy being advocated by the adherents of market socialism. Thus, he apparently concluded (correctly) that the economic reforms were fraught with important political consequences. Those economic reforms . . . envisaged judging enterprises primarily by efficiency as measured by market criteria. To achieve efficiency, the dinar was to be devalued and the goal was set of convertibility by 1970. The country's borders, furthermore, were to be opened both to the in-migration of capital (especially under the aegis of Yugoslav-foreign joint ventures) and to the out-migration of workers. Ranković evidently feared that, as a result of the economic reforms, Yugoslavia would be integrated into Western Europe and into the capitalist international market, the problems of internal political control would be increased, the Yugoslav citizenry would be exposed to Western influences, and a more Western-oriented foreign policy would ensue — all of which Ranković opposed. Instead, he appears to have stood for an entirely opposed line: the continuation of 'political' factories, the discouragement of foreign investment and close ties with the socialist states. Finally, his behavior conjured up fears, most notably in Croatia, that his dominance in post-Tito Yugoslavia would bring about a return of Serbian dominance . . .

The victors were not content, however, to limit themselves to the purging of Ranković and his cohorts. Ranković's ouster was followed by a series of institutional alternations designed to prevent a similar occurrence (use of the secret police to try to strengthen his position) and to provide an institutional context in which economic reform and political decentralization might flourish.

14.   Also, the character of state investment changed.

TABLE 2
Investment in fixed assets financed by different levels
(in percent)

	1953	1955	1960	1962	1964	1966	1970	1972
Federation	97	73	60	51	19	40	55	10
Republics	2	14	11	15	22	20	20	70
Communes and districts	1	13	29	34	59	40	25	20

Source: Dubey (1975).

15.   Nevertheless, the picture remained quite complicated. The allocation of

funds continued to be influenced by considerations other than simply the 'profitability' of projects. Government policies and viewpoints of founding members of banks, who were also the chief borrowers, exercised considerable influence. There were also strong tendencies toward concentration. In 1966 there were 111 banks, which were reduced to 64 by 1970. These mergers resulted in the emergence of some very large banks with practically a national field of operation. Banks came in for increasing criticism as being too powerful in determining the allocation of funds and being a serious obstacle to greater autonomy of workers' self-managed enterprises.

16.   The stress on economic objectives and on institutions such as monetary and financial institutions — in order to facilitate the rational allocation of resources and to increase productivity and income — is motivated in part by genuine interest in raising the material standards of workers and the society as a whole. Thus, as suggested later, there may arise a genuine dilemma here between economic gains and gains in democratic participation and equality.

17.   Social ownership means neither state ownership nor workers' ownership, but diffusion of ownership among producers, consumers, and collectivities in Yugoslav society. Thus, ownership as a socio-economic category is not vested in any particular holder. No societal actor holds the rights of social ownership, not even the Federation. However, the law recognizes a special property right which it refers to as the 'right-to-use'. Under this, workers are vested with management of the means of production and the right to dispose of the products (IILS, 1972:133). That is, the authority to manage property is delegated to more or less autonomous enterprises and institutions which, in turn, are managed by the workers directly or through their elected organs of self-management (see footnote 21) (Hunnius, 1973:274).

The Yugoslav property concept appears to facilitate a shift from emphasizing the rights of 'property owners' to stressing the duties as well as rights of 'property users' vis à vis other social actors. This contributes to generating a broadly based social network regulating and intergrating the resource, information and value flows between and among different spheres of social activity. Such a regulatory network and social integration is difficult, if not impossible, to achieve under capitalist institutions with their restrictive interpretation of property rights and assignment of costs and benefits.

18.   In the case of an enterprise consisting of less than 30 persons, there would be no elected workers' council. The whole working community acted as a council. This arrangement was also legally permissible in any working community with no more than 70 persons. In the case of enterprises with more than 70 persons, the workers' council had to consist of a minimum of fifteen persons, with no maximum specified.

When an enterprise had less than 10 working members, there was no managing board, but above that number a managing board consisted of a minimum of 5 persons, again without any maximum. Prior to 1974 the director of the enterprise attended meetings of the workers' council and was a member of the managing board.

19.   It is worth reminding ourselves of Yugoslavia's limited resources initially, that it undertook this experiment not as one of the rich lands of the world, but as one of the poorest and least developed in Europe (see section 4).

20.   This contrasts with the development of 'soviets' in the Soviet Union which were supported by a social movement. The process of centralizing and bureaucratiz-

ing society was carried out over the opposition of, and struggle with, parts of that movement: Kronstadt, workers' opposition, etc. Such self-governing movements did not exist in Yugoslavia. (For a discussion concerning the 'imposed nature' of self-management in Yugoslavia, particularly in relation to the shaping and dynamics of the social system, see Golubović [1971].)

21. This argument attempts to go beyond the issue of imposed versus emergent basis for Yugoslav self-management institutions. The key elements in the argument are: (1) Yugoslav society, on the basis of the historical experience of the liberation movement, acquired certain social structural potentialities and corresponding cultural elements; (2) the political leadership activated and transformed these in the face of a serious challenge to Yugoslavia, and their position in it, acquiring legitimation for the struggle against Stalin and the Cominform; and (3) although the leadership was instrumental in activating and reshaping these potentialities and cultural elements for their purposes, the latter nevertheless led to developments and movements not entirely under their control. Thus, both the continuity and discontinuity of self-management in relation to earlier developments can be identified. This corresponds to a certain extent with the argument of Rus (1977:2) that self-management was continuous with the liberation movement. Although the initiative for self-management originated from above, it was not simply a system of 'imposed democracy', because it had its own real social base in the liberation movement:

> Thus, self-management was not only the voluntary act of the political elite, which could in this way acquire legitimization for its struggle against Stalin and the Cominform, but was at the same time a transformation of the liberation movement, based on *political* participation, into a labor movement, which would now be based on the economic participation of those employed.

22. Wage, income and consumption differentiation illustrates this point. Basic wage differentials, taken as averages, are low both within enterprises and even nationally (see Table 3). The spread in average incomes between different skill levels at the national level is less than 1 to 3. Wage incomes differ in most enterprises by a factor of 1 to 4 (only about 7 percent of Yugoslav enterprises had a spread of 1:6 in 1970) (Vušković, 1976:31). This is little compared to capitalist societies. But the cumulation of regional, sectoral and skill differentiations leads to much larger spreads, up to 1:15 (Vušković, 1976:33).

In addition, income is only one criterion of social differentiation. It does not indicate consumption of educational services which appears to be the major intergenerational transmission mechanism of position and status in communist societies where private ownership of the means of production has been largely abolished. Also, other bases of social differentiation, relating to political and cultural aspects of social life, contribute to substantial differences among employees.

23. Ignorance about self-management institutions themselves is widespread. Large numbers of workers have been found unable to give an account of problems treated by self-management bodies. As many as one-fifth were found to be unfamiliar with the formal self-management structure of the company, and an equal number of them could only state a few things about it (Tanić, 1972).

TABLE 3
Average personal incomes by level
of skill or education
(unskilled workers = 100)

Level	Year			
	1963	1968	1970	1976
Manual				
Highly skilled	188	169	182	166
Skilled	142	130	137	128
Semi-skilled	117	106	108	104
Unskilled	100	100	100	100
Non-Manual				
University	273	258	273	244
Advanced	231	188	199	175
Secondary	191	161	166	146
Lower grade	138	131	136	118

Source: Statistički godisnjaci Jugoslavije.

But these figures reflect only basic wage incomes and do not take into account overtime and family earnings. Nor do they reflect differences due to profit-related wage bonuses, enterprise-owned apartments with nominal rents, company cars, expense accounts (allowed for much coveted foreign travel), and other enterprise allocated consumables.

The lack of knowledge and often interest is partly a result of the system having become 'too complicated for most of the workers who have to operate it', although knowledge varies according to the type of worker and type of factory (Riddell, cited in Pateman, 1970).

24. One of the most systematic interpretations of the bases of managerial influence within Yugoslav work organizations is given by Županov (1971a). Participation in discussion at work unit levels is twice as great as in discussions at the enterprise level (43 percent compared with 20 percent) (IILS, 1972:144). A survey in Slovenia in 1968 (in 111 industrial and mining enterprises) showed that workers were interested in the following issues: 72 percent in personal income matters, 61 percent in the business results of the enterprise, 40 percent in welfare facilities, 34 percent in development of the enterprise, 16 percent in the organization of production and work relations, 10 percent in personnel policy, 5 percent in the work of self-management bodies, 2 percent in irregularities in the enterprise, 1 percent in retirement income (IILS, 1972:152).

25. Highly skilled and skilled manual workers make up more than 50 percent of the membership of workers' councils and 46 percent of the membership of boards of

management (see Table 4). This strengthens the trend toward intensive industrialization and rationalization of work (IILS, 1972:145):

> They tend to strive for occupational advancement and so to draw nearer to the technical intelligentsia; they also tend by their roles, attitudes, ideology, and social perceptions, to influence other workers and the non-manual employees.

26. The majority of prices were controlled until the 1965 reforms.

27. This viewpoint ignores the sources of the growth and its impact on working conditions and work environment, a theme we shall return to later. Increased productivity and higher incomes, benefiting many, may be purchased at the expense of some workers' health and welfare. Greater influence of less skilled workers could lead to preferential improvements of their workplace conditions instead of, possibly, wage increases for all.

28. Without a more precise definition of 'worker', one is unable to conclude from this that there is not 'workers' control' or self-management. It is 'white collar' workers and highly skilled workers who appear to exercise disproportionate influence over self-management processes. In other words, the split between skilled and unskilled workers may be greater than that between skilled workers and managers and engineers.

29. On the other hand, the accumulation and rotation of offices and positions in different spheres of social life (especially political and economic, but probably including the socio-cultural) by individual actors facilitates the coordination of decisions in the different spheres.

30. Salaried workers (39 percent) along with students, military, etc (20 percent) dominate the League of Yugoslav Communists, while workers remain a minority (34 percent) — and an even smaller minority of its leadership (Horvat, 1969).

31. Nor does the establishment of quotas or the banning of leading managers from self-management and social management bodies (as under the 1974 Constitution) solve the problem. For this does not in itself improve the ability of production workers to participate in fact and effectively in key decision-making processes. However, it does explicitly define a conflict between manager/cadre groups and shop-floor workers. This has effects of its own.

32a. Županov (1972) suggests that self-management operates as 'collective entrepreneurship', where self-management has come to imply autonomy from the environment. At the same time, workers' influence on decision-making and planning is acknowledged ideologically but in practice is depreciated in the name of efficiency.

32b. Because of the *potential* ideological and socio-political context in which managers operate, their role is not as clearly or as exactly defined as in capitalist systems. Obradović (1976:30) points out in the case of Yugoslavia:

> His power is rather high, but *illegally so*. He has to be versatile and find the legal rationale for all his actions. According to J. Županov, . . . he manipulates various interests and groups watching closely the rationale of his behavior in the institutional, legal, and ideological sense. In many actions he is relying on organizations outside the company. In the first place on the banks and socio-political organizations, sacrificing there a part of his autonomy.

One interpretation of the success of strikes in Yugoslav work organizations suggests that strikes make the illegitimate power exercised by management obvious: the strike is oriented against management. But management is institutionally defined as simply the executive organ of self-management bodies. The strike points up a lack of worker control due to weak or ineffective self-management bodies.

Such a paradoxical situation gives legitimation to political bodies outside the enterprise to intervene because 'something is wrong with self-management' (much as near-bankruptcy or bankruptcy brings outside intervention in the case of enterprises operating under capitalist institutions). This intervention is made against the management and in the name of workers (the legitimate holders of enterprise power). To avoid such intervention management tends to quickly meet the demands of striking workers. The success of strikes in Yugoslavia is an indicator of management concern about and eagerness to maintain autonomy. (Županov, 1971b).

In this context, it should be pointed out that approximately 80 percent of the strikes last less than 1 day and 35 percent 3 hours or less. The strikes typically involve small numbers (a few hundred), who are usually production workers (79.6 percent) (this data comes from a study of Jovanov, 1973). That is, only exceptionally are technicians and members of the administrative staff involved. A major factor underlying Yugoslav strikes appears to be the low economic status and unfavorable market position of an enterprise (Obradović, 1976:31). The highest frequency and intensity of strikes are in the metal, metallurgy, and textile sectors.

33.   The stability of social hierarchization in the economic sphere depends to a large extent on parallel or corresponding conditions within the socio-cultural and political spheres, for example, legitimation to support managerial/technical elitism and autonomy (see Chapter 5). The outcome of struggles and developments in these spheres determines whether or not a compatible — and even reinforcing — context for economic structure and processes will obtain (see discussion in section 5).

In other words, ideological and legitimation processes must address and resolve the substantial gap between reality and ideal, the divergence between the actual perceived distribution of power and aspirations for the normative or ideal one, democratic participation. Thus, some theoreticians (e.g. Bilandžić) argued that self-management should be something analogous to parliamentary democracy. Practically, this means that workers and their representatives would not be involved in day to day operations but only elect competent managers who are to fulfill their responsibilities and programs. At the same time, Rus (1972) found some evidence that the ideal distribution was adapted to be more compatible with the real one during the course of the 1960s. Initially, workers felt that all members of the enterprise should participate equally in decision-making. However, by the end of the 1960s workers had come to more and more accept the oligarchic status quo and no longer sought equal participation (Rus, 1972; Zukin, 1975). This can be interpreted as a lowering of democratic aspirations under pressures from market rules and forces (for a discussion of the consequences of tension between ideal and reality in social systems, see Sekulić, 1975).

34.   Self-managed enterprises operating under conditions of market competition cannot regulate effectively technical innovations and system change with a view to developing self-management institutions. Technologies and other instruments of production (e.g., assembly lines), division of labor, and development strategies and

paths are selected for their comparative advantage in market competition, and not for their contribution to, or compatibility with, self-management institutions and values.

The pressures to adopt more capital intensive technologies, to increase enterprise size (see section 4), and to adopt new organizational forms (such as divisionalization) adapted to modern market conditions and development are not as much a matter of worker choice as 'given' by the conditions and forces of markets. Participating in the world economy and the international division of labor generates particularly intense pressures — pressures that do not originate in or are not subject to regulation by Yugoslavia — toward efficiency, larger industrial units, more advanced technologies, and higher degrees of professionalization. These tendencies move decision-making and planning upward and away from shopfloor workers (Hunnius, 1973:314-15). And differences in function, outlook, and power within enterprises are amplified. Expressed in another way, the democratization of the internal structure of work organization, motivated and guided by ideological and political goals, comes into conflict with external arrangements and developments associated with market competition and forces.

35.   In spite of 'social ownership', advantaged enterprises retain control over 'their' positive gains, while disadvantaged enterprises have in practice very limited rights to the benefits others gain, nor do they receive substantial compensation for relative losses. 'Solidarity transfers', e.g., through the 'fund for aid to underdeveloped republics and autonomous regions' are defined in monetary terms, rather than in terms of a multi-dimensional concept of costs and benefits suggested here. They have quite a limited regional impact on the actual process of differential accumulation and uneven development, if any at all (see Chapter 5).

36.   The major problem facing the political leadership of Yugoslavia — and a problem for the federation as a whole — was and continues to be the backwardness of substantial regions of Yugoslavia as well as the diversity of, and long-established conflicts among, the Yugoslavian peoples. Yugoslavia has been and remains a complex multi-national society with pockets of extreme underdevelopment among some of its sub-populations and with enormous socio-economic and cultural gaps between the wealthiest and poorest regions.

The most socio-economically underdeveloped regions of Yugoslavia, Bosnia-Herzegovina (with 1 percent of the total Yugoslav population), Macedonia (8 percent), Montenegro (3 percent), and Kosovo (6 percent), lie in general to the south of the River Sava. These regions were either part of the Ottoman Empire or buffer zones in the defence of Europe against Ottoman expansion. The more developed northern and western republics and provinces, Slovenia (8 percent), part of Croatia (22 percent) and Vojvodina (10 percent) were under Central European influence and formed part of the Austro-Hungarian Empire. Prosperity was greatest in Slovenia and in a small number of urban areas in Croatia (including Dalmatia) and in the rich agricultural area of the Vojvodina. Little industrial development had taken place in Serbia (26 percent). In general, one should bear in mind the substantially different socio-economic structures inherited by the Yugoslav revolution, ranging from industrial capitalism in the north to feudal structures in the south. This suggests the structural bases of many political conflicts (Bičanić, 1973).

37. An atomized self-management society has difficulty dealing effectively with collective action problems and societal coordination, since self-managed enterprises and other work organizations do not produce social integrative mechanisms within themselves. In practically every sphere where coordination is required at levels above self-managed enterprises, other work organizations, and local socio-political units (communes), there have been substantial problems. In capitalist societies, the state has become a key institution in the efforts to provide integrative and stabilizing mechanisms (see Chapter 5), but this solution has become increasingly unacceptable ideologically in Yugoslavia (see section 5 concerning efforts to develop functionally equivalent institutions).

The point here is that the differential accumulation of material (as well as socio-cultural and political resources) by different groups, enterprises, as well as political/administrative units of communes, regions and republics, is, in the long-run, incompatible with socialist objectives and, moreover, threatens the basic cohesion of a multi-national society such as Yugoslavia and the reproduction of its self-management institutions. The likelihood of realizing social cohesion and collective commitment of societal actors to the maintenance and development of a self-management society is increased to the degree that inequalities and patterns of uneven developments do not become extreme, that inequalities which do occur are generally viewed as temporary and correctable 'dysfunctionalities' (not fixed or basic characteristics of the institutional set-up or society), and that most social groups, if not all, have opportunities to exercise meaningful control over the system so as to re-negotiate and to correct felt injustices.

38. Personal income differences arising due to varying capital endowments contradict the notion that all capital is supposed to be socially owned (Dubey, 1975).

39. Typically, corporate size increases effectiveness in competition with other enterprises, particularly in international markets where multi-national corporations play a major role (Sacks, 1976). Sacks (1976:387) has shown that Yugoslav firms in general grew substantially in size during the period 1958-71. Early in this period there were indications that they were already large by international standards. This evidence is consistent with Sacks's hypothesis that firms in a market socialist system find competitive advantage in large size, but unwillingness to establish new enterprises may also be a factor.

40. Zimmerman (1976) stresses the intense and articulate dispute about 'the proper organization of Yugoslav society'. 'This not only entailed a confrontation of different interests and methods, but a confrontation of different, broader concepts of problems of the socialist society' (Marko Nikezić, former foreign minister and 1971-72 president of the Serbian Party, quoted in Zimmerman [1976:72]).

41. The growth of industrial output averaged over 10 percent per year, agricultural output fluctuated declining by 5 percent in 1970 and increasing 9 percent in 1971. Overall, from 1947 to 1972 the social product increased 4.8 times with a yearly rate of growth of 6.6 percent. The yearly rate of growth was not even, as suggested earlier: the lowest rate (2 percent) occurred in the first period covering the break with the Soviet Union, and the fastest rate of growth (8.5 percent) was in the following decade during the time the economy changed over to a decentralized market economy and to self-management of work organizations (Rus, 1977).

42.   The percentage (1966) prices are indicated below:

TABLE 7
Exports as percentage of GNP

1952	1961	1965	1970
10.3	14.3	18.2	20.7

43.   The rapid economic development, based on high rates of investment, was achieved in part at the expense of personal incomes preceding the 1965 reforms. Thus, the growth of personal income of the employed for the entire economy was for this reason significantly less than the growth of the social product through 1963. Only from this period onwards did personal spending grow parallel with the growth of social product (Rus, 1977:17). Rus suggests that because of this development, conflicts within enterprises decreased, whereas strikes had grown in number from 1952, reaching their peak in 1965 (Jovanov, 1973). Rus writes (1977:17):

> Where earlier management together with political organizations within enter-
> prises strongly insisted on as great as possible investments and as low as possible
> salaries, the situation today tends toward negotiating and compromise. The
> reason that greater social unrest did not appear in the earlier periods despite
> relatively low incomes, may be found, among other things, in the relatively
> greater equality of personal incomes for various categories of workers.

44.   The growth of unemployment is indicated in Table 8. This data must be viewed in the context of the rapid growth of the economy. The number of employed increased 2.5 times in the last 20 years. Every year, on the average, 124,000 new work places were opened, so that the total number of employed grew in the period from 1.7 million persons to 4.2 million (Rus, 1977). But this growth was insufficient to keep up with the rapid growth of employable adults (due both to population growth and rapid urbanization).

TABLE 8
Growth of unemployment in Yugoslavia

	1957	1964	1975
Total Number	116,000	212,000	502,000
Percentage of unemployed in relation to all employed	2.7	7.9	12.0

45.   Inflation has been a chronic problem of the Yugoslav system and reflects (1) the operation of a market system in the context of (2) the power and motivation of

workers of individual enterprises to raise wages and pass the costs on in the form of higher prices and (3) the provision of easy credits by the banking system to make this possible on a continuing basis, thereby reducing the chances of 'zero-sum conflicts' (Černe, 1971).

TABLE 9
Inflation rates

	1956	1965	1970	1972	1973	1974	1976	1977
Rate of inflation in percent calculated on the basis of retail prices	3.3	39.1	10.7	16.7	18.7	24.7	6.7	12 (est.)

Source: Rus (1977).

46.   For instance, economic competition and unequal accumulation and development patterns stimulated nationalistic tendencies in the context of a policy decentralized to the republican level. This was particularly manifest in Croatia's relation to Serbia. At the same time, economic competition tended to increase the influence of the managerial/technical elites (Bilandžić, 1974).

47.   Belgrade University was occupied in 1968. The Zagreb University strike, which took place in 1971 (see later discussion), was coupled with a demand for a Croatian currency and had clear nationalistic overtones. Non-party and Croatian nationalist types had won earlier in the year leadership of the Student Federation at Zagreb University and at republican level and led the strike. Their inability to mobilize workers in factories to strike limited its overall impact and averted the chances of civil war (Rusinow, 1977).

48.   This was particularly manifest in the expansion, and increasing political importance, of *Matica Hrvatska*, a Croatian cultural organization which had played a 'distinguished and aggressive role in developing Croatian national consciousness during the "Slav awakening" and the bitter nationality struggles of the last decades of the Habsburg monarchy' (Rusinow, 1977:276-77). In less than a year's time during 1970-71, a membership drive resulted in growth of the organization from 2,323 members in 30 branches to 41,000 in 55 branches. Political publications were also initiated (Rusinow, 1977).

49.   That is, the interpretation of self-management and relative stress on different features of it varies among these groups.

50.   The rising influence of the technocracy was also connected to increasing conflict within the political elite. Some argue that the conflict was limited to a narrow circle at the top of the party (Bilandžić, 1974). The subject of the struggle was the further development of the economic system. The main factions were apparently those supporting the development of greater centralization and state regulation and opposition to the market economy, on the one hand, and, on the other, the self-management faction and economic technocrats supporting the view that all aliena-

tion of surplus value from the producer is contrary to self-management. The technocratic faction and, indirectly, the self-management faction supported the autonomy of self-managed enterprises and their internal technostructure.

51. The development was different in the different republics: in the case of Serbia, de-etatisation of state capital (Table 1) led to a concentration of power in the hands of Belgrade banks and foreign-trade companies. The technocratic elite in the economy was tied to technocrats or technocratically oriented members of the political leadership of Serbia. In highly developed Slovenia, where the influence of financial viewpoints and groups was strong, the official policy advocated the 'shareholders' model' of self-management. (This is the notion that inputs into the enterprise are not only work but capital, that within the management of the enterprise, holders of capital should be represented also, and that capital owners should enjoy income [Županov, 1975].) Moreover, in Slovenia, there emerged claims for national autonomy. In the case of Croatia, such expressions took extreme forms (see footnotes 47 and 48), including demands for the admission of Crotia to the United Nations and for the formation of a National Bank of Croatia whose governor would be sent to Washington for credits (Zimmerman, 1976:66; Rusinow, 1977). The emerging nationalistic movement in Croatia was supported not only by the traditional intelligentsia but by technocrats concentrated in the largest enterprises and banks in Croatia who felt disadvantaged vis à vis Serbia and the Federation as a whole.

It was argued that the 'surplus value of Croatian labor' was being 'expropriated' by Belgrade banks, Belgrade-based foreign trade enterprises and bureaucracy. Although Croatia produced 27 percent of the Yugoslav social product, 30 percent of its industrial production and 36 percent of its foreign currency earnings, Croatian banks controlled only 17 percent of Yugoslavia's total bank assets. Serbian banks controlled 63 percent. The three largest banks in Yugoslavia among the top ten were in Belgrade. Four of the ten largest foreign trade enterprises were also located in Belgrade and together had an annual turnover at that time of 23,500 million (old) dinars, compared to the 2,000 million of Zagreb's one large firm in this sector (Rusinow, 1977:323).

Such analyses underlay the demands in Croatia for separate republican foreign currency regimes, so that each republic could keep what was earned or remitted in its territory, buying and selling as needed in a free all-Yugoslav (in fact interrepublican) currency market (Rusinow, 1977:297).

52. Zimmerman (1976:74) contrasts the position of Tito, Stane Dolanc, and Kardelj with Nikezić's (see footnotes 47 and 48):

> For them [Tito, Dolanc, and Kardelj] the lessons of the Zagreb [University] strike were dramatically opposed to those derived by Nikezić. For Nikezić, the need was for a policy approved by the masses and for greater democratization; for Tito and Dolanc, the main danger was liberalism. Their policy prescriptions were those typically associated with the Leninist tradition. Democratic Centralism must be observed: 'We have forgotten that . . .' Tito declared, 'and that fact is one of the basic causes of the situation in our country.' In the words of the now famous September 18, 1972 letter by Tito and the LYC Executive Bureau: 'There has been a fair amount of wavering, inconsistency, and deviation from

the principles of democratic centralism.' Moreover, 'Cadre policy has also been neglected', Tito said. As the letter expresses it, 'The League of Communists must consolidate its role and influence in the field of cadre policy . . . Responsibility for constructive social and state affairs [must]be entrusted to people who will perform these duties in the interest of the working class and the development of socialist self-management.' To ensure such an occurrence, the party, in the words of the letter, must be 'transformed into the kind of organization of revolutionary action that is capable of translating its stands and policy into life more efficiently.' 'We have never believed,' Tito declared, 'that organized democratic institutions in the state and society represent separation or disassociation of the League of Communists from the obligations and the responsibility to act as an ideo-political force in an organized manner: . . . Communists in all institutions should implement the LCY policy.' Finally, opportunism must be fought: 'The toleration of views and political conduct that are at variance with the ideology and policy of the League of Communists' must be terminated.

53.   The dominant political leadership's ability to introduce such reforms and to rewrite the Constitution and change basic laws, thus restructuring the institutional set-up and changing the 'rules of the game', indicates their meta-power capabilities with respect to Yugoslav society.

54.   The Croatian 'nationalist leaders' were dismissed in 1971. Stane Kavčić, prime minister of Slovenia in 1972, one of the major political figures most committed to efficiency, market solutions and decentralization (along with close economic ties to Europe, which also came under criticism during this period) was removed in 1972. Marko Nikezić, former foreign minister and in 1971-72 president of the Serbian Party, a prominent advocate of extending democratization, resigned in 1972 and was removed from the party in 1974. (In 1971 he had emphasized, concerning the Croatian developments, the importance of 'freeing ourselves from our own Communist conservatism which, being unable to respond to the changed needs of society, would try to master the difficulties of the present stage by returning to the old norms and relations, to a renewal of ideology and a renewal of the party and so forth' (cited in Zimmerman, 1976:73; also, see Rusinow, 1977).

15 of the 52 members of the party presidency conferred at the 9th Congress were no longer members by the time of the 10th Congress. Eight resigned under attack for serious deviations and seven had lost their party membership (Rusinow, 1977:336). Removals were not only carried out at the top political levels. Rusinow (1977:330) reports that in Belgrade alone some 200 enterprise directors were replaced in the two year period between mid-1972 and mid-1974, many of them after losing party membership.

Neutralism and professionalism in all walks of life were vigorously attacked, at the same time that central party control over newspapers and weeklies was greatly enhanced (Zimmerman, 1976:76). Zimmerman reports that the mass media were particularly promising sources for the discovery of 'technocrats, anarcho-liberals, and nationalists.'

55.   Self-management communities of interest are required by law in the fields of education, health, research and cultural activity, on the community and republican levels. They are planned for and administered by delegates from production

organizations which finance social services and by delegates who are employed in the corresponding social services. Collectively and on an equal basis both sets of delegates decide about yearly and middle-range plans of work for the social service, as well as about financing the realization of these plans. In this way, work organizations, through their delegates, have a direct influence on the financing and development of social services.

56. The reforms altered or re-established certain power relationships in the economic sphere as well as between the economic and political spheres. For instance, members of the managerial and technical elite have been blocked from participating in the Communal and Associated Labor Chambers. At the same time, delegates to these chambers have been 'deprofessionalized' through the requirement that they keep their ordinary jobs during their term of office (the lack of time and experience would tend to enhance the opportunities for party members to exercise influence).

Directors of enterprises are to be elected from a list of one to three candidates proposed to the workers' council by a commission. (Directors are now referred to as 'individual management organs' to avoid the 'bourgeois- technocratic connotations' of director (Rusinow, 1977:329). The commission is composed of an equal number of enterprise representatives and of communal assembly appointees. This represents a return to the pre-1964 system which had commune participation in the nominating commission. This system had been criticized earlier as unjustifiable political interference in workers' rights (Rusinow, 1977:129). Also, the 10th Party Congress reaffirmed the party's right to 'intervene' in decision-making and selection of officers by the commission.

In general, during the 1950s leading economic actors consulted politicians before making important decisions. Then, during the liberal phase, the opposite occurred. Assemblies after 1963 tended to be dominated by the managerial-technical elite and by professional politicians with regional and local constituencies (such politicians tended to be oriented more to 'special' and even 'nationalistic' interests than to Yugoslav party and party discipline interests). Now, once again, political leaders oriented to the top leadership appear to be preeminent.

57. These institutions were introduced in the 1974 Constitution as a major new technique for coordinating and regulating social relationships and exchanges by agreements or contracts. They are intended to serve as functional equivalents to state planning, compatible with self-management principles of social organization in that they negate both the lack of social control over the liberal market and hierarchies of state planning. Social compacts are contracts between government organs, economic chambers, trade unions, and other collective actors, and concern such matters as price policy, the policy of personal incomes, employment policy, and planning. Self-management agreements regulate relations between and among work organizations, whether these relations concern cooperation in production, the business integration of enterprises into a larger company, the creation of banks on the part of work organizations, the instituting of economic chambers, or even penetration (by Yugoslav enterprises) in foreign markets. Economic relations between work organizations which bear on the policy of salaries and on personnel policy in work organizations are also regulated by such agreements.

58. Proposals to return to centralized planning and control would, in our view, be a step backward away from the liberation of work and the liberation of political

power. Such centralized controls would inhibit the development of democratic relations among those engaged in production. Democracy must be learned, practised, and maintained through everyday processes. Moreover, centralized controls fail to realize and utilize for the collective good the potential interest of producers in their work and in the operation of their work units. They also discourage the development of conscientious, responsible attitudes toward work and social ownership. Finally, such solutions only exacerbate problems of status differentiation and hierarchization in society. Even problems of uneven development may be left unsolved.

59. Self-management has been institutionalized as a societal value and pattern of social relationship and activity. This has constrained and biased possible restructuring and institutional innovation that could have been effectively initiated by the political leadership. This is another way of saying that the meta-power of the political leadership was, in part, constrained by conditions which they had helped bring about. And these constraints provide a certain logic and continuity to current Yugoslav development.

60. In other words, destratification of power within organizations may be closely connected to stratification of power in the global system (the establishment or maintenance of meta-power). But at the same time there are immediate social welfare benefits in the form of the equalization of personal incomes within and between organizations. For example, the introduction of social compacts concerning income distribution contributes to bringing about destratification of incomes within and between enterprises and branches. There is still a basic dilemma between the power to liberate and the liberation of power. On the one hand, a political leadership itself acts to establish and develop self-management and participatory democracy at the same time that the realization of these goals and values ultimately implies a negation to a greater or lesser extent of the power of the leadership.

61. As we see it, a major task for societal analysis is to identify contradictions and conflicts occurring, or likely to occur, in a particular institutional arrangement, and to specify and analyze the dilemmas these present. On the basis of this examination, one may be able to develop concepts and strategies to deal with the dilemmas and to contribute to producing and developing desirable societal structures and processes. For instance, one aim here would be to indicate areas where constraints and regulatory processes could be imposed on market and other key social institutions in order to facilitate the development of self-management institutions and values. Among the areas for the exploration of such social control are the following: (1) the design and use of technology which is compatible with genuine self-management. Along such lines, Fusfeld (1978:8) proposes (i) technologies that rely on decision-making abilities of workers at all levels, in place of the present pattern of routinizing individual work; (ii) technologies that facilitate shifting of individual workers and groups between jobs; (iii) technologies that bring workers together into small groups. (2) The exercise of constraints and regulation of market forces and developments which work in opposition to, and dominate, self-management forms and processes within enterprises. (3) Exploration of the effects of size on self-management practices and specification of optimal size for effective self-management practice. (4) Indication of limits to the division of labor (and the types of division of labor) compatible with full development of self-management. (5) The establishment of learning and socio-cultural conditions and processes in family,

community and work as well as in the usual cultural and educational institutions in such a way as to be compatible with the full development and reproduction of genuine self-management. (6) The establishment of political institutions and the effective practice of politics in ways compatible with the development of self-management.

62. Ionescu (1976:33) suggests that a major dilemma facing all Eastern European societies hinges on the contradiction between socio-economic forms which are emerging and the established political forms:

> The real object of the contradiction is the necessity to adapt Leninist structures to the technological revolutions that have swept the industrial world since the second world war. By now it is universally clear that the industrial-technological society, with its built-in corporate structures and therefore with its essential need for expanding pluralization, can no longer live within the narrow Leninist boundaries or parameters.

REFERENCES

Baće, M. (1949), 'O nekim pit anjima kritike i samokritike u SSSR,' *Kommunist*, 3, No. 6.

Baumgartner, T., W. Buckley, T. R. Burns and P. Schuster (1976), 'Meta-Power and the Structuring of Social Hierarchies,' pp. 215-88 in T. R. Burns and W. Buckley (eds.), *Power and Control*. London: Sage Publications.

Bendeković, J. (1975), 'Analiza sistema investiranja u SFRJ Poslije 1965,' *Ekonomski Pregled*, 26, Nos. 3 and 4.

Bičanić, R. (1973), *Economic Policy in Socialist Yugoslavia*. Cambridge: Cambridge University Press.

Bilandžić, D. (1973), *Ideje i praksa društvenog razvoja Jugoslavije*, Beograd: Komunist.

—— (1974), 'O kriznom razdoblju u razvoju samoupravljanja u Yugoslaviji,' *Pogledi*, No. 11-12.

Bon, E. (1975), 'Viewpoints on the Yugoslav Model of Socio-Economic Development.' Unpublished manuscript.

Bošnjak, V. T. R. Burns, S. Saksida, and D. Sekulić (1978), *Dialectics of Societal Planning and Change: Studies of Planning, Conflict, and Democracy*. Unpublished manuscript.

Černe, F. (1971) 'Komparativna motivno-funkcionalna analiza našeg kolektivno-samoupravnog sistema,' in: *Samoupravni ekonomski socijalistički sistem*, Beograd: Savez Ekonomista Jugoslavije.

Dedijer, V. (1971), *The Battle Stalin Lost*. New York: Viking.

Denitch, B. (1976), *The Legitimation of a Revolution: The Yugoslav Case*. New Haven: Yale University Press.

—— (1977), 'Notes on the Relevance of Yugoslav Self-Management', pp. 141-60 in: M. R. Haug and J. Dofny (eds.), *Work and Technology*. London: Sage Publications.

Deutscher, I. (1972), *Stalin*. Harmondsworth, Mddx.: Penguin.

Drulović, M. (1973), *L'autogestion à l'épreuve*. Paris: Fayard.

Dubey, V. (1975), *Yugoslavia: Development with Decentralization: World Bank Report*. Baltimore and Boston: Johns Hopkins University Press.

Fusfeld, D. R. (1978), 'Workers' Management and the Transition to Socialism'. Paper presented at the First International Conference on the Economics of Workers' Management, Dubrovnik.

Golubović, Z. (1971), 'Ideje socijalizma i socijalistička stvarnost,' *Praxis*, No. 3-4.

Gorupić, D. and I. Paj (1970), *Workers' Self-Management in Yugoslav Undertakings*. Zagreb: Ekonomski Institut.

Horvat, B. (1969), *An Essay on Yugoslav Society*. New York: International Arts and Sciences Press.

Hunnius, G. (1973) 'Workers' Self-Management in Yugoslavia,' in G. Hunnius, G. D. Garson, and J. Case (eds.), *Workers' Control*. New York: Random House.

International Institute for Labor Studies (1972), *Workers' Management in Yugoslavia*. Geneva: International Labor Office.

Ionescu, G. (1976), 'The Modern Prince, Its Princes, and its Condottieres,' *Studies in Comparative Communism*, 9:27-34.

Jerovšek, J. (1969), 'Struktura utjecaja u općini', *Sociologija*, No. 2.

Jovanov, N. (1973), 'Odnos štrajka kao društvenog sukoba i samoupravljanja kao društvenog sistema,' *Revija za Sociologiju*, No. 1-2.

Kalogjera, D. (1975), 'Samoupravni sporazumi i društveni dogovori — mehanizmi samoupravne integracije udruženog rada,' *Ekonomski Pregled*, No. 3-4.

—— (1977), 'Planning under the System of Workers' Self-Management.' Paper presented at the 2nd International Conference on Participation, Workers' Control and Self-Management, Paris.

Obradović, J. (1972), 'Distribution of Participation in the Process of Decision-making on Problems Related to the Economic Activity of a Company in Zagreb,' *Participation and Self-Management*, 12:3-17.

—— (1976), 'Sociology of Organization in Yugoslavia,' *Acta Sociologica*, 19:23-35.

Pateman, C. (1970), *Participation and Democratic Theory*. Cambridge: Cambridge University Press.

Pijade, M. (1949), 'Veliki majstori licemjerja,' *Borba*, 22, 29 September, 5, 6 October.

Randonjić, R. (1975), *Sukob KPJ sa Kominformom*. Zagreb: Centar za aktuelni politički studij.

Rus, V. (1972), *Odgovornost in moč v delovnih organizacijah*. Kranj: Moderna Organizacija.

—— (1977), 'Yugoslav Country Context.' Unpublished manuscript.

Rusinow, D. (1977), *The Yugoslav Experiment: 1948-1974*. Berkeley: University of California Press.

Sacks, S. R. (1976), 'Corporate Giants under Market Socialism,' *Studies in Comparative Communism*, 9:369-88.

Sekulić, D. (1975), 'Motivacija i socijalna akcija,' *Revija za Sociologiju*, No. 3.

Stojanović, S. (1973), *Between Ideals and Reality*. New York: Oxford University Press.

Tanić, Z. (1972), 'Dimensions and Factors of the Apperception of Self-Management,' *Prva medjunarodna konferencija o participaciji i samoupravljanju*, Zagreb.

Vušković, B. (1976), 'Social Inequality in Yugoslavia,' *New Left Review*, No. 95, January-February, pp. 26-44.

Zimmerman, W. (1976), 'The Tito Succession and the Evolution of Yugoslav Politics,' *Studies in Comparative Communism*, 9: 62-79.

Zukin, S. (1975), *Beyond Marx and Tito: Theory and Practice in Yugoslav Socialism*. New York: Cambridge University Press.

Županov, J. (1969), *Samoupravljanje i društvena moć*. Zagreb: Naše Teme.

——— (1971a), 'Samoupravljanje i društvena moć u radnoj organizaciji,' in J. Jerovšek (ed.), *Industrijska sociologija*. Zagreb, Naše Teme.

——— (1971b), 'Industrijski konflikti i samoupravni sistem,' *Revija za Sociologiju*, No. 1.

——— (1972), 'Employees' Participation and Social Power in Industry,' in: *Prva medjunarodna konferencija o participaciji i samoupravljanju*, Zagreb.

——— (1975), 'Evolucija i involucija samoupravnog poduzeća — jedan nacrt za tipološku analizu,' in *Proizvocne organizacije i samoupravni sistem*, Grupa, Sistem i čovjek Zagreb.

II
THEORETICAL STUDIES

4

HIERARCHY AND DEMOCRATIC AUTHORITY

Peter Abell
University of Birmingham, UK

INTRODUCTION

'Come the revolution' — we are frequently told — then hierarchical social structures will disappear; in the free democratic society the need for such structures, which are essentially the repressive instruments of those in power, will no longer exist. Accordingly, hierarchy will be relegated to the prehistory of mankind and we can look forward to the wholly edifying spectacle of men and women coming together in freely formed associations carrying out their business in the spirit of equality, mutual respect and freedom. Is this merely a pipe-dream or does it contain an element of truth?

Whether or not a society entirely devoid of hierarchical ordering can ever be realized I leave aside, but in the light of current interest in most industrialized countries (and some non-industrialized ones also) in 'participation', power-sharing, self-management and so on, a more modest analysis of the relationship between the principle of hierarchy and 'democratic authority' in work organizations seems not inappropriate. Does an organization based upon genuine democratic principles imply a non-hierarchical structure? Or, if not, do the social functions of hierarchy change under the imposition of such principles? Clearly much will rest with our definitions of these concepts, but before I make any attempt in this direction I should like to place my analysis in an historical context.

I believe that, however haltingly and uncertainly, we in advanced industrial societies, are entering the age of democratic industrial authority — an age in which the traditional forms of industrial authority are either breaking down or becoming so modified as to render them completely unrecognizable. The unholy alliance of downright repression, manipulation, paternalism and professional competence is being progressively challenged by new sources of power and legitimation, which, at their heart are egalitarian and democratic — in fact, we are in part witnessing the demise of Max Weber's rational legal form of legitimation and thus, in many respects (though not all) of his rational bureaucratic form.[1]

Just as Weber, at the turn of the century, was able to claim a general tendency toward what he termed 'societal rationality' and the concomitant rational bureaucratic administrative structures, we can detect a tendency toward democratic authority structures. Weber was able to document a decline in the importance of traditional and charismatic sources of legitimation, so, likewise, we can chart the decline in rational-legal forms of legitimation.

I should hasten to emphasize that one should not think in all or none terms; Weber was able to speak of mixed forms of legitimation and democratic authority structures will likewise incorporate elements of legal rational forms of legitimation and perhaps even charismatic and traditional ones as well. This is for two reasons; firstly, since we live in a transitional period between the pre-eminence of legal rational and the pre-eminence of democratically legitimated structures, pure types[2] are not fully operative. Secondly, just as legal rational bureaucracies were staffed by professionals with specified technical skills of one sort or another, so democratic structures have also to find an appropriate role for such personnel. In fact the tension between legitimation through competence and through democratic rights is, in my opinion, one of the central problems we will increasingly face in the closing decades of the century.

One only has to look at the fierce polemics in universities over the last few years, concerning the rights of students to participate in university governance and to control aspects of the curriculum, to recognize the contemporary importance of this tension. Sociologists have documented the difficulties that professionals can face in bureaucratic organizations of the sort Weber had in mind

(Cotgrove, 1970); these are, however, in my opinion going to fade into insignificance in the forthcoming years, when compared with the new challenges posed by pressures for democratic legitimation. The so-called crisis of middle management is yet a further instance of this tension which is very much with us already.

WEBER'S IDEAL TYPE

Weber believed he was able to classify the administrative structures in organizations in terms of the dominant mode of legitimation of the necessary[3] inequality in their internal power distributions. An individual (or group) was said to possess power (*Macht*) to the degree that his (its) own will could be enforced despite resistance.[4] He recognized, however, that for reasonable stability this 'power' had to be seen as legitimate by both those who were exercising it and particularly by those subject to it. There are a number of problems with these rather simple concepts, but they are sufficiently precise for our present purposes. So the source of authority (i.e. legitimized power inequality) becomes the defining characteristic of an organization. Weber was adamant that all organizations faced a problem of compliance and thus the need for an authority structure. Furthermore, he was also quite explicit that authority worked to the advantage of the 'rulers' of an organization Surprisingly enough he never actually defined what he meant by bureaucracy and sometimes uses the term in a restrictive sense to mean an administrative system based upon legal rational authority and at other times in an extended sense to mean any administrative structure irrespective of its form of legitimation (Albrow, 1970). A further point should also, perhaps, be emphasized; Weber used the term 'bureaucracy' to denote the administrative structure of an organization, not all of its members. Roughly speaking, he drew a tripartite distinction between (a) the rulers (owners, leaders, etc.); (b) the administrative staff; and (c) the general membership — and, strictly speaking, applied the term bureaucratic only to the second. This usage of course reflects both the structure of the joint-stock company — with owner(s), managers and operatives[5] — and public administrative structures supposedly at the behest of government. Despite this tripartite division, the term 'bureaucracy' has been used by many of Weber's commentators to include both 'operatives' and administrators and with the changes wrought by developments in twentieth century technology and the parallel attenuation of the distinction between 'work' and 'administration', this is, perhaps, more useful.[6]

Similarly, with the emergence of the concept of a self-managed enterprise (which, incidentally, I see as the central organizational form of the age of democratic authority) it is not always useful to draw a distinction between the owners or 'rulers' and the administrative staff. Unless, therefore, I need to make some precise distinctions I will tend to use the term bureaucratic organization which will normally cover both administrators and operatives and sometimes owners, etc.

The precise meaning which Weber attaches to the ideal-type (legal-rational-bureaucracy) has caused some controversy, but I am not here concerned with details, since there seems to be sufficient consensus, at least on the major elements of his conception. Few, I suspect, would disagree with the following list of propositions slightly adapted from Albrow (1970):

W1. The officials (administrators) are personally free, observing only the impersonal duties of their offices.

W2. There is a clear hierarchy of offices with requisite authority and sanctions.

W3. The functions of the offices are clearly specified.

W4. Officials (administrators) are appointed on the basis of a contract which specifies their rights and obligations in terms of written rules (technical and legal).

W5. Officials are selected on the basis of a professional qualification.

W6. Officials have a money salary graded according to position in the hierarchy.

W7. The official's post is his sole or major occupation.

W8. There is a career structure, promotion is possible by merit according to judgement of superiors in the hierarchy.

W9. The official may appropriate neither the position nor the associated resources.

W10. The official is subject to a unified control and disciplinary system based upon the hierarchy of offices.

These ten propositions are listed separately and, thus, might appear to stand as logically independent descriptors. Such an interpretation would, in my opinion, be unfortunate, comprising a failure to recognize the internal logic whence the concept of 'hierarchical ordering of offices' plays an all-pervading role.[7] It seems to me to be worthwhile to attempt a reconstruction of the logical infrastructure of Weber's ideal type, trying to demonstrate the role that 'hierarchy' plays; but before I do this the time has come to be more precise about the concept itself.

DEFINING 'HIERARCHY'

Everybody is familiar with the simple idea of a hierarchical ordering — organizational charts of one sort or another are immediately recognizable (in our culture) and there is a natural way of speaking of the 'top' and 'bottom' of such charts, thus the relationship between positions is one of super and subordination. In its most straightforward interpretation a hierarchy (tree)[8] may be defined in any one of six equivalent ways.

A tree is a graph[9] consisting of $N > 1$ points which (Berge, 1962):

1. is connected[10] and possesses no cycles;
2. contains no cycles and has $N - 1$ arcs;
3. is connected and has $N - 1$ arcs;
4. contains no cycles, and if an arc is added which joins two non-adjacent points, one (and only one) cycle is thereby formed;
5. is connected but loses this property if any arc is deleted;
6. every pair of points is connected by one and only one distinct path (sequence of arcs).

Thus, although the idea of a 'tree' is intuitively rather simple it contains a surprisingly varied range of elementary mathematical properties.

The question we must ask is — why are organizations so often based upon this principle? And in so doing, ponder the implications of the above six properties. If we construe organization as necessarily involving the coordination of N activities (see below) then there are $N(N-1)/2$ possible symmetric relations between all pairs of activities. If we further assume that, in some sense, the maintenance of relations is a costly activity[11] then we can immediately see one appeal of hierarchy: it replaces $N(N-1)/2$ by $(N-1)$ costly relations, whilst still maintaining overall connectivity (i.e. the grounds for coordination). In fact, in virtue of (5) a hierarchy is a unique structure on a set of activities in that it maintains overall connectivity by a minimum number of relations. Further, since by (6) every pair of activities is connected by only one path, the structure contains no redundant connections and thus also eliminates the possibility of conflicting 'messages' along different routes.[12] So (ceteris paribus) in a world where (a) coordination is necessary and (b) the maintenance of relationships is costly — hierarchical trees are minimal cost structures.

From an organizational point of view, the three important properties of any given hierarchy are its size, its spans of control and its depth. In an organization of size N, with a uniform span of S and depth of n the three properties are related as follows:

$$N = \sum_{i=1}^{n} S^{i-1}$$

Thus, if we fix any two the third is determined. The building blocks of a hierarchy are spans of control — a number of subordinates with one and only one superordinate.

I should mention here other possible hierarchical structures defined over a set of points, which are rather more complex than the simple tree (i.e. they may have more relations [arcs])like the upper and lower semi-lattices which I will return to below, but for the moment, in the context of our analyses of the role hierarchy in Weber's ideal type, it is sufficient to stick with the simple tree.[13] So let us now turn to the underpinnings of Weber's ideal type, paying particular attention to the role of hierarchy.

THE ROLE OF HIERARCHY IN
WEBER'S IDEAL TYPE

The ten Weberian propositions can be construed as resting upon a series of deeper-lying assumptions relating to hierarchy. These assumptions in part derive from the value system of those industrial (and other) societies[14] which Weber was describing, and in part reflect cognitive processes that are perhaps almost universal to man. It seems to me important to unravel these two aspects, so that we can clear the way for an analysis of an 'ideal-type' which we might expect to replace the Weberian one as these societies mature into what I have termed the age of democratic industrial authority.

A.1. Collective (Organized) activity is resorted to since the goals so pursued can be more readily obtained than by individual action.

Thus, the costs (if any) of collective effort are more than off-set by the benefits. Rationality would dictate that organized action will take place to the point where the benefits equal the costs at the margin. Putting things this way immediately raises the whole vexed question of the relationship between Weber's ideal type and organizational efficiency — in particular the relationship between his concept of (legal) rationality and efficiency. Albrow (1970) has pointed out that many of Weber's interpretors have, in his opinion wrongly, equated Weber's idea of rationality (*Zweckrationalität*) with means/ends efficiency. Albrow argues that Weber was not offering a theory of organizational efficiency, merely describing a contemporary process whereby legal-rational activity (independently defined) was becoming embodied in administrative practice, leaving open the question as to its 'efficiency'. Thus, he writes:

> Each of the propositions involved in his [Weber's] pure type of bureaucracy referred to a procedure... Any such procedure was for Weber intrinsically rational, irrespective of its relation to organizational objectives. In short, he was not offering a theory of efficiency but a statement of the formal procedures which were prevalent in modern administration.

Be this as it may, what seems to me to be of importance is that a tradition has evolved which has interpreted Weber to mean that rationality (in his sense) is conducive to organizational effectiveness (independently measured). This tradition has been extremely fruitful theoretically and empircally enabling us to specify reasonably

precisely where legal rational bureaucratic organizational structures are and are not efficient. Thus, even if Weber did not intend
his ideas to be used in this way, they have, in fact, proved, when so
used, most insightful. Furthermore, it is difficult to believe the in-
eluctable trend toward rational-legal bureaucracy, which Weber so
admirably described, was in fact taking place without some idea of
organizational efficiency informing those involved in building the
administrative structures of the time — they were not imposing
legal rational structures for the mere love of them! I, therefore,
have no compunction in adopting A.1, and its implied notions of
means/ends rationality, as one of the intellectual underpinnings of
Weber's ideal type.[15]

A.2. Collective action implies a
division of Tasks

Following contemporary organizational theorists, by task I mean a
process of transforming a set of inputs (material or symbolic) into a
set of outputs by the application of appropriate technologies.[16] This
is nothing more (when taken in conjunction with A.1), than a statement of the venerable concept of the division of labour. But it is
here that we encounter (implicitly in Weber) the most profound influence of hierarchical thinking. Collective action is institutionalized in an organizational structure which (in virtue of A.1) is concerned with some global task(s). Characteristically, this task is,
hierarchically, decomposed into a series of sub-tasks each of which,
if rationally/efficiently pursued, contributes to the fulfilment of
the global task; thus, the decomposition will normally generate a
series of interdependent tasks.[17] At this stage the decomposition is
not to be thought of at the actual level of the division of labour, but
rather as a cognitive process reflecting one way in which human beings attempt to solve complex problems (i.e. think about effecting
global tasks). I will term this the 'cognitive function of hierarchy.'
The above few sentences might appear so obvious to the reader as
to be barely worth the effort. The 'obvious', however, often has a
habit of concealing the profound and it seems to me that the very
ease with which we (in our culture) handle the idea of task-
decomposition, demonstrates the endemic nature of hierarchical
thinking to our cognitive processes.

Clearly, most organizations (bureaucracies) are established to solve a more or less complex problem and the question arises as to whether the 'hierarchical solution' of complex problems is in fact endemic to man, and if so, why? Further, if it is endemic, what implications does this carry for the actual division of tasks/labour in organizations? But before I consider these difficult issues, it is worth noting how 'deep' in human consciousness hierarchical 'reasoning' really goes. One has only to mention axiomatic reasoning, a mode of thought which has come to dominate Western man. From a set of axioms one deduces a set of theorems — one, as it were, unpacks the implicit complexity in the content and interrelationship of the axioms. There is nothing 'new' in the deduced propositions, they are merely a restatement of that which is 'already there'. Axiomatic reasoning has, at least since Greek antiquity, held some sway in Western culture and with the intellectual defeat of Baconian inductivism in the late seventeenth century — particularly at the hands of Newton — it largely became the abstract standard by which other intellectual procedures were to be judged. Thus a value entered the consciousness of Western man, proclaiming the intellectual superiority of axiomatic reasoning above all others. Even the chaotic process of the world had to be organized into nomological axiomatic systems.

Furthermore, the way we actually classify the world around us is almost invincibly hierarchical. Most taxonomic systems naturally lend themselves to a hierarchical structure with a 'downward' relation of contrast and upward one of inclusion. All the evidence suggests that hierarchical modes of thinking and cognitive organization of the phenomenal world are not unique to Western man but are much more widely distributed. Recent developments in cognitive anthropology (Tyler, 1969) and the analysis of kinship (White, 1969) testify to a deep reliance on hierarchical principles in many different cultures. If we can take the work of Levi-Strauss seriously, then man's cultural world derives from an endemic sequential application of 'binary opposition' which clearly generates a tree structure. And much more seriously, Chomsky's transformational grammar also rests upon an explicit hierarchical foundation.[18]

In one way or another, hierarchical structures seem to be at the very foundation of our ways of thinking and apprehending the world around us. But why? Are there any deeper-lying processes at work, or should we conclude that this reflects the structure of the mind itself and search no further? We may, I believe, analyze the processes involved rather more deeply by looking at human problem solving; intuitively[19] we can, I think, determine three salient cognitive processes in problem solving.

If a problem is intractable globally then:

a) Decompose the problem into sub-problems.

b) Find a solution for each sub-problem in isolation.

c) Combine the sub-solutions into a global solution to the problem.

This sounds rather trivial, but the simple description conceals a number of important issues:

1. Of the (presumed) variety of possible ways of decomposing the problem which should be adopted? The answer is, in part, involved in a specification of (b) and (c).

2. One should decompose the problem in such a way that the sub-problems are solvable in isolation (or nearly so[20]).

3. One should decompose the problem in such a way that the solutions can be reconstituted to solve the global problem. These twin constraints impose certain practical restrictions upon problem solving — a heuristic, as it were. They reduce the variety of possible decompositions, for there is no use in decomposing a problem into relatively easily solvable sub-problems which cannot be reconstituted into a global solution.

Let us examine (b): the important point here is the criterion of independent solution; the sub-problem must be solved without constant reference to the other sub-problems. The hierarchical decomposition of problems into sub-problems is, in effect, a way of holding complexity constant, it enables us to ignore (for the moment) the rest of the problem. The solution must be built (in virtue of (c) into a global solution, but the combination of sub-solutions must depend only upon the solution to the sub-problem, not upon its internal complexity.[21] So, principle (c) is also a way of holding complexity constant.

This leaves (a) — how do we know how to locate sub-problems which have the interrelated properties (b) and (c)? There are no universal rules here — if there were then the problem could be entirely routinized and correspondingly would lose much of its complexity. But one factor of crucial significance for our analysis resides with an additional constraint — any sub-problem must be less complex than its supra-problem, for if it were not there would be no cognitive gain in making the decomposition in the first place. Although the idea of the complexity of a problem is itself rather difficult, it seems that it is a correlative of heterogeneity and, conversely, the less complex a problem then the more homogenous it is.[22] Thus, principle (a) usually implies a progressive internal homogenization of the sub-problems with hierarchical decomposition. It is immediately evident that homogenization of this sort takes place in any taxonomic hierarchy — contrast within a given class becomes finer and finer.

The cognitive functions of hierarchy are thus intimately connected with the way we solve problems and, as we have seen, organizations are structures institutionalized precisely for the purpose of problem solving. It is, therefore, not surprising that hierarchical structuring penetrates them so deeply. Given man's proclivity for hierarchical problem solving and notwithstanding a contemporary emphasis on 'lateral thought', etc., it seems likely that organizational design will to some extent continue to reflect this proclivity. It is interesting in this context that organizations like the Kibutzim, animated by an extremely strong egalitarian ethic, still exhibit a hierarchical design, though if we are to believe Tannenbaum et al (1974), their hierarchies are very uneven, varying in depth in the same organization. But clearly a more important question is — need the cognitive function of hierarchy be translated into a division of labour? I will return to this point presently.

A.3. The Division of Tasks implies a need to coordinate Tasks

Clearly, sub-tasks must be coordinated under the rubric of (c).

A.4. Principles A.2 and A.3 imply a division of labour which (a) reflects the hierarchical division of tasks and (b) generates a need for coordinative roles.

This is, in a sense, the most fundamental inference in Weber's ideal type and it should be emphasized that it is an empirical inference:[23] we move from the cognitive realm to the world of labour — a division of problem solving becomes a division of social roles and the functions of individuals and groups. The cognitive function of hierarchy is translated into a hierarchical division of labour. So the second function of hierarchy is to establish a coordinated division of labour, and the principles (a) (b) and (c) are then likewise translated into the world of practical activity. Let us examine the implications of this translation. It implies a process whereby the task performance of any sub-part of an organization should be carried out in reasonable isolation from other sub-parts and, secondly, that only the summary performance (i.e. solution) of the sub-part should enter into descriptions of the coordinative interactions of any sub-part with other sub-parts. So the performance of the total system should depend only on the summary performance of sub-parts (Simon, 1962). The essential feature of the division of labour in a hierarchically structured organization is that the complexities of the internal operations of any sub-part should only enter the interactions with other parts in summary or aggregate form. In accordance with our above analysis, it normally follows that sub-parts should be internally as homogeneous as possible. In effect the internal homogenization of an organizational sub-part — which in extrema means the individual — enables the summary performance of the part to be readily ascertained without too much loss of local information in terms of a relatively simple set of parameters. The emphasis on standardized procedures and rules — for many the quintessence of bureaucracy — became necessary precisely because of the hierarchical coordination of tasks. Hierarchical coordination means coordination downwards and the venerable epithet, 'rules down, information up', comes into its own. The problems facing the peak coordination, or any coordinator further down a hierarchy, are two-fold: firstly, to specify and set the tasks of sub-parts in relation to the global task (the task-decomposition structure) and secondly, to monitor and coordinate the performance of these tasks, attempting to ensure they do, in fact, ultimately contribute optimally to the global task. In order that he should not crowd his information processing capacity, the coordinator will (ceteris paribus) attempt to standardize the functions of his subordinates which will in general reduce the volume and complexity of information flowing upwards, whilst still enabling him to estimate the performance of the subordinate in relation to the global task. It is, of course, only organizations facing very routine task environments which can be 'rule governed' in this sense (Lawrence and Lorsch, 1969; Burns and Stalker, 1966) and as environments become less and less predictable the subordinate has to be given discretion. Nevertheless, the coordinator still needs relatively uncomplex information flows to enable him to fulfil his coordination function adequately. If this is not feasible, then his optimal span of control is accordingly lowered and (for a given size) the depth of the organization increases with all the attendant problems of control-loss (Williamson, 1970). There is thus a constant pressure within hierarchically structured organizations towards homogenization which, not surprisingly, has become one of the central maxims of classical management theory.[24]

A.5. The need to coordinate will set up a distribution of information needs.

The information needs of an organization based upon principles A.1 to A.4 are those that enable each task performer to fulfil the obligations of his task such that his performance may adequately contribute to the global task. Since we may assume the generation and transmission of information is costly,[25] 'rational' organization will (a) only generate and transmit information appropriate to sub-task performance and coordination, (b) use the least cost (connected) transmission mechanism, namely the hierarchy. So, here, we encounter the third function of hierarchy: it provides (under the assumptions) a least cost coordinative function.

A.6. Within the division of labour there will be a diversity of interests; in particular concerning the distribution of costs and benefits in pursuing the organizational goal.

**A.7. If individuals are rationally self
interested then it is in their interest
to maximize their benefits and
minimize their costs[26] as
organizational participants.**

Although Weber was not entirely explicit about the divergence interests within organizations, it is clear he regarded bureaucracies as
systems in which 'power' (and thus divergence of interest, according to his own definition of this concept) is an essential ingredient.

**A.8. Thus (in virtue of A.6 and 7),
organizations have the need of a
control function (over and above
the coordination function).[27]**

Weber's ideal type assumes the control and coordinative functions
should coincide and so the hierarchy should, where appropriate,
take on a control function as well.

**A.9. In virtue of the control function of
hierarchy a source of power is
required which is correlative with
the hierarchy.**

**A.10. It is desirable that the source of
power be legitimized into a
source of authority.**

Weber clearly recognized 'knowledge' within the division of tasks
(labour) as the source of legitimate power — 'Bureaucratic administration signifies authority on the basis of knowledge. This is
its specifically rational character'. Since legitimation is something
that is bestowed by those over whom power is exercised and since
power is correlative with hierarchy, it follows that the hierarchy has
an additional upward legitimizing function.

In summary then, we can recognize five major functions of 'hierarchical ordering' in Weber's ideal-type:

(a) the cognitive function (division of tasks);
(b) the division of labour function;
(c) the coordinative function;
(d) the control function;
(e) the legitimizing function;

It is also clear from Weber's ten propositions that the hierarchy has the further functions of:

(f) providing a basis for differential salaries (W6);
(g) providing the basis for a career orientation (W8);
(h) providing a basis for selection and promotion (W8).

That each function should be correlative with hierarchy must be regarded as a series of assumptions reflecting a certain constellation of values. It is, I hope, clear though that the concept of hierarchical ordering plays a crucially central role in the 'logic' of Weber's ideal type.

THE PARTIAL DEMISE OF
STRICT HIERARCHY

Weber was, of course, writing over half a century ago and in the intervening period — one of rapid technical and social change — many modifications have taken place in organizational structures. In work organizations a trend, so brilliantly charted by Chandler (1962) from the entrepreneurial to multi-functional and then to multi-divisional, and thus backward and forward vertical integration and finally horizontal conglomeration, has taken place. Attendant upon this, a gradual process of economic concentration has occurred with an increase in average company size, though not necessarily plant size (Prais, 1977). This has had the effect of attenuating the proportion of market interfaces in capitalist economies, replacing them by administrative (and, thus, hierarchical) interfaces and increasing the average depth of companies. Thus, in one sense, we have witnessed a secular trend towards an increasing incidence of deep hierarchies;[28] they have not, however, uniformly taken on the various functions which I outlined above.

Although the architecture of organizations large and small is still characteristically based upon hierarchical task decomposition structures, there has been some resistance to the implied homogenization of activities. At the individual operative level, demands for job enrichment, enlargement, etc., have perhaps begun to reverse the trend. And, at the department and plant and subsidiary company level a number of studies have indicated that subordinate demand for diversity of activities (e.g. decision making) is an important factor in calculating the overall level of decentralized discretion (Thomas, 1977).

Furthermore, the increasing complexity (and rate of change) of the social and technical environment of organizations has led to an often begrudging recognition that some 'problems' are not best addressed through the medium of hierarchical decomposition — and certainly not through a hierarchical division of labour. This has led to an institutionalization of such things as 'project teams', 'trouble shooting groups' and matrix organizational structures, which in various ways circumnavigate the cognitive and coordinative functions of hierarchy. Though too much should not, in my opinion, be read into these developments as they still all take place within the overall context of hierarchical control and coordination.

Despite our earlier reservations about linking rational legal structures with (economic) efficiency, a number of important studies (Burns and Stalker, 1966; Lawrence and Lorsch, 1969) have spawned a general theoretical model whereby rational legal bureaucratization is effective only to the degree that organizations face reasonably certain decision making environments. Where environments are uncertain then 'bureaucratic structures' tend to be ineffective and must be replaced by ones which place much less reliance on hierarchical coordination. For instance, the communication pattern tends not to conform to the hierarchy and is invariably much richer in linkages than in bureaucratic structures. It has recently been shown (Abell and West, 1977) that the probability of cross-level, and inter-span connections occurring increases logistically with task uncertainty of the communicator's role.

All these tendencies seem to suggest that hierarchical coordination is no longer invariably the rule and, indeed, it has become common practice in organizational theory to distinguish between the formal hierarchy and the informal communication and coordinative structure (Daniels, 1972).

THE CONCEPT OF RATIONAL DEMOCRATIC AUTHORITY

In its broadest interpretation democratic authority is the process whereby the distribution of power in a system is legtimized in terms of democratic process.[29] So, I will define democratic authority as democratically legitimized power and, where it is in the rational self-interest of individuals to partake in a system based upon such power, I will speak of rational democratic authority. What is the logical structure of the concept of democratic legitimation?

All societal processes of legitimation are a response to a basic question which takes the form: what are the grounds upon which an actor willingly[30] surrenders his autonomy to another? Or, why does an actor accept a decision which is not in accord with his own preferences? Weber recognized three main sources of legitimation, thus types of authority — traditional, charismatic and legal rational — the latter claiming predominance in legal rational organizations. I want to outline the basic features of rational democratic authority. I assume:

D.1 That individuals are self-interested (at least in part).[31]

D.2 That individuals under conditions (and only under these conditions) of *cognitive autonomy* are to be regarded as the best judges of their own self-interest.[32]

D.3. Condition A.1 holds (for if it did not there would be no reason for collective effort).[33]

D.4 Conditions A.6 and A.8 hold (there is, thus, a need for [i] a control function, [ii] a source of legitimized power).

The rational democratic legitimation of power distributions in such a system must take account (in the context of D.1, 2, 3) of four principles[34] (Dahl, 1970).

D5. The principle of absolute political equality.
The principle where all members[35] of the system have the right to

directly participate with equal power (i.e. normally equal voting rights) in all decisions affecting the organization.[36]

D.6. The principle of representation.

The principle whereby individuals have the right to surrender all or part of their rights of participation and power to chosen representatives, or delegates.

D.7. The principle of special competence.

The principle whereby it is recognized that certain decisions call for specialized skills.

D.8. The principle of efficiency.

The principle whereby it is recognized that some concept of goal fulfilment is the raison d'être of the system.

D.9 Principle D.5 takes precedence over principles D.6, 7 and 8.

Consider a system in which D.5 operates — in virtue of D.1 we must assume that individuals will have to face situations where the decision outcome does not represent their interests (preferences). It is at this point where the need for legitimation enters. Paraphrasing our earlier query concerning legitimation — why should a rationally self-interested individual accept a decision if he is 'out-voted'? Well, first of all, he must have the right of withdrawing his services[37] and he will presumably do this at the point where the costs (to him) of remaining equal the benefits (at the margin!). He has the right to make this decision but the organization must guarantee the conditions of cognitive autonomy (D.2) such that he can rationally make this decision.

If, however, the individual decides to stay, then he may rationally surrender his autonomy by accepting the democratically determined decision outcome, i.e. give legitimation to the collective body. The source of this legitimation springs from the individual's right to participate, the guarantee of cognitive autonomy and right of withdrawal. Of course, in anything except the smallest organization it is physically impossible for all members to be involved in all decisions (Dahl, 1970), and thus it will at some point be within the rational self-interest of individuals to surrender their decision making autonomy to representatives.[38] But the degree to which this happens must be subject to D.5 itself.

Furthermore, individuals, either directly or through representation, may rationally surrender their autonomy to those whom they deem (principle D.5) more competent (D.7) than themselves to make certain decisions. Similarly for efficiency; in both cases the individual will surrender autonomy to the point where (from his point of view) the costs of doing so exceed the benefits. But since this point will in general not be consensual, the agreement must be arrived at through principle D.5. It seems, however, that to prevent the 'tyranny of the majority' there must be an additional principle (privacy):

D.10 The principle whereby the individual has certain specified right to a limited set of personal or private decisions.

The collectivity must guarantee this area of private choice.[39]

Thus, by way of summary: in a system based upon the principles of rational democratic authority the distribution of power will be legitimized by a process where the principles of representation, competence, efficiency, act as constraints upon the principle of participative and political equality with guarantees of (i) a certain level of privacy and (ii) the grounds for cognitive autonomy.

A NOTE ON ORGANIZATIONAL ALTRUISM

Before we examine how the principles of democratic authority might affect the hierarchical structuring of organizations, I should, perhaps, make a few comments on the possibility of individuals having motives other than self interest. I assumed above (D.1) that individuals were self-interested and further that conflict is endemic. I will be criticized for failing to take into account the possibility of altruistic motives.[40] The ethical principle 'from everybody according to their ability, to everybody according to their needs' would, if practically realizable, certainly change the basic structure of an organization. Though I count myself amongst those for whom this ethical injunction carries much weight, I see little likelihood of its becoming the sole animating ethical principle in the foreseeable future. Insofar as individuals are altruistically committed (to an organization) then they will seek to minimize their benefits and maximize their burdens, but, presumably, the latter only to the point of equality, since to take more of the burden than equal share is to deny one's fellows the equal privilege. Presumably in an altruistic system (based upon scarce resources) a coordinative but not a control function will be required. We would, thus, still face issues concering the appropriateness of hierarchy.

DEMOCRATIC AUTHORITY AND HIERARCHY

If the principles of rational democratic authority were applied to an organization, how would this affect the various functions of hierarchy which we earlier outlined? Indeed, would we tend to expect any hierarchical structuring at all? I will examine each factor in turn.

The Cognitive Function

Even in a society dominated by democratic forms of authority, organizations will surely be set up with the purpose of performing tasks (i.e. solving problems) and it is difficult to believe that the hierarchical solution of problems can be entirely eliminated from human thought processes. Nevertheless, the principles of democratic authority suggest certain features of organizational design:

(a) The actual design of the task-decomposition should be subject to the participation principle D.5, allowing for democratically agreed competence and efficiency constraints.

(b) Since those who will have to work the organization are involved in its 'design' it is likely that the task-decomposition will not take the homogeneity principle to the same degree.[41] The decomposition will, therefore, in general, one supposes, involve some criteria of 'job enrichment' or 'enlargement' which corresponds to principle D.10.

The Coordinative Function

We demonstrated that the legal-rational hierarchy was, under reasonable assumptions, a least cost (i.e. efficient) structure of information transmission in which the volume and nature of the information distribution is dictated by the criteria of competence. Organizational participants receive and transmit information only to the level at which they can perform their tasks adequately.

An organization based upon the principle of rational democratic authority has, on the other hand, to generate and transmit information such that the principles of cognitive autonomy are fulfilled — and accordingly individuals may be deemed to be the best judges of their own interests. So information must be guaranteed to each individual such that he can formulate and signify his preferences in the context of the basic principles of equality, representation, etc.[42]

Needless to say, the distribution of information will be entirely different in organizations structured on legal rational and on rational democratic principles. But the question still remains as to whether the flows should follow hierarchical routes or not. This will, however, in large part be dictated by the division of labour function, so we now turn to this.

The Division of Labour Function

If we still expect, under the imposition of rational democratic authority, a hierarchical task-decomposition (albeit modified) then would we expect this to be translated into the division of labour in the manner of the rational legal organization? One answer to this is to say, yes, but where every role in the hierarchy is subject to 'constrained' principles of democratic process. So the organization would look topographically very similar to a legal rational organization except that it would have roles which are either (a) elected functionaries or (b) consultative bodies of one sort or another involving processes of direct and representational democracy. Alternatively, one may say no — organizations will have no vertical division of labour except for a superimposed 'democratic body' so the depth of the organization would be 2 with a span $(N-1)$. This is the extreme form of direct or representational democracy and is (under rational principles) only likely in very small organizations. We may, perhaps, fruitfully think in terms of a continuum running from this extreme case $(S = [N-1]$, $n = 2)$ to another extreme where the hierarchy is similar to the rational legal type but the role incumbents are subject to election differentially constrained by criteria of competence, efficiency and privacy. There are thus a multitude of possible structures lying between the two poles, each of which may be erected under the general rubric of constrained political equality. It is perhaps of interest to note in passing Lenin's remark: 'Wanting to abolish authority in large scale industry is tantamount to wanting to abolish industry itself' (Engels, 1959).

As organizations grow in size and complexity, it may become increasingly necessary to distinguish between their political and executive hierarchies (for example, Yugoslavia). We can imagine, for instance, a political structure along the following lines: each work-section democratically elects a section council, section councils elect workshop councils, which in turn elect works councils, which then elect the supreme decision making body. This political structure will then construct (appoint) an executive (= coordination/control [see below]) hierarchy. Clearly the possibilities here are very varied, but lack of space precludes a fuller anlaysis.

There is, however, one principle of coordination with much to recommend it: The coordinative function in the division of tasks should allow for the consultation of all possible sub-sets of task performers.

If this principle were applied, bottom up as it were, then the organization could be depicted as a two-level structure where the 'upper' level would be the set of all logically possible combinations of participants. Clearly, in anything but the smallest organization this structure is unlikely, but if the principle is repeatedly applied such that all possible combinations at any level have a least common superior who is democratically elected (again constraint by competence, etc.) the organization would have the structure of an upper semi-lattice (Berge, 1962; Friedel, 1967). This would seem to me, in principle, the most likely 'hierarchical' ordering in democratically structured organization. It embodies the principle of self-coordination, something which is, in my opinion, central to the wider concept of self-management.

Returning finally to information flows: if there is the slightest shred of truth in the last paragraph then one would expect information flows (sufficient for cognitive autonomy) to follow the arcs of the semi-lattice.

The Control Function

A number of commentators have explicitly assumed that with the advent of democratic regimes the need for an organizational control function will disappear. Marx, for instance, clearly distinguished between what he termed supervision (i.e. control) and coordination — the former being one type of unproductive labour:

> All labour in which many individuals cooperate necessarily requires a commanding will *to co-ordinate* [my emphasis] and unify the process, and functions which apply not to partial operations but to the total activity of the workshop much as that of an orchestra conductor. This is a productive job, which must be performed in every combined mode of production.

but also:

> ...supervision [of] work necessarily ensues in all modes of production based on the antithesis between the labourer, as the direct producer, and the owner of the means of production...the production process is simultaneously a process by which the capitalist consumes labour power.

Marx, of course, believed that with the non-exploitative organization of work the supervision function would no longer be required. Is this likely? Well, if we first of all continue to assume that individuals are rationally self-interested, I think not. Consider an organization based upon principles of democratic authority producing a flow of income. Further, assume the organization is of such a size that all the organizational sub-tasks are not performed in a 'face to face' relationship and the contribution of the individual task-performer to the total task is correspondingly small. Now we may assume that under the imposition of a rational democratic regime the flow of income is a bounded public good (within the confines of the organization). This being the case, as for all such goods, it is in the rational self-interest of the organizational participant to maximize his share of the income and minimize his costs (i.e. his work-effort [Olsen, 1968]). If this line of reasoning is allowed, then it would appear that even in a democratically structured organization there would be a need for a control function of some sort, to guarantee that the rationally self-interested participant performs his task.

There are two arguments opposing this reasoning. Firstly, if we relax the assumption of 'self-interest' and replace it by an assumption of bounded-altruism, then the individual is committed to his 'fellow participants' and the control function would be accordingly redundant; the coordinative function would, of course, remain. In fact as I pointed out above, altruistic motives would lead to equality of real 'income' within an organization. Whether or not work-organizations can be constructed which are based upon altruistic motives must be an open question. But what we can safely say is that to the degree that such motives replace 'self-interest' then the control function in an organization is accordingly attenuated.

The second argument concerns the assumption that work-effort is a cost. Democratically constructed work-organizations may be able to so change some (if not all) forms of work such that their fulfilment is regarded as a benefit rather than a cost. It seems to me, however, unlikely that this process can go all the way, though it may be that one of the major benefits of genuine democratization will be the change in task design and thus the increased likelihood of 'work as a benefit' motivation.

As we saw earlier, one of the central assumptions of the Weberian type concerns the hierarchical coincidence of the coordinative and control functions. The principles of rational democratic authority, however, would dictate that, insofar as there is a need for control then there is no reason to suppose it should necessarily follow the structuring principles of coordination (e.g. a semi-lattice). The structuring of the control function should be independently arrived at through the principles of equality representation, competence and efficiency. But the latter may, of course, determine a certain overlap in control and coordinative roles.

The need for organizational control raises issues concerning the basic lines of conflicting interest within organizations. Although it is beyond the scope of this paper to consider capitalist, managerialist, or state command economic systems, it does appear to me that the growth of rational democratic principles will increasingly militate against each of these. There will be a strain toward a consensual objective function within work organizations which is impossible with maximands like profit, managerial income, or state revenue. As far as I can see, the economic system most compatible with the principles is that so brilliantly outlined by Vanek (1970) whereby organizations are governed according to the five principles of self-management[43] in a socialist market economy. Though I might say I am not as sanguine as Vanek concerning the internal harmony of organizations operating under his assumptions.

THE NEW IDEAL TYPE — RATIONAL DEMOCRATIC ORGANIZATION

Finally, using the aforegoing analysis, I should like to outline the salient features of the new 'ideal type' of organization — like all such types it involves accentuation, but I believe in the coming decade it will progressively replace the Weberian rational legal type in industrialized and perhaps industrializing countries. A rational democratic organization[44] will have the following properties (which should be compared with W1-10):

1. Members of the organization will be personally free to leave the organization, but if they remain they must fulfil their duties as politically equal participants and the duties of their task.
1.1 All members have the right to information such that they can rationally pursue their own self-interest (cognitive autonomy).
1.2 All members of the organization have a right to participate with equal voting power in all decisions. But members may decide to delegate decision making under the principles of (a) representation, (b) competence, (c) efficiency. Members have a right to revoke such delegation.
1.3 Members have a right to some basic level of privacy.
2. Organizations will attempt to distinguish between coordinative and control functions. Coordinative and control roles will be structured (under the rubric of 1) according to the principles of representation, competence, efficiency and privacy.
3. The functions of all roles will be as clearly specified as is feasible.[45]

4. Members are democratically appointed (1.2) on the basis of a contract.

5. Qualifications will be a constraint on the democratic process of appointment.

6. The distribution of income pension rights, etc., will be decided democratically.

7. The individual may play more than one role in the organization as a consequence of democratic process (1).

8. The career structure will be subject to democratic process (1).

9. Members may appropriate neither the role nor the resources which go with it.

10. There will be a (unified?) control and disciplinary system sanctioned by democratic authority.

I recognize the sketchy nature of my analysis, a number of important issues concerning changing membership, relations between organizations, protection of minorities, the role of trade unions, etc., all of which have an important bearing upon the structuring of organizations and their decision making, have been given little attention. Furthermore, the possibilities inherent in the concept of self-coordination have not been explored in any detail. I hope to take up these various issues elsewhere.

NOTES

1. I must emphasize at this point that Weber saw no necessary contradiction between rational legal authority and democracy. In fact one of his most important contributions to the development of social criticism lies with his rejection of the older tradition (Mill, Michels) which saw bureaucracy and democracy as antipathetic.

2. The logical structure of Weber's concept(s) of ideal-type has, of course, generated a great deal of discussion. It seems fairly clear, however, that for Weber it was always unlikely that an ideal type would 'exist' in its fully developed form, since in its abstraction it always involved a process of accentuation.

3. It is, I think, important to recognize that despite some commentators' claims to the opposite, Weber clearly recognized organizations as resting upon incipient conflict and thus the use of power.

4. This is, of course, the famous Weberian definition of power which has proved so fruitful in subsequent empirical and theoretical efforts to use the concept. It clearly rests upon the notion of opposing interests or preferences.

5. Weber seems to have been entirely clear about what we now term the separation of ownership and control. However, a bureaucratic structure was, for Weber, an instrument by which the policies of the owners (rulers) were rationally translated into activity by the members. We might note at this point that Weber was entirely open to the idea that the 'rulers' should be appointed by democratic process. Thus the bureaucratic civil service, at the behest of democratic government. He seems, however, to have been less certain when it comes to industrial organizations.

6. Marx's distinction between mental and manual labour is, of course, germane here. Attempts to analyze organizational structure from this perspective seem to run into difficulties also (Abell 1977).

7. I am not suggesting Weber makes this explicit.

8. I will use the term hierarchy to mean a tree which is technically well defined, see, for instance, Berge (1962).

9. A graph is defined in terms of (a) a set of points (vertices) and a set of arcs (lines) connecting at least one pair of points. See Berge (1962).

10. Connected means there is a sequence (path) of arcs between all pairs of points in the graph.

11. I will return to this assumption presently.

12. It is traditional to interpret hierarchies in terms of 'commands down' and 'information up'. Clearly, in a more complex hierarchical structure than a 'tree' one could get conflicting commands and also information taking different routes through the structure which may be subject to differential distortion (see below).

13. Weber was, I think, clearly meaning us to interpret hierarchy in terms of trees. In a number of places he refers to organizational charts.

14. This is, of course, not surprising. Weber was attempting, in his analysis of bureaucracy, to show how wider social beliefs and values were increasingly being adapted to and adopted by organizations (bureaucracies).

15. It is, I think, correct to say with Albrow that Weber's prime concern was (a) to describe the essential elements of legal rational authority and (b) to show how these were increasingly being adopted in administrative structures. Weber's intent was, thus, primarily descriptive (and perhaps predictive). In this sense it can be argued he was not himself concerned with the 'efficiency' of the administrative structures. But it does seem clear that Weber was describing a historical process in which the participants themselves were coming to see rational-bureaucracies as the most efficient organizational instruments for realizing specified ends. They were, as we now know, only partly correct (Pugh, Merton, Gouldner, etc.) Thus Weber's 'theory' of rational bureaucracy was in his hands essentially descriptive, but in the hands of contempoprary practitioners essentially normative.

16. See Abell (1975) for a fuller statement.

17. The task-decomposition structure (Abell 1975) is, usually, hierarchical for reasons I explore below. It may be viewed as a structure in which the relations of interdependence are of two types: (a) vertical coordination of activities (to effect the

global task), (b) horizontal flow of goods and services. This is a simplification, but I do not need a more complex picture for present purposes.

18. Transformational grammar is perfectly hierarchical in its application. The movement from deep structure to surface structure is, thus, also hierarchical.

19. Anybody who has been involved in proving a new theorem will, I am sure, recognize the following account.

20. Clearly, one might have for some problems to solve within tolerance.

21. If it did there would be no point in decomposing the global problem into sub-problems.

22. I do not pretend to be more than touching on these issues. Even if I were capable of making a deeper analysis it would, I suspect, take me into a diversion of inordinate length. Complexity usually implies (a) a large number of 'variables' and (b) many relations (of varying form) between them.

23. In the sense that there is no logical reason why the cognitive function of hierarchy should be translated into a division of labour.

24. The contemporary trends towards participation, job enlargement, etc., must be regarded as opposed to this maxim and part of the general trend towards democratic authority structures (see below).

25. The theory of teams, for instance.

26. I suppose one should say at the margin.

27. One way of defining a whole series of issues away (e.g. by some Marxists) is to assume either perfect consensus or altruistic motives. I will return to these possibilities later.

28. This trend has been complicated by changes in average spans in work organizations (Woodward, 1965; Blau, 1955).

29. Note this does not necessarily imply equality of power.

30. I introduce willingness here to distinguish legitimation from compulsion.

31. I will briefly discuss altruistic motives below.

32. The conditions of cognitive autonomy are easy to specify informally in terms of 'requisite information to form preferences, in line with one's interests'. However, when one looks at this rather more deeply a number of problems arise (Abell, 1977). Throughout this paper I will use the term rather informally as sufficient information to guarantee that the individual is the best judge of his interests. I am obviously trying to rule out the application of D_2 where the individual is manipulated.

33. One may argue the actual decision to engage in collective effort should be subject to democratic process (see below). This raises the question concerning an individual joining an already established organization — presumably he must be allowed to propagate ideas concerning dissolution of the organization.

34. In principles D5, 6, 7 and 8 I follow Dahl (1970).

35. Members might be defined as all those who have an interest at stake (Dahl, the principle of affected interest). In a highly interdependent economy, however, this might extend the membership very widely indeed. In this paper I will not draw a precise definition of membership, but I would like to draw the attention of the reader to the current debate concerning who should have a stake, particularly in work organizations. Should the consumer, the supplier, etc? My own prejudice is for including only those that actually work in the organization, recognizing that even this can be ambiguous.

36. Again there are rather acute definitional problems along similar lines to (35).

37. One would, at this point, have to examine the alternatives open to him. I will assume, however, that all alternative organizations are permeated by the same principles of democratic authority.

38. Here, and in what follows, I am not concerned with the fine details of democratic alternatives (representation, deputation, rote, direct democracies and so on). Organizations would, one supposes, experiment with various mixes of these alternatives.

39. Clearly democratic majorities can tyrannize individuals or minorities. One will need, therefore, safeguards against this, an organizational (or societal) bill of rights might be appropriate, involving D.10. This requires special, detailed consideration.

40. Some Marxists have seen the revolutionary socialist transformation of society as coincidental with the introduction of altruistic motives (at least to the boundaries of the working class).

41. The principle of privacy may be constitutionally designed to prevent this.

42. The list of 'requirements for democracy' (Dahl, 1971) would be appropriate here.

43. The essential features are (a) maximization of income/employee, (b) equal participation by all members in all decisions, (c) a democratically agreed income schedule, (d) market economies.

44. As before, I will not distinguish between the administrative structure and operatives, so the appropriate term is 'organization' rather than 'bureaucracy'.

45. Depending on environmental predictability.

REFERENCES

Abell, P. (ed.) (1975), *Organisations as Bargaining and Influence Systems*. London: Heinemann.

—— (1977), 'The Many Faces of Power and Liberty: Revealed Preferred Autonomy and Teleological Explanation'. *Sociology*, 13.

—— (1980), 'On the General Theory of Social Class'.

Abell, P. and V. West (1977), 'The Bureaucratisation of Organisational Structure' (mimeo). London: Imperial College.

Albrow, M. (1970), *Bureaucracy*. London: Macmillan.

Berge, C. (1962), *The Theory of Graphs and its Application*. London: Methuen.

Blau, P. (1955), *The Dynamics of Bureaucracy*. Chicago: University of Chicago Press.

Burns, T. and C. M. Stalker (1966), *The Management of Innovation*. London: Tavistock.

Chandler, A. (1962), *Strategy and Structure*. Cambridge, Mass.: MIT Press.

Cotgrove, S. and S. Box (1970), *Science, Industry and Society*. London: Allen and Unwin.

Dahl, R. A. (1970), *After the Revolution*. New Haven, Conn.: Yale University Press.

Dahl, R. A. (1971), *PolyArchy, Participation and Opposition*. New Haven, Conn.: Yale University Press.

Daniel, W. W. (1972), 'Changing Hierarchies at Work', *The Listener*, 7 September.

Engels, F. (1959), *Marx and Engels' Basic Writing in Politics and Philosophy* (ed. E. Fleuer). New York: Doubleday.

Friedel, M. (1967), 'Organizations as Semi-lattices'. *American Sociological Review*, 32, 46-54.

Lawrence, P. R. and J. W. Lorsch (1969), *Organisation and Environment*. Homewood: Richard D. Irwin.

Olsen, M. (1968), *The Logic of Collective Action, Public Goods and the Theory of Groups*. New York: Schoken.

Prais, S. J. (1977), *The Evolution of Giant Firms in Britain*. Cambridge: Cambridge University Press.

Simon, H. A. (1962), 'The Architecture of Complexity', *Proceedings of American Philosophical Society*, 106, No. 6.

Tannenbaum et al (1974), *Hierarchy in Organizations*. San Francisco, Calif.: Jossey Bass.

Thomas, K. (1977), 'Belief Determinants of Decentralisation,' (mimeo). London: Imperial College.

Tyler, S. A. (1969), *Cognitive Anthropology*. New York: Holt Rinehart and Winston.

Vanek, J. (1970), *The General Theory of Labour Managed Market Economies*. Cornell: Cornell University Press.

White (1969), *The Anatomy of Kinship*. New Jersey: Prentice-Hall.

Williamson, O. E. (1970), *Corporate Control and Business Behavior*. New Jersey: Prentice-Hall.

Woodward, J. (1965), *Industrial Organisation*. London: Oxford University Press.

5

WORK, POLITICS, AND SOCIAL STRUCTURING UNDER CAPITALISM:
Impact and Limitations of Industrial Democracy Reforms under Capitalist Relations of Production and Social Reproduction

Tom Baumgartner
Université de Louvain, Belgium

Tom R. Burns
Universities of Oslo, Norway and Stockholm, Sweaen/Scandinavian Institutes of Administrative Research, Sweden

Philippe DeVille
Université de Louvain, Belgium

INTRODUCTION

The point of departure of this paper is the notion that work, work processes and organization must be seen in the context — economic, political, and socio-cultural — of a capitalist totality. This totality is characterized, at the same time, by contradictions and dynamics changing parts and whole. A major aim of the paper is to model and analyze several of the mechanisms whereby capitalist structures and processes, particularly those relating to work, are reproduced and transformed. Such modeling is intended

Authors' note: We are grateful to Bengt Abrahamsson, Russel Hardin, and Lars Erik Karlsson for their helpful comments and criticisms of an earlier version of this paper. Burns' research for this paper was supported by a grant from the Work Protection Fund, Sweden, for a project, 'Co-determination and structural change in an organizational perspective' (Burns and Per Hugo Skärvad, principal investigators, Scandinavian Institute for Administrative Research).

to enable us to describe and assess the properties, development patterns, and strategies-for-restructuring of capitalist totalities. A specific concern in this context is an analysis and evaluation of several industrial democracy reforms and, in particular, of their role in contributing to the maintenance or basic transformation of capitalist society. The limitations and potentialities of such reforms are assessed in terms of standards based on the concept of the eventual liberation of work. By the liberation of work is meant a systemic redistribution of power whereby workers gain decision-making control over work and its products, the organization of work, and the work environment (institutional context).

Part One of the paper examines several aspects of the restructuring of capitalist society. In this context we consider industrial democracy reforms as instances of system restructuring and adaptation. An initial assessment of certain limitations of these reforms is outlined. Part Two focuses on the capitalist system of economic production and distribution and the processes of accumulation and uneven development which characterize it. In this part of the paper we outline briefly several of the key concepts and principles guiding our approach to describing and analyzing social systems as dynamic totalities. Part Three addresses itself to capitalist reproduction and transformation as a function of transactions — resource, information, and value flows — between sub-systems in capitalist society. We return in Part Four to a critical treatment of industrial democracy reforms, some of their limitations and potentialities, in terms of the liberation of work. In this context we take up the question of societal transformation — and the liberation of work, in particular — and try to indicate those concerns which movements and strategies of liberation might address.

I ASPECTS OF THE ADAPTIVE
RESTRUCTURING OF
CAPITALISM

1. System Restructuring and Dialectics:
A Selective Overview

A social system does not typically operate or develop unimpeded.

Different groups of actors make different assessments and disagree about development patterns and tendencies. For instance, uneven development and stratification under capitalism — where particular classes, economic sectors, and regions enrich themselves at the expense of others, or without spreading substantial benefits to others — generate discontent and powerful opposition movements (labor, regional, and ecological movements are examples), at least within democratic societies. The emergence of these movements often directly or indirectly results in socio-economic policies and institutions designed to regulate or remedy such developments. Welfare and labor legislation, collective bargaining institutions and regulation of labor markets, anti-trust and monopoly controls, regional policies and public works, and regulatory agencies of all types exemplify such restructuring. In many instances, they offer some relief to those who are losing out in capitalist development.

The structuring of capitalist society has been, and continues to be, a consequence of class conflict and the continuous need to provide for the reproduction of capitalist domination. But increasingly such restructuring is also the consequence of political decisions and action concerning the accumulation and distribution of resources, the shaping and regulation of social structure and its direction of change (Jones, 1975:34).[1] Not only do political processes and the state influence stratification patterns and their development, but they contribute to structuring social interests and defining lines of social conflict.

State regulatory institutions and policies are typically formulated in such a way as to achieve a smoothly functioning capitalist system and to reproduce its characteristic processes and relationships. In particular, processes of accumulation are enabled to continue effectively; asymmetries of the socio-economic order, above all unequal social control over resources and resource allocation through private property institutions, are substantially upheld. State activity — and its continuing expansion — are financed by transfers from capitalist production and continued accumulation (see Part III). Nevertheless, the regulatory institutions, policies and transfers often result in unintended consequences, which may contribute to destabilization and conflict in capitalist society.

The following paragraphs discuss: (1) the regulation of instability of the economic system; (2) the regulation of resource and power accumulation of enterprises; and (3) the regulation of labor/management conflict. Section 2 takes up industrial democracy reforms as instances of restructuring efforts to make the capitalist system function more effectively, as well as more critical responses to capitalist conditions and development.

(1) Regulation of Instability of the Economic Sub-System

From the beginning of the Industrial Revolution, the capitalist system, in both its national and international forms, has experienced a number of economic and political crises which threatened its survival. But, at the same time, in dealing with these crises, capitalist societies have shown a remarkable ability to promote strategies and to design societal (i.e. political and economic) regulatory processes as institutional arrangements serving to preserve system stability.

A recent paper (DeVille and Burns, 1977) examines the process of creating and developing state regulatory mechanisms designed to counteract or overcome instability in the capitalist system, instability which in various forms has characterized it during the course of its development. Regulatory processes, it is argued, may, to a greater or lesser extent, stabilize the system temporarily, but they also make for potential instability over the long run by creating conditions for new contradictions and conflicts to emerge. What was conceived of as a stabilizing measure may itself become a destabilizing factor.

Financial crises and monetary regulation in the US provide an illustration of this. A series of banking regulations was introduced (beginning in 1863 with the National Banking Act and culminating with the Federal Reserve Act of 1914). Prior to 1860, apart from a few unsystematic attempts at regulation which never endured, the banking system and the money market could be described as free of institutional regulation (of course, there was regulation by market forces). A national currency did not actually exist. This resulted in a complicated system of clearing houses dealing with almost 10,000 different currencies which were private bank notes! With increasing industrialization and the ever-growing interstate commerce, such a situation could not persist, not only because it was cumbersome but also because it was unstable. In the absence of any restrictions or regulation of credit expansion, banks (especially the 'wildcats') overcommitted themselves. Defaults were frequent, resulting in recurrent panics and banking crises.

Effective supervision by the centralized Federal Reserve System (FRS) of money and banking in the US was established by 1914. This contributed to the stable, rapid economic growth up until the Great Depression of 1929. But the FRS could not prevent collapse of the banking system and the persistence of the Depression. Indeed, in its concern for monetary stability, the FRS amplified the crisis. It raised the discount rate in 1931, increased the reserve requirements imposed on member banks in 1936, and in general throughout the period let the money stock steadily decline. This led eventually to substantial changes in ideas and values, to the search for new regulatory processes and techniques better equipped, at least within the context of a capitalist system, to deal with the instability of the capitalist system. In other words, the assessment of monetary institutions as a failure in dealing with the problems of the Great Depression set the stage for the 'Keynesian Revolution' and the emphasis on more direct intervention of the state in the capitalist system. In the worlds of policy and scholarship alike, money was relegated to a minor role and stress was placed on fiscal policies (government expenditures and taxation) as the instruments to regulate the entire macro-economic environment. In this context, the principle was more or less established that business cycles had to be brought under control by means of specific fiscal policies generated through and implemented by the state. A new conceptual framework, Keynesian theory, emerged to both justify and guide the capitalist state in its policy formation and regulatory activity. The apparent success of such policies and of the Keynesian framework led in the 1960s to the widespread belief that problems of instability in the capitalist system had been basically solved.

The recent failure of macro-policies and government regulation to deal with the dual problem of maintaining full employment and achieving price stability has led to even more direct government intervention in the system, for example, income policies, various forms of wage and price regulation, subsidies, joint public/private ownership, and nationalization.[2] It has also led to serious questioning of the Keynesian framework and attempts to restructure it or to develop a new, more effective, theory.

(2) Regulation of Uneven Resource
Accumulation and Concentration

The concentration of resources and economic power in the hands of particular groups or such concentration in particular areas of a country has frequently evoked pressures to establish regulatory institutions designed to limit such developments.[3] These constraints are observable in the case of anti-trust laws and policies, regional development policies, land-use planning, etc., all measures designed to prevent the growth and abuse of power, and to reduce social conflicts arising from this. Typically, regulators are introduced after the fact, that is, after a period of extreme economic concentration and uneven development. In the case of US capitalist development, first horizontal mergers of enterprises were regulated. The emergence of vertical mergers called forth new regulations to deal with such concentration. Recent reinterpretations of anti-trust law have been the basis of efforts to check concentration through conglomeration. Presently, some attempts are being made to limit the influence of large corporations upon the political process through their ability to finance political campaigns and to penetrate government and legislative policy-making.

In general, one observes that:

(i) the concentration of power and uneven development under capitalism often evoke discontent and social movement — or the threat of such reactions — to limit or reverse these developments. This is particularly the case in societies with well-developed democratic norms and institutions, a strong labor movement as well as other movements concerned with protecting class, regional, environmental, and other interests (see footnote 3).

(ii) Such reactions (or their potential) lead to the establishment of regulatory institutions to limit or regulate further concentration of power and uneven development tendencies.[4]

(iii) But the existing concentration of power and uneven development, which has resulted from the operation of mechanisms — now to be controlled — provides the basis on which a new round of power concentration and uneven development may take place based on new or other mechanisms (see footnotes 4 and 5). Because the established regulators only partially, if at all, constrain the new mechanisms (for they were developed for other mechanisms), powerful enterprises and groups are often relatively free to exploit the new mechanisms. The dynamic interplay between partial constraints (imposed by an ever-expanding regulatory apparatus) and new mechanisms of power concentration and uneven accumulation enable power concentration and uneven development to proceed.

Regulatory institutions and policies, ostensibly designed to limit particular destabilizing or conflict generating developments in capitalist societies, typically result in unintended consequences.[6] Thus, not only do regulatory processes often fail to control new developments and related contradictions and conflicts, they may even contribute to such effects by modifying perceptions, norms and values, and by changing incentive and opportunity structures. Social actors re-assess and re-orient their activities. New goals and claims may be articulated, new action strategies considered, and 'the rules of the game' transformed. All of this becomes the basis for the emergence of new conflicts and new potentialities for system restructuring.

(3) Conflict Regulation

Capitalist systems of production and distribution are characterized by underlying sources of conflict linked to the structure of the system: institutionalized differences in power, functioning and outlook (see Part II). Key decisions are made by employers and managers in opening or closing a workplace, determining the type and level of production and employment, introducing particular forms of technology and work organization, rationalizing production, determining directly and indirectly qualitative and quantitative aspects of the work environment, and allocating resources (surplus revenues and profits) (Hyman, 1976; Burns, 1976b).

Labor reacts to its subordination to capital in various ways. Above all, power struggle and conflict between capitalists/ managers and workers over the conditions and terms of employment are characteristic features of relations of production and the economic sub-system. These conflictive tendencies are not easily suppressed, particularly if effective work motivation and productivity are to be maintained (see section 2). The state or its agencies attempt to regulate the conflictive relationships by establishing interaction conditions and rules to facilitate communication between the labor market 'partners', to inhibit conflict escalation and violence, and in general to maintain a satisfactory level of cooperation and productivity (i.e. with a minimum level of strikes, slowdowns, and other forms of labor unrest) in the face of inherent conflict.

The long and continuing lines of factory and workplace acts and labor market legislation are sufficiently known and understood in their effects on working conditions and management/labor interaction. Parallel to this is the tendency of encouraging settlement by mediation, arbitration or other peaceful means, embracing intermediate forms such as 'compulsory' bargaining and mediation, and the extension of collective agreements reached in a major part of an industry throughout the whole of it (Stone, 1966: 412-413; Burns, 1976b). As Dahrendorf points out (1957:230):

> Conciliation, mediation, and arbitration and their normative and structural prerequisites are the outstanding mechanisms for reducing the violence of class conflict. Where these routines of relationship are established, group conflict loses its sting and becomes an institutionalized pattern of social life.

That the regulatory apparatus has not fully succeeded in preventing or consistently controlling labor unrest in capitalist societies of the West is pointed up not only by recent waves of wildcat strikes and factory takeovers (Burns, 1976b), but by increasing rates of absenteeism and new types of demands (e.g. regarding quality of the work environment, participation in management, etc.). The existing collective bargaining apparatus has not been designed or has proved itself incapable of dealing effectively with these emerging problems.

The partial failure of collective bargaining and other labor market institutions to deal with emergent problems and functional requirements relating to 'labor' under modern production conditions provides the context for our discussion of the industrial democracy reform movement in advanced capitalism.

2. Industrial Democracy Reforms

The following discussion first identifies several types of industrial democracy measures . In general, these entail attempts to restructure certain aspects of capitalist social organization. Second, it identifies a few of the divergent social interests and movements behind such restructuring efforts. Finally, for the purpose of critically assessing industrial democracy reforms, criteria and guidelines based on a holistic concept of the liberation of work are introduced and applied.

Diverse Reforms

A variety of measures fall under the category of industrial democracy: (i) job redesign, job enrichment, redesign of technology and production methods, work humanization programs, autonomous work groups. (ii) Work and factory councils in which workers (or often their union representatives) sit together with management in order to obtain information and possibly (although less frequently) to discuss and decide issues related to the immediate work environment, that is the context in which workers are required to fulfill their production tasks. (iii) *Mitbestimmung*, co-gestion and co-determination measures associating workers with decision-making functions in enterprises. (iv) Profit sharing and ownership participation. (v) Self-management, autogestion, and self-government.

The first two categories entail changes in substantive conditions and in relations of control over the immediate work environment. They affect the micro-level, taking as given the basic worker/management differentiation and existing private property institutions. They are intended to overcome antagonisms and conflicts in the relations of production by giving workers greater control over their immediate work environment and by improving communication. The last three categories are directed by varying degrees at the ownership and control principles implied by private property institutions.

The measures indicated in (iii) and (iv) are ostensibly designed to minimize the social differentiation between capitalists/managers and workers, by making workers (typically, their trade union representatives) into managers and capitalists, respectively. Profit sharing/ownership participation, in particular, is intended to interest workers in investment (in lieu of wage increases) and in the profitability of their enterprise and thus achieve at the aggregate level the same effect in improved motivation, attention, and sense of responsibility that job enrichment programs try to accomplish at the micro-level.

Self-management is a system where all members of the work organization participate in decison-making and control of the enterprise, its policy-making and planning. (This form of industrial democracy is discussed in greater detail in Baumgartner, Burns, and Sekulić in this volume.)

Diversity of Interests and Forces in
Back of Industrial Democracy Reforms.

The matrix of interests and pressures for the restructuring of capitalist enterprises referred to as industrial democracy reforms is a complex one. Different ideological perspectives, and socio-economic and political interests are involved. Any reform typically represents the outcome of complex struggles and negotiations involving multiple actors and diverse interests. Thus, perceptions of the reform's role within capitalist society and the degree of commitment to its extension or future development may differ radically. Pressures for industrial democracy reforms (with many contradictory facets) arise for several interrelated reasons, which include among others:

(i) *Democratic culture.* There is incompatibility between socio-cultural values and norms concerning human equality, self-reliance, and freedom, and the hierarchical and constraining nature of social control in capitalist systems of production.[7] Indeed, the work place is the most authoritarian milieu in democratic societies (with the obvious exception of the military and total institutions such as prisons and mental hospitals). Employees are compelled to lead a double existence: outside their work they may enjoy considerable liberties, independence and self-confidence, although their capacity to structure and restructure social life to any significant degree is quite limited; in their places of work they are subject to strict authority and control, particularly those at the lower end of the hierarchy, and to forces of technological and social organizational change over which they have little or no control — in Touraine's phrase, 'dependent participation.'

Capitalist production, as a distinct non-democratic social order, has difficulties in legitimizing itself in democratic societies. (In this sense, one may speak of a basic contradiction between certain characteristic features of the economic sub-system and of the socio-cultural and political sub-systems, see Part III.) Indeed, capitalist forms of authority tend to be limited to economic affairs. In political and legal areas, there is obvious competition with democratic ideas.[8] Opposition to particular aspects, and even the totality, of the capitalist order is endemic, especially in Europe where well-developed labor movements are found. This opposition manifests itself in attempts to control or restructure such institutions. In this struggle an appeal is made on grounds, among others, of democratic norms and values (Burrage, 1972).

(ii) *Defense and promotion of workers' interests.* Workers themselves, their representatives, and groups oriented to working class problems struggle to a greater or lesser degree to structure the work environment, working conditions, and power capabilities within enterprises in a way more in line with workers' needs and interests, or in a few instances even with utopian visions. For many workers, this struggle is on a day to day basis. Increasingly, as the standard of living and level of education of the work force increase and as new concepts and norms about proper work conditions emerge, workers are less likely to accept rigid controls, job stress, dequalification and monotony, which were considered normal in the past. As Marrow points out (1975:35-36) (see also footnote 10):

> The feelings of restlessness, anger and hatred that creep out of the factories and shops and office buildings, and into the streeets and homes of Americans, come from jobs that provide no challenge or variety, and from bosses who are inconsiderate and autocratic. The on-coming generation has new doubts about the ideas of efficiency. They are unwilling to pay the crushing price of loss of pride, mind-killing monotony, dehumanization and stress diseases in return for the highest wages in history.

(iii) *Contradictory developments within the capitalist system.* There are developments within capitalism itself generating pressures for improved work environments and industrial democracy reforms:

— reduction of apathy or 'negativism' of workers who are involved in production processes where the means of production entail very substantial investments and where proper attention and maintenance of equipment by workers is essential or where quality control of products by workers is needed;

— encouragement of cooperative attitudes and reduction of industrial conflicts is important to minimize production costs, maintain a favorable public image, or to meet delivery times or other performance demands. The shift in priorities among some segments of the labor force (referred to in[ii] above) makes problematic the effectiveness of past control strategies and patterns.[9] New strategies for regulating and integrating workers into the production process are called for, and some industrial democracy reforms, as suggested earlier, appear to meet this requirement;

— more effective or optimal utilization of human resources of the enterprise, especially where human resources are significant factors as in knowledge production, non-standardized production with maximum problem-solving demands on production units, and creative production activities generally.

Modern production (capital and knowledge intensive) increasingly requires motivated workers, regular attendance, attentiveness to quality and to the proper functioning and maintenance of equipment, and fuller utilization of human problem-solving capabilities. (Ironically, more automated production, which displaces workers, often requires increased worker responsibility and attentiveness.) However, in a broad range of work conditions under capitalism, the control of worker performance and output tends to be increasingly costly due to low motivation, absenteeism, and unpredictable acts such as wildcat strikes.[10] This has stimulated an interest on management's side to reform working conditions and, indeed, to involve workers more in enterprise functioning so as to improve their 'work attitudes' and to minimize control costs. A common argument from progressive managements, consultants, and academic researchers is that increased worker participation in structuring and managing the work setting and, indeed, in participating in enterprise management generally, will not only not harm productivity and management functions, but improve them. The argument goes that there will be better information flow, greater self-adjustment possibilities and creative problem-solving. In this light, the measures can be seen as organizational measures to improve capitalist performance and to legitimize capitalist institutions.

At the same time, there is a distinct and present danger that these social innovations, introduced as more efficient organizational technologies (job enrichment, autonomous work groups,

Mitbestimmung, etc.) in the context of modern production systems, may ultimately undermine (or threaten to undermine) capitalist relations of production. On the other hand, apathy and individual strategies such as missing work or switching jobs in order to cope with unsatisfactory working conditions do not generally threaten capitalist relations of production, although they may increase costs and reduce productivity in certain production settings. The dilemma facing managers is often between economic goals related to productivity, profitability, and capital accumulation, on the one hand, and on the other, political and ideological objectives relating to maintaining capitalist relations of production ('quantitative' versus 'qualitative' efficiency in Gordon's terms [1976]).

The contradictory or dual implications of many industrial democracy reforms are suggested by the divergent interests involved in the formulation and implementation of industrial democracy reforms. Those who view industrial democracy reforms as preliminary steps in building a new non-capitalist order assume a cumulative or evolutionary development whereby capitalist relations of production will be transformed (in a piecewise process). Such optimism may or may not be well-founded. What is called for is an analysis of the way the reforms operate and develop within capitalism as a totality, the extent to which they restructure fundamentally capitalist relations of production and characteristic processes, and interfere with or supplant social reproduction of capitalist institutions. In the absence of such an analysis, one must suspect the type of development described in section 1: regulatory mechanisms designed to control uneven developments fail to deal with emergent structures and processes of capitalism. As a result, the reforms only give the illusion of initiating a process of social transformation.

3. Critical Assessment of Industrial Democracy Reforms

Work is social action in a particular social context. By the liberation of work is meant a redistribution of power and control whereby workers gain decision-making control over work and the work environment. This notion has several interrelated features (see Figures in Part III):

— capacity to structure and restructure work relations and production processes in which they are involved;[11]
— control by the direct producers over the products of their work processes. Products include spin-offs and spill-overs of productive activities;[12]
— control over the behavior and future development of the enterprise;
— the capacity to participate in control over the economic, political, and socio-cultural environments of the enterprise, which shape its development possibilities.

On the basis of this systemic view of the liberation of work, Table I offers an assessment of different industrial democracy reforms with respect to their contributions to the various facets of liberation defined above. The contribution to one facet of work liberation by a reform is indicated by an X under the relevant criterion. Xs in parentheses indicate potentialities for a limited degree of increased control. Often, however, such potentialities may be difficult to realize in practice, and indeed the difficulties may reflect efforts on the part of managers to restrict the potential effects of a reform.

This table is meant only to be suggestive. A more detailed analysis of each reform, for example the type of analysis outlined in Baumgartner, Burns and Sekulić (see Chapter 3) in the case of self-management, is required in each case.

To be able to make a more precise and systematic assessment of industrial democracy reforms in the context of a capitalist totality, a framework must be developed. The purpose of the framework is to describe and analyze control relationships and structures as well as reproduction processes under capitalism. In particular, two inter-related questions are of concern: (1) the manner in which a system of production and exchange produces and distributes resources and develops societal action capabilities among the actors involved; and (2) the processes whereby unequal distribution and accumulation tend to be reproduced. Parts II and III, respectively, are addressed to these tasks.

TABLE 1
Assessment of industrial democracy reforms in terms of work liberation criteria

Industrial democracy measures	Control criteria				
	Control over labor process	Control over products of labor process — Revenue	Other valuables (e.g. managerial expertise)	Control over future development	Control over economic political, and socio-cultural environments of enterprise
Worker designed job enrichment, work process; autonomous work groups	X				
Mitbestimmung, co-determination, cogestion					
Board of directors level		(X)		(X)	
Shopfloor level	(X)	(X)			
Profit sharing/ ownership participation		X			
Self-management	X	X	(X)	X	(X)

II CAPITALIST RELATIONS OF PRODUCTION AND DEVELOPMENT PATTERNS

1. Theoretical Introduction

Capitalist societies not only produce goods and services and allow capital accumulation to continue. They tend to produce uneven development, wealth as well as poverty, advanced as well as backward sectors. In connection with uneven development and the structuring and restructuring of work as well as other spheres of social action, social reactions, movements, and conflicts are also produced. Many of these features of capitalist societies, if uncontrolled or unregulated, would act to undermine capitalist economic institutions. Part I examined briefly the role of the state in regulating and controlling uneven development, instability and conflict in capitalist systems.

In this part and Part III we outline a theoretical approach with which to investigate and analyze capitalism as a dynamic totality. A basic premise of the approach is that the maintenance and the reproduction of capitalist socio-economic structures and processes depend on structures and processes in the political and socio-cultural spheres and on the set of relations — the flow of resources, information, and values — between the spheres.[13] That is, the complex interrelationships and flows between societal sub-systems not only largely characterize a social system as totality, but play a substantial role in its reproduction (and provide potentialities for its transformation).

Several of the key concepts and principles of our approach are outlined below. Although the discussion is relatively abstract, the notions introduced provide specific guidelines in the construction of models of capitalist relations of production and of the reproduction of the capitalist totality.

1. The social process of capitalist production generates multiple outcomes. These include effects in the sphere of economic production and distribution as well as in other spheres of social action; in addition to intended effects there are unintended, spin-off and spill-over effects.

2. Because of property rights (or more generally control rights) and their positions and roles in the division of labor and exchange

processes, actors or classes of actors have qualitatively and quantitatively different linkages to the products, including the various spin-offs and spill-overs from production and exchange processes. Of course, these products include goods and services as well as possibly revenue gained from the sale of goods and services.

3. Consequently, there is differential accumulation of capability, resources, and social power among the different actors or classes of actors. In other words, the distribution of benefits and costs of production and exchange activities are unequal.

4. This differentiation translates into uneven development capabilities — the differential ability among actors — to shape or take advantage of action opportunities and to avoid or overcome traps (vicious circles). Such uneven development supports reproduction and elaboration of power differences.

5. In the context of analyzing ways in which systems of social production can both reflect and produce unequal power structures, we try to formulate a model of social reproduction. Social systems are human constructions, that is, artificial. They require continual reproductive and structuring activities in response to changes in their environments. We speak of social reproduction when stability or maintenance of characteristic societal relationships and processes occur. This entails their maintenance during a given time period as well as the production or acquisition of necessary and sufficient resources for their perpetuation in subsequent time periods. Thus, social reproduction depends not only on replacing means of production and on the maintenance and replacement of actors (reproduction of labor power). It also entails structuring the context in which social activity takes place, e.g., in the case of economic production, structuring the political and socio-cultural spheres.

Thus, our investigation of social reproduction (and transformation) centers on the interactions between societal sub-systems: economic, political, and socio-cultural. Specifically, we look at whether or not, and if so in what ways, resource, information and value flows shape compatible or incompatible developments in other sub-systems. Social reproduction of institutions depends on compatible or corresponding developments.

6. An institutional arrangement not only generates particular intended outcomes. There are also various spin-offs and spill-overs which operate to reproduce the arrangements, as well as effects

operating to undermine or transform the existing system. Often these are unintended consequences of the policies and actions of dominant groups (DeVille and Burns, 1977).

7. Actors or categories of actors adversely affected by the operation or development of the institutional set-up may be able to socially articulate their disadvantage and discontent, e.g., in terms of norms and values about fairness or equity (or other ideological grounds). They may also be organized and mobilize to carry out social action to change the institutional set-up or at least certain undesirable features of it (undesirable from their viewpoint). These activities usually bring them into conflict with those having an interest in or commitment to the reproduction. That is, conflict arises concerning the maintenance (or reproduction) as opposed to the restructuring and possible transformation of the institutional set-up. Such conflict can interfere with or obstruct reproduction processes, setting the stage for social transformation.[14]

2. A Class Model of Economic Production and Distribution in Capitalist Systems

In this section a simple class model of production and distribution under capitalist institutions is formulated (see also Baumgartner, 1978). The model specifies differences in social structural positions among actors in the division of labor and in related exchange activity. Moreover, there is unequal distribution and accumulation of benefits and costs of productive activity among the different classes and sub-classes of actors exchanging with one another. Resources (surpluses) accumulate more at certain points (i.e. with certain classes or sub-classes) than others.

Figures 1 and 2 represent systems of resource flows and capability development which reflect the inequality in structure and in process in capitalist systems. The models represent three critical aspects of capitalist production and distribution (Carchedi, 1975):

— The complex relations of production whereby the actors or classes of actors in the system — the owners or managers of capital [A] and the sellers of labor power [B] — are differentiated in their power and control possibilities at the same time that they are bound together in a structured system or totality.

— The differentiation in function between the owners or

managers of capital (see footnote 17) and the sellers of labor power. The former use power based on control over, and technical knowledge about, the means of production in order to plan, structure, and manage the production process, the type of technology employed, the organization of work and work processes, etc. Workers or employees submit their labor power to managers to be directed and managed as part of the total process of production. And, in this, they carry out the concrete operations (work) of transforming physical and symbolic inputs into outputs through applying appropriate technologies.

— The differentiation in gains and losses among the actors or classes participating in the production/distribution system, e.g., the expropriation of surplus products and values.

Employer/employee exchange under capitalism is unequal — and exploitative — in a structural sense.[15] The employee submits his or her labor power to the control of the employer. The latter provides the employee with part of the revenue derived from operating the means of production and supplying goods and services to 'consumers' (see Figure 1). B has the right to use as he or she sees fit the income received from the employer. But, in general, the income B obtains offers only short-term, consumption benefits.[16] For the most part, it is provided and utilized individually in personal consumption (and the reproduction of labor). A worker or workers as a class gain little or no structural power from the personal incomes they receive. They certainly do not provide a basis for bargaining with managers or with other power agents in society.

A, on the other hand, retains exclusive control over the physical means of production X. At the same time, he gains control over the labor power Y of the employees he hires and over the economic and non-economic products, spin-offs and spill-overs, resulting from the operation of the means of production, in particular:[17]

— the products (YX) of this production;
— the revenue R gained from the sale of products;
— transfers T to the political sphere (which we might think of as management knowledge and skills as well as real resources applicable to activity, that is production, in the political sphere);
— aspects relevant to socio-cultural production Z, such as legitimations of the social differentiation and ranking of actors in social life or legitimations of private property control relationships.

FIGURE 1
Structure of unequal exchange
between employer and employee

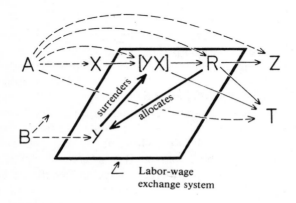

Labor-wage
exchange system

⟶   Flow of production and use of revenue
---⟶ Exertion of control
⟶   Processes in the exchange relationship

Dashed lines indicate control over a given resource, or over spin-offs and spill-overs. Solid lines indicate transformation processes and flows, that is, production, selling, use of revenue, production of spin-offs and spill-overs. The short dashed line originating at B and pointing in the direction of X is intended to suggest the exercise of partial control by B over X (in the sense of workers' co-determination; see also footnote 20).

Clearly, Bs give up to A more than simple labor power. A gains control over the multiple social (economic and non-economic) products, (YX), R, T, and Z, resulting from productive activities.[18] These appropriated products tend to enhance A's long-term action capabilities and structural powers to shape and reshape relationships and processes in the sphere of economic production as well as in socio-cultural and political spheres. In contrast, B's opportunities are diminished, above all in the economic sphere, to develop long-term action capabilities and to acquire meta- or structural powers to shape and reshape social structures and processes.[19] As a result, [A] maintains and develops its social powers relative to [B] as well as to more static groups in the society, such as those associated with less dynamic or less rapidly developing productive activities. The accumulation and extension processes provide the bases of power in new economic domains (production settings as well as markets) as well as in cultural and political-administrative spheres (e.g., in the latter case by trading economic concessions and favors for political and regulatory advantages) (see Part III). The uneven accumulation and development of societal power in this manner is a major factor in class A's domination over class B and in the reproduction of capitalism, although often with new features.[20]

3. Uneven Development and Dual Economy Phenomena

Capitalist enterprises operating in market systems tend to differentially accumulate resources and to develop unequally. Such uneven development occurs at different societal levels:

— between enterprises — e.g., between advantaged enterprises, such as conglomerates, and disadvantaged enterprises — in the same sector;

— between sectors, e.g., between industrial and agricultural sectors or between enterprises in advanced sectors and those in backward sectors;

— between regions which are differentiated by their different production profiles (the sectors characterizing regions) as well as by the relative advantages or disadvantages of enterprises in a given region as opposed to the enterprises of other regions.

FIGURE 2
Unequal exchange between capital and labor
and between center and periphery enterprises

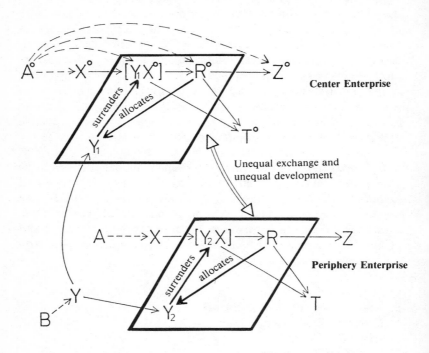

The model of Figure 1, which represents the unequal exchange and development between actors of class A and those of class B may be elaborated to distinguish between different sectors of the economy or sub-classes of agents in capitalist production. As a beginning, one may distinguish between owners or controllers of center and periphery capital, A^O and A respectively. The former tend to cover durable manufacturing, capital goods, advanced technology, and knowledge and professional service industries, whereas the latter are found in agricultural production, incompletely processed materials and agricultural production, non-durable manufacturing, and sub-professional services.[21]

Figure 2 represents the uneven distribution and accumulation of resources, through unequal exchange, among different classes and sub-classes of actors exchanging with one another:

— between capital and labor;

— between center and periphery enterprises (advanced and backward capital).

Below we refer to certain of the characteristic features of the capitalist production and exchange system which contribute to its reproduction and development tendencies with respect to the center/periphery duality:

1. *Capital.* The quantity and quality of capital is unequally distributed between center and periphery exterprises (X^O and X respectively). For example, the latter exhibit less capital intensive production than the former.

2. *Labor.* The labor allocated between center and periphery enterprises (Y_1 and Y_2, respectively) usually differs qualitatively. That is, center enterprises are better able to attract human resources and to develop them to a greater extent through education and knowledge production than periphery enterprises.

3. *Revenues.* Center and periphery enterprises have different levels of revenue (R^O, R) and gains per unit of input (capital and labor). Specifically, center enterprises usually achieve a greater surplus revenue and a higher rate of return on investment than periphery enterprises. The different levels of revenue and returns on inputs results in unequal allocations:

— to capital owners;

— to reproduction and development of the means of production;

— to labor income necessary to maintain and reproduce labor power;
— to transfers and taxes (T^O,T) paid to public institutions;
— to transfers of resources to socio-cultural processes.

As suggested above, center enterprises produce and supply capital goods, advanced technology, and processed consumer goods with high value added, based on capital intensive processes of production. On the other hand, the periphery tends to produce and supply in return incompletely processed raw materials and agricultural products, and consumer products with low-value added, based on the use of cheap labor in labor intensive processes.[22]

4. *Wages.* Center enterprises are more likely to offer higher wages, better working conditions and fringe benefits, and employment security than periphery enterprises. This is reflected in the structure of wages (and wage costs) (r^O,r), between the two categories of firms.

5. *Capital accumulation.* Periphery enterprises typically fail to either accumulate substantial surpluses or to attract capital (loans, equity capital, etc.) to the same extent as center enterprises.

6. *Exchange.* The exchange between center and periphery enterprises — whether direct or indirect (through market processes) — results in different rates of capital accumulation as well as different spin-offs and spill-overs favoring the economic development of center enterprises over periphery enterprises. Such exchange is unequal to the extent that the production of periphery enterprises results in relatively weaker market (bargaining) position, less economic gain per unit of labor and capital input, less potentiality to develop new technologies, fewer possibilities or incentives to develop a skilled labor force and management.

7. *Development Potentialities.* Class A is internally differentiated in terms of A's relationships to qualitatively varying productive and exchange activities and their social consequences (there is corresponding differentiation within class B). This differentiation both reflects and promotes unequal structural advantages and development capabilities, symbolized, for instance, in the pairs (R^O,R), $(r^O r)$, (T^O,T), (Z^O,Z) and capital (X^O,X) in current as well as future phases.

The labor and capital inputs into production processes of center enterprises tend to be superior, quantitatively and qualitatively, to the inputs into periphery enterprise processes. This increases the relative chances of center enterprises to compete successfully with periphery enterprises in international as well as in more local markets for factors of production and for buyers of products in the cases where they produce the same or substitutable products. In addition, center enterprises tend to pull input prices up to the disadvantage of peripheral enterprises which have fewer economic resources as well as potential resources through credit facilities to afford higher prices.

As suggested earlier, center enterprises typically enjoy qualitatively and quantitatively superior results (e.g., R^O, T^O, Z^O) from production/exchange activities than periphery enterprises. Especially noteworthy are differential accumulation and development of capital, management knowledge and skills, technology and overall development capabilities (R&D investment and activity), different standards of living for workers, and different levels of legitimation and capability of influencing political conditions (e.g., through high taxes and other transfers to the state and political organizations).

While center enterprises are able to accumulate and expand their power and control over resources such as advanced technologies and production processes, higher quality labor, finance capital, the weaker, peripheral enterprises tend to lose out relatively in the process, unable to compete as successfully for, or to develop to the same degree, the forces of production, finance and human capital and support structures.[23] For instance, center enterprises, due to their accumulation and development potentialities, are more likely than periphery enterprises to exert a total agglomerative pull, in attracting:

— favorable support from communities and government agencies dependent on or attracted to the possibilities of relatively more substantial and secure revenues. This support can take the form of providing favorable legal and tax conditions as well as support structures such as transportation, training and education, research and information facilities, etc., which are geared to the needs of center enterprises;

— physical resources, equity capital, credits;

— human resources.

All in all, center enterprises gain to a greater extent than peripheral enterprises in action capabilities and structural advantages in the political economy of capitalist production and distribution. And, therefore, the former are in a better position than the latter to structure productive relations and their environments more favorably to their reproduction and development, other things being equal. Also, this differentiation implies unequal development — or capability for development — of the forces of production. In this sense, the owners and managers — as well as, to a substantial degree, workers — of advanced production systems gain surplus values at the expense of the owners and managers (and workers) of backward production. Of course, a few peripheral enterprises may, by virtue of finding a niche and effective management, achieve substantial 'upward mobility.' But the basic center/periphery structure favoring the former over the latter remains and tends to be reproduced.

III CAPITALIST REPRODUCTION

1. Introduction

Part II concerned the manner in which the capitalist system of production and exchange distributes resources and differentially develops societal action capabilities. This part of the paper examines the processes whereby capitalist institutions, the relations of production and accumulation processes, are reproduced.

Reproduction of the system depends in part on replacement of machinery and reproduction of labor. Such processes would be indicated in Figures 1 and 2 by circular loops from products (YX) or revenue to means of production and from wages back to labor power, respectively.[24] Reproduction also entails the continual structuring of the conditions and context of the economic sub-system in a way (so as to make it) compatible with its essential structures and processes. In particular, it requires structuring processes in other spheres of social action, which ensure that the capitalist production/exchange system is not fundamentally changed in the face of restructuring forces and movements (Part I). Critical here is control over real resources as well as knowledge resources such as management and technical competence. In particular, resources available from surplus revenues may be used to gain political advantage or to support state activities, e.g., in welfare, educational, and other areas, and to prevent or retard any transformational tendencies or developments incompatible with capitalism (especially, as embodied in center enterprises).

The interrelationships among societal sub-systems play a major role in the reproduction and transformation of social structures and processes (see Part II, section 1). The key principle underlying the analyses here is that the maintenance and reproduction of capitalist relations of production and processes depend on their socio-cultural and political contexts, just as the capitalist economy contributes to shaping processes and structures in its political and socio-cultural contexts. Earlier, we suggested the complex forms such inter-sphere linkages may take, particularly between the political and economic spheres: we also stressed the role of the state in regulating and controlling instability, uneven development and conflict. The structural and ideological context of capitalist relations of production is the topic of section 1. Section 2 examines the flows and linkages between the economic sub-system and political and socio-cultural sub-systems, indicating the structuring and meta-power aspects of such flows. Section 3 concerns itself with the relation of sub-system concordance to social reproduction.

1. The Structural and Ideological Context of Capitalist Relations of Production

Capitalist control over material and non-material resources is based on networks of social relations outside the economic sphere. An actor or class of actors is implicitly or explicitly recognized by others in the networks to have control rights over the resources. This is the structural and normative context of control relations and, in particular, of property ownership. The rights of ownership — to do with property as the owner sees fit, such as the right to sell it — are socially defined and sustained opportunities for control over it.[25]

The structural context of property rights and of the employer/ employee relationship in capitalist society maintains and reproduces unequal control over the means of production as well as over the multiple valuables and power resources derived from operating them (see Part II, section 2). The ideology and norms relating to private property and related notions such as 'free enterprise' provide a general normative pressure and substantial networks of supporters (in formal as well as informal positions) who can be mobilized to protect basic capitalist social and material arrangements. Of course, definite 'support structures' are also formally organized and charged with the responsibility of preventing disruption of the system: judicial, administrative and police branches of the state. They function both explicitly (by legal directives, e.g., to protect private property and the prerogatives of the owners and managers of private property) and implicitly (by a set of assumptions underlying policies and operations with respect to business enterprises) to maintain the position of employers. This provides capitalists with more or less autonomous control over private property and the rights to operate firms without undue or dysfunctional interference from workers, consumers, or the general public. In particular, the police and courts of the capitalist state as well as political groups identified with capitalist institutions operate to guarantee that, should ideology and persuasion fail, the structure of socio-economic relations and the configuration of constraints outlined above are maintained 'by other means', namely 'legitimized force'. When in the contemporary capitalist state we say that A 'owns something', we actually know that his ownership rests on property laws that are sanctioned by a government. In fact, of course, they (A) do better than control it; they have the judicial and police powers of state on their side to sanction individuals who would illegally take the property away (Adams, 1975:41).

The basis of support for the maintenance and reproduction of structures and processes in the economic sphere are also ideological, institutional, network and exchange links, convergent interests. For example, the economic importance of business enterprises — their role in providing employment and capital accumulation — to a community and to government revenue (as well as to party financing) gives them political leverage to counteract community and employee pressures as well as government attempts at control. They can effectively threaten the government, community, or an employee group with movement of their 'private plants' elsewhere or with a 'necessary' contraction of operations or employment, unless the government or community ceases 'interference'. Were the government or courts to initiate policies and decisions which jeopardize business confidence and well-being, serious economic instability and social problems would result with adverse effects on employment, tax revenue, and political climate.

The well-being of corporations and financial institutions under such circumstances becomes identified with the national interest (Stone, 1971:32) (as well as with the political interest of those in government who are eager to keep or advance their positions).

Hence, although there may be considerable divergence in interest about specific issues and problems (economic or social), there is a well-understood shared interest of the government executive and of the corporate executive to keep the capitalist system functioning. The same holds in the case of labor union leaders.[26] This convergence of 'general interest' and commitment to the effective functioning of the system serves to maintain through structuring activity capitalist structures and institutions (with minor corrections and reforms deemed essential to effective performance and to perpetuation of the system). This shared commitment among the highest circles of society is an essential aspect of system reproduction.

2. Interrelationships and Flows between Economic, Political and Socio-Cultural Sub-Systems and the Process of Societal Reproduction

Control of the economic system of production and distribution implies that A is able to intervene and to influence, intentionally or unintentionally, events and developments in other spheres of social action. This is accomplished not only through the use of real resources (e.g., allocations of revenue as discussed above) but also through controlling evaluation criteria, legitimations, and related developments associated with production processes. For instance, capitalist managers structure the division of labor in the production process, that is, the way in which jobs and functions are allocated, above all between physical, and managerial and mental work. This is not only an organization of production for economic and technical purposes.[27] It produces and reproduces the unequal distribution of technical and managerial knowledge and skills which are particularly important bases of social status and hierarchy in modern societies.

The structuring under capitalism of the production process — in particular, the division of labor in that process — has taken planning, management, communications, and other control functions from workers. These are activities relating to higher cognitive levels of precision, categorization, language development, abstraction, and complexity. This limits the possibilities of workers to develop such competence (or to use it if acquired, for example, through formal education). The underdevelopment of labor in this and related respects assures not only continued subordination to a technocratic elite in the work place — even if workers are given the rights to participate in decison-making activity — but also their subordination in poli.ical and socio-cultural spheres, where the possession of these capabilities is of strategic importance. Thus, the structuring of the production process, the underdevelopment of the knowledge and action capabilities of labor, contribute to the reproduction of work relationships in other spheres of social life. (We are not claiming that this is invariably intentional nor that countervailing processes do not exist.)[28] Moreover, the underdevelopment of labor (in the areas of competence referred to above) makes for relatively weaker language, cognitive training, and cognitive development for working-class children in the course of family socialization and pre-school learning. This is often reinforced during the schooling process. In this way class relations are to a greater or lesser extent reproduced inter-generationally (Tropea, 1977).

The mutual reinforcement between conditions and developments in the economic sphere and those in the socio-cultural sphere — and the implications of this for social reproduction — is pointed up in a number of ways other than the division of labor. For instance, the use of certain types of technology may enhance the emergence or maintenance of a technocratic value system. The decision to produce (or create) some products and not others has obvious implications in affecting social 'tastes and preferences', e.g., regarding individual means of transportation, individual family housing units and in general, goods and services designed for individual consumption. (This is not to speak of the use of resources to directly shape and influence 'tastes and preferences' through such strategies as advertising, marketing, etc.)

Such privatization of consumption, relations of consumption, and in general community life inhibits the development of ties of solidarity, of group consciousness and of organization among workers (as consumers and citizens) outside the workplace. And this condition, as we will argue later, contributes to the reproduction of the capitalist system.

Part of the revenue of enterprises, the transfers T, enters into the transactions between the economic and political spheres. The specific forms which such transfers can take are many: taxes, social security contributions, bribes, contributions to finance the election campaigns of politicians, in some systems the financing of interest group associations primarily charged with lobbying and other political activity.[29] Transfers are an input in the production process of political decisions, rules, laws, etc. insofar as the realization of such decisions requires resources (salaries, buildings, information systems, etc.). It is also an important input in the sense that many political decisions would remain empty if not backed up by the availability of finances for the purchase of human and physical resources required in their execution and administration. And thus many political decisions would most likely cease to be valued outputs from the political sphere.[30]

Transfers — and their production — provide a substantial legitimational aspect. The ability to produce increasing revenue for the state (or to generate the real resources for state activity), both for political production activities as well as for the self-reproduction of the state administrative apparatus, offers one justification for the capitalist mode of production. This aspect of transfers — or perhaps it is more meaningful to speak of this aspect of the economic sphere itself — contributes to structuring in a fundamental way the relationships between the economic sphere and the other spheres of social action. Hence, the strong theoretical and practical arguments in favor of seeing the economic sphere within capitalist societies as the dominant one.

Revenue also assures the reproduction of labor and capital through allocation of wages (consumption goods) for workers and depreciation (capital goods) for enterprises. But revenues allocated, for example, to wages are also incomes. And incomes are inputs into social processes generating different action opportunities, life chances and consumption patterns, and status differentiation of different occupational groups. That is, the very distribution of income and wealth through capitalist relations of production contributes to the structuring of social differences in society. At the same time, status differentiation is an output of the socio-cultural sub-system. It reflects certain values, legitimation principles, and social distinctions derived from the socio-cultural sphere, for instance, such notions as appropriate standards of living — and hence, appropriate levels of income — for different categories of actors. These socio-cultural elements operate to shape policies and practices in the economic sphere. In particular, they contribute to making certain structures of functions and of wages appear 'fair' or socially acceptable (legitimized), as in the assignment of functions as well as in the allocation of revenue for wages between managers and workers and among workers according to occupation, sex, religion, ethnicity and race.[31] As Hyman (1976:30) points out:

> Such ideologies of occupational worth, it has often been argued, exert a considerable influence on the processes of wage and salary determination (since they affect both what employees are prepared to accept, and what employers consider reasonable to concede). These legitimations of income differentiations, in turn, mesh closely with the broad structure of class inequality and the distribution of social power which it incorporates. Processes of power, prestige and ideology thus interact intimately in the labor market.

3. Sub-System Correspondence and Reproduction

The economic sphere partially shapes, through real resource transactions and value and norm formation, the socio-cultural and political context in which capitalist enterprises operate. In this way, socio-cultural and political processes mediate the self-reproducing structuring processes generated by the economic sphere, e.g., processes relating to the technocratic value system and the privatization of consumption. The effectiveness of these mediating effects depends on the compatibility of social structure and processes in the economy with those in the socio-cultural and political spheres, i.e. whether or not parallel or similar hierarchical systems obtain. This is to say that resource, information, and value production in the economic sphere will play an effective role in reinforcing and reproducing capitalist production relations and processes provided that structures and processes in the socio-cultural and political spheres (i.e. its context) are concordant or compatible. In general, structural concordance or correspondence enhances the effectiveness of resource transfers and value and norm processes generated from economic production. This is a key factor in the reproduction of capitalism.

Inputs into political and socio-cultural production are not controlled entirely by capitalist managers. To the extent that workers can and do produce their own political and socio-cultural organizations, that is workers and workers' movements have resources (including wages) beyond those necessary for the pure reproduction of labor power, we may observe the phenomenon of the displacement of the conflict process from one sphere of social action to others: that is, from the economic to the political and socio-cultural spheres. The conflictual relationship between capitalists and workers is reproduced in the other spheres of social action and creates in each of them a similar pattern of relationships and processes, although the formal actors involved might be defined differently in the various spheres. In everyday language, we might speak about political parties, voters, citizens, lobbies, and politicians with respect to the political sphere; and elites, consumers, the elderly, the young, different ethnic groups, etc. for the socio-cultural sphere. (In the latter case, the general level of organization of individuals and groups in the sphere may be relatively low.) Whatever the degree of arbitrariness of these labels, they indicate that social actors structure and identify themselves differently in relation to different spheres of social action. At the same time, it should be stressed that there may be considerable overlap in terms of the individual persons and groups involved (the significance of such overlap is discussed below).

In sum, the dominance relationships, concepts and values associated with capitalist production may not be realized or find compatible parallels in the political and socio-cultural spheres. On the contrary, they may be contradicted, e.g., opposed by actors committed to articulating and realizing, through cultural and political struggle, democratic norms and the humanization of work. Such opposition may, under conditions of institutionalized power, contribute to some restructuring of capitalist forms of organizing production through industrial democracy reforms, or reforms of the work environment, as discussed earlier. This is not to say that these reforms transform capitalist relations of production and key processes, for instance, by abolishing, through the establishment of self-management institutions, the distinction between employer and employee.

On what conditions or factors does structural concordance — or its absence — depend?

1. The greater the overlap of elites, the more likely structural concordance will obtain. As suggested earlier, consumers in the

socio-cultural sphere are often fragmented or disorganized. The conflictive relationship between capitalists and workers may be only weakly, if at all, reproduced in the socio-cultural sphere.[32] Thus, workers (as consumers and often as citizens) have few opportunities or even incentives to form sentiments of solidarity and to organize outside of the workplace, that is, to conceive of and to realize a viable alternative based on solidarity and cooperation with others. (Of course, cooperative movements and workers' recreation and sports clubs represent countervailing tendencies.) In particular, their impact on educational research, and national and international communication systems, may be quite limited, although activities and developments in these areas influence to a substantial degree the future developments of society.

2. High consensus (shared ideology and understandings) and overlap or network ties between elites in economic, political, and socio-cultural spheres is conducive to reproduction. On the other hand, increased differentiation and incongruence between elites in different spheres may threaten it. Such situations give rise to alternative or competing bases of elite legitimation, the polarization of elites, and the reduction in their ability to cooperate in adapting or bringing about non-basic restructuring in response to crisis or external challenge. In a word, meta-power disequilibrium obtains.

3. Inputs in the socio-cultural production process are not only the material resources, values, and information from the economic sphere. Conflicting values and beliefs, legitimations, tastes and preferences, and other socio-cultural elements are produced and reproduced through a number of different processes and structures: through processes associated with economic production and distribution (the topic of earlier discussion); through socialization and the reproduction of traditions, customs, and conventions; through religious beliefs and practices; through the perceptions that actors have of their positions and changes of position within the social system; through conflict processes within economic, political, as well as socio-cultural spheres of social action. These multiple and alternative inputs in the socio-cultural production process, thus, are not completely determined by economic conditions and processes. Other factors in socio-cultural production may work in opposition to providing conditions conducive to the reproduction of economic relations and processes. Moreover, economic relations and processes may generate conditions — such as unintended socio-cultural and political developments — which

operate in opposition to reproduction and development of structures and processes characteristic of the economic sphere. It was pointed out earlier that the maintenance of capitalist institutions is made difficult in societies with strong democratic and egalitarian norms and values, because there obtains a high degree of incompatibility between structures and processes in the economic sphere (a hierarchical order) and political democratic structures and processes (see Part I, section 2).

It can now be seen more clearly under what conditions structuring or meta-processes taking place between two or more spheres of social action might contribute on the one hand to morphogenic tendencies and transformation and, on the other, to stability and reproduction of the system. To exemplify this, let us take the extremely simple case where the structural concordance between conflictual relationships and processes in the two spheres is substantial. For instance, elites in the socio-cultural sphere (E) are high status, high income groups closely linked to managerial elites and capitalists (A). Consumers (C) are closely related to dominated 'production groups' and workers (B). To the extent that the As control the resource transfers and the value and legitimation flows — at the same time that the Es control other key conditions and inputs of the socio-cultural system relevant to structuring of the economic sphere — to that extent the outputs such as the technocatic value system and status differentiations of the socio-cultural system would tend to be compatible with the reproduction of both the economic and socio-cultural subsystems of production. The compatibility reflects the concordance of relationships and processes in the two spheres:

— the concordance of the unequal distribution of power between capitalist/socio-cultural elites, on the one hand, and workers/consumers, on the other (that is, the social relations in the two spheres);

— the concordance of production processes in the two spheres. Concordance between the two spheres is maintained in part through transactions (communication, coordination, and exchange) and structuring processes going on between them.

The treatment here of the interactions between economic, political and socio-cultural sub-systems has in no sense been complete. Our discussion has been limited to consideration of a few resource, value, and knowledge flows with the aim of illustrating our methods of modeling and analysis of societal reproduction. We have tried to suggest a few of the ways in which the economic sub-system contributes — through resource, value, and knowledge flows to other spheres of social action — to the production (and reproduction) of structures and processes in socio-cultural and political spheres. These structures and processes tend to be compatible with those in the economic spheres. At the same time, the outputs of the political and socio-cultural spheres contibute to the reproduction — and adaptation — of capitalist relations of production and processes in the economic sub-system. Thus, social hierarchy in enterprises is partly maintained and reinforced through outputs, e.g., differences in competence and status, resulting from educational and other socio-cultural production processes. Similary, 'productions' of the political sphere tend to maintain and reinforce conditions conducive to capitalist organization of work and related processes.

IV TRANSFORMING OR REFORMING
CAPITALISM: STRATEGY
AND CRITIQUE

1. Industrial Democracy Reforms:
System Maintaining or System
Transforming Strategies

In Part I we introduced a definition of the liberation of work and a scheme to assess industrial democracy reforms in terms of the definition. The framework and analyses presented in Parts II and III imply that a basic question to be asked of industrial democracy reforms is, 'To what extent do such reforms provide workers with structural or meta-power?' More specific questions are the following:

— To what extent does a reform restructure control relationships with respect to production processes, the organization of production, products, and strategic spin-offs and spill-overs of production? (see Figures 1 and 2).

— To what extent does increased control by workers over their labor and systems of production, provided by a reform, allow them to extend their control and power over other spheres of social life, in particular the political and socio-cultural spheres?

— To what extent do the reforms give workers control over reproduction processes and the possibilities to shape new 'rules of the game' and institutional arrangements?

The intent of our earlier discussion was to shed some light on these questions.

(i) As already suggested in Table I, many industrial democracy reforms must be assessed unfavorably in relation to these questions. Reforms such as *Mitbestimmung*, co-determination and the like, represent only increased influence, within the existing institutional arrangements, not extensive control (either in the legal or technical sense) over relations of production, production processes and products. While such initiatives may be seen as a step toward the liberation of work, the gap between the most favorable assessment of such reforms and the liberation of work as defined earlier is substantial. Even changes in power relationships around the production process, e.g., through workers' acquisition of participatory decision-making rights, typically leaves meta-power distribution unchanged. That is, there is little or no change in the capability to structure power relationships between workers and managers in enterprises, to restructure the production process, the organization of production, or the distribution of its products, or to reshape the institutional context of production. Even highly developed self-management systems may fall far short of this standard (see Chapter 6).

(ii) Table I refers to direct effects of industrial democracy reforms on the distribution of power and control in work life. There may also be indirect changes mediated through political and socio-cultural processes. Thus, reforms introduced in work organizations, although they have minimal direct impact on the distribution of power and meta-power, can have, ultimately, structuring effects on such organizations through their influence on political and socio-cultural processes. For example, worker representation on the boards of directors of enterprises has probably had minimal impact on the management and control of enterprises (see Table I). Nevertheless, it can be argued that this institutional arrangement could have important socio-cultural and political implications over the long-run by changing public images of workers and labor union leaders, their role in work life, and their potential roles in the future. To put it succinctly, workers as well as the public might develop new conceptions of working people (or, at least, of their representatives), e.g., legitimizing their broader participation in societal decision-making processes. Similarly, through co-determination and various forms of participation in management, workers' self-image can be changed to the extent that they are able to discover and develop their capacity to make decisions, plan and manage. This would entail the acquisition of new skills, knowledge, and attitudes which, for instance, enhance political participation and initiatives in cultural affairs. Such changes are likely to lead to new goals and demands, and the perception of new action possibilities and opportunities for initiating change.

But these ramifications and developments would be unlikely in contexts where access to and influence over educational and mass media facilities and socio-cultural processes by workers and their representatives are generally limited; or where there are similar restrictions on political expression and opportunities for influence. In general, one expects that the same measure leads to different outcomes in different political and socio-cultural contexts. For this reason, the argument that a reform will have substantial indirect or derived effects must be traced and analyzed in different spheres of social life, political, socio-cultural, and ultimately back to the economic. In this way, one is in a better position to judge the ultimate potential of a reform to contribute to the liberation of work under conditions where it does not directly change power relationships.

(iii) The creation of participatory structures and processes at various levels (workplace, enterprise management, and society) does provide new platforms for individual and collective expressions by workers and of their interests. However, past experience in industrialized capitalist countries seems to indicate that participation has been accompanied more by integration than by emancipation of workers.[33] This may be less a direct function of the participatory arrangement itself than of the fact that workers basically accept the traditional criteria of decison-making and action, 'rules of the game' and other constraints as given. That is, an ideology about the logic of enterprise activity and development binds the parties together.

Thus, one should not only explore the possibility of changing power relationships relating to work life but the possibilities and strategies to change the dominant ideology and logic of evaluation, decision-making and social action in the social organization and management of production (i.e., capitalist logic). Such concerns suggest the importance of struggle and innovation in the socio-cultural sphere. Of specific concern here would be the development of alternative concepts, information and accounting systems, technology, forms and processes of work organization in capitalist enterprises which could contribute to emancipatory processes.

(iv) Many industrial democracy reforms are major achievements for workers in capitalist societies in that they contribute to improving the physical and mental health conditions of workers, their security, etc. (e.g., the Norwegian and Swedish work environment laws providing legal protection against physical as well as psychological stress). Moreover, such changes, which are valuable in themselves, can also contribute to bringing about alterations in concepts and norms regarding the nature of work, work processes, and work environment. Such socio-cultural changes may over the long run have structural impacts.

But almost all measures fail to provide workers with an extensive set of powers and meta-powers. In this sense, the reforms can be judged as basically structure-maintaining changes (or as not structure-transforming in intent). Although they often entail concessions to workers, they do not in any direct way fundamentally challenge structural features of capitalist institutions. To go beyond system maintenance and reproduction functions, industrial democracy reforms must attack two of the major interrelated features of capitalism:

— unequal distribution of gains and losses as a result of workers' lack of extensive controls over work, the organization of work, its products, and the institutional context in which work takes place;

— capitalism as a dynamic totality, and the control relationships and structuring processes which reproduce the totality.

2. The Global Process of Liberation in Complex Social Systems

Our models of capitalist institutional arrangements indicate that the liberation of work and the liberation of political power must be simultaneously and dialectically related: they are different facets of the same fundamental process, the progressive equalization of power and meta-power among social actors. In terms of the perspective outlined here, this implies keeping in mind a dynamic totality.

(i) *Multiple Spheres.* The liberation of work requires activity and movement not only in the economic sphere but in the political and socio-cultural spheres as well. This enables the formation and development of concepts and values as well as institutional rules and conditions which would facilitate the achievement of greater demociatic control over work life. Moreover, this may contribute to the development of democratic concepts and practices in other spheres of social action.

(ii) *Multi-level.* Liberation activity entails complementary social action at different levels:

— at the enterprise level to extend control over the social process of production to redesign jobs and work organization and to gain control over the products of labor in the broadest sense;

— at the level of structuring the political, legal, and socio-cultural contexts of work organizations or enterprises.

In the first case, it is the day to day activity in their place of work which may provide workers with the competence and confidence for work liberation. In the second case, political action may be oriented to shaping societal legislation, government policies, and new institutional arrangements. In this sense, the object is to establish macro-conditions facilitating liberation activity at the micro-level. Such action may be realized through voting or through influence exercised via national labor unions and socialist parties.[34] Local political action to reinforce industrial democracy norms in enterprises may also be of considerable importance. Action involving the articulation of concepts, values, and norms about the nature of work, the work environment, democratic work relationships, etc., may also be carried out at different levels in the socio-cultural sphere: for instance, through mass media activity as well as through schools and other local learning and socialization processes, including such activities within work organizations themselves.

(iii) *Holism.* Liberation thus takes on a systemic or holistic property (through multi-sphere, multiple level social activity and social movement). Due to the complex inter-linkages between spheres and between levels in social systems, it is essential that different problem-solving activities and movements be seen in relation to one another. Although for tactical purposes, one may have to proceed in piecemeal fashion, the dangers of such moves should be identified and emphasized. On the one hand, struggle and success at the enterprise level may be constrained or encapsulated because of market, legal, socio-cultural or other constraints within which the enterprise operates. On the other hand, legislated macro-changes may have minimal impact because workers are unorganized or unable (due to the lack of competence and confidence) to make effective use of the opportunities provided by such legislation (e.g., they lack necessary knowledge, skills, and well-defined goals).

(iv) In general, macro-level changes, e.g., through societal legislation, will be insufficient in themselves, when local-level conditions and processes negate or contradict the objectives or intentions in back of the macro-level changes. Similary, a local-level initiative and development may be constrained or negated by macro-level factors. Thus, an incompatibility or mismatch between macro-level conditions and processes and those on the micro-level may contribute to blocking or undermining a genuine development toward the liberation of work — or at least cumulative and amplification effects may be retarded. Similar constraints may arise between one sphere of social action and another. What this suggests is that efforts be directed to developing holistic concepts and strategies to bring about the transformation of social systems for the purpose of human liberation.

NOTES

1. For instance, income structure (and specifically, the structure of wages and prices) is coming under increasing influence of government policy ('income policies'). One result of this is that the government tends to be looked to (and blamed) concerning questions of distributive justice and market failures of various types. This tendency is, of course, much more comon and more explicit in capitalist systems where,as in Sweden, the state plays a pervasive regulatory role in the economy as well as in the society as a whole.

2. The relationship in advanced capitalism of the state to the economic sub-system is a complex one, involving processes of interpenetration as well as differentiation and relative autonomy. That is, there are substantial pressures on the state to become involved in concrete economic affairs, as well as pressures and constraints limiting such involvement. Instances of the state limiting its involvement or withdrawing from existing involvements are indicated in a variety of ways: (i) avoidance of formal price and wage controls; (ii) periodic reduction of the level of intervention, for instance, some movement away from the high rate of the late 1960s; (iii) encouragement of private institutional equivalents to state activity or special institutional arrangements with only partial state involvement (e.g., special semi-autonomous public enterprises).

3. While labor and regional social movements are examples of sources of such pressure, it is worth recalling that farmer and small business groups have also played prominent roles — and in some instances continue to play an influential role in the opposition to the tendencies toward concentration of capital and resource control in capitalist development. Although they may not have challenged the principles of private property rights, they have opposed the growing dominance of monopoly capital, systems of credit, distribution, marketing, and government policies which favored large capital over small.

4. Of course, this control is typically not directed at the uneven accumulation itself, but at the misuse of the power and its immediate effects resulting from unrestrained, uneven accumulation.

5. Technological as well as legal changes may favor the exploitation of a new process of concentration.

6. State response to capitalist crisis and the incentives for regulating a dynamic (structurally changing) economic sub-system entails the following (DeVille and Burns, 1977):

(i) In response to crisis or regulatory failure, learning and innovation processes occur on the practical as well as theoretical levels. New institutional regulatory arrangements as well as theoretical models with which to describe and determine policies are created and developed. These are designed to maintain a smoothly functioning system and to stabilize the core social processes and structures in the system. In particular, state regulation is oriented, to a substantial degree but not exclusively, toward: (a) continuance of capital accumulation as well as maintenance and reproduction of the asymmetrical social relationships in production and accumulation (see Models I and II, Figures 1 and 2, respectively); and (b) preserving the sociopolitical stability of the system. (These two functions may be simultaneously compatible and contradictory [DeVille and Burns, 1977]).

(ii) Over any extended period of time incompatibilities arise between the regulatory system and the regulated economic sub-system.

(iii) These incompatibilities arise from the fact that the regulatory system is designed to regulate certain relationships and processes of a particular economic system. The regulated system undergoes further restructuring for two reasons: first, the regulated system's internal development continues as a function of unregulated structures and processes (see Part II); second, the regulatory system itself brings about changes in processes and relationships in the regulated system, often in unintended ways. That is, regulation has unintended consequences which ultimately tend to limit the capability and effectiveness of that regulation. When serious instabilities arise which cannot be effectively controlled by means of the established regulatory system, a crisis occurs. That is, there is a control failure. Out of this crisis comes further experimentation and learning and the creation of new regulatory mechanisms (see sub-sections [1] and [2]).

7. This reflects contradictions between organizing principles: the principle of administrative or control hierarchy and that of egalitarianism and participation in decisions which affect one's life. This opposition is a general phenomenon in social life today, with increased demands in a number of areas of social action for ordinary people to participate in the conduct of societal affairs. Production, labor union life, government, and other institutions all reflect these tensions.

8. The capitalist order is typically not defended on grounds of its intrinsic good, that is its good per se. But rather it is defended on grounds that it is efficient or assures maximum economic growth, providing benefits for a majority of the population. Or it is defended on the basis of meritocratic criteria which are held to be consistent with (certain) democratic norms.

9. The Special Task Force established by the US Secretary of Health, Education, and Welfare reported in *Work in America*, 1973, that:

...a significant number of American workers are dissatisfied with the quality of their working lives...As a result, the productivity of the worker is low...Moreover, a growing body of research indicates that, as work problems increase, there may be a consequent *decline in balanced socio-political attitudes* (emphasis ours).

10. Of course, the articulated dissatisfaction of workers with their working conditions and work environment may not be high. Indeed, pressure from workers to gain greater control over their work and work environment and to feel that their work activity is important may be weaker than many of us would like to believe. Workers have other options to structure their world and life experiences: e.g., demand higher income with which to enjoy leisure time activities; withdraw fom unsatisfactory work environments, either temporarily (absenteeism or cognitive withdrawal of various sorts) or permanently (moving from one working place to another). Workers' level of satisfaction with their work is based, of course, on their conceptions of work and expectations shaped to a large degree by models, norms and values generated within the capitalist system (see Part III).

11. Production is a transformation of a set of inputs, material as well as symbolic, into a set of outputs through the use of labor applying particular technologies.

12. Spin-off and spill-over products include those products which impinge on the activities and conditions of other production units as well as on other spheres of social action. For example, in the latter case, this could entail transfer payments to communities, the use in political activities and decision-making of managerial knowledge and capabilities acquired in the process of planning and controlling enterprises, and legitimation and prestige derived from being involved in particular tasks or occupying particular positions (see Part II).

13. Three spheres of social production are considered here: economic, political-administrative, and socio-cultural. These spheres or societal sub-systems are linked through a complex set of relationships, flows, and dependencies. The maintenance and transformation of economic structures and processes depends on structures and

processes in the political and socio-cultural spheres; and vice versa. Sub-systems and system components are linked to one another in the usual causal and feedback loops as well as through structuring linkages and processes. Structuring is an operator on processes, functions and relationships rather than on variables. In this sense, structuring represents a higher order, that is meta-form of determination or causality.

A major factor in the structuring of social systems is human action itself. That is, humans through their activities, intentionally and unintentionally, structure societies and the particular social institutions characterizing those societies.

14. In general, reproduction of a social system results when those committed to its characteristic structures and processes have sufficient will, intelligence, and resources to counteract restructuring forces and activities from outside as well as fom inside the system. Shifts of power and control over resources among actors with different concepts or models of desirable or effective institutional arrangements are major factors in the transformation of institutions.

15. Although our arguments here refer ostensibly to contemporary capitalism with private ownership and management of the means of production, it may, with appropriate modifications, be extended to industrial societies without significant private ownership (e.g., the socialist countries of Eastern Europe). Inequality in control over the means of production (as represented in Figure 1) is justified in most East European countries by ideology (e.g. concepts such as 'dictatorship of the proletariat' and 'rational socialist management') and sustained institutionally in ways similar to those found in capitalist societies (see Part III).

16. This is not to overlook the fact that the capitalist division of labor and exchange systems have often provided obvious advantages to subordinate or dependent actors, e.g., in the form of immediate consumption goods. However, such 'advantages' must be clearly distinguished from long-term structural gains and capability development which accrue to members of [A]. (In other words, the major concern here is with the power and meta-power consequences of the division of labor and exchange, not the subjective feelings and interpretations of those involved, e.g., the satisfaction of employees with their wages are socially defined on the basis of a prevailing ideology as 'fair' or 'satisfactory'.)

17. This analysis is structurally as well as temporally over-simplified in that it fails to distinguish within the classes [A] and [B]; for example, between managers of conglomerates and multi-national corporations and small businessmen (see Part III), or between technicians and other professional employees and blue collar workers.

Concerning the latter distinction, it is often pointed out that, although legal ownership rests with the stockholders, effective economic control, that is the power to dispose of the means of production and of labor power, often rests with top managers and technocrats. The latter, by virtue of their knowledge, skills, and education, occupy strategic positions in the control over, and development of, economic and technical developments in a modern industrial society. Therefore, they belong to or are closer to group A in Models I and II (Figures 1 and 2) than to the class of Bs who, as blue collar and office employees, are more likely to be 'dependent participants'.

Top managers and technocrats operate at present within the ideological and institutional constraints of capitalism. However, their knowledge and skills and bargaining power based on their importance to the effective functioning of the system put them in a more favorable position than most 'employees' to get the system to serve their interests.

18. Thus, employees create or contribute to the creation of resources and valuables which they do not receive or do not get paid for. This constitutes the origin of surplus products and values which are appropriated by the managers and owners of capital.

Some products or valuables, e.g., those related to knowledge accumulation or skill development are not so much a matter of non-payment as non-opportunity to gain them in production settings. Of course, revenue might well be devoted to purposes of special education and acquisition of valuable skills.

19. Meta-power is the capability of structuring and regulating an institutionalized area of social action. It entails, therefore, the ability to manipulate or to transform the institutional famework and 'rules of the game' of social action. Meta-power is therefore distinguished from power exercised within a given institutional order (Baumgartner et al., 1976).

20. Of course, with the development of effective trade unionism and the social democratic welfare state in many contemporary capitalist societies, a definite restructuring of the relations of production diagrammed in Figure 1 has been accomplished; in particular, employees have gained some influence over certain aspects of the operation of the means of production, especially their working conditions (this shift is indicated by the short arrow from B to X). But the basic structures and processes of capitalism remain substantially unchanged, in spite of the numerous important, and in many instances, beneficial reforms under the development of 'welfare capitalism'.

21. It is not merely a matter of the production and trade of agricultural goods and raw materials, as opposed to manufactured goods, but a question, in part, of the political and economic context in which production and exchange take place. Also of relevance are the power and development potentialities associated with the production and exchange of diffcrent types of goods in different contexts. This is pointed up in the case of agricultural producing countries such as Denmark and New Zealand or the OPEC oil producing countries.

22. Note that productivity increases may have substantially different consequences in the different contexts of A^O and A. In the case of A^Os, they would be reflected in increased profits (and also possibly increased wages). Such productivity increases may not lead to substantial gains in profits, wages, etc. in the case of peripheral enterprises (this is often the case in agriculture where productivity growth lowers prices).

23. A variety of factors may have contributed to such a pattern (that is, Gunnar Myrdal's process of 'cumulative causation'): initially favorable market position and terms of trade, strong control over strategic factors of production and the production process, and attraction of capital, political and economic support from the state, and so forth.

The key notion here is that the comparative advantage, success, and profitability of an enterprise is to a large extent a function of its ability to control — or develop control — over relevant factors and resources in its environment: factors of production, customers, as well as the political and socio-cultural environments (political support, freedom from legal and normative constraints, technology, knowledge and patents, and human resources generally).

24. The reproduction costs for capital (X^O and X) and labor (Y_1 and Y_2) are greater for center enterprises than for peripheral ones. But typically these costs are not born correspondingly by center and periphery enterprises, respectively. For instance, the cost of capital reproduction may be redistributed through taxation and fiscal policies. This also holds true in many instances for technology development, and research and development generally. Similarly, the costs of labor reproduction (e.g., relating to education and job training) may be borne in part by the state.

The distribution of reproduction costs can have a substantial bearing on uneven development. In particular, the fact that reproduction costs for labor and the means of production are greater for center enterprises than for periphery enterprises may, under suitable conditions, play a role in center/periphery reversal (see Alker et al., 1979).

25. Property and ownership, of course, have a range of meanings and forms in different social systems, depending on what complex of control rights are socially established and maintained.

26. We do not overlook, however, the pressures within the labor movement to restructure and even transform the system, and the dilemmas which labor leaders experience between system-maintaining and system-changing efforts.

27. As suggested by an earlier discussion, social distinctions in the work place may not serve any technical need or function. Rather, ideological and control functions may be served:

— compliance with general status distinctions (e.g., sex, age, and race) and rules prevailing in the society;
— divide and rule strategy to undermine solidarity and fragment workers (through status hierarchization and promotion of competition) so as to maintain domination in the relations of production.

28. For instance, labor unions and labor movement groups may establish educational institutions and carry on activities to offset, in part, the 'cutural hegemony' of capitalism. The intensity and effectiveness of such movements vary considerably among countries.

29. Some forms of transfer (T) are partly controlled through the outputs of the political system, i.e. taxes are a legal obligation only partially within the enterprise's discretion to define and manipulate through its profit figures. Other forms (e.g., financing of interest group associations and lobbies) are completely within the power of individual enterprises, at least the executive organs of collective interest organizations supported by enterprises, managers, and capital owners.

30. This argument points to an interesting overlap between the political and economic spheres (which holds for other spheres as well). Much political action and interaction is also economic action and interaction, certainly in the sense given to economic production in capitalist GNP accounts. This is another instance of the multi-faceted nature of social action.

31. Capitalist managers staff positions, allocate prerogatives and benefits based on certain general norms and legitimation principles relating to status distinctions. Hyman and Brough (1975) argue that norms of fairness are social values which legitimize existing inequalities, disguise conflicts of interest and thus buttress the

position of those who possess material power in society and control production. Indeed, those with material power exercise influence in the cultural sphere, shaping and maintaining more or less successfully institutions and practices conducive to legitimizing and stabilizing a political economy based on socio-economic private ownership of the means of production and inequality. This contributes to the production and reproduction of social values and norms which reinforce their material interests (Hyman and Brough, 1975).

32. In other words, this entails a failure to shape and develop a socialist alternative which comprehends society as a dynamic totality.

33. This is certainly the case of job enrichment, work humanization and autonomous work groups which, as experiences with these reforms have shown, can be relatively easily integrated into established structures and processes of capitalist organization of production. Rasmus (1974) argues that job enrichment, autonomous work group arrangements, and participation programs are in general designed to give workers greater responsibility for production without real independent control over the decisions that determine production and the powerful contextual factors. They assume responsibility for eliminating work stoppages, absenteeism, tardiness, turnover, etc. In practical terms, this leads to workers encouraging each other to work harder, recommending the elimination of 'unnecessary' jobs and the replacement of old jobs with new machinery and equipment, and workers disciplining each other. The work force as a group thus carries out voluntarily a number of tasks that were previously the responsibility of management.

34. Of course, the history of the labor movement indicates just such multi-level and complementary activity to structure and regulate the conditions of work. On the one hand, there has been pressure for general statutory regulation of employment: minimum wages, unemployment benefits, pensions, sickness benefits, and in some instances regulation of dismissals. Also, statutes have imposed minimum standards for the avoidance of accidents and industrial diseases (Clegg, 1976). On the other hand, workers' collectives through bargaining and day to day struggle in their work places also structure and regulate conditions of work.

REFERENCES

Adams, R. N. (1975), *Energy and Structure*. Austin, Texas: University of Texas Press.

Alker, H. Jr., T. Baumgartner and T. R. Burns (1979), 'Center/Periphery Relationships and Their Reversal in the World System.' *Alternatives: A Journal of World Policy*, in preparation.

Baumgartner, T. (1978), 'An Actor-oriented Systems Model for the Analysis of Industrial Democracy Measures,' pp. 55-77 in R. F. Geyer and J. van der Zouwen (eds.), *Sociocybernetics*, Vol. I. Leiden: Martinus Nijhoff.

Baumgartner, T., T. R. Burns, and P. DeVille (1978), 'Conflict Resolution and Conflict Development,' in L. Kriesberg (ed.), *Research in Social Movements, Conflict, and Change*. Greenwich, Conn.: JAI.

—— (1979), 'Actors, Games, and Systems: The Dialectics of Social Action and System Structuring,' in: Scott G. McNall (ed.), *Theoretical Perspectives in Sociology*. New York: St. Martin's Press.

Baumgartner, T., W. Buckley, T. R. Burns, and P. Schuster (1976), 'Meta-power and the Structuring of Social Hierarchy,' in: T. R. Burns and W. Buckley (eds.), *Power and Control: Social Structures and Their Transformation*. London and Beverly Hills, Calif.: Sage Publications.

Burns, T. R. (1976a), *Dialectics of Social Systems: The Reproduction and Transformation of Social Institutions*. Working Papers: Institute of Sociology, University of Oslo, Oslo.

—— (1976b), *Strikes and Social Change: Industrial Conflict and Restructuring of Management/Labor Systems*. Unpublished manuscript.

Burrage, M. (1972), 'On Tocqueville's Notion of the Irresistibility of Democracy,' *European Journal of Sociology*, 13:151-75.

Carchedi, G. (1975), 'Reproduction of Social Classes at the Level of Production Relations,' *Economy and Society*, 4:361-417.

Clegg, S. (1976), *Collective Bargaining*. Oxford: Oxford University Press.

Dahrendorf, R. (1957), *Class and Class Conflict in Industrial Society*. Stanford, Calif.: Stanford University Press.

DeVille, P. and T. R. Burns (1977), 'Institutional Response to Crisis in Capitalist Development,' *Social Praxis*, 4:5-46.

Gordon, D. (1976), 'Capitalist Efficiency and Socialist Efficiency,' *Monthly Review*, 28:19-30.

Hyman, R. (1976), *Industrial Relations. A Marxist Introduction*. Mystic, Conn.: Verry Lawrence.

Hyman, R. and I. Brough (1975), *Social Values and Industrial Relations: A Study in Fairness and Inequality*. Oxford: Basil Blackwell.

Jones, T. A. (1975), 'Modernization Theory and Socialist Development,' in M. G. Field (ed.), *Consequences of Modernization in Communist Countries*. Baltimore, Md.: Johns Hopkins University Press.

Marrow, A. J. (1975), 'Management by Participation,' in E. L. Cass and F. G. Zimmer (eds.), *Man And Work in Society*. New York: Van Nostrand Reinhold.

Morgan, E. S. (1978), 'The Great Political Fiction,' *New York Review of Books*, 9 March: 13-18.

Rasmus, J. (1974), 'Why Management is Pushing "Job Enrichment",' *International Socialist Review*, December.

Stone, A. (1971), 'How Capitalism Rules,' *Monthly Review*, 21:3-36.

Stone, J. (1966), *Social Dimensions of Law and Justice*. Stanford, Calif.: Stanford University Press.

Touraine, A. (1972), Cited by T. Bottomore, 'Three authors in search of a proletariat,' *New York Review of Books*, 6 April, p. 31.

Tropea, J. (1977), 'Language, Socialization, and Social Reproduction.' Paper presented at a Conference on Language and Society, Oslo, Norway, September 1977.

Wright, E. O. (1976), 'Class Boundaries in Advanced Capitalist Societies,' *New Left Review*, No. 98, pp. 3-41.

6

LIMITED EFFECTS OF WORKERS' PARTICIPATION AND POLITICAL COUNTER-POWER

Veljko Rus
University of Ljubljana, Yugoslavia

I SELF-MANAGEMENT AS CLASS OR META-CLASS SYSTEM OF PARTICIPATION

The goal of Yugoslav self-management is not only the humanization of work, industrial peace, higher wages, a better work environment, and a greater system of trust among managers and workers; the goal of self-management is above all the political emancipation of the working class and the domination of the same, within the framework of a self-management system. In this sense, self-management is only a special form of the dictatorship of the proletariat. 'For us the dictatorship of the proletariat is so, not the dictatorship of the state apparatus, or of state despotism, it is rather — according to its essence — a revolutionary form of an unquestionably leading role of the working class, or rather of the historical interests of the same in a managing society' (Kardelj, 1976). Thus, the goals of the Yugoslav self-management are explicitly political. They are directed towards such a distribution of political power as will make possible the establishment of the long-term interests of the working class.

In spite of such clear goals, the implementation of them in the given historical circumstances meets with several difficulties. The fundamental problem in this connection is: who is the actual carrier of the long-term interests of the working class: all the working people, the working class, or the League of Communists? The implications of this question are not only of a theoretical nature, they are rather political and they decide the nature of the dictatorship of the proletariat.

The same difficulties appear at the level of empirical investigations: the working class and all the working people employed in the public sector are used as synonyms. Such a broad definition is most appropriate because in a propertyless society, it is hard to define what is and what is not the working class. Also, the constitution continually emphasizes the leading role of 'the working class and all the working people'. We have, therefore, to do with an ambiguous formulation of the working class, which is probably used purposely because it makes possible a flexible definition of it, with regard to the rapidly changing circumstances in Yugoslav society.

However, this ambiguous formulation, 'the working class and all the working people', institutionalizes a contradiction which is going to become more and more outstanding in the future. This contradiction is based on a double conception of self-management.

1. According to the first concept self-management is a meta-class system setting up work as the dominant and universal value, and establishing work as the criterion of the distribution of income and as a base of emancipation of working individuals, regardless of the job they execute.

2. According to the second concept, self-management is not a universalistic meta-class system, but a particularistic and class-oriented system. In this case, it is not a question of establishing work as the supreme value in society, but primarily domination of those strata or groups which are the carriers of the long-term interests of the working class.

The implications proceeding from these two concepts are extremely far-reaching in a political sense as well as in an economic and cultural sense.

II ACTUAL AND DESIRED
PARTICIPATION

In our empirical research (Rus, 1974[1]) we could not take into account all these problems. We tried to explore only which are the main conditions for effective workers' participation and whether employees could change the distibution of power to their benefit by participation. We were interested to know whether the participation of employees led only to humanization of work relations or also to their political emancipation.

The above questions have been measured by several indices related to different dimensions of the participation. We have analyzed the effects of participation at two organizational levels (the level of plant and the level of a working group), and further, the effects of participation on various issues of decision making (concerned with cadres, organization, and economics), and the effects of different modes of participation (giving proposals, decision taking, control over implementation of decisions, etc.). Besides this, we have tried to establish what are the aspirations of employees for participation, since it is expected that the differences between the actual and desired participation are quite relevant for estimating the future development of self-management in Yugoslav enterprises.

Table 1 gives information about the intensity of workers' participation at the plant level. Two characteristics of actual participation are visible from this table:

(a) that participation is not intensive, since the indicators oscillate between 1 and 2 (that means between very seldom and seldom participation);

(b) that the intensity of participation in the sphere of business decisions (the first four decisions) and in the sphere of social decisions is almost exactly the same. To these two findings, one more fact should be added (which cannot be derived from Table 1), and that is that the intensity of workers' participation is almost exactly the same in all of the examined enterprises.

The low intensity of participation is in accordance with our expectations; it is evident that the long-term plan cannot be frequently

TABLE 1

**Actual participation of employees at the level of basic organization (plant) and their aspirations.
Seven industrial organizations and two market organizations representative sample for each organization
(N = 842); year 1974.**

Issue	Actual (mean)	Aspirations (mean)
Formulation of long-range plan	1,39	1,95
Investments in equipment	1,44	2,00
Introduction of new products	1,46	2,15
Selling products	1,51	2,11
Nomination of top management	1,69	2,15
Nomination of candidates for W.C.	1,93	2,31
Formulation of criteria for hiring and firing	1,39	1,95
Criteria for income distribution	1,51	2,50
Decisions about bonuses	1,42	2,36
Housing policy	1,27	2,23
Norms for quality and quantity of work	1,44	2,28

1 = very seldom; 2 = seldom; 3 = frequent; 4 = very frequent participation.

discussed, and that the leaders and delegates to self-management bodies are elected only once in several years, etc. Even if the interest of workers in decisions is great in this sphere, and if all of the conditions are given for the realization of their interests, we cannot expect an essentially more frequent, or rather, more intense participation in the future.

The findings of our research are very similar to those obtained by Arzenšek (1970) and Možina (1971); Arzenšek's interpretation is different from ours, but it is not contradictory to it. According to Arzenšek, the small differences in the intensity of participation among enterprises are a consequence of the fact that the traditional and autocratic style of leadership still continues to predominate in Yugoslav enterprises. Tannenbaum's research supports, to some extent, Arzenšek's interpretation, since it indicates that autocratic leadership is more expressed in Yugoslavia than in other countries (Tannenbaum, 1974). In this case, the low participation would be a consequence of the conflict between an exceptionally democratic institutional structure and paternalistic behavior of the executive hierarchy.

Table 1 also contains the data regarding the aspirations of workers for participation at the plant level; the basic characteristics of their aspirations are:

1. The wishes of workers for cooperation are greater than their actual participation.
2. The aspirations of workers for cooperation in social decisions are greater than for cooperation in business decisions.
3. With regard to the intensity of aspirations, the differences among enterprises are greater than the differences in the actual participation.

The more intense aspirations represent a real possibility for the further development of self-management in Yugoslavia. On the other hand, we must call attention to the fact that the aspirations are not essentially higher than actual participation. We estimate this finding to be favorable as well, because we suppose that modestly higher aspirations provoke greater activity of the workers, while substantially higher aspirations would provoke workers' disappointment with their existing situation, frustration, and dissatisfaction. We also consider to be of importance the finding that the aspirations of workers are more selective than their actual participation: they are more directed to participation in social decisions than to participation in business decisions. In these aspirations we see important trends toward more selective participation of workers, which makes possible a more intense influence in a narrower scope of activity. The selective participation of workers in strategically the most important spheres can essentially increase the effectiveness of participatory activity and, at the same time, reduce the use of time and energy.

Our findings regarding the aspirations at the level of enterprise are basically identical with the findings of Možina (1971). Higher and more selective aspirations are thus probably a rather stable phenomenon with Yugoslav workers.

The actual and aspirational participation at the level of a working group is given by Table 2. It shows:

1. that the indices of actual participation of workers at the level of a working group are only insignificantly greater than on the plant level;
2. that variations in participation among enterprises are also exceptionally small (these data are not listed); and
3. that the participation of workers in the field of the organization of work (the first three decisions) is greater than in the sphere of social problems.

The same findings apply to the workers' desired participation at work-group level:

1. the aspirations for participation at this level are not greater than the aspirations for participation at the level of the plant;
2. the aspirations for participation in organization of work are greater than those for participation in social issues of a work group;
3. aspirations are greater than participation.

We did not expect that the actual and desired participation of employees at the level of the work group were just as small as those at the level of the plant. We had expected an essentially greater par

TABLE 2
**Actual participation of employee at the level of work group and their aspirations.
Seven industrial organizations and two market organizations; representative sample (N = 842); year 1974.**

Issue	Actual participation	Desired participation
Formulation of monthly plan of production	1.50	2.30
Distribution of tasks among workers	1.74	2.44
Work time (holiday, shifts, breaks)	1.62	2.46
Hiring of co-workers in work group	1.52	2.37
Firing of co-workers from work group	1.30	1.90
Nomination of foreman	1.46	2.27
Conflicts resolution within work group	1.59	2.15

1 = very seldom; 2 = seldom; 3 = frequent; 4 = very frequent.

ticipation at the level of work groups because we supposed that workers are more interested in the immediate working surroundings, that they have more experience and so also more possibility for cooperation in the sphere of their daily work, and because we suppose that the problems at this level are more short-term and, therefore, subject to more frequent decisions.

The low actual participation at the level of work groups could be explained by the fact that in the preceding period Yugoslav self-management was expressly of a representative system, oriented to the activity of workers' councils (W.C.) at the level of the plant or enterprise. In connection with this, the institutional possibilities of workers' participation at plant level were essentially greater than those at the level of a working group. The participation at the level of a work group was mainly spontaneous and informal; it depended on the leadership style of middle and low management.

If, by the above hypotheses, we can explain the low degree of actual participation of workers at the level of work groups, the same hypotheses cannot explain as well the low aspirations of workers for participation at this level. It is possible that the aspirations of workers have not been activated as yet, since they think the present situation cannot change; it is also possible that the nature of problems does not permit more frequent participation, and it is possible that by participation at this level, workers cannot realize their essential interests. Further, statistical analysis (to be treated below in Table 5), will show the hypothesis about non-activated needs to be the most relevant one. This hypothesis is supported by the high correlations between aspirations and actual participation: the more intense the participation of workers, the higher are their aspirations. If participation of workers is low, aspirations for participation are low as well.

In addition to this, we have been surprised by the fact that workers are more oriented towards participation in organization of work than towards participation in regulating group interactions. This orientation of workers is contrary to the theory of human relations and other socio-therapeutical schools.

Such an orientation cannot be treated as 'workers' technocratism' because we know that at the level of the plant, workers' aspirations are oriented to social and not to business problems. The different orientation of aspirations at these two levels can be explained by the different function of participation at these two levels: at the level of the plant, workers' participation is more defensive and preventive (oriented to protection of workers' interests), while at the level of a work group it is more offensive and active — oriented more to fundamental working problems from which also other social consequences proceed. Intense aspirations related to distribution of tasks to some extent support our interpretation; it is evident that the amount of income, the quality of work, and the group with which the worker cooperates depend on the distribution of work tasks.

The data of Tables 3 and 4 refer to the desired forms of workers' participation at the level of plant and also at the level of a work group. The data of these two tables show nothing essentially new with regard to the data which we have already treated in connection with workers' aspirations. They are only a verification of previous data and an indicator of internal validity of previous findings. There exists a high positive correlation between intensity and quality of participation: the more intense is the workers' participation, the higher forms of participation they desire. This relation has not only been discovered in this research but, rather, has been obtained in some previous research projects (Rus, 1964).

Correlations which refer to intraitem analysis of actual and desired participation of workers are all statistically significant. Differences occur only in intensity of correlations:

1. The most intense correlations can be seen among the aspirations for participation in various decisions inside the same level of an organization. This means: workers who wish to participate more intensely in one kind of decision at the plant level or at the work group level wish to cooperate more frequently also in other decisions. Thus, aspirations are not sporadic, but rather systemed and forming an integrated whole.

2. The correlations among aspirations for participation at both levels are also intense; the correlations between aspirations for participation at plant level and at the level of work groups prove that workers perceive participation as a uniform complex.

3. All the correlations among particular indicators of actual participation are still always significant at both levels; thus, participation is not only an integrated aspirational system, but also an integrated behavioral system; participation in one decision increases the probability of participation in other decisions as well.

TABLE 3
Aspirations of employee according to the mode of participation (plant level). Seven industrial organizations and two market organizations; representative sample (N = 842); year 1974.

Issue	Aspirations about mode of participation			
	wish to be informed only	wish to discuss	wish to decide	wish to control implementation
Formulation of long-range plan	51.7	22.7	7.0	5.5
Investments in equipment	44.7	27.3	12.1	5.0
Introduction of new products	45.1	25.3	12.8	5.7
Selling products	50.1	20.8	8.4	6.4
Nomination of top management	41.6	27.2	13.4	6.3
Nomination of candidates for W.C.	36.0	30.4	18.3	6.9
Formulation of criteria for hiring and firing	40.1	27.1	13.4	6.9
Criteria for income distribution	30.2	32.7	20.9	10.2
Decisions about bonuses	32.9	33.7	17.6	7.6
Housing policy	36.5	27.0	13.3	11.4
Norms for quality and quality of work	37.1	29.1	16.0	7.7

Percentage of employees who do not like to participate in any of above mentioned modes is not inserted in table but could be counted as a difference between other modes and total 100 percent.

TABLE 4
Aspirations of employee according to the mode of participation (work groups level). Seven industrial organizations and two market organizations; representative sample (N = 842); year 1974.

Issue	Aspirations about mode of participation			
	wish to be informed only	wish to discuss	wish to decide	wish to control implementation
Formulation of monthly plan of production	49.9	27.6	10.1	4.2
Distribution of tasks among workers	37.5	34.0	15.7	5.8
Work time (holiday, shifts, breaks)	32.8	37.4	17.2	5.2
Hiring of co-workers in work group	35.5	32.4	17.8	4.6
Firing of co-workers from work group	43.1	26.6	10.6	3.1
Nomination of foreman	37.2	32.3	15.9	5.0
Conflicts resolution within work group	39.4	30.0	12.5	4.2

4. Correlations among indicators of participation at group and plant levels are, in most cases, significant. Decision making about personal income and about working norms at plant level is most closely related to decision making at the level of a work group. Participation in these two spheres of decision making at the plant level is, thus, of highest strategical importance for participation at the work group level.

5. The significant correlations between actual and desired participation are not so frequent: approximately one-half of all the possible correlations are significant. Some forms of participation are more important for future development than others. Actual participation in those spheres which refer to business decisions at plant level, and those referring to labor problems at the work group level are most closely related to aspirations. Participation in these two spheres, thus, significantly stimulates also aspirations for further participation.

Regardless of the various possible directions of interpretation of the above correlations, we can say that participation in one sphere generates participation in another. We can say further that actual participation generates greater aspirations for participation and that greater aspirations for participation generate also more actual participation.

The whole complex of participation is thus revealed as a self-generating process, or rather, as a self-reinforcing complex.
If this statement is correct, or if it can be generalized, then we can say that the conditions for participation are not essential. What is essential is its constitution which, in most cases, will lead to self-generating processes of participation. This hypothesis is also supported by the fact that the analyzed enterprises have been extremely heterogeneous both with regard to their size and their technology and with regard to education of employees: in our cases, heterogenous conditions do not create heterogeneous processes of participation. This means that participation as a self-generating process is relatively independent of the socio-technical environment. This conclusion has been proven also by the fact that those workers who have previously been members of workers' councils now participate more intensely, and simultaneously have greater aspirations for further participation.

III CONTINGENCIES OF
PARTICIPATION

If we now look at Table 5, we can see that there are only a few variables which influence greater or smaller participation. Out of 18 variables included in our research, only status variables and those variables which measure vertical relations are significant predictors. However, these status variables (income, education, level), and variables measuring the relations between superiors and subordinates do not influence the intensity of participation at the plant level; they only influence the intensity of participation at the work group level. If we take into account the relatively high degree of formalization of participation at the plant level and the precise criteria of candidating the members of self-management bodies (which are based on the principle of representation of all the groups and on the principle of exclusion of top managers from self-management organs), then it is understandable that status variables cannot influence the intensity of participation at plant level. Highly institutionalized participation at this level explains also why vertical relations do not influence self-management activities. If we generalize these hypotheses, we should expect similar effects of legislative regulation to take place at the level of work group activity. Greater formal regulation of workers' participation at this level should also prevent discriminatory effects of status and leadership contingencies: the more participation is formally regulated, the lower differences in participation among workers with different status will be and the higher the independence of their participation from leadership style.

The absence of statistically significant correlations among demographic characteristics (sex, age) and participation is interpreted as the proof of universality of self-management, or rather as evidence that demographically different populations have been made equal in the self-management system.

Unexpected also were statistically non-significant correlations between work environment (formalization of work, interdependence at work, formalization of work tasks) and the intensity of participation. This finding complements the above-mentioned fact about similar intensity of participation across enterprises, even though their technology is essentially different. It looks like the participatory system depends more on the social structure

TABLE 5
Seven industrial organizations and two market organizations; representative sample (N = 842); year 1974.

Variables \\ Participation		Plant Level		Group Level	
		Actual	Desired	Actual	Desired
Personal variables	value orientation	.	.	.	.
	sex	.	.	.	.
	age	.	.	.	.
Status variables	education	.	+ + + + + + +		+ + + +
	income	.	+ + +	+ + + +	+ + + +
	status	.	+ + + +	+ + + + + +	+ +
Behavior variables	earlier members of WC	+ + + + + + +	+	+ + + + + +	+
Work environment	formalization of work	.	.	.	.
	monotony	.	.	+	.
	personal development	.	.	.	.
	interdependency	.	.	.	.
Leadership	participatory leadership	.	.	+ + + +	.
	protectiveness of leader	.	.	+ +	.
Peer relationship	competitiveness of workers	.	.	.	.
	cooperation	.	.	.	.
	indifference	.	.	.	.
Active influence upon	co-workers		.	+ + +	.
	supervisors		.	+ + + + + +	.
	members of WC	+ + + +	.	+ + + +	.
	political function	+ + + +	+	+ +	.
	top management	+ + + + +	.	+ + + + +	.
Passive influence from	co-workers	.		.	.
	supervisors	.		.	.
	members W.C.	+	+ + + +	+ +	.
	political function	.	+ +	.	.
	top management	.	.	.	.

*Crosses mean statistically significant correlation coefficients.

than on technology, more on the power relations among organizational groups inside work organizations and, of course, among strata outside it, then on technological complexity. This assumption is supported by several empirical researches which all prove technological non-determinism of social systems in work organizations (Perrow, 1970; Mohr, 1971).

We have also been surprised that peer relations among fellow workers do not influence either actual or desired participation. On the basis of these findings, we assume that horizontal relations are conditioned more or less culturally and not organizationally, that is why they do not vary across organizations.

IV PARTICIPATION AND POWER

In the bottom part of Table 5, we present correlations between power and participation. In our case, power is interpreted as a dependent variable with regard to participation, even though the opinion that power is really an independent variable is more and more frequent (Županov, 1972). This turn in the interpretation of the relation between power and participation is based on the fact that the distribution of power has not essentially changed in Yugoslavia, even though the self-management system has operated over 25 years. According to Županov, participation presupposes a more or less equal distribution of power; if power is distributed unequally, if it is centralized and hierarchical, then effective workers' participation is not possible.

Even though the above theory is logical, it has not been proven by Yugoslav research up until this time. It is a fact that the distribution of power in Yugoslav enterprises is relatively more equal than in other countries. But this equalization exists only (Tannenbaum, 1974) on the level of enterprises at which there are operating workers' councils, committees of W.C. and executive committees of W.C. If at lower levels power is still always hierarchically distributed, this is a consequence of the fact that self-management in Yugoslavia has been mainly limited to the level of enterprises.

Our findings call attention to the fact that in some cases there exists a very close relation between participation and power, whereas in some other cases no relation has been found; the relations between participation and active power are very close, whereas there are barely any significant relations between participation and passive power.[2] The relations between power and aspirations for participation are also very rare; from this we can come to the conclusion that aspirations have not had significant influence on the perception of the relations between power and actual participation.

If we attempt to interpret these findings so that we consider participation as independent and power as an outcome variable, we can say that with participation, the workers' influence on the other members in an organization increases (active power) whereas the influence of other members on the workers does not decrease.[3]

The most appropriate interpretation of these different effects could be the following: greater participation generates greater influence of the worker on his environment, it does not, however, curtail the influence of other members, since the influence of others primarily depends on status and means, which do not change due to workers' participation.

In addition to this explanation an alternative one is possible also: the passive power is not based on the system of interpersonal relations, but rather on the system of impersonal relations. If this is true, no relation between passive power and participation can be expected. Even though we directly questioned the workers regarding the influence of individual groups upon themselves, and about their influence on such groups, it is possible to assume that in the first case workers perceive more status power, and in the second more participatory or behavioral power. Since status is based on the entire system of allocation of resources and, at the same time, reflects also the stratification structure of the entire society, passive power can also be explained as that power which cannot be essentially changed by participation. Participation of one or another group can, temporarily, change the relation of power, but the effects are not permanent and soon disappear.

A more or less stable status structure is conditioned above all by allocation of means, by distribution of decisions, by selection of employees, by defining the channels of communications, by internalization of professional and business goals, etc. Status relations, thus, reflect some impersonal system of power with permanent, indirect and impersonal effects; since it is indirect and impersonal, it cannot be perceived as a separate system, but only in combination with another system. That is why it is probably correct to call it a system of metapower (Baumgartner et al., 1976), founded on metachoice, which cannot be essentially influenced by employees' participation.

If this hypothesis about coincidence of the personal and impersonal system of power is confirmed, and if the relative independence of status power on participatory power appears, then the problem of the relation between participation and power would appear in an entirely new light. In this case, participation would be the generator of redistribution of behavioral power: participation of workers could democratize interpersonal relations among workers and leaders, but it could not change status power in the enterprise as a whole. Participation would create greater integration of workers at the level of interpersonal dynamics, but it would not work in the direction of emancipation of workers with regard to the impersonal system of metapower.

In this case, changes should be induced in two entirely opposite directions: in the direction of increasing participation, making possible a democratization of daily mutual relations, and in the direction of political control of metapower in the sense of creation of contrapower against the present dominant coalitions which are carriers of this system of metapower.

The problem of the coincidence of two systems has been raised in sociological literature by Baumgartner's article (already mentioned), and also by Michel Crosier (1963) who has established that the direct relations among all the groups at all levels are friendly or at least fair, the indirect relations among groups at different levels, however, are hostile. Crosier has explained this phenomenon by transformation or sublimation of conflicts which are generated within particular levels to the higher level. With this he has indicated that the system of personal relations can be essentially different from the system of indirect or impersonal relations. If we turn his explanation and show how impersonal status dependences are transformed into personal conflicts which block any interaction, we would complete his picture of bureaucratic organization as a double, mutually dependent and at the same time symbiotic structure of power.

The need for the symbiosis of the two systems in an hierarchical organization problably lies in the fact that the democratized interpersonal system of power activates and motivates the members of an organization; it gives to them the possibility of initiative and the possibility for self-regulation of mutual relations. On the other hand, the function of the impersonal system is to guarantee a relatively stable distribution of power. The changes taking place in interpersonal relations do not affect the stability of status structure of power.

Without the symbiosis mentioned above, the status distribution of power would be completely rigid and, as such, psychologically unacceptable for employees, since they would perceive it as a permanent and insurmountable dependence which can cause only apathy or resistance. With a relative independence of the interpersonal system of power from the status system of power, there appears actual, and temporary, redistribution of power which can represent an important source of initiative and creativeness for the members of an organization.

This symbiosis of two power systems can perhaps also explain Clark Kerr's statement that the basic contradiction of contemporary society lies in the fact that more and more initiatives are expected from employees in their working places, while at the same time their working places are more and more subordinated to the entire system upon which they have no essential influence (Clark Kerr, 1971). Employees have more and more freedom for participation within a less and less free system; the impersonal status system tolerates and even stimulates active power, but because of the impersonal nature of its existence, it prevents emancipation of workers from it.

V THE ROLE OF POLITICAL ORGANIZATIONS IN THE SELF-MANAGEMENT SYSTEM

As we have seen, direct participation of workers is not a satisfactory condition for their political emancipation. This should be reached by other means. The counterpower based on control of political organizations could be one possible way toward the greater equalization of status power. However, the belief held by the Yugoslav political elite that by direct workers' participation, the complete emancipation of workers could be reached, led to the theory that political organizations within the system of self-management are not necessary any more. The Communist Party was removed from work organizations and the activity of the union was substantially diminished, so that the influence of the Communist Party in the years 1969 and 1971 was smaller than the influence of the management groups (see Table 6). At the end of this period, even the foremen had more influence than the party, while the influence of the union was even smaller than that of the party.

The political activity of the union was mainly limited to the yearly assembly and to collecting membership fees. The union did not perform the role of protection of workers' rights; in some cases it even became an instrument of the management. Management frequently exercised moral pressure upon workers through the union, so that some unpopular changes in connection with incomes, reorganization and firing have been explained and supported by the union itself. The opinion that the union was no longer necessary in a developed self-management society and would accordingly disappear, together with the Communist Party and the state, was spread more and more among union leaders themselves; Bogdan Kavčič (1972) reports that 39 percent of trade union presidents in enterprises doubted or did not know whether the union was necessary any more.

Three consequences of the described depoliticization have been registered at the end of the period called liberalism:

— the domination of management over workers' councils;
— the uncontrolled power of top-management and staff in work organizations (see Table 7);
— differentiation and substratification of the blue collar workers.

Among all of the above-mentioned consequences, the differentiation of the working class was the most dangerous for the existence of the self-management system. It happened that in some organizations, the power distance was smaller between skilled workers and supervisors than between skilled and unskilled workers. Furthermore, the skilled workers have been largely over-represented in the workers' councils. Thus, in Yugoslavia in 1972, 49.7 percent of the members of W.C. were skilled workers and only 15.5 percent semi- or unskilled workers, though at the same time 38.2 percent of the employees were semi- or unskilled workers and only 31.8 percent skilled workers.

TABLE 6
Internal active influence: 100 individual organizations; respondents: employees (N = 3000); years 1969, 1970, 1971.

Groups	Actual influence			Desired influence		
	1969	1970	1971	1969	1970	1971
General director	3.91	4.02	4.05	4.14	4.23	4.27
Top management members	3.69	3.77	3.83	3.96	4.07	4.10
Workers' council	3.40	3.55	3.53	4.16	4.27	4.30
Executive committee of W.C.	3.38	3.52	3.41	3.90	4.04	4.05
Middle management	3.41	3.49	3.45	3.87	3.89	3.95
Supervisors	3.05	3.16	3.14	3.65	3.75	3.79
Communist Party	3.13	3.11	2.97	3.57	3.64	3.69
Union	2.80	2.97	2.82	3.67	3.90	3.89
Workers	2.60	2.81	2.75	3.62	3.71	3.85

1 = very small; 2 = small; 3 = medium; 4 = great; 5 = very great influence.

TABLE 7
Eleven industrial organizations in Slovenia; respondents members of Workers' Council (N = 171); year: 1974.

Groups	% of members of W.C. who said that groups are not sufficiently controlled
General director	39
Top management members	60
Professionals (staff)	59
Members of W.C.	18
Functionaries of League of Communists	41
Functionaries of union	26
Heads of plants	39
Supervisors	34
Skilled workers	25
Unskilled and semi-skilled workers	22

Reactivation of political organizations was necessary because it became clear that the system of self-management was more and more controlled by management. Workers' participation could not be politically effective if it was not supported by the counterpower of the political organization.

On the other side, the reactivation of the Communist Party and the union also brought about the possibility of reactivating political bureaucracy. The whole system of self-management was faced by the question of how to liquidate liberalism and yet preserve democracy, and how to establish more equal distribution of status power, yet not to establish some kind of political or etatistic domination over the system of self-management.

The answer to this question was that the increased role of the Communist Party and the union should be accompanied by greater socialization of these organizations. While these organizations should increase their control over the self-management system and build greater counterpower to management in work organizations, they should not make any symbiosis with the state apparatus. Political organizations should be integrated into a self-management system and, at the same time, separated from the state apparatus.

The new constitution, adopted in 1974, institutionally defines the socialization of political organizations. The role of the Communist Party should be socialized above all by its integration with the Socialist Alliance and the union. A closer connection of the party with the Socialist Alliance and union makes possible democratization and openness of the party, since through the media of voluntary organizations, it must develop methods of persuasion and not the coercive methods as established through the media of the state apparatus. The closer collaboration of the party with the union will also strengthen the role of the latter and decrease the apolitical character of it.

The second element of the socialization of the party lies in the fact that the new constitution institutionalizes the role of political organizations (the party and trade unions). Within this, political organizations assume also formal and public responsibility; their role has become legitimate and, thus, also responsible; this means that socialization of power increases together with the growing status power; institutionalization of responsibility becomes an essential condition for socialization of power.

The third element of the socialization of political power lies in the incorporation of political organizations into the institutional system of the state. This, however, does not mean growing etatism in political organizations, since they are integrated into the representative and not into the executive system of the state. Political organizations are, namely, given a special place in the new representative system, which is called the delegate system. Besides working organizations and local communities, political organizations also form their delegations at all of the levels of the institutional system. In this way they should strengthen the delegate system in relation to the executive apparatus and, at the same time, should insure the promotion of equality, solidarity and other long-term interests of the working class inside the delegate system.

With the new constitution, the union assumes many functions inside working organizations and also at the level of inter-organizational relationships. The union should no longer be a politically neutral organization, controlled by the local management, but should, according to the provisions of the constitution, perform the following functions within work organizations:

(a) it should assume the responsibility for forming the lists of candidates for all the leading and self-management organs in enterprises;

(b) it should have the role of mediator in case of strikes and other conflicts among employees, for which no formal procedure has been anticipated;

(c) it should support the newly established system of workers' control which supervises both the top management and workers' councils if they follow agreements and other self-management regulations;

(d) it should pay special attention to the work environment and security at work.

The role of trade unions will be of no lesser importance in regulating mutual relations among work organizations: trade unions will initiate, regulate, criticize and suggest changes for social compacts and self-management agreements. The trade unions should be responsible for bringing in accordance the development plans, and for the formation of the principles of distribution of income; they should insure the principle of solidarity and unity of the working class and establish its long-term interests.

By all of these institutional changes the counterpower should be built into the status system and, therefore, the geater equilibrium of the whole status power should be re-established. The behavioral power of workers, based on their direct participation, should be placed by these changes into a more proper frame of status power.

NOTES

1. This research is based on secondary data analysis of nine work organizations and on primary data collected by representative sample of 842 employees.
2. Active power is exercised by a focal group upon the other groups within an organization, while passive power is exercised by other groups upon the focal one. In this case, workers are the focal group.
3. In this article, influence and power are taken as synonymous to avoid theoretical discussions about their conceptual differences.

REFERENCES

Arzenšek, Vladimir (1970), *Komparativna analiza participacije in socialnih vrednot*, Ljubljana: Institut za sociologijo in filozofijo v Ljubljani.

Baumgartner, T., W. Buckley, T. Burns and P. Schuster (1976), 'Meta-Power and the Structuring of Social Hierarchies,' in T. Burns and W. Buckley (eds.): *Power and Control*, London: Sage Publications.

Crosier, Michel (1963), *Le phenomene bureaucratique*. Paris: Edition du Seuil.

Kardelj, Edvard (1976), Delo, ponedeljek 19. aprila, Ljubljana (speech in the Assembly).

Kavcic, Bogdan (1972), 'Položaj sindikata v delovni organizaciji,' *Teorija in praksa*, Vol. 9, No. 10.

Kerr, Clark (1971), 'Post-Scriptum a l'industrialisme et le travailleur industriel,' *Revue Internationale du Travail*, Vol. 106, No. 6.

Mohr, Lawrence (1917), 'Organizational Technology and Organizational Structure,' *Administrative Science Quarterly*, Vol. 16, No. 3.

Možina, Stane (1971), *Interes samoupravljalcev za odločanje*, Ljubljana: RCEF.

Perrow, Charles (1970), 'Departmental Power and Perspective in Industrial Firms,' in M. N. Zald (ed.), *Power in Organizations*, Nashville, Tenn.: Vanderbild University Press.

Rus, Veljko (1974), *Empirična analiza samoupravne aktivnosti v devetih slovenskih TOZD-ih*, Ljubljana: FSPN.

Tannenbaum, Arnold (1974), *Hierarchy in Organizations*, San Francisco: Jossey Bass Publications.

Županov, Josip (1972), 'Soudlučivanje radnika i socialna moč u industriji,' *Organizacija i kadrovi*, Vol. 6, No. 5.

7

SYSTEMS OF DOMINATION, ACCOMMODATION AND INDUSTRIAL DEMOCRACY

Eric Batstone
University of Warwick, UK

The practice of industrial democracy has generally failed to match expectations. Works councils and joint consultative committees provide few opportunities for worker power. Worker representation at board level in companies has generally 'had little effect on anything'. Experience is similar under self-management and in worker co-operatives (Batstone, 1976).

Numerous explanations have been put forward for this state of affairs. Many so-called 'democratic' schemes are very weak: for example, workers may have only consultative rather than decision-making rights and then only in a limited number of areas; they may not have equal representation with management or shareholders on various bodies; worker representatives may be bound by restrictive rules of confidentiality; worker representatives may be structurally isolated from the key power-points within worker organizations more generally; and so on. Few would deny that the correction of these weaknesses is important. Similarly, it is clear that the larger structure of society limits the extent to which any meaningful form of industrial democracy can become a reality.

Other explanations for the limited success of democratic practice stress that a period of learning and experimentation is inevitable. Again, this is quite true. But the nagging question is whether this period will lead to an extension or diminution of democratic expectations and experience. For while there are undoubtedly a range of factors in society which are favourable to industrial democracy, there are others which work in the opposite direction.

It may also be suggested that it is impossible to achieve a totally democratic form of industrial organization. A degree of hierarchy is inevitable, for work has to be co-ordinated and skills and expertise will be differentially distributed among people. But even if one takes this point into account, it can scarcely be argued that the experience of the 'democratic' operation of industrial enterprises matches what might reasonably be expected.

In this paper, I want to focus upon certain aspects of industrial organization which are important obstacles to industrial democracy. In some senses, much of my discussion can be seen as pursuing argument similar to those of Michels (1962) in his 'iron law of oligarchy'. 'Who says organization, says oligarchy.' However, it would be wrong to suggest that those obstacles cannot be overcome. The point is that unless we are aware of them and actively attempt to resolve the problems they raise, then the future of industrial democracy is a dismal one. As Selznick argues:

> The point of anti-utopian criticism is not that it denigrates ideals. Rather it asks that such ideals as self-government be given their proper place in human affairs. Ideals are definers of aspirations. They are judgment upon us. But they are not surrogates for operative goals. The latter have the special virtue, and suffer the peculiar hardship, of striving to be reasonably adequate renderings of the moral ideal while taking due account of the human condition and the historical setting. A practical goal that does not rise to opportunities is unworthy; but one that ignores limitations invites its own corruption (1966; x-xi).

My arguments draw quite strongly upon my own research experience, particularly in relation to worker directors (Brannen et al., 1976; Batstone and Davies, 1976) and constitute the early stages of planning a further research project in the area of industrial democracy. More specifically, in this paper I attempt to consider a few points which can be derived from the work of Max Weber. The first of these is the way in which power derives from rules, these in turn reflecting a larger system of domination (for a discussion of this interpretation of Weber, see Clegg, 1975). Taking this as a starting point, I argue that the whole nature of organizational arrangements is political not merely in terms of the differential distribution of authority, but also — and more importantly — in terms of the permeation of rules, roles and procedures by particular sets of values, goals and priorities. Unless these procedures and rules are dramatically changed, the possibility for democratic practice is inevitably limited.

The second part of my argument can be conveniently located in Weber's distinction between formal and substantive rationality. 'Substantive rationality cannot be measured in terms of formal calculation alone, but also involves a relation to the absolute values or to the content of the particular ends to which it is oriented' (1947: 185). In other words, the system of domination by rules and procedures may be incomplete or become misdirected. The distinction between formal and substantive rationality means that organizational behavior involves a continual 'negotiation of order'. This may provide some opportunities for democratic influence, but it seems that often coalitions which determine the direction of organizational activity serve to cut worker representatives out of the key processes of decision-making.

DOMINATION AND ROUTINIZATION

It is obvious, but important, to note that organizational behavior occurs within a larger context. That larger context imposes constraints upon the extent to which particular courses of action can be consistently pursued in the long-term. Unless some form of external aid is forthcoming, for example, a company which fails to make a profit cannot survive indefinitely in a market economy.

However, the larger structure of the economy does not totally predetermine enterprise behaviour. Competition in a market economy may be strong or weak; in addition, there is invariably *some* room for manoeuvre in terms of the goals pursued. A number of authors have argued that, within capitalist economies, the dominant goals pursued by companies have changed as control has shifted from owners to a professional management. The accuracy of this view is not the point at issue here. Rather, the example is used to suggest that there may be conflict among groups in terms of whose priorities should dominate, and, within limits, the outcome of such conflict may not endanger the continued existence of the enterprise.

The problem is how far the larger context of industrial activity does constrain options. Certainly it constitutes a structure of domination which has to be taken account of by actors. For them it is a fact of life (although possibly susceptible to some manipulation) (Weber, 1968: 33). Given this larger institutional context, further systems of domination are built up in the form of organizations to achieve the ends of their creators. By laying down rules and procedures an attempt is made to create a largely taken-for-granted world for the participant such that his behaviour furthers the goals of those in control of the organization. Routinization, the very essence of organization, builds in assumptions and priorities such that some interests and issues are highlighted and others squashed. This feature of organization can be conveniently considered in terms of two areas: the notion of expertise and the nature of accounting systems.

THE NATURE OF EXPERTISE

A crucial element in Weber's ideal type of bureaucracy is that the incumbents of positions should have the requisite ability and expertise. The way in which these skills are defined rests ultimately upon the priorities fostered by those who control the organization and by the larger system of domination. Many new forms of expertise are specifically sponsored by the state or industry; those which are not may quickly find themselves 'taken over' and shaped by the dominant groups within industry. Haber, for example, has shown how the grand claims for scientific management have become modified so as not to endanger the position of higher management but to further their purposes (1964).

Put at its crudest, unless particular areas of activity are defined as problematical (or potentially so) then experts will not develop. For example, in Britain over the past few decades there has been a remarkable growth in the number of personnel and industrial relations specialists. This growth of a body of 'experts' can only be understood in the context of companies believing that workers' actions are becoming increasingly important and are obstructing corporate goals. The rise of industrial relations as a specialism does not define worker action as legitimate or as a proper democratic expression. Rather it seeks to 'deal with', 'control', 'induce' workers to be fully committed to 'enterprise goals'. Challenges by workers are seen 'as indications of moral weakness, sectional greed, blind conservatism, or simply an inability to grasp the fact that times have changed. Most of the responses defined as "management's labour problems" are open to be stigmatised in this way' (Fox, 1974: 349). These are the sorts of assumptions built into the role of industrial relations manager. 'Problems' are reflected in the shape of the evolving skills.

Marcuse has argued that 'Specific purposes and interests of domination are not foisted upon technology "subsequently" and from the outside; they enter the very construction of the technical apparatus. Technology is always a historical-social project: in it is projected .what a society and its ruling interests intend to do with men and things' (1968:223-4). I am trying to suggest that the same is true of expertise more generally. However, this is not to say that no types of expertise can be diverted to other sets of purposes. In principle, it seems possible to divide expertise into a number of kinds. First, some bodies of 'knowledge' and skill have meaning *only* because of the larger system of domination. Any successful attempt to change the priorities of industrial activity would therefore require the demise of this kind of expertise. Second, other types of skills may not be intrinsically biassed although their historical development has reflected the priorities of dominant groups. Industrial democracy would therefore require a thorough rethinking of the knowledge which has been built-up to remove the bias built into its evolution (Elliott and Elliott, 1976). Third, there may be some types of expertise which could fit quite easily into a fully democratic organization. (But while skills may be intrinsically neutral they can achieve a political hue from the larger context in which they are pursued [Baritz, 1965].)

It would be difficult to establish the relative importance of these three kinds of expertise without a good deal of careful study. But there seems little doubt that many specialisms would fall into the second category, for knowledge does not simply grow; conscious endeavours have to be made to achieve understanding. The development of knowledge therefore reflects the purposes of those in a position to sponsor and control the pursuit of knowledge. And the specialist or expert becomes accustomed to working within a particular perspective and set of essentially political assumptions. The latter point has been frequently made in relation to computer technology. It *can* be used for democratic purposes, but the great majority of computer technicians employ their skills to facilitate the goals of a corporate elite. The same point is evident in discussions of the rise of a new, technological working-class. It is argued that the technical experts of the 'post-industrial society' will begin to demand that their skills be used to more socially constructive ends. Evidence in support of this view is as yet limited. More relevant to the present discussion is the implication of this thesis that in the past and present (if not in the future) technical experts have taken for granted the perspectives embodied in their more general work situation. The purposes to which they put their expertise, and hence its pattern of development, reaffirm particular priorities and the existence of a hierarchical structure.

It has often been argued that scientists and professional groups hold values which contradict the primary goals of employers. Scientists are committed to the advancement of knowledge and professionals to their own ethics and the good of the community. However, the degree of conflict can be easily exaggerated. Research indicates that many scientists in industry demonstrate rather less commitment to wider values than those, for example, who pursue academic careers. In addition, controls upon research scientists can effectively constrain their freedom to pursue goals other than those of dominant groups (Cotgrove and Box, 1970). Professional autonomy rests upon a monopoly over the right to engage in the relevant area of activity; this depends upon some form of organizational edict and relative weakness on the part of clients. But within an industrial enterprise the client is also the sponsor: he can remove or qualify the monopoly of the professional.

Nevertheless, it is still probable that experts seek a degree of autonomy. Relative freedom from larger constraints is the key characteristic of an occupation termed a profession or a craft. The terms 'profession' and 'craft' have less to do with intrinsic skills than the ability to enforce a certain exclusivity. The claim to expertise is largely a political exercise aimed at improving security, status and other rewards. By his political activity, the professional seeks to define what may be crucial political issues as essentially technical matters which can be safely and properly left to him. The attempt to maintain a monopoly and the claim to competence may also serve to prevent the development of more useful means to resolve problems or methods which would get to the roots of problems rather than simply tinkering with symptoms. Such criticisms are commonly levelled against craft groups. But it applies with equal, if not greater, force to many professions (and other expert groups): the medical profession is one obvious case. Some specialisms also have an interest in the continuation of particular problems. For example, industrial relations experts would soon be out of jobs if labour problems ceased to exist (or ceased to be defined as 'problems').

It is clear that experts do occasionally achieve a good deal of power in some companies and on particular occasions (Wilensky, 1967). But dominance by a group of experts may often be limited by the conflicting interests and perspectives of different types of expertise. More important in industry is the structure of the enterprise. Experts are also managers with their own hierarchy. At the peak of these hierarchies selection appears to be based not so much upon the readiness to protect expertise as the readiness to accept the assumptions of the dominant management team (Nichols, 1969). There exist, therefore, trusted brokers who can mediate between specialisms and general management.

Brokerage roles are all the more important because experts develop their own codes of practice, bodies of theory and language. In part, these are necessary in order to create and develop expertise and bodies of knowledge. They may also be part of a strategy to achieve exclusiveness and autonomy. But for whatever reason they arise, their effects are the same: they act as barriers against intrusion by outsiders. Brokerage is therefore crucial.

The current nature of expertise creates numerous problems for industrial democracy. As I have argued, it is necessary to identify the political bias in specialisms and attempt to correct them. This is not likely to happen unless a concerted effort is made and the very foundations of some bodies of expertise are seriously challenged. But in most societies the brokers who can most easily undertake this task are part of the more general management team and may therefore have rather limited sympathy with the cause of industrial democracy. Even if the management team is threatened by democracy, the brokers can still take the option of retreating into the mystifications of their specialisms in order to maintain power. The end result of attempts at democratization could therefore be an extension of the autonomy and power of experts whose perspectives and skills run counter to the interests of workers, and this may be legitimized by apparently democratic structures. This argument is not to deny totally the validity of 'expertise'; rather, it is to suggest that its limits are problematical.

ACCOUNTING SYSTEMS AS VOCABULARIES OF MOTIVE

The previous section has discussed one aspect of organization: the routinization of the dominant group's goals in terms of expertise. Another aspect is the setting up of procedures which facilitate the division of tasks, the flow of information, the integration of activities and the overall assessment of performance. This occurs in the belief that it is possible to calculate (or gain calculable proximations to) and predict aspects of corporate activity which will further the ordained goals of the organization. Company procedures embody a conception of a larger body of political purposes, if only imperfectly. This is most obviously true of accounting systems. Given the importance of financial viability for a capitalist enterprise, it is logical that a key feature of routinization should be an attempt to maintain a close check upon the inflow and outflow of cash. Systems of data collection and interpretation are therefore set up — more or less competently — which reflect the priorities thought to lead to profitability.

Accounting systems do far more than simply record aspects of financial performance. To the extent that they constitute a key feature of organizational procedures, they determine the terms of legitimate debate. Discussion focusses upon financial criteria; other factors are, of course, relevant but they either derive their meaning from the pursuit of profit or act merely as secondary constraints. At the least, accounting systems constitute an important means of setting the terms of debate within an enterprise, for they place primacy upon capital rather than labour.

The more general meaning of the term 'account' indicates this clearly. As Scott and Lyman point out with reference to the sociological importance of talk:

> Our concern here is with one feature of talk: its ability to shore up the timbers of
> fractured sociation, its ability to throw bridges between the promised and the
> performed, its ability to repair the broken and restore the estranged. This feature
> of talk involves the giving and receiving of what we shall call *accounts*.
>   An account is a linguistic device employed whenever an action is subjected to
> valuative inquiry. Such devices are a crucial element in the social order since they
> prevent conflicts from arising by verbally bridging the gap between action and
> expectation. Moreover, accounts are 'situated' according to the statuses of the
> interactants, and are standarized within cultures so that certain accounts are ter-
> minologically stabilized and routinely expected when activity falls outside the do-
> main of expectations (1968:46).

As these authors remark, the idea of an account has a certain resemblance to Weber's notion of a motive as a socially 'adequate ground for the conduct in question' (1947:98-9). C. Wright Mills has developed this idea in his discussion of vocabularies of motive. He points out that 'men discern situations with particular vocabularies' and they anticipate the consequences of actions in terms of these same vocabularies: 'In a *social* situation, implicit in the names for consequences is the social dimension of motives. Through such vocabularies types of societal controls operate' (1967:441-2).

A number of examples may be useful in developing this feature of accounting systems. In one large multinational company the key features of the monthly balance sheet are stocks, balances, profits and six ratios: sales to capital, profit and sales, profit to employees, sales to stock, sales to debtors, and sales to employees. This system makes, it is claimed, 'every manager in the group acutely conscious of fractions of a penny, and personal responsibility for profit has been raised to virtually unparalleled peaks'.

Management by exception, particularly when linked to detailed operating plans, indicates the nature of accounting systems as vocabularies of motive. Achievement of targets as laid down in the plans is its own legitimation; the fact that the targets may be partial and not in fact lead to a very high level of profitability ceases to be important. As long as the manager achieves the forecast level of performance, no questions are asked of him. It is only when he fails to do so that he has to explain his actions. His justifications for failure may well be primarily oriented to the detailed features of the accounting system; and endeavours to improve performance will, of course, be oriented to the operating plan, for this constitutes the vocabulary of motive.

The importance of this aspect of accounting systems is also seen when comparisons are made between the priorities, activities and language of managers operating under different control systems. For example, in one engineering plant the control system placed a great deal of emphasis upon reducing the amount of scrap. This was reflected in managers' behaviour; they continually tried to minimize scrap and their discussion was dominated by this priority. In another similar factory the control system did not include scrap levels but focussed upon achieving high levels of output. Breakdowns and labour disputes were the dominant concerns of these managers; scrap rarely entered into their priorities.

The manipulation of accounting systems is perhaps the best indication of their role as vocabularies of motive, for the act of manipulation recognizes that the system of cost controls constitutes the main means of legitimating activity. So, for example, in one plant studied, production managers had budgets relating to wages and manning, overtime, special allowances for workers, and so on. In order to win worker co-operation they might be forced to provide additional allowances. When, however, they had reached the maximum on this budget, they put further allowances under some other budgetary heading. In the same way, production and maintenance managers each had their own budgets for breakdowns and repairs. Particularly when they approached their allowed expenditure in this area, production managers attempted to persuade the maintenance manager to agree to putting the costs of breakdowns on his budget. These attempts to manipulate procedures recognize their importance in setting the terms of 'legitimate' debate (Weber, 1968:32).

Accounting systems therefore operate as vocabularies of motive in a number of ways. They reflect the priorities of the dominant groups and indicate to more junior managers the way in which they are expected to behave. They set the terms of debate. Achievement of plans and targets is its own legitimation, and, generally, management attempt to do exactly that. Where they feel they cannot do so, then managers often attempt, by manipulation or other means, to provide accounts of their actions in terms of the dominant vocabularies of motive. At a more general level, the power of these vocabularies is to be seen in the arguments which workers employ in relation to their employers when there are proposals to close their plant. As one study found, workers invariably argue that their plants are profitable or could become so in the company's terms. 'In other words the arguments against closure put to the corporation were primarily of an economic nature; they were *argumenta ad hominem* based upon the values and priorities of the corporation itself...the structure of power required that workers adopt the sorts of arguments which were legitimate in the eyes of the powerful' (Brannen et al., 1976:206).

I have argued that procedures within companies tend to set the terms of debate and the vocabularies of motive. The implications for industrial democracy are obvious. It is necessary not only to change the persons who formally hold power but also to ensure that new priorities are reflected in accounting systems. Otherwise the perspectives of those whose role is the identification of problems and the formulation of solutions are likely to counter the aims of the democratic formality of the organization. Again, this is no easy task, but it requires at the minimum that systems such as social audits are given as much weight as conventional accounting procedures.

CHANGE AND ACCOMMODATION

There is a strong tendency towards industrial concentration in the capitalist economy. Competition means that some firms grow, and others die. Even when large size is not accompanied by specific advantages such as economies of scale, there is still a tendency for industrial concentration to increase (Prais, 1976). As companies have grown in size, they have been forced to develop more routinized procedures and have made greater use of those considered to be 'experts'. Chandler has argued that it is possible to trace a typical pattern of changing organizational structure in American companies as new strategies have been adopted (1962).

Large enterprises developed with the growth of the railroads and required new forms of administration. By the late nineteenth century other large enterprises were finding it necessary to divide their organizations into a series of specialized functions. In addition, increasing organizational size and complexity led to the development of a professional management. Under this new direction, companies sought to maintain or improve their position by seeking new

markets and sources of supplies or by expanding their range of products. Geographical expansion and diversification created problems for the old functional system of administration. Even at the
highest levels of the organization, the specialists became over-
involved in day-to-day problems while no-one was able to take an
overall perspective which was essential for long-term planning and
assessing company performance. Accordingly, Chandler argues,
companies began to adopt a multidivisional structure with four different types of executive position. At the top of the organization a
general office was established, manned by general executives and
staff specialists, to 'co-ordinate, appraise and plan goals and
policies and allocate resources for a number of quasi-autonomous,
fairly self-contained divisions'. Each division dealt with one major
product or a particular geographical area; it had its own central office made up of a number of departments, each responsible for a
major function. In turn, the departmental headquarters 'coor-
dinates, appraises and plans for a number of field units. At the
lowest level, each field unit was a plant or works, a branch or
district sales office' (1962:9). Such a multidivisional structure is
becoming common in Britain (Channon, 1972) and in the rest of
Europe (Franko, 1974).

The implications of such a company structure are clear. The
room for lower level bodies to develop their own policies is formally limited: they can only (legitimately) operate within the constraints set by the general and central offices, and at the same time
procedures are established which guide, and act as a check upon
their actions. Specialists, often divorced in terms of background,
skill and geographical location from those in the operating units,
play a major part in policy formulation. The role of procedures and
experts which has been discussed above becomes that much greater.
Strategic decisions are based less upon the performance of individual operating units or divisions than upon how key members
of the general office conceive the overall interests of the company
(Brooke and Remmers, 1970). Conflicts of interest are therefore
likely, and it is by no means certain that lower levels of the
organization will not seek to manipulate procedures and act independently, believing that the accounting system fails to take account of important facets of their organizational activity. In other
words, a disjunction exists between formal and substantive rationality.

The Partial Nature of Formal Rationality

Despite the growth of expertise and routinization, the formal rationality of organization is inevitably incomplete in terms of meeting the substantive goals held by the dominant group. Systems of formal rationality contain the assumption that it is possible to calculate events and in order to do this they build in further assumptions of frequently limited validity concerning their subjects. Alfred Marshall made this point strongly in a rather different context:

> In my view every economic fact, whether or not it is of such a nature as to be expressed in numbers, stands in relation to cause and effect to many other facts, and since it *never* happens that all of them can be expressed in numbers, the application of exact mathematical methods to those which can is nearly always a waste of time, while in the large majority of cases it is positively misleading; and the world would have been further on its way forward if the work had never been done at all (1901).

A similar point is made by Stobaugh in discussing company attempts to develop rating scales for determining a country's investment climate. He points out that the various elements in the rating scale may in reality have different effects on different projects and that the climate may change during the life of a project. Some companies have attempted to allow for these difficulties but, Stobaugh concludes, 'in practice such corrections become so complicated and arbitrary that they mainly serve to highlight the difficulties in assigning proper weights and in selecting a proper risk premium' (1969).

In the same way that much organizational endeavour is oriented towards making the environment more predictable, so is much thought given to reducing uncertainty within it. Duties and responsibilities of individuals should be predictable. In other words, the essence of organization is that a person in one position can act on the assumption that his behaviour will fit neatly with, and be consistent with, the behaviour of others. The activity of each organization member is theoretically limited and oriented to particular goals. This provides a basic paradox of organization. An industrial enterprise typically attempts to change — to grow, to become more profitable within a changing situation — but its organization may work against this aim precisely because it seeks to limit the amount of innovative activity on the part of most of its members. This paradox exists both because of the limits of responsibility involved in organizational position and because of the bias noted previously in the sorts of organizational priorities, information-collection and analysis procedures which are created (Wilensky, 1967).

A further limit to formal rationality is that rules are by their very nature general. In any situation, the actor has to define the rules as relevant and may have to choose between conflicting rules (Batstone, 1976a). Even when an actor attempts to achieve his superior's ends rather than his own, the application of rules is a problematical process (Zimmerman, 1971). But rules may also be used by actors as a means of diverting organizational purposes for they may provide a defence and hence a source of power for members of an organization (Crozier, 1964). I have already touched upon this aspect in discussing the strategies of experts, but the use of rules as a defence and an obstruction is much more widespread. In many organizations, activity is only saved from absurdity because members consistently break rules. It is for this reason that 'working to rule' can be such an effective sanction. Miller and Form make broadly similar points concerning the nature of organization:

> Although formal organization is designed to subject production to logical planning, things never seem to go 'according to plan.' This is evidenced by the many 'problems' managers encounter. They find that no matter how carefully they organize, despite the concern in anticipating problems, unanticipated ones always arise. For these eventualities formal organization offers little guidance because it is created as a guidepost for the routine, the typical and the foreseeable (1951).

It is not surprising, therefore, to find that managers spend a good deal of time on activities which they do not define as central to their task; indeed, much of their time is spent in undertaking 'abnormal' tasks. The point is that normality, as seen by managers, appears to be a rare event (Burns, 1954). Consistent with this, it has often been found that managers spend a great deal of their time in contact with each other: since organizational procedures fail to provide the requisite understanding, they have to engage in networks of contacts which will provide some insight into what is happening (Dubin, 1962). Management activity does not conform to rational models of decison-making; rather, it is often characterized by brevity, variety, fragmentation and superficiality (Mintzberg, 1973).

Accommodation and Negotiation

In the preceding section I have pointed to the inevitable incompleteness of routinization. As a consequence, managers are forced to develop networks of relationships through which they can reach some understanding of events within the enterprise. Such knowledge relates not merely to technical issues and events, but also to the changing fortunes of various factions within the company. It is not just idle chatter when managers discuss events and personalities within their companies. They are building up and developing notions of the real power structure and thereby they can more effectively determine their own courses of action.

It is clear that there is a continual 'negotiation of order' in organizations. Action and inaction are always problematical. Negotiation is inevitable, for 'order is something at which members of any society, any organization must work. For the shared agreements, the binding contracts — which constitute the grounds for an expectable, non-surprising, taken-for-granted, even ruled orderliness — are not binding and shared for all time. . .the bases of concerted action (social order) must be reconstituted continually' (Strauss et al., 1971: 103-4). Negotiation occurs throughout an enterprise; its existence is indicated, for example, even at the 'lowest' levels in industry by the development of 'informal' agreements, custom and practice, and 'ca' canny' (Brown, 1977). Such lower-level negotiation may often constitute an evasion of, or accommodation to, the larger system of domination (Roy, 1954); its by-product may be to prevent major problems coming to the attention of those in superordinate positions.

The extent to which negotiation serves to 'warp' the organizational structure seems to vary considerably. The actual process of decision differs according to such factors as ownership, history, organizational environment, the detailed nature of formal control systems, and so on. Burns and Stalker, for example, found that in the same industry the more adaptable companies had a more organic form of organization which largely ignored the niceties of function, status and formal responsibility. The fluid pattern of networks recognized that constantly changing conditions gave 'rise constantly to fresh problems and unforeseen requirements for action which cannot be broken down or distributed automatically arising from the functional roles defined within a hierarchic structure' (1961:121).

Patterns of negotiation often mean that real decision-making does not occur at points in the organizational structure which constitutionally have such powers. This is clearly seen in the case of many boards of directors. As the National Swedish Industrial Board concluded, 'the substance of power is vested in management and not the board of directors. ...in many cases the board of directors is a passive institution, an institution "in the hands of" the managing director and his assistants' (1976:27). Similar conclusions were reached in a British survey of board room practice (British Institute of Management, 1972:3) and in a number of American studies (e.g. Mace, 1971; Gordon, 1961).

There are a number of reasons why the board, at least where shareholdings are widely dispersed, should play such a small role in the negotiation of order. Managers (including in this term full-time executive directors) are 'experts' who inevitably achieve considerable influence because of their formal role which provides them with authority, detailed knowledge (of a kind) and information (Mechanic, 1962), and with large resources in terms of personnel. Boards, which generally meet only rarely, are at a severe disadvantage (Batstone, 1976:21). Furthermore, management typically originate and formulate proposals (Gordon, 1961:128). They are able to 'shape' problems so that what would be basic issues to some are sketched over or become hidden assumptions (March and Simon, 1958; Carter, 1971). Proposals and accounts may therefore be designed as much to 'screen' as to illuminate (Pahl and Winkler, 1974:109; on self-management enterprises, see Benson [1974:259-62] for a similar argument). Finally, the room for decision-making is also reduced by the manner in which past decisions serve to cut out present options.

The networks of negotiation have significance in two respects. First, they may change the pattern of power within the organization: the distribution of power is therefore problematical, and this will be discussed in a moment. Second, it is through negotiation that policies may be determined and then 'dressed up' to have a wider legitimacy. Networks are crucial to successful manipulation. In this respect, the rules and procedures within a company may become simply rituals (Cleverley, 1973). For example, companies often lay down minimum rates of return for investment projects: unless these are met, then no project will be accepted. But interviews show that managers quite openly admit that they 'cook the figures' in order to ensure that their own hunches and preferences meet the formal requirtements. As Cleverley notes, if the requisite rates of return are increased, the figures relating to any proposal 'will be improved accordingly'. But by manipulating the organizational vocabularies of motive, groups of managers make it difficult for others to challenge their proposals: 'there is no way in which the person analyzing the project can contest those figures — unless he can find a flaw in the performance of the projection rituals' (Cleverley, 1973:77).

The process of formulating plans and proposals is itself a very political process. The reduction of alternatives and the gradual commitment to particular options is in part a reflection of the relative power of different individuals and groups. At the same time this process has implications for the future balance of power: the decision to invest in a particular plant strengthens the power of managers in that plant, while the decision to reduce the level of activity in a plant is likely to reduce the power of its managers. Moreover, the evolution of a proposal serves to strengthen the unity of the 'winning' coalition as its members make further political investments in its success and their careers become closely tied to the final acceptance of the proposal.

The significance of these political processes can be seen in the case of a number of companies merging. Over a period of time one former company, which I will call Zedco, came to dominate the new corporation even though it accounted for only a minor part of the new organization. Investment tended to be disproportionately concentrated upon former Zedco plants. And, when other plants were allocated large capital projects, there was a strong tendency for former Zedco managers to be appointed to key positions in those plants. The key decision-making groups had become dominated by former Zedco managers and this was reflected in the investment and appointment policies of the new corporation.

From the viewpoint of the dominant Zedco group their appointment policy was quite logical. They trusted their former Zedco colleagues and shared common priorities and assumptions; there was also a pre-existing network of relationships. Negotiation could therefore occur more easily if key positions were held by Zedco men. But this policy had further consequences. As the Zedco network became more important, managers from the other merging companies felt themselves increasingly isolated; they found they could not get their 'voices heard in the magic circle'. They lacked the contacts to feed their wishes into the deliberations of the Zedco experts at the general office. Consequently, decisions tended to become even more biassed towards those establishments run by former Zedco managers, those which were already receiving a disproportionate amount of investment funds. This example shows clearly, then, the way in which the networks of negotiation permitted manipulation of procedures and thereby fostered particular courses of action as against others.

If networks are so significant, it is clearly important to know what factors affect membership. Networks are likely to overlap and also vary according to issue. Generally, managers will seek out those whose aid is essential to their stratagems and seek to minimize the involvement of those likely to obstruct their endeavours (Batstone et al., 1977). While management coalitions may sometimes include workers or other outside groups (e.g. Chandler, 1964), there will be a tendency to exclude these sorts of people. Where they are powerful, then a variety of strategies may be used to prevent them becoming too fully involved in the key management coalition. Middlemen (Bailey, 1969) may be used in an attempt to gain some idea of worker attitudes without having to give them access to 'the inner circle'. Or specific institutions may be set up to give workers a voice but to isolate them from the real decision-making processes. Even when workers are put onto formally key bodies, these may become isolated from the key networks as managers shift their political activities to other points in the organization (cf. Selznick, 1966). For the essence of networks is that they are flexible and fluid; their key activities may easily be shifted from one committee to another, or to the dining room or to informal discussions at any location or time. It is therefore difficult to keep them in check.

Membership of key coalitions is not solely dependent upon power. It is also likely to be influenced by the occupancy of roles which bring persons together frequently: this suggests that key coalitions will be made up of those who are relatively senior in the organizational hierarchy. This proximity also means that key coalition members tend to operate on broadly similar sets of information. They are also likely to develop common perspectives on the way in which the company operates and should operate. Finally, proximity in the organization may facilitate the development of trust, a vital ingredient if coalitions are to be united and effective. For if the coalition is to attempt to cut others out of decision-making and is to seek to create a veneer of inevitability around the outcome of its deliberations, it has to be sure that no member will betray its activities. For example, if a member were to reveal the real political considerations underlying a particular proposal, then disaffected groups would have something on which to base concerted opposition. There may, of course, be occasions on which key coalitions break up and then others, including workers, may have an opportunity to play a real role in influencing policy. But if top management are careful in their selection and socialization procedures and insuring that no one member becomes too disaffected, 'institutional integrity' can be maintained (Selznick, 1957).

The importance of shared perspectives and trust at the higher levels of organizations is seen clearly in the emphasis commonly placed by top management upon the acceptability of their colleagues and upon mutual trust. This explains why in most multinationals boards are made up solely of persons from the 'home' country of the company. As the chairman of a multinational explained: 'We have to be able to speak freely together, and trust each other implicitly' (Tugendhat, 1973:234). If key groups are suspicious of 'foreigners' they are likely to be even more strongly opposed to the possibility of workers becoming formally involved in key decisions. This appears to be so; in their evidence to the Bullock Committee on worker representation at board level in Britain, many companies demonstrated the fear that worker directors would break up the 'effective working relationships' which had developed among the company elite.

It is little wonder, then, that where worker directors are required by law some companies shift the locus of real decision-making away from areas in which the worker director might become involved (Batstone, 1976:26). (Often this is not necessary because the board is relatively insignificant.) Where this is not done, then pressures are imposed upon worker directors to accept the priorities of the dominant group. The acceptance of these priorities often ap-

pears to be the quid pro quo for anything resembling membership
of the key coalitions (Batstone, 1976:25). But, even so, worker
representatives may seldom become fully integrated into the central
networks since they do not conform totally to the criteria for
membership of the team. A crucial problem for industrial
democracy, then, is exactly how one attempts to change the key
networks within companies.

CONCLUSIONS

In this paper I have attempted to look at a few aspects of organizational behaviour which are likely to be significant obstacles to industrial democracy unless they are consciously taken account of
and concerted attempts made to overcome them. Specifically, I
have stressed the manner in which the growth of expertise and the
nature of procedures within companies embody particular assumptions and priorities which may be inimical to any significant
democratic expression. I have also argued that the networks central
to the development of corporate strategy are often of such a kind
that worker representatives either find it difficult to become involved in them or have to change radically their world-views in order to
achieve any significant degree of involvement.

Nor are these problems confined to partial schemes of industrial
democracy common in many European countries. They apply with
similar force to more radical systems. For the formal institutionalization of worker co-operatives or self-management does not
overnight remove history. Experts still rely upon a traditional body
of knowledge; procedures may be only marginally changed; and if
managers still hold their positions their closed networks may still
have great significance. Indeed, it is possible that the power of experts and top management increases under so-called democratic
systems. Not only may traditional educational systems foster the
old assumptions of expertise, but the expert and the manager may
find their roles strengthened precisely because democratic forms
can be used to legitimate and buttress oligarchic practice. Such
eventualities may occur through the conspiratorial activities of
managers opposed to democratic notions. But they may equally occur through the best of intentions: experts may sincerely believe

that their 'knowledge' is important and fail to recognize the bias involved in that knowledge. Similarly, managers may fail to realize the full implications of a democratic structure and — advertently or inadvertently — use it as a means of manipulation; and accounting systems may still embody notions of the priority of capital rather than labour. The end result may therefore be a growing disillusionment on the part of all, or an even greater managerial dominance garbed in a democratic rhetoric. This may reflect itself not only within the industrial enterprise but also in the wider society (e.g. Vuskovic, 1976; Pateman, 1970).

It is not, therefore, sufficient to develop democratic models of organization based upon philosophical notions and constitutional niceties. These are, of course, important; but in addition it is necessary to have a fuller sociological understanding of the way in which organizations actually operate before engaging in social engineering. One further note of caution might usefully form the conclusion of this paper. We who study industrial democracy tend to define ourselves as experts and the arguments concerning expertise which I have outlined above apply with equal force to us. There is a danger that we, with the most noble of intentions, foster the growth of a new paternalism.

REFERENCES

Bailey, F. G. (1969), *Stratagems and Spoils: A Social Anthropology of Politics*. Oxford: Blackwell.

Baritz, L. (1965), *Servants of Power*. New York: Wiley.

Batstone, E. (1976), 'Industrial Democracy and Worker Representation at Board Level: A Review of the European Experience', in Batstone and Davies, 1976.

Batstone, E. (1976a), 'Making Out in a Bank'. Duplicated paper.

Batstone, E. and P. L. Davies (1976), *Industrial Democracy: European Experience*. London, HMSO.

Batstone, E., I. Boraston and S. Frenkel (1977), *Shop Stewards in Action; The Organisation of Workplace Conflict and Accommodation*. Oxford: Blackwell.

Benson, L. (1974), 'Market Socialism and Class Structure: Manual Workers and Managerial Power in the Yugoslav Enterprise', in F. Parkin, ed., *The Social Analysis of Class Structure*. London: Tavistock.

Brannen, P., E. Batstone, D. Fatchett and P. White (1976), *The Worker Directors: A Sociology of Participation*. London: Hutchinson.

British Institute of Management (1972), *The Board of Directors*. Management Survey Report No. 10. London.

Brooke, M. Z. and H. L. Remmers (1970), *The Strategy of Multinational Enterprise*. London: Longman.

Brown, G. (1977), *Sabotage*. Nottingham: Spokesman Books.

Burns, T. (1954), 'The Direction of Activity and Communication in a Departmental Executive Group.' *Human Relations*, VII, 73-9.

Burns, T. and G. M. Stalker (1961), *The Management of Innovation*. London: Tavistock.

Carter, E. E. (1971), 'The Behavioural Theory of the Firm and Top-Level Corporate Decisions'. *Administrative Science Quarterly*, XVI, 413-28.

Chandler, A. D. (1962), *Strategy and Structure: Chapters in the History of the Industrial Enterprise*. Cambridge, Mass.: MIT Press.

Chandler, M. K. (1964), *Management Rights and Union Interests*. New York: McGraw-Hill.

Channon, D. F. (1973), *The Strategy and Structure of British Enterprise*. London: Macmillan.

Clegg, S. (1975), *Power, Rule and Domination*. London: Routledge and Kegan Paul.

Cleverley, G. (1973), *Managers and Magic*. Harmondsworth, Mddx.: Penguin.

Cotgrove, S. and S. Box (1970), *Science, Industry and Society*. London: Allen and Unwin.

Crozier, M. (1964), *The Bureaucratic Phenomenon*. London: Tavistock.

Dubin, R. (1962), 'Business Behaviour Behaviourally Viewed', in G. B. Strother, ed., *Social Science Approaches to Business Behaviour*. London: Tavistock.

Elliott, D. and R. Elliott (1976), *The Control of Technology*. London: Wykeham.

Fox, A. (1974), *Beyond Contract: Work, Power and Trust Relations*. London: Faber & Faber.

Franko, L. G. (1974), 'The Move Toward a Multidivisional Structure in European Organisations', *Administrative Science Quarterly*, XIX, 493-506.

Gordon, R. A. (1961), *Business Leadership in the Large Corporation*. Berkeley: University of California Press.

Haber, S. (1964), *Efficiency and Uplift: Scientific Management in the Progressive Era, 1890-1920*. Chicago: University of Chicago Press.

Mace, M. L. (1971), *Directors: Myth and Reality*. Boston, Mass.: Harvard University Press.

March, J. G. and H. A. Simon (1958), *Organizations*. New York: Wiley.

Marcuse, H. (1968), *One Dimensional Man*. London: Abacus.

Marshall, A. (1901), Letter to A. Bowley. *Memorials*. London.

Mechanic, D. (1962), 'Sources of Power of Lower Participants in Complex Organisations', *Administrative Science Quarterly*, VII, 349-64.

Michels, R. (1962), *Political Parties*. New York: Free Press.

Miller, D. C. and W. H. Form (1951), *Industrial Sociology*. New York: Harper.

Mills, C. W. (1967), 'Situated Actions and Vocabularies of Motive' in I. L. Horovitz, ed., *Power, Politics and People*. New York: Free Press.

Mintzberg, H. (1973), *The Nature of Managerial Work*. New York: Harper & Row.

National Swedish Industrial Board (1976), *Board Representation of Employees in Sweden: A Summary from a Survey*. Stockholm: Liberförlag.

Nichols, T. (1969), *Ownership, Control and Ideology*. London: Allen & Unwin.

Pahl, R. E. and J. T. Winkler (1974), 'The Economic Elite: Theory and Practice' in P. Stanworth and A. Giddens, eds., *Elites and Power in British Society*. London: Cambridge University Press.

Pateman, C. (1970), *Participation and Democratic Theory*. Cambridge: Cambridge University Press.

Roy, D. (1954), 'Efficiency and the Fix', *American Journal of Sociology*, LX, 255-266.

Scott, M. B. and S. M. Lyman (1968), 'Accounts', *American Sociological Review*, XXXIII, 46-62.

Selznick, P. (1957), *Leadership in Administration*. New York: Harper & Row.

Selznick, P. (1966), *TVA and the Grass Roots*. New York: Harper & Row.

Stobaugh, R. B. (1969), 'How to Analyze Foreign Investment Climates', *Harvard Business Review*.

Strauss, A., D. J. Murray and D. C. Potter (1971), 'The Hospital and its Negotiated Order' in F. G. Castles et al., eds., *Decisions, Organisations and Society*. Harmondsworth: Penguin.

Tugendhat, C. (1973), *The Multinationals*. Harmondsworth: Penguin.

Vuskovic, B. (1976), 'Social Inequality in Yugoslavia', *New Left Review*, VC, 26-44.

Weber, M. (1947), *The Theory of Social and Economic Organization*. Trans. T. Parsons and A. M. Henderson. New York: Free Press.

Weber, M. (1968), *Economy and Society: An Outline of Interpretive Sociology*. New York: Bedminster Press.

Wilensky, H. (1967), *Organizational Intelligence*. New York: Basic Books.

Zimmerman, D. (1971), 'The Practicalities of Rule Use' in J. D. Douglas, ed., *Understanding Everyday Life*. London: Routledge & Kegan Paul.

III

STRATEGY AND
CRITIQUE OF STRATEGY

8

ON THE NATURE OF CAPITALIST-INITIATED INNOVATIONS IN THE WORKPLACE

Gerry Hunnius
Atkinson College and Faculty of Environmental Studies, York University, Toronto, Canada

I. THE CRISIS IN COLLECTIVE BARGAINING IN CANADA: SYMPTOMS, REALITIES, AND RESPONSES

Ever since the mid 1960s attacks on collective bargaining have been mounting in Canada. The Woods Report[1] published in December 1968, reported that: 'The result verges on a crisis of confidence in the present industrial relations system'.[2] The visible symptoms include a rash of strikes,[3] rejection of negotiated contracts by the rank and file union membership, disruption of public services, occasional violence during strikes and a public predisposition to put the major part of the blame for this 'problem' on the unions. In particular, unions are being blamed for increased inflation.[4]

Author's note: Prepared for the International Conference on *Possibilities for the Liberation of Work and Political Power,* The Inter University Centre of Post-Graduate Studies, Dubrovnik, Yugoslavia, 31 January-3 February, 1977.

In a submission to the Woods Report, the Canadian Chamber of Commerce stated that collective bargaining functioned best when there was a reasonable balance of power between management and labour. They concluded that this balance was currently lacking — labour had become too powerful.[5] Organized labour, of course, holds the opposite view. It seems obvious that organized labour is by definition a junior partner in a capitalist state. To this we must add the political fact that in many respects labour legislation in Canada is more restrictive than in other industrialized capitalist nations. The legislative ban on strikes during the term of an agreement, for instance, encourages employers to exercise their 'residual rights' once the agreement has been signed. They feel free to do anything the agreement does not specifically rule out, regardless of the effects on their employees.[6]

I believe we can safely assume that the gentlemen of the Canadian Chamber of Commerce are fully aware of these facts. Their statement about an alleged imbalance in favour of organized labour has, I would argue, one purpose only: to keep the balance permanently tilted against labour. Statements of that kind serve only two related functions: they put pressure on governments to maintain the present imbalance and they attempt to influence the media and the general public. Virtually all employer organizations proclaim that collective bargaining is an essential part of Canada's present socio-economic-political system.[7] The Woods Report concludes as follows: 'We are convinced that these are deeply held views which reflect a realization on management's part that modern-day capitalism could not survive without free collective bargaining and an independent trade union movement'.[8]

It seems clear that the leading employer organizations realize fully the systems-maintaining function of unions and collective bargaining. At the enterprise or plant level management's responses are far less unified and range from acceptance of unions and collective bargaining to reluctant toleration and outright hostility. The latter view is particularly evident among small non-union establishments. Acceptance and support of collective bargaining is almost universal among unions in Canada. They see it as a vehicle for worker advancement within the system.[9] The major thrust of the criticism of the adversary system, and of collective bargaining in particular, has come from governments, supported by the media. Given the function of the state in capitalist society, it is perhaps not surprising to see governments taking the initiative in this matter.

As usual, it was Prime Minister Trudeau who was most outspoken about what bothered the government. In a recent meeting in Belleville, Ontario, he noted that collective bargaining was no longer fulfilling its function in a situation where unions negotiated an agreement but the members then went out on wildcat strikes. 'This is a very basic problem', he said, 'That the unions and the employers have to face together'.[10] Of course it is a basic problem, it deals with the question of how to maintain an obedient and disciplined workforce; it deals, in short, with the capitalist's need to control the process of production. The solution, according to Trudeau, has to be faced by unions and employers together. But how? The solution emerged quite clearly at a recent national convention of the Liberal Party in a resolution which urged 'the government to establish a royal commission to study and recommend ways of bringing some measure of industrial democracy to Canada as a way of replacing the adversary system of labour-management relations with something more cooperative and productive.'[11]

It may be of some historical and political significance to turn our thoughts for a moment to the Federal Republic of Germany. It was in 1965 that Chancellor Erhard proclaimed the new ideology of the *formierte Gesellschaft*. Free competition was no longer an adequate regulator of the economy and should be replaced by the cooperative 'formierte Gesellschaft'. Erhard described the future society as follows:

> The 'formierte Gesellschaft' (organized society or liberal corporatism) is based on the cooperation of all groups and interests and is constituted not out of authoritarian pressure but out of its own power and will. This means that this society no longer consists of classes and groups which want to push through their own exclusive goals but that it is...according to its own nature cooperative. ...The society will strengthen state authority to the extent that necessary reforms and the establishments of priorities for solving social tasks will be acknowledged. ...[12].

Or, as Jürgen Habermas has pointed out: 'Based on high and rising levels of productive forces, industrially developed societies have ex-

panded social wealth. This in turn lends realism to the consideration that the antagonistic sharpness of competing needs may be
blunted in view of a continued, if not increasing, pluralism of interests and in line with the definite possibility to satisfy these
needs'. A 'society living in abundance' makes obsolete 'compromises dictated by scarce resources'.[13]

The similarity between the remarks by Erhard and those of the
Canadian Prime Minister quoted earlier are important. While the
social and historical circumstances of the Federal Republic of Germany and of Canada must be considered, the commonality facing
both capitalist nations at different historical times are strikingly
similar: in short, they boil down to the question as to the most
viable strategy to maintain capitalist rule.

Prime Minister Trudeau's remarks of May 1975, and his subsequent 'musings' about a 'new society', were fleshed out by repeated
statements of senior civil servants of the Federal Department of
Labour who have argued in favour of an industrial relations system
with stronger emphasis on the 'mutuality of interests' of all parties
(labour, employer and government). A recent article by the labour
reporter of the *Globe and Mail* reads as follows:

> A proposal by an industrial relations consultant that Canada emulate West Ger-
> many in bringing together key groups in the economy for regular consultation
> has been endorsed by federal Deputy Labour Minister Thomas Eberlee as a step
> toward placing collective bargaining on a rational basis.[14]

Similar statements have been made in the past by Assistant Deputy
Minister of Labour, William Kelly.

Organized labour in Canada, as well as in the United States, has
always been hostile to proposed innovations of this kind. The
change in the policy of the Canadian Labour Congress,
documented in 'Labour's Manifesto for Canada' makes the
gradual introduction of some form of co-determination in Canada
more likely. Labour's Manifesto for Canada was approved by the
11th Constitutional Convention of the Canadian Labour Congress,
held in Quebec City, 17-21 May 1976.

'Labour's Manifesto for Canada' points out that organized
labour has always set a price at which it would support the
'system'. Historically, this has included the right to unionize and
the right to free collective bargaining. Looking ahead at the 'post-

control society' (after the termination of wage and price controls), the Canadian Labour Congress proposes its version of tri-partism and national planning to the Federal Government's emerging liberal corporatism. Tri-partism, for the Canadian Labour Congress, means full partnership status for labour, along with government and business. 'Full partnership means that national planning must include more than an incomes policy in which only wages and salary are restrained...' 'A prerequisite of tri-partism must be that management gives up its unilateral right to determine investment and pricing policies. Labour must not willingly enter into any arrangement where only half the income equation, i.e. wages, is to be determined.... To enter into a tri-partite agreement under such adverse circumstances would indeed be using the union organization as an arm of both business and government to restrain the workers'.[15] It is significant that organized labour, at the level of the Canadian Labour Congress, has taken a public position on the danger of co-optation under a liberal corporatist system.[16]

A few brief remarks must be made at this point about the Manifesto and its likely fate in the near future.

— The Manifesto counters the increasing centralization of power in the Federal Government by demanding the centralization of power within organized labour in the hands of the Canadian Labour Congress. The obvious alternative to a fragmented labour movement, namely the mobilization of the working people of Canada, is not even considered in this Manifesto. There is clearly an important political difference between a united movement based on informed grass-roots support, local initiative and power and one which is based on structural centralization where effective decision-making is removed from the membership. The Manifesto, if implemented, would give the Canadian Labour Congress a piece of state power without creating the working class base for it.[17]

— What is completely missing in the Manifesto is a concern with the conditions of work on the shop floor and the office dealing with the blue and white collar blues which have by now been adequately documented. Most of the proposals and counterproposals made so far ignore the growing dissatisfaction of Canadian workers with the conditions and organization of work. A recent survey, entitled *Canadian Work Values*,[18] finds that intrinsic aspects of work such as having sufficient informa-

tion and authority, opportunity to develop abilities and problems of supervision are of more importance to Canadians than
extrinsic features such as salary or comfortable surroundings.

It seems obvious that these findings, popularly labelled blue and
white collar blues, are not unrelated to work stoppages and other
manifestations of worker discontent. To the degree that worker
participation in management, industrial democracy, job enrichment and similar innovations of the human relations approach to
management have been discussed recently in Canada, they have
emanated either from individual 'progressive' capitalists, or from
politicians and senior civil servants. Organized labour in Canada
has on the whole remained suspicious or uninterested in such innovations. Their suspicions rest on the belief that such innovations
have usually turned out to be manipulative ploys of management.
Their disinterest, on the other hand, was summed up recently by
the Secretary-Treasurer of the Ontario Federation of Labour when
he stated that worker participation and cooperation will be useless
unless they can bring about full employment. 'When the time
comes for [workers] to be let go, they'll let go', he said, 'you can't
get security out of meetings'.[19]
— The opposition to a tri-partite decision-making body with
equal power to labour, business and government has been very
strong. Its implementation is very unlikely indeed. The Federal
Government has flatly refused to share decison-making power
with labour; parliamentarians of all parties are opposed to any
new centre of power which they fear would by-pass parliament;
an increasing number of trade unionists are opposed to the centralization of power within organized labour proposed in the
Manifesto while others see the entire plan as a political sell-out
of Canadian workers.
While the tri-partite power sharing of the Manifesto seems to be
dead for the time being, it is reasonably certain that the Federal
Government, supported at least by a few provincial governments,
will move ahead slowly with the introduction of a series of innovations, borrowed and adapted from the Federal Republic of Germany. It is not too difficult to see why the West German model appeals to 'progressive capitalists' and politicians in Canada. A recent
report, produced for the Federal Department of Labour, states, for
instance that the Concerted Action Program, the Council of

Economic Advisors, and various aspects of the co-determination program have resulted in 'reducing the level of expectations in collective bargaining', and have made it possible to reach agreements without great difficulty. The author of this report argues that worker involvement in traditional management functions, such as the large-scale employee lay-offs in the coal, steel and iron industries, 'prevented serious labour-management disruptions [read: strikes] in those industries'.[20] In terms of the class struggle and the role of the state in advanced capitalist society innovations of the kind we are discussing here cut across the two main functions of the state: that of accumulation and of legitimation. In this case, the legitimation function of the state is directed particularly at organized labour. It is essential for the capitalist system to get the support of organized labour for the continued expropriation of surplus. While expropriation is to be maintained, the relations of production are to undergo certain changes; or to put it differently, the mechanisms of expropriation are changing.

Since work in capitalist society is unable to satisfy the non-material needs of working people, consumerism as a way of life, as an ideology, was consciously fashioned by corporate capital to channel and transform these desires, hopes and dreams into monetary values. Edward Filene, who in the early 1930s had developed a reputation as 'the mouthpiece of industrial America', argued that, industry could 'sell to the masses all that it employs the masses to create'.[21] Such a development required a 'selective education which limited the concept of social change and betterment to those commodified answers rolling off American conveyer belts'.[22]

Collective bargaining, restricted as it was to monetary issues, fulfilled this function admirably. The increased purchasing power of unionized workers must be seen in the proper context. For many non-unionized workers, the unemployed, and many senior citizens real income has declined. The gap in income between the rich and poor in Canada has increased between 1946 and 1971.[23] Corporate profits in Canada between 1926 and 1960 have increased more in relation to the GNP than total labour income.[24] Much the same has happened in Britain.[25]

We have observed before that absenteeism, turn-over rates, sabotage, strikes and rejection of contracts by the union membership are increasing rapidly in Canada. The Federal Government has clearly drawn different conclusions from these phenomena than the

unions have. While the latter continue to demand more pay and increased leisure time as the main answer to the growing unrest of the
rank and file workers, the government seems to have taken recent
attitude studies more seriously. The *Canadian Work Values* study
shows that 'the single most important consideration in the minds of
Canadians proved to be interesting work'. 'In general, it would
seem that intrinsic aspects of work such as having sufficient information and authority outweigh the importance of extrinsic features
such as salary or comfortable surroundings'.[26] Given our 'monetiz-
ed' consumer culture and the restrictive nature of collective
bargaining which encourages monetary demands and largely pro-
hibits bargaining for the intrinsic aspects of work mentioned in the
attitude study, it is quite likely that demands for higher wages are in
fact manifestations of needs and desires which either remain un-
articulated or are pragmatically dismissed as unobtainable under
the present system of capitalist production.

The response by the Canadian state must be seen in the context
of the Marxist definition of the function of the state under
capitalism. It seems compelling to see the government's initiative as
being in the best long-term interest of corporate capital. The very
fact that the initiative originates from the government and not from
corporate owners means that the proposed innovations will have to
be politically acceptable in terms of electoral politics. Governments
are, after all, accountable to an electorate while corporations are
not.[27]

Government initiatives seem to move along two parallel and
inter-related lines. On the one hand there is the attempt to incorporate certain features of the West German model of industrial
relations; on the other hand the Federal Government has already
begun several 'quality of worklife' types of innovation in the civil
service.[28]

The literature on the West German co-determination model is extensive. Since we are primarily interested in the system-transforming
potential of such innovations, I will restrict myself to a few relevant
observations, largely of a negative nature. The executive board of
the West German Trade Union Federation (DGB) has clearly stated
that: 'A general conception of co-determination of this type
presupposes a system of free enterprise based on the principle of
free market economy'.[29] In the view of many critics, the develop-

ment of trade unions towards corporatism has found its culmination in co-determination.[30] Moving from the general to the specific,
one of the features of the West German model which is likely to be
introduced in Canada in some form is the works council. A number
of 'problems' seem to have developed in the Federal Republic of
Germany:

1. The representation ratios are fixed by law. In larger plants
they allow for at least 570 employees per councillor and in some
cases the representation load is even heavier. Face-to-face
knowledge of shop problems and handling of grievances is almost
impossible under such conditions. The problem is intensified by the
fact that as councillors tend to keep 'white-collar' office hours, late
and night shift workers are left without the benefit of councillors.[31]
Whatever solidarity might have existed at the time of election of
councillors will likely have eroded within the first year of their
term.

2. Skilled and long-service workers tend to dominate the Works
Councils. Female workers, shift workers as well as foreign workers
are under-represented. The long tenure of councillors (3 years) frequently continues indefinitely.[32] This democracy of 'notables' does
not seem too different from the experience of Yugoslavia where apparently highly skilled workers and technicians dominate most
organs of self-management within enterprises.

3. Fürstenberg concludes that 'the works council is a marginal
institution at the crosspoint of three large interest groups: management, trade unions and the employees of the enterprise. Only in a
few cases will it be possible for one of these groups to constantly
use the works council for its own purposes'.[33]

It should be pointed out that the works council (*Betriebsrat*) is
the independent representative of all workers in a given establishment. The employer is not represented in the works council. The
original intention was for the works council to be the voice of all
the employees in a given enterprise. It is thus somewhat disturbing
to hear that, 'only in a few cases will it be possible for one of these
groups to constantly use the works council for its own purposes'.

One other aspect of interest to the Government of Canada as well
as several provincial governments, is the practice of appointing or
electing employees to the Board of Directors of publicly and
privately owned enterprises or institutions. It is thus relevant to
look at the experience in West Germany where the practice of

workers' representation on supervisory boards has been in operation for some time. Several points should be made:

1. Parity representation on supervisory boards has existed in the coal mining and steel industries for some time. It has recently been extended to all German companies with more than 2,000 employees; but there are two restrictive provisions:

(a) At least one employee representative must be nominated by the so-called *leitende Angestellte* (employees with managerial functions).

(b) In conflict situations (i.e. in case of a tied vote) the chairman casts the deciding vote and the chairman is always nominated by the shareholders.[34]

The facts speak for themselves. To call this type of capitalist control 'co-determination' is absurd.

2. The labour members of the supervisory board are restricted by law from accepting any obligations to the union or work force that has elected them.[35]

3. While the legal function of supervisory boards includes the control of the managing board (the 'real' decision-maker), in practice, especially when business is booming, the 'actual activities of supervisory boards do not amount to much more than co-ordination, advice, and formal ratification of decisions already made by the managing board'.[36]

Since the managing board is in reality the real decision-making body, it is relevant to look briefly at the function of the labour director, who in practice is nominated by the unions. The labour director is responsible both for effective managment *and* effective representation of the workers' point of view.[37] The problems associated with this particular innovation have been numerous:

(a) On the whole, it has worked 'smoothly' largely because almost all labour directors 'behaved'. Their practice and ideology has proven to be no danger to business interests.[38]

(b) While the labour director is supposed to provide a link between works councils and management, he is in practice pledged to silence (as are the labour appointed members of the board of supervision) if the competitive position of the enterprise could be adversely affected by the dissemination of such information.[39]

(c) Fürstenberg concludes his comments on the labour director by stating that: 'Experience has shown that the labour director can handle his difficult situation only by attempting to become fully integrated in management and socially recognized by his colleagues on the board'.[40]

Are such innovations system-maintaining? Do they offer a potential for radical transformation of capitalist rule? There would seem to be at least three inter-related questions which must be considered:

1. Are such innovations compatible with the continuous control of capital over labour?

2. The problem is posed in the following way by one observer: 'What essentially distinguishes invasion from incorporation is the continuing existence of an independent power base, the mobilization of which remains permanently on the agenda'.[41] Does co-determination facilitate or hinder the existence or emergence of an independent power base within the organized workforce?

3. The question of consciousness has occupied Marxists for a long time. How does it change from trade union consciousness to class consciousness and finally to revolutionary consciousness? Is the notion of 'false consciousness' viable? Is consciousness cumulative? Do several instances of workers' solidarity and power produce an 'explosion' of consciousness?

There are no empirically tested answers to any of these questions. We will offer some tentative answers in the concluding remarks to this presentation.

II THE LONG ARM OF THE JOB: WORK AND POLITICAL POWER

Any debate of revolutionary (system-transforming) change must of necessity proceed on the basis of certain assumptions. Without much elaboration I want to state several, to me compelling, assumptions which will form the basis for our subsequent analysis and discussion.

1. It is not necessary for all classes to share the dominant social values. It is sufficient for the maintenance and stability of a system of social power if those actually sharing in societal power develop consistent societal values.[42]

2. Despite contradictions and divisions, such homogeneity of values and ultimate aims does in fact exist within the corporate rul-

ing class of the advanced capitalist countries.[43] In his analysis of the linkages between the Canadian state and the capitalist class, Leo Panitch sees a confraternity of power:

> . . .an ideological hegemony emanating from both the bourgeoisie and the state which is awesome, which is reflected in the sheer pervasiveness of the view that the national interest and business interests are at one, and which certainly ensures the smooth functioning of the relationship between the state and the capitalist class.[44]

3. Stability and maintenance of the system not only require essential unity in the ruling class but also the absence of such unity in the working class. It is precisely the lack of value-consensus within the working class which keeps them compliant.[45]

4. This lack of consensus within the working class can only be explained adequately by the Marxist theories of 'pragmatic role acceptance and manipulative socialization'. Despite all the criticism, I find the concept of 'false consciousness' compelling.[46]

5. A new class and ultimately a revolutionary consciousness in the working class is not only strategically (organizationally) essential for a successful revolutionary transformation of capitalist society, it is also imperative for the qualitative make-up of socialist society. Carl Boggs in his study of Gramsci's *Prison Notebooks* writes:

> Gramsci stressed that while subordinate classes might establish political, military, or even economic domination, this could be catastrophic for the future of socialism if it were not firmly rooted in a new popular consciousness. At worst such a revolution would lead to unprecedented violence and human sacrifice, at best to a formal bureaucratic order along the lines of a caste or priesthood.[47]

6. If revolution requires a united proletariat and a divided capitalist ruling class, the revolutionary task of our time is to unite the heterogeneity in the working class,

> around opposition to the corporate ruling class and to develop its particularized grievances into explicit socialist consciousness and practice by demonstrating their common root in capitalist property relations. This in turn requires revolutionary theory that encompasses both the specific situation and the concrete, historical occasion of the entire world proletariat. Revolutionary theory mediates between and unites individual feelings, introspective understanding, social vision, historical consciousness, and political strategies and tactics.[48]

For a long time I have viewed the world of work as being governed by laws and practices totally at variance with those pertaining in the rest of (liberal) society. The capitalist division of labour with its corresponding hierarchy of managerial control, embedded in the unequal power relationship between capital and labour, seemed so dramatically different from the realities of civil society with its civil rights, individual and political freedoms and the accountability of rulers to the ruled. No doubt the differences are real and should not be dismissed. In a very real sense, however, these differences are differences in degree, not in kind. The correspondence between civil society and the world of work turns out to be very close.

A reading of liberal democratic theory from Schumpeter to contemporaries like Bernard Berelson and a corresponding examination of the realities of democratic life in the industrialized liberal democracies of Western Europe and North America shows that the essentials of elite (i.e. capitalist) rule pertain in both workplace and civil society. The rule of capital over labour is out in the open in the sphere of work where it is only partially modified and mystified by the existence of unions.[49]

The mystification process in civil society is far more widespread and sophisticated. It has, on the whole, also been more successful. The functions of the state, the system of representative democracy including voting and the multi-party system, the notion that the free enterprise system works in the long run for the benefit of all citizens, the benevolent nature of social welfare legislation and many other processes and institutions are still seen by a majority of citizens as benefiting everyone and as being essentially democratic. Their system-maintaining functions are on the whole successfully mystified or hidden. Apathy, for instance, must clearly be viewed as system-maintaining. The viability of the capitalist political system, it would appear, depends on the apathy and non-participation of the 'masses'. As one leading American social scientist has pointed out, 'what seems to be required of the electorate as a whole is a distribution of qualities along important dimensions. We need some people who are active in a certain respect, others in the middle, and still others passive'.[50] The system-maintaining function of apathy in the workplace has been recognized since Adam Smith. For the worker, on the other hand, apathy is a personal and immediate 'solution' to a public or structural problem. As a private remedy for a structural defect, apathy is eminently rational behaviour. Herzberg once remarked that idleness, indifference and irresponsibility are healthy responses to absurd work.

Apathy, idleness, shoddy workmanship, absenteeism, increased turn-over rates and sabotage are individual responses to structural realities which in turn are part and parcel of the normal functioning of the capitalist mode of production.[51] We need to ask a number of questions at this point:

1. To what degree, if any, does work (particularly in a factory) affect a worker's life away from work?

2. What relevance, if any, does the answer to this question have in terms of system maintenance or transformation?

3. Is there a link between the apathy, frustration or anger of the individual worker and collective action by workers? If so, what is the nature of this linkage?

4. What is the system-transforming potential of such collective action?

(a) The evidence here is fairly clear. There seems to be a direct carry-over effect. Meissner, for instance, states that:

> When choice of action is suppressed by the spatial, temporal and functional constraints of the work process, worker capacity for meeting the demands of spare-time activities which require discretion is reduced. They engage less in those activities which necessitate planning, coordination, and purposeful action, but increase the time spent in sociable and expressive activities.[52]

Arthur Kornhauser's study of 407 auto workers found that workers with low job satisfaction, 'were often escapist or passive in their non-work activities: they watched television; did not vote; and did not participate in community organizations'.[53] The reverse side of the coin also seems to hold according to research done in Norway. Elden reported that 'We have consistently found that democratized authority structures result in more workers attempting to control their own lives, both in the plant and beyond'.[54]

(b) The system-maintaining effect of apathy and non-participation in political life by members of the working class (i.e. the masses) has been discussed before.[55] To what extent the opposite side of the coin ('workers attempting to control their own lives, both in the plant and beyond') is potentially system-transforming, is less clear. We shall return to this question later on.

(c) Common sense would tell us that there must be a link between individual frustration and anger and collective action. The evidence might not satisfy an empirically oriented social scientist but I find it compelling enough to argue that the potential for a transformation of individual protest into collective action exists given a number of factors the nature of which we do not fully understand. The case of the Vauxhall workers at Luton is one example of such transformation. It is by now so well known that I do not need to repeat it here.[56] Another example of a similar nature has been reported by Martin Glaberman. It deals with the no-strike pledge given by the labour leadership during the second world war when the United States was attacked.

What happened in the United Auto Workers (UAW) was this: The no-strike pledge was given by the labour leadership without consulting the union membership. The UAW, because of its more democratic history, decided to put the issue to a vote at its annual convention in 1944. The three positions put before the convention, including one in support of the no-strike pledge, were all voted down. The furious and confused UAW leadership figured that the cure for democracy was more democracy and decided to hold a referendum. A secret ballot was mailed to the home of every member of the UAW. It was a simple question this time: Are you for or against the no-strike pledge? The vote took place early in 1945 and the members of the UAW voted two to one to reaffirm the no-strike pledge. The problem was that, before the vote, during the vote, and after the vote, a majority of auto workers were on strike. The two to one majority in favour of the no-strike pledge was not an absolute majority of the entire UAW membership. The workers that went on strike, on the other hand, *were* an absolute majority of the UAW.[57] The UAW and the Vauxhall cases are by no means isolated examples.

What lessons can we draw from this, apart from the fact that the Vauxhall experience casts doubts on the usefulness of sociological attitude surveys of individual workers? Gorz suggests that a 'potential of frustration and revolt lies permanently dormant within the working class and that, in so-called normal periods, no one knows how deeply the working class feels oppressed, exploited, frustrated and dominated'.[58] Glaberman adds that what workers, 'think and do in the presence of fellow workers is not necessarily the same think that they will think and do as isolated citizens — as one man with one vote'.[59] As an individual voter or as an isolated individual facing an interviewer, the worker feels powerless because he is powerless, but collectively he feels powerful because he is powerful. He knows that collectively workers can shut down a plant, he knows that the shut-down of his plant will in turn force the shut-down of other plants. Quite apart from the psychological dynamics of mass meetings and mass action, the worker is aware of his power when he acts in solidarity with others.

(d) The system-transforming potential of such collective action is evident but the weight of system-maintaining counter measures is enormous. Collective actions, particularly those of a spontaneous rank and file origin, occupy only a small part of the workers' experience and time. For most of his life, at work as well as away from work, he is in the position of a powerless isolated individual.

Given the potential collective power of the working class, it is not surprising that the ruling class does everything in its power to forestall or limit the opportunities for workers to test their collective strength. At the point of production this takes the form of the minute division of labour, the fragmentation of tasks, the classification of jobs, the division of mental and physical work — in short, the fragmentation of the work force. Large plants, such as the Mirafiori plant of Fiat at Turin are now being broken up and replaced by smaller, widely dispersed units, and job enrichment in its various forms further fragments the workforce.

The fear of the bourgoisie of the potential collective power of the working class borders on paranoia. Huw Beynon, in his study of the English working class, remarks that the mass meeting is anathema to many people. 'Few things raise middle class Britain to a greater show of moral outrage than workers packed into large halls, voting on important issues by a show of hands'.[60]

The ruling class throughout the capitalist world has clearly grasped the danger which working class solidarity and consciousness poses to the established order. Two separate, but interrelated, aspects of the liberal-democratic tradition will illustrate this point. The demand and the achievement of univeral suffrage and more specifically the secret ballot is usually seen as a class victory of democratic forces. But as S. Rokkan has pointed out, it was something of a double-edged weapon. He noted that '. . . the primary motive for the introduction of the ballot system was to make it possible to escape sanctions from superiors; this was the essence of the Chartists' early demands and has always been a basic concern of working-class movements. . . .' But, he adds: 'What has been less emphasized in histories of electoral institutions is that provisions for secrecy could cut off the voter from his peers as well as his superiors. . . . by ensuring the complete anonymity of the ballots it became possible not only to reduce bribery of the economically dependent by their superiors but also to reduce the pressures towards conformity and solidarity within the working class'.[61] As Miliband notes, concentration on the act of voting itself, in which formal equality does prevail, helps to obscure the actual inequality of influence among citizens in capitalist society.[62]

Another related aspect of the liberal-democratic tradition is more obviously directed against the emergence of working class solidarity and action. I am referring to the practice to prohibit the reaching of decisions by a show of hands or in any manner other than by the secret ballot. The Labour Relations Act of the Province of Ontario (Canada) states: 'A strike vote or a vote to ratify a proposed collective agreement taken by a trade union shall be by ballots cast in such a manner that a person expressing his choice cannot be identified with the choice expressed'.[63] Again, we must note how an obviously democratic innovation which merits support also performs a system-maintaining function by isolating the individual workers from other workers, thus reinforcing his feeling of isolation and powerlessness.

The pressures, the legal limitations, and the incentives to think and to act alone and in isolation from your peers, are formidable. How can they be overcome? I believe that the Vauxhall and the UAW experience, as well as that of countless wildcat strikes, contract rejections and the occasional community-based mass action supports the assumption, formulated by Mann as follows, that 'The working class is more likely to support deviant values if those values relate either to concrete everyday life or to vague populist concepts,[64] than if they relate to an abstract political philosophy'.[65] Let me conclude on this point by quoting from the remarks of a trade union activist in California:

...let me clarify my attitude toward the question of boredom and alienation as contributing factors to the rising discontent (of workers). I do not 'dismiss' these factors. Far from it. But I am aware that workers do not strike or take other action in response to 'alienation' or 'boredom' as such.... Working people know better than to strike against abstract and intangible conditions like boredom and alienation. These factors are real but must first be given a concrete expression and meaning. Discontent over boredom and alienation is therefore often contained and expressed in concrete demands to end speed-ups and mandatory overtime, improving safety and health conditions, deal with dictatorial foremen, and so forth.[66]

Before proceeding further we need to consider briefly some of the societal institutions and processes outside the world of work. There are a number of reasons why this seems pertinent in the context of attempting to isolate and discover system-maintaining forces as well as system-transforming potentialities. There is first of all the undeniable fact that the locus of social control (over the masses) has shifted since the beginning of the nineteenth century. From an almost total concentration on work (the division of labour) it has now been extended to cover every area of a worker's life. Stuart Ewen argues that, 'the factory had not been an effective arena for forging a predictable and reliable work force'.[67] 'Up to that point (second decade of the 20th century), much of indigenous working-class culture had resisted capitalist growth in general and the invasion of capitalism into their work and lifestyles in particular'.[68]

The second point to be made deals with a complex set of seemingly contradictory phenomena. On the one hand, to quote Robert Dubin, 'The industrial workers' world is one in which work and the work-place are not central life interests for a vast majority'.[69] In other words, work is a means to an end; the real world begins after work. As a consequence of this, it has been suggested that, 'community, not class (not even job) is the adequate unit of analysis'.[70] The labour movement in general, particularly in the United States and Canada, has acted in support of the notion that life begins after work. The Protestant work ethic, with its emphasis on the intrinsic value of work as an end in itself, has not found much support from the labour movement.[71]

There are a number of problems with this view. In terms of revolutionary strategy the entire weight of Marxist analysis suggests that the potential for revolutionary consciousness and action is highest in the workplace. Recent attitude studies have also thrown doubt on the notion that 'life begins after work' can be interpreted to mean that work has become a necessary evil (means) to be suffered only because it allows for enjoyment and happiness during leisure hours. The most recent Canadian study on the work ethic and job satisfaction shows very clearly that workers value the intrinsic aspects of work ahead of extrinsic features, such as wages.[72] More casual observations of the behaviour patterns of retired people and of workers who suddenly find themselves the recipients of large amounts of money (e.g., from a lottery) would seem to confirm the view that work is more than just a means to an end. As stated earlier, the phenomenon is complex and does not lend itself to easy generalizations.

The important question, it seems to me, is to locate the source of the workers' feeling of powerlessness, if indeed there is one primary source. Proudhon, for instance, saw the feeling of deference and inferiority that possessed the working class, as a fundamental problem.[73] He essentially located the source of this compliance in the workers' experience in the workplace. Paradoxically, he felt that this deference could only be overcome by education.[74]

Given the reality of powerlessness of individual workers away from work as contrasted to the potential of collective action and thus power at the point of production, is it not possible that the source of this deference and powerlessness lies primarily outside the organization of work? Or to put it differently: are not the actual relations of power between labour and capital relatively more favourable to labour within the workplace (as contrasted to civil society)? Is not the socialization of the consumer more pervasive and more successful than that of the producer? The fact that the same individual experiences capitalist rule as a producer from eight in the morning to five in the afternoon and as a consumer for the rest of the time, makes it only more difficult to unravel the problem.

III SOME THOUGHTS OF A STRATEGIC NATURE

Before we turn to an analysis of the system-transforming potential of contemporary innovations in the organization of work (e.g., job enlargement, job enrichment, socio-technical systems approach, participative management, etc.), we must take a brief look at the forerunner of these innovations: the human relations approach to management. Who introduced these innovations and why? What have been the effects of these innovations? What has been the reaction of organized labour? We will then look at the main characteristics of contemporary innovations as well as the system-maintaining nature of newly introduced control mechanisms. Almost without exceptions, these innovations have been introduced by employers and management. While the reasons for introducing these innovations have varied to some degree, they have usually included all or most of the following:

In the case of the earlier forerunners of the human relations approach (Welfarism or Industrial Betterment) in the United States during the early 1900s, three factors seem to have significantly motivated employers to experiment with such innovations.

— It was used by employers to 'eliminate labour unions in those establishments where they existed, or to undermine the possibility of their existence through the gamut of benefits that management granted their employees'.[75]

— It offered employers an alternative to unionism and collective bargaining, which at that time 'was losing its claim to universality'.[76]

— It was profitable to the employer. It tended to reduce the turnover of employees and the occasional outbreak of open conflict. The slogan publicized by the president of National Cash Register, 'it pays', was repeated by many other senior managers from coast to coast.

With the rise of the human relations approach proper (from the time of the experiments at the Hawthorne Works of the Western Electric Company) other factors gained in prominence. Insulating employers from unionization, however, has remained an important reason for introducing such innovations, particularly in small and medium-sized enterprises and institutions.[77] The main reasons, however, would seem to have related to the inability of Taylorism or scientific management to provide satisfactory solutions to 'labour problems' (i.e. labour unrest and declining productivity). Deskilling of jobs and the rising level of educational attainment of the work force persuaded employers to shift their emphasis from the stick to the carrot (from Taylorism to human relations) without, however, surrendering control over the workforce and the process of production.[78] The rapid growth of the service sector, where people deal with other people rather than with machines, accelerated the introduction of these innovations.[79] Labour dissatisfaction with the conditions of work manifested itself by increased absenteeism, high turnover rates, poor workmanship, slowdowns and sabotage.[80] Virtually all these innovations show an increase in worker satisfaction and a corresponding increase in enterprise productivity and profits.[81]

These innovations usually include all or some of the following characteristics:

1. The creation of 'autonomous' and partially self-managed work groups. These groups are ideally small enough to allow for face-to-face communication and direct decision-making without the intermediary of elected or appointed representatives or supervisors.

2. Job specialization and rigid job classifications are downgraded in favour of job enlargement and job enrichment. Activities formerly performed by separate departments (e.g., maintenance) are now built into an autonomous team's responsibilities. Certain limited managerial functions (e.g., quality control and aspects of personnel work) are performed by members of the autonomous work team. The notion here is to include functions requiring 'higher order human abilities and responsibilities' in every set of tasks to be performed by the work teams.

3. Frequently, we can observe the introduction of certain egalitarian notions (e.g., on wage scales) within each work group. Individual competition is often downgraded in favour of group competition.

4. Supervisors and foremen are sometimes withdrawn or their function changed to that of a facilitator and communicator (between management and the work teams and between different work teams).

5. Information previously withheld from the workers is now made available more freely.

6. Physical facilities are created which reflect the new philosophy (e.g., separate dining halls for managers and employees are replaced by common facilities).

7. Profit sharing is frequently introduced to increase the workers' stake in the prosperity of the enterprise.

8. Involvement of workers in coordination and wider decision-making (beyond the internal functioning of the work group) is occasionally encouraged.

9. In some non-unionized enterprises employers have encouraged the setting up of associations encompassing everyone employed in the enterprise. Through their elected executive and their various committees, these associations begin to assume the functions of management. In one Toronto-based enterprise,[82] the association functions as the bargaining agent with management. Since management is also part of the association, they sit in effect on both sides of the bargaining table. While the managerial rights clause is usually held in reserve (one assumes for occasions where the employee-dominated association would make demands incompatible with the interests of the employer), the tendency is to allow the new association to make most decisions previously made by management.

The attempt of the employer is to find an 'accommodation between the demands of the organization and the technology on the one hand, and the needs and desires of its members on the other, so that the needs of both are jointly maximized'.[83] The break with the earlier and now discredited human relations approach is slight but real. The human relations approach ignored the question of power altogether and instead juggled status and prestige categories in an attempt to induce employees to identify with the goals of the corporation. To a very limited extent, and restricted to sharply and narrowly defined areas on the shop floor, the new job enrichment approach does deal with power and thus potentially with dynamite.

Management has recognized that participation pays off. The truth that in order to maintain control they must share it, has been difficult for management to accept. It is important to realize that our critique of job enrichment is not directed against the specific innovations (e.g., the creation of autnonomous work teams, rotation of jobs, etc.). Such innovations would in all likelihood be part of a worker-imposed system of self-management. What is of critical importance here is the question of power. Who introduces what changes for what ends? Job enrichment introduced by employers leaves overall control in the hands of the bosses. The introduction of these innovations has, in many instances, replaced certain aspects of the minute fragmentation of jobs with a variety of innovations which have in practice blurred the detailed division of labour and reduced the lowest levels of the hierarchy of managerial control. At the same time, new and more sophisticated mechanisms of social control have emerged, including the following:

The existence of autonomous work groups within the undertaking will make it more difficult to present a united front in pressing union demands. One observer notes that, 'A strike in an autonomous work group is less disruptive than a united, plant-wide strike'.[84] The autonomous work teams at the new Volvo assembly works at Kalmar, for instance, have their own individual workshops (i.e. assemply points). Each work team has its own changing and rest rooms.[85] There are separate doors for entry and exit for the members of each work team.[86]

Not only is a strike in an autonomous work group less disruptive for management (it hardly poses a threat at all), these new innovations will make it much more difficult for workers to exercise their collective strength at the plant level. If in fact workers of one autonomous group never have occasion to meet with workers from other groups, a very important pre-condition for collective action will have been destroyed. The new condition of the worker will now more closely resemble his isolation and powerlessness outside of work (as consumer).

We have repeatedly cited evidence throughout this paper of attempts by the capitalists to undermine or prevent the solidarity of the working class. Techniques, such as those described at Volvo, are clearly part of a changing system of social control. The control function of management has not evaporated. By a variety of techniques such as profit sharing, the physical separation of workers from each other, the shifting of responsibility from lower management to work teams without a corresponding increase in their decision-making power which is limited to matters internal to the function of each teams, and by the introduction of competition between teams, by these and other techniques, management attempts to create a new and more sophisticated process of integration and control.

The last point requires further explanation. The most recent and comprehensive national (US) survey on job satisfaction was conducted by the Survey Research Center at the University of Michigan in 1969. Preliminary analysis has led several critics to conclude that workers evaluate their jobs by comparing their jobs to other jobs they have had or to jobs their friends now have. They do not compare their jobs, apparently, to some hypothetical national norm. If that is true, it would seem to follow that the elimination, or reduction, of differences between groups (which are now separated in space) will do very little to eliminate dissatisfaction among workers, while the elimination of differences within groups can be expected to become a priority for employers.[87] The creation of autonomous work teams, coupled with a stress on egalitarianism within the group, has in fact become an increasingly popular aspect of job enrichment type innovations.[88]

The reaction of organized labour in Canada and the United States has been overwhelmingly hostile to innovations of this sort. Among the main reasons would seem to be the following:

1. One observer has pointed out that 'Individual job enrichment, as proposed by Herzberg, attacks some of the very bases of trade union action. It is intended to appeal to the worker's individualist motivations and to reduce his material demands. Above all, Herzberg considers that job restructuring should not be discussed with the workers or unions, since consultation of this sort should cover what he calls questions of ''hygiene'' and not those of ''motivation''.'[89]

2. Job enrichment type innovations in non-unionized undertakings offer a realistic strategy for preventing the unionization of the workforce.[90]

3. Job enrichment frequently has led to a reduction in employment. When job enrichment was introduced at General Foods the workforce was cut by nearly 40 percent and at AT and T by an even greater amount.[91]

4. The setting up of autonomous work groups generally leads to an increase of production per worker (the individual's workload is increased).[92]

5. Trade unionists, particularly the leadership, are strongly wedded to the adversary role of unions and the collective bargaining method of labour-management relations. Participation in management, and the sharing of responsibilities for the success or failure of the enterprise, are viewed as being unacceptable by many trade unionists, given the fact that ultimate power in the enterprise and the economy remains in the hands of the employer and the state. Trade unionists do not want to sit on 'both sides of the bargaining table'.

6. The trade union leadership in particular fears that job enrichment type innovations, if sufficiently widespread, will undermine the functions and the power of the trade union movement.

7. Finally, the very fact that these innovations (at least in the past) have been introduced by employers makes trade unionists, at least in Canada and the United States, very suspicious.

One feature which has aroused some interest in terms of its system-maintaining or transforming potential is the idea of co-ownership for labour.[93] The German Acts concerning Capital Accumulation in Workers' Hands (1961 and 1965), the *comunidades industriales* in Peru and the wage earner investment funds in Sweden[94] are all indications of a fairly new addition to the more orthodox innovations discussed earlier.

While the system-maintaining impact of such innovations might well be similar to that of individual profit sharing innovations (closer identification of the worker with the success of the undertaking), the transforming potential raises more complex issues. I am not discussing here the long-term implications of counter-acting or even reversing the current trend towards concentration of ownership in the hands of an ever smaller number of corporate capitalists, although this is an important issue in itself. What I would like to raise is the potential of such innovations for immediate collective and anti-capitalist action by the working class. Zimbalist reports one such example when he comments on the contradictions of employee stock ownership in Peru. This plan, 'entails applying 10 percent of yearly profits to the purchase of stock for the workers up to 49 percent worker ownership...' It has generated 'substantial unrest amongst anxious workers who have protested that employers are covering up profits. Workers have gone on strike demanding open books and an acceleration of the stock transference process'.[95]

The dynamics involved in the Peru experience would seem to be of potential strategic importance. In different circumstances this phenomenon has been described as 'the revolution of rising expectations,' or the 'domino theory,' which was widely used in rationalizing United States' aggression in Vietnam. The 'theory' amounted to the belief that if Vietnam was allowed to fall to the communists, the rest of South-East Asia would follow and the communists would soon stand on the shores of California. An obvious question emerges in relation to the various innovations we have been discussing. It is this:

If in fact work satisfaction increases after the introduction of
such reforms, and if in fact production and profits increase,
then why have these innovations not spread to all capitalist
enterprises and institutions? The conventional wisdom, after all,
postulates that the maximization of profits is the name of the
capitalist game!

The answer might well be, as Andre Gorz and Stephen Marglin
have suggested, that capitalists will use the most efficient
technology only in so far as it is compatible with the maintenance
of social control over the workforce and the entire process of production. The capitalists may well fear that these innovations, which
they have been compelled to introduce reluctantly and sporadically,
will threaten their overall control and power.

There is a basic and important contradiction in the job
enrichment/industrial democracy type of innovations. In order to
survive, capitalists must use the most efficient technology
available. And here we have a case where capitalism has produced a
technology which it seems unwilling to utilize except in special circumstances. They are unwilling to utilize it because they fear that
power and control might escape their embrace if workers are encouraged to make their own decisions on the shop floor, if the
managerial hierarchy is weakened, if minimum skill requirements
are replaced by an increased emphasis on higher skills and responsibilities, if in short the system of production in order to function
comes to rest more openly on the consent and initiatives of the
worker. Might not the workers, collectively, respond in the manner
of Peruvian workers by demanding more autonomy, more control
and more power? Is it too far-fetched to assume that these same
workers will begin to question the very function and purpose of
capitalist ownership and management?

In the majority of cases where job enrichment has been introduced by management, all or some of the following characteristics
have been present.

— The enterprise has been in financial difficulties of some kind,
usually attributed to 'labour problems'.

— Job enrichment has been introduced by 'progressive management' as a more viable alternative to increased doses of Taylorism.

— In many cases in the past innovations have been watered
down or discontinued after the initial crisis was overcome.

These facts would seem to support the notion that capitalists have been aware of the potential unfolding of the 'domino theory'. What can set the domino theory in motion is not so much the exact location of the battlelines (i.e. where the hierarchical division of labour ends), but the process of initiating change. Any shift in the power relations within an enterprise presents a threat to owners and their management.[96] The unfolding of the domino theory may thus cause irreparable damage to the capitalist owner long before the expropriation of private property. It is more than likely that if workers had a substantial say in the goals as well as the organization of the work process, the accumulation of capital would cease to be the dominant function of production. As soon as workers begin to redistribute surplus into higher wages, the creation of safer and more satisfying working conditions, increased leisure, and increased quality in production, the very mechanism which keeps capitalism alive would be threatened.

It is in the correspondence between family, schooling and work that another capitalist contradiction with revolutionary potential seems to emerge. The class sub-culture of students (and their families) is strengthened by schools, and the labour market translates these differences of class culture into income inequalities and occupational hierarchies. Assuming that capitalists will feel compelled to accelerate the introduction of job enrichment and 'industrial democracy' type of innovations on a massive scale, we can expect the demand by industry for more highly skilled workers to increase. Not only will these workers have to be more highly skilled, they will have to exhibit characteristics and behaviour patterns quite different from those required in the past. Instead of obedience to authority they will have to be creative and capable of autonomous action; individual competitiveness will have to be replaced by co-operative behaviour; narrow specialization by a general understanding of a much wider area of the process of production. As Gorz has pointed out,

> the problem for big management is to harmonize two contradictory necessities: the necessity of developing human capabilities, imposed by modern processes of production, and the political necessity of ensuring that this kind of development of capabilities does not bring in its wake any augmentation of the independence of the individual, provoking him to challenge the present division of labour and distribution of power.[97]

Gorz believes that this represents, 'a tissue of explosive contradictions, for to attempt to teach ignorance at the same time as knowledge, dependence at the same time as intellectual autonomy within narrow limits, is to expose oneself — if one cannot enforce a rigorous segregation — to the risk of seeing these limits and this ignorance challenged'.[98]

It may well be that this is what the European Association of National Productivity Centres had in mind when they stated that 'rising educational standards' were one of the main reasons explaining the 'thrust for "industrial democracy" in the 1960s'.[99] Current literature dealing with this issue tends to confirm the view that, at least in Canada and the United States, changes in schooling in the 1960s are related to the increase in dissatisfaction among blue and white collar workers. This increase in dissatisfaction has in turn been related to the accelerated introduction of job enrichment type of innovations.

If the foregoing assumptions are valid, one would expect the state (in capitalist society) to take the initiative in attempting to solve the emerging crisis. Both in Canada and the United States, such initiatives by the state are in fact taking place. The response is more clearly organized and defined in the United States, where the US Government has funded a major research project dealing with the 'Educational Requirements for Industrial Democracy'.[100]

IV CONCLUDING QUESTIONS
AND REMARKS

The complexity of the problems compels me to conclude my paper with more questions than answers. The implications of the research done by Meissner and others (that the experience of constraint and isolation at work carried over into free time) would seem to be clearly system-maintaining, particularly so if we agree with Berelson that the apathy of the masses is essential for the maintenance of political stability. The research reported by Elden (democratized authority structures at work result in more workers attempting to control their own lives, both at work and beyond) would seem to have a clear system-transforming potential. But this would only be the case if the change from authoritarian to more democratic authority structures is accompanied by, or results in, a change in the consciousness of the affected worker. The capitalist system might well be capable of absorbing a substantially larger number of citizens who 'seek to control their own lives'. While Berelson has accurately perceived a contemporary reality, his normative conclusions are not necessarily correct.[101]

A similar problem exists in evaluating the revolutionary potential of such events as the uprising of workers at the Vauxhall works in Luton, wildcat strikes, the UAW no-strike vote and similar experiences elsewhere. Are explosions of militancy of this nature accompanied by changes in the consciousness of the workers involved? Michael Mann, for example, argues that, 'Collective action will normally "fail," or appear to achieve only limited ends, but its real significance lies in the growth of class consciousness through everyday experiences'.[102] If no expansion of consciousness takes place during these moments of militancy, can we expect such events to have a cumulative effect which will eventually trigger off the proletarian revolution? Andre Gorz has argued that there can be no cumulative effect, 'of a series of gradual reforms if they are introduced over a long period and without a very sharp trial of strength based on a considered strategy'.[103] The Vauxhall events as well as wildcat strikes, on the other hand, do represent a trial of strength and an assertion of the collective power of workers, but they are not normally based on a 'considered strategy'. We are still relatively ignorant as to how, and under what conditions, consciousness expands.

I have indicated on a number of occasions that capitalist socialization directed at the citizen as a producer is not as effective as capitalists would undoubtedly like it to be. The assumption has been that socialization of the citizen as consumer has been much more effective. There is, however, at least some evidence (in Canada) that the citizen as consumer exhibits at times 'deviant' values which may well have a potential for system-transforming consciousness and action. It is revealing that despite the public opinion poll craze rampant in Canada, no survey had ever been undertaken to find out what people think of the media as a whole. The Senate Committee on the Mass Media undertook such a survey. Here are a few of the results:

— Close to half of newspaper readers suspect that criminal elements influence the news.

— Three out of ten Canadians feel that the media are not sufficiently critical of government.

— About two-thirds of the sample felt that 'big business' was to blame for press bias, and four out of ten felt that newspapers serve the interests of advertisers or the government, rather than the public at large.[104]

— Only one in five Canadians believe they are getting unbiased reporting of the activities of politicians.[105]

'Shocking' as the *Report on the mass media* has been, it suffers from a number of severe shortcomings which are more or less inherent in any reports which have been requested and are controlled by the spokesmen of the same economic interests they are supposed to investigate. Three shortcomings in particular are of relevance here:

1. Publication, distribution and dissemination of the findings are in effect restricted to a small number of individuals (e.g., why didn't Information Canada disseminate the findings of such reports?).

2. Much of the material collected is left out of the final report. This has been true of the *Report on the Mass Media* as of other similar reports.

3. Such reports rarely question the underlying reasons for the various malpractices and shortcomings they criticize.

While one should guard against reading too much into the results of this survey, they do nevertheless seem to indicate an existing or emerging consciousness about the nature of capitalist institutions.

In conclusion, I want to look at one institutional aspect of capitalist society: the separation of work and life. This split between our place in the social division of labour and the sphere of personal life seemingly divorced from the mode of production,[106] constitutes an enormous obstacle to the realization of class consciousness and revolutionary action. As Mann points out, according to this liberal market view of ethics and society, 'freedom and justice are best secured by "breaking down" man's needs and activities into separate segments (work, consumption, politics, etc.) and providing each one with a separate market in which individuals can express their preferences and realize their needs.'[107] For consciousness to expand (from trade union to class and revolutionary consciousness), the workers must first understand the nature of the economy, then make 'connections between his work and his family life and between his industrial and his political activity'.[108] Revolutionary consciousness and action also presuppose that the workers see socialism as a viable and superior alternative. To quote Mann once again,

> This new society conditions the form of the revolution itself: collective experiences herald the new collective organization of production. Hence 'explosions' must be in the direction of collectivism, firstly in the form of sentiments of solidarity with other workers, and secondly in the grasping by workers of an alternative socialist ideology.[109]

The segmentation of life in capitalist society offers no collectivist experience outside the world of work. Outside his place of work, the worker (as consumer/citizen) is powerless and feels powerless. He has no opportunity to 'form sentiments of solidarity' with other 'consumers'. He has no opportunity to conceive of a viable alternative based on collectivism, cooperation and solidarity with others. His fragmented existence, based, except in his experience with other workers at work, on the individualism and competition of the market system does not allow the realization of total human values. Human communities, on the other hand, require people who participate as total persons rather than as partialized and specialized role-players or position-holders.

This dichotomy in the experience of the citizen in capitalist society is not only a system-maintaining obstacle, it is also the reason why the potential for revolutionary socialist action is essentially limited to the sphere of work. The collectivism, solidarity and potential power experienced by the citizen as producer allow for collective revolutionary action and the initial expansion of consciousness, while the individualism, the isolation and the powerlessness experienced outside the world of work do not. Whatever radical potential may emerge is diverted into system-maintaining institutions or processes (e.g. political parties, voting, etc.) Thus the segmentation of life is reproduced in the very class which is destined to overcome it. Socialist politics should be more concerned with overcoming the social, political and cultural dimensions of the fragmentation of life in capitalist society, instead of concentrating all efforts at nationalizing the 'commanding heights of the economy' and taking over state power. The present wave of capitalist-initiated innovations in the workplace opens opportunities not only to de-mystify the motives, nature and likely effect of such innovations, it also offers opportunities to expose the interrelationships and connections between work and non-work areas of life. An understanding of this correspondence, especially between work, family, education and 'politics,' would seem to be an essential first step in exploding the myth of the allegedly separate and autonomous nature of these aspects of social life.

The whole debate of 'socialism from above or from below' is of importance now. If the consciousness and action of members of the working class is to expand in a revolutionary direction, all intermediaries between the workers and the 'enemy' must be exposed and where necessary, by-passed or removed (unless they perform a specific defensive function). This does not counterpose 'spontaneity' to 'leadership'. Leadership and organization are essential, as national planning will be in a socialist society.

What it means in terms of strategy is that the struggle must be carried out and controlled directly by working people and their recallable delegates. Union leadership in this struggle is consistent with direct democracy only as long, and only up to the level, where direct rank and file participation and control exists. The same holds true for other existing or emerging organs of struggle. To state the ideal is easy — to implement it is incredibly difficult.

NOTES

1. *Canadian Industrial Relations*, The Report of Task Force on Labour Relations, Privy Council Office, Ottawa, December 1968 (subsequently cited as *The Woods Report*).

2. Ibid., p. 3.

3. In 1975, Canadian strike statistics were second only to those of Italy. Donald Rumball, 'Worker Participation in Canada?' in *The Labour Gazette*, Vol. 76, No. 8 (August 1976), p. 429.

4. *The Woods Report*, op. cit., p. 3.

5. Ibid., p. 92.

6. Cf. Ed Finn, *Beyond the Adversary System in Labour Relations*, Industrial Relations Centre, Queen's University, Kingston, 1975, pp. 7-8.

7. *The Woods Report*, op. cit., p. 90.

8. Ibid. p. 91.

9. Ibid., pp. 91-21. The recent (October 1975) introduction of wage and price controls, which in practice have turned out to be largely wage controls, have only strengthened organized labour's determination to demand the return of 'free collective bargaining'.

10. William Johns, 'System of bargaining is defective, PM says,' *The Globe and Mail*, 26 May 1975.

11. *The Globe and Mail*, Editorial, 4 May 1976.

12. Quoted in Rob Burns, 'West German Intellectuals and Ideology,' in *New German Critique*, No. 8 (Spring 1976), p. 13.

13. Jürgen Habermas, 'Strukturwandel der Öffentlichkeit,' Neuwied am Rhein: Luchterhand, 1962, p. 254, quoted in W. Müller and C. Neusüss, 'The Illusion of State Socialism and the Contradiction between Wage labor and Capital,' in *Telos*, 25 (Fall 1975), p. 33.

14. *The Globe and Mail*, 25 May 1976.

15. *Labour's Manifesto for Canada*, Canadian Labour Congress, Ottawa, 1976, p. 10.

16. Time/space problems have prevented me from including a more detailed examination of the social functions of unions and more specifically of collective bargaining. Such an examination would have shown in some detail how unions and collective bargaining have been reduced to their present system-maintaining status.

17. Leo Panitch, 'Labour's Manifesto,' *This Magazine*, Vol. 10, No. 5-6 (November-December 1976), p. 11.

18. M. Burstein et al., *Canadian Work Values: Findings of a Work Ethic Survey and a Job Satisfaction Survey*, Information Canada, Ottawa, 1975.

19. Quoted by Richard Dunstan, 'Power-sharing prime topic at labor-management seminar,' *The Barrie Examiner*, 8 October 1976.

20. Charles J. Connaghan, *Partnership or Marriage of Convenience?*, Labour Canada, Ottawa, n.d., pp. 23-24.

21. Quoted in Stuart Ewen, *Captain of Consciousness: Advertising and the Social Roots of the Consumer Culture*, New York: McGraw-Hill, 1976, p. 54.

22. Ibid.

23. Leo Johnson, *Poverty in Wealth*, Toronto: New Hogtown Press, 1974.

24. M. C. Urquart and K. A. H. Buckley (eds.), *Historical Statistics of Canada*, Toronto: The Macmillan Company of Canada, 1965 (reprinted 1971), p. 130. For an up-to-date analysis, see Arthur Donner, 'Balance of income shifts because of recessions,' *The Globe and Mail*, 16 May 1975.

25. Richard Hyman, *Strikes*, London: Wm. Collins Sons and Co. Ltd. (Fontana) 1972, pp. 85-89. It should also be noted that the labour share is considerably higher in Britain than it is in Canada.

26. M. Burstein, et al., op. cit., pp. 29 and 30.

27. There have been several innovations in job enrichment and 'participative management' in the private sector. In many instances little is known about these experiments (the Aluminium Company of Canada at Kingston is one such example).

28. Essentially these innovations seem to be patterned on successful job enrichment experiments in the United States. Too little is known about them to allow for a more definitive analysis.

29. D. G. B. Executive Board, 'Co-determination in the Federal Republic of Germany,' in G. Hunnius et al., *Workers' Control: A Reader on Labor and Social Change*, New York: Random House, 1973, p. 196. See also Friedrich Fürstenberg, 'Workers' participation — the European experience,' in *The Labour Gazette*, Vol. 76, No. 8 (August 1976), p. 427.

30. Cf. Helmut Schauer, 'Critique of Co-determination,' in Hunnius et al., op. cit., p. 223.

31. R. Herding, *Job Control and Union Structure*, Rotterdam: Rotterdam University Press, 1972, p. 323.

32. Ibid., p. 329. See also Fürstenberg, op. cit., p. 425.

33. Fürstenberg, op. cit., p. 426.

34. Ibid., p. 427.

35. Herding, op. cit., p. 322.

36. Fürstenberg, op. cit., p. 427.

37. Ibid., p. 426.

38. Herding, op. cit., p. 321.

39. Cf. Schauer, op. cit., p. 213. Schauer does not specifically mention the labour director but speaks generally of labour appointed members of supervisory boards and joint production committees (*Wirtschaftsausschuss*).

40. Fürstenberg, op. cit., p. 426.

41. Richard Hyman, *Marxism and the Sociology of Trade Unionism*, London: Pluto Press, 1971, p. 50.

42. Cf. Michael Mann, 'The Social Cohesion of Liberal Democracy,' in *American Sociological Review*, Vol. 35, No. 3 (June 1970), p. 435.

43. Cf. Ralph Miliband, *The State in Capitalist Society*, London; Weidenfeld and Nicolson, 1969, p. 196.

44. Leo Panitch, 'The Role and Nature of the Canadian State,' paper presented to the Annual Meeting of the Canadian Political Science Association, Laval University, 2 June, 1976, p. 12.

45. Mann, op. cit., pp. 436-37; Miliband, op. cit., pp. 195-96.

46. Mann, op. cit., pp. 423-37. For an analysis of manipulative socialization, see Miliband, op. cit., chapters 7 and 8. See also, Michael Mann, *Consciousness and Action Among the Western Working Class*, London: Macmillan 1973.

47. Carl Boggs, 'Gramsci's "Prison Notebooks" — Part 2,' in *Socialist Revolution*, Vol. 2, No. 6 (November-December 1972), p. 46.

48. The editors of *Socialist Revolution*, 'The Making of Socialist Consciousness,' reprinted in Richard C. Edwards et al. (eds.), *The Capitalist System*, Englewood Cliffs, NJ: Prentice-Hall, 1972, p. 504.

49. The complex nature and function of unions and of collective bargaining in the United States and in Canada had to be deleted because of lack of space.

50. Bernard Berelson, 'Survival Through Apathy,' in Henry S. Kariel (ed.), *Frontiers of Democratic Theory*, New York: Random House, 1970, p. 71.

51. I am indebted to John Keane for some of the thoughts on apathy. Cf. John Keane, 'Worker Control, Self-Management, and Secondary Industry: The British Experience,' undated manuscript.

52. Martin Meissner, 'The Long Arm of the Job: A Study of Work and Leisure,' in *Industrial Relations*, Vol. 10, No. 3 (October 1971), p. 260.

53. Quoted in Andrew Zimbalist, 'The Limits of Work Humanization,' in *The Review of Radical Political Economics*, Vol. 7, No. 2 (Summer 1975), p. 53.

54. J. M. Elden, 'The Work Revolution,' *Working Papers for a New Society*, Vol. 1, No. 2 (Summer 1973), pp. 90-91. Cf. Zimbalist, op. cit., p. 53 and Steven E. Deutsch, 'Issues in Comparative Research on Labor and Work Democratization,' paper prepared for the *4th World Congress of the International Industrial Relations Association*, Geneva, 6-10 September 1976, p. 13 and Melvin Kohn, *Class and Conformity: A Study in Values*, Homewood, Ill.: Dorsey Press, 1969, p. 192.

55. Cf. Berelson, op. cit.

56. Cf. Andre Gorz, 'Workers' Control Is More Than Just That', in Hunnius et al., (eds.), *Workers' Control: A Reader on Labour and Social Change*, New York: Random House, 1972, pp. 332-34.

57. Martin Glaberman, 'The Role of Work and Working Class Consciousness,' in A. H. Turritin (ed.), *Proceedings of the Workshop Conference on Blue-Collar Workers and their Communities*, York University (Toronto), 10-11 April 1975. Reprinted in *Our Generation*, Volume 11, No. 2 (Winter 1976).

58. Gorz, op. cit., p. 335.

59. Glaberman, op. cit., p. 131.

60. Huw Beynon, *Working for Ford*, London: Allen Lane (Penguin Books), 1973, p. 305.

61. S. Rokkan, 'Mass Suffrage, Secret Voting and Political Participation', in *Archives Europeenne de Sociologie*, Vol. 2, No. 1 (1961), p. 143; quoted in Miliband, op. cit., pp. 193-94.

62. Miliband, op. cit., p. 194.

63. *The Labour Relations Act*, revised statutes of Ontario, 1970, chapter 232 as amended by 1975, chapter 76, February 1976, p. 39.

64. By vague populist concepts, Mann refers to 'vague simplistic divisions of the social world into "rich" and "poor".' The problem, according to Mann, is that the deviant values which are expressed in concrete terms corresponding to everyday reality and the vague populist notions of rich and poor, worker and boss, are separate. One is concrete and the other is vague. There is no political philosophy uniting the two in the working-class consciousness. Mann, op. cit., p. 436.

65. Ibid., p. 432.

66. Jack Rasmus, 'Setting Gonick straight,' in *Canadian Dimension*, Vol. 10, No. 4 (September 1974), p. 42.

67. Ewen, op. cit., p. 18.

68. Ibid. The remarks refer to the United States of the 1920s.

69. Quoted in Herding, op. cit., p. 299.

70. Ibid.

71. Cf. Bertil Gardell, *Quality of Work and Non-Work Activities and Rewards in Affluent Societies*, Reports from the Psychological Laboratories, The University of Stockholm, No. 403 (December 1973), p. 5 ft.

72. Burstein et al., op. cit., p. 30.

73. P. J. Proudhon, *De la capacité politique des classes ouvrières*, Paris: M. Rivière, 1924. Quoted in R. W. Jones, 'Selected Aspects of Class and Revolutionary Consciousness with Special Reference to Anarchist and Marxist Perspectives' (unpublished manuscript), Toronto, August 1975, p. 60.

74. P. J. Proudhon, *General Idea of Revolution in the Nineteenth Century*, London: Freedom Press, 1923, quoted in Jones, op. cit., p. 61.

75. Bruno Ramirez, 'Collective Bargaining and the Politics of Industrial Relations in the Progressive Era, 1898-1916,' unpublished PhD dissertation, University of Toronto, 1974, p. 230.

76. Ibid., p. 236.

77. Cf. James W. Rinehart, *The Tyranny of Work*, Don Mills, Ontario: Longman Canada Limited, 1975, p. 150.

78. Ibid., p. 138. See also Zimbalist, op. cit., p. 54.

79. Rinehart, op. cit., p. 84.

80. According to the US Bureau of Labor Statistics, absenteeism rose by 35 percent between 1961 and 1972; Zimbalist, op. cit., p. 54.

81. Cf. Paul Blumberg, *Industrial Democracy: The Sociology of Participation*, London: Constable, 1968, p. 123. Special Task Force to the Secretary of Health, Education and Welfare, *Work in America*, Boston, Mass.: the MIT Press, 1973, p. xvii. Zimbalist, op. cit., p. 54.

82. Supreme Aluminium Industries Ltd. For a detailed account see, Jacquelynne Mansell, 'Workers' Participation: A Case Study of Supreme Aluminium Industries Limited', Student Discussion Paper No. 3 (April 1976), Faculty of Environmental Studies, York University, Toronto.

83. Louis E. Davis, 'Job Satisfaction Research: The Post-Industrial View,' in Louis E. Davis and James C. Taylor, *Design of Jobs*, Harmondsworth, Mddx.: Penguin Books, 1972, p. 170.

84. R. Tchobanian, 'Trade Unions and the Humanisation of Work', *International Labour Review* Vol. III, No. 3 (March 1975), p. 205.

85. Reported by a group of German trade unionists from the IG Metall, in Innis Macbeath, *The European Approach to Worker-Management Relationships*, London: British-North-American Committee, 1973, pp. 83-84.

86. *Lotta Continua*, 28 July, 1973. (Interview with three Volvo workers), translated for the author by Bruno Ramirez.

87. Christopher Jencks et al., *Inequality: A Reassessment of the Effect of Family and Schooling in America*, New York, Basic Books, 1972, pp. 247-50.

88. A good example is the General Foods pet-food factory in Topeka, Kansas, which opened in 1971. Richard E. Walton, 'How to counter Alienation in the Plant', *Harvard Business Review* (November-December 1972), pp. 70-81.

89. Tchobanian, op. cit., p. 203.

90. Management spokesmen of Supreme Aluminium Industries Ltd. in Toronto openly admit this.

91. Jack Rasmus, 'Job Control. . . . Not Job Enrichment,' in *Canadian Dimension*, Vol., 10, No. 3 (July 1974), p. 31.

92. Tchobanian, op. cit., p. 204.

93. We are not discussing here profit sharing by individual workers, the social effect of which is clearly system-maintaining.

94. Cf. Rudolf Meidner, *Wage-earner Investment Funds*, Summary of a discussion paper for LO's study campaign, autumn 1975, Swedish Trade Union Confederation, Stockholm, 1976.

95. Zimbalist, op. cit., p. 57 ft. Open books has been a traditional worker control demand in Britain.

96. S. Marglin, 'Work, Technology and Social Change,' address at York University (Toronto), 1 April 1974.

97. Andre Gorz, 'Capitalist Relations of Production and the Socially Necessary Labour Force,' *International Socialist Journal* (August 1965), p. 422.

98. Andre Gorz, *Strategy for Labor: A Radical Proposal*, Boston, Mass.: Beacon Press, 1967, p. 108.

99. European Association of National Productivity Centres, *Industrial Democracy in Europe: The current situation*, Working document, Brussels, March 1976, p. 6.

100. This research has been funded through a grant from the National Institute of Education, Department of Health, Education, and Welfare, United States Government (NIE Grant No. NE-G-00-3-0205), 1 September 1973 — 31 August 1976). The research was carried out by the Portala Institute (Menlo Park, California) to be relocated later to the Center for Economic Studies at Palo Alto, California.

101. See, for example, the scenario developed by Robert Dahl, *After the Revolution: Authority in a Good Society*, Basingstoke: The Macmillan Press, 1973; London and New Haven, Conn.: Yale University Press, 1970.

102. Michael Mann, *Consciousness and Action Among the Western Working Class*, p. 47. For a critical evaluation of the Vauxhall experience and other similar events, see Mann, ibid., pp. 48-54.

103. Andre Gorz, *Socialism and Revolution*, New York: Doubleday Anchor Books, 1973, p. 151.

104. The Special Senate Committee on Mass Media, *The Uncertain Mirror: Report of the Special Senate Committee on Mass Media*, volume I, Ottawa, 1970, pp. 83-84 and *Good, Bad, or Simply Inevitable?*, volume III, pp. 26-28.

105. Ibid., Volume III, pp. 26, 48-49, 62 and 77.

106. Cf. Eli Zaretsky, 'Capitalism, The Family, and Personal Life — Part 2,' in *Socialist Revolution*, Vol. 3, No. 3 (May-June 1973), pp. 83-88.

107. Mann, op. cit., p. 19.

108. Ibid.

109. Ibid., p. 48.

9

SELF-MANAGEMENT — STRATEGY FOR AUTONOMY OR INTEGRATION?

Finn Valentin
University of Copenhagen, Denmark

I THE CONCEPTUAL PROBLEM

The articles in this anthology are contributions to the Conference on 'Liberation of Work and Political Power', that was held at the Dubrovnik Inter-University Centre in 1977. In this chapter, I will attempt to discuss the relationship between the central concepts in the title of the conference. What is the relationship between, on the one side, 'liberation of work' and, on the other, the 'control of political power'?

This is a problem that requires further explication. It must be related to some specific historical questions and conditions, and the concepts must be clarified. Delimiting this article along the historical dimension is easy to account for. We will discuss problems that can be considered as part of the current phase of western capitalism. It will be the developments of the 1960s and 1970s that will be analyzed. The article will discuss Denmark as an example of the problems that will be broached. On the other hand, delimiting the problem's main concepts is a more complicated matter. What do we mean by 'liberation of work', and by 'control of political power'? It is thought-provoking that much of the discussion of this subject in the last decade — including most of the contributions with scientific intentions — attempts to probe the subject without clear definitions of these key concepts. Naturally, this hampers clarity and precision in the scientific and political dialogue.

In the meantime, this weakness is understandable, because all the difficulties of the subject seem to be concentrated in the problem of definition. Right off, it appears, perhaps, simple to define 'liberation' and 'control' as extensions of the behaviorist tradition. Here, both concepts refer to the ability of an individual/group to influence variables in its/their environment according to their own preferences. The more the influence over the greater number of variables, the more the control and freedom that can be attributed to the individual, according to this behaviorist viewpoint. If this kind of definition is useless for our purpose, it is naturally because the very nature of our sphere of inquiry cannot be reduced to coequal 'variables'.[1] By virtue of modern forms of management (autonomous groups, etc.), today's worker can be said to have increased his possibility for influencing more variables in his environment. But this has not brought him one step closer to the control of political power. With his voice as political citizen, he has increased his influence over social areas in the explosive development of the state sector throughout the 1960s and 1970s — without it bringing him one step closer to the liberation of work. In other words, not all variables and interconnections are equally interesting for our problem.

Social science has still not been able to produce a precise understanding of the relationship between micro and macro levels, so that unambiguous, relevant concepts can be extracted. Here we will content ourselves by pointing out the aspect of the concepts that is central for this article. The crux is the concepts' relationship to the dimension that consists of economic property and the forms of appropriation linked to production. Put more concretely, it concerns the workers' legal rights to the means of production, and to the products produced. By 'liberation of work,' we mean the process whereby the workers extend their rights to include ownership of the products and means of production. This extension is then considered the real precondition for saying that the workers have the freedom to frame the production and labor processes on their own. Corresponding to this, we understand 'control of political power' to mean the process whereby the working class, through the state, dissolves the property relations of capitalism. Several other

kinds of property relations can replace these. For example, ownership can be handed over to the state. Or it can — in a variety of
concrete ways — be handed over to the actual producers, by which
the economic prerequisites for the liberation of work, in the above
sense, are established. Thus we see that there is no unambiguous
relationship between 'control of political power' and 'liberation of
work'. The working class can dissolve capitalist property relations
by way of political power, but it is in only one of the variations of
the further development from there, that ownership — and with it
decision-making power over the work process as a whole — is
handed over to the actual producers.[2]

It is important to emphasize that this extension of the workers'
power to the process of production, and in society as a whole, must
be understood as a process. Hereby we underline the main point in
this way of presenting the problem: the worker will never obtain
that power by a sudden and abrupt radical change in the power
structure. We are talking about an objective that is obtained
gradually, by taking one step after another. The main problem then
arises: how can we determine if the previous steps are part of the
correct process? Are they taking us in the right direction? The prior
steps do not, by themselves, lead to an economic foundation for a
new basis of power. At best they can manipulate the prerequisites
so that, many steps later, we can make the great leap.[3]

In other words, we are in an area where what counts, most of all,
is avoiding bourgeois social science's tendency to particularize a
subject. We cannot deal with the central aspect of our problem if
we isolate the question of the liberation of the process of production from the greater change in the state's basis of power. It is
useless to answer the one question with 'political science,' and the
other with theories about the worker in the process of production
(theories of organization, management, motivation, etc.).[4]

We can make our problem even more precise. The change of the
state's basis of power, and the state's change of capitalist property
relations are essential in the revolutionary process. That process
will be brought about by a multitude of precursors, where the existing order will appear unable to meet the demands of the population in a number of areas (prices, employment, planning, social service, housing and environment, etc.). The system will accommodate some of these demands in its attempts to stabilize itself.

This accommodation can take many forms, all of which aim at restoring the capitalist order.

In the following, we will analyze some examples from Denmark in the 1960s and 1970s. These examples will show how demands and problems arise that cannot be met by the institutions of society. The working class, through political parties and the labor movement, has put pressure on the system that could produce new institutions. These new institutions are characterized by three things:

1. They offer a kind of solution to the problems and demands that have arisen.

2. They institutionalize a new power area for the working class. They contain elements of increased influence and political power.

3. But at the same time, they integrate the working class into the capitalist order in new forms that restore and legitimize that order.

The examples try to illustrate the dialectic between reform and revolution. The working class can expand its power, management and control over certain areas through reforms. The same reforms can — in a wider perspective — contribute to the restoration and legitimization of the capitalist order. The problem in the present chapter is to put this dialectic between reform and revolution within a general characterization of the present phase of capitalism, and then illustrate it with the Danish examples.

It would be proper to mention that the problem for the chapter, as it is defined here, can only be considered worthwhile on the basis of certain prior assumptions. The first of these assumptions is obvious enough, that the author's normative preference for the possible social development that is discussed here, is shared. It is a political choice that lies outside the subject of scientific evaluation. Meanwhile, with this choice cleared up, the scientific social-theoretical discussion of the understanding of the relationship between these power-changing social pressures can be reopened.

The second set of assumptions is perhaps less obvious. Our problem is naturally interesting only if one assumes that the gradual extension of the producers' self-management is not a simple evolutionary process — in the extension of self-management itself there is no guarantee that it will automatically continue to be extended. This kind of notion about the self-expanding capacities of self-management is found, though, in a number of varying disguises, both in the political and scientific discussion of the subject. I shall mention two examples taken from hypotheses about the micro and macro levels respectively.

Reference is frequently made to theories of 'level of aspiration' on the micro level. According to these, a limited extension of the producers' self-management will raise their level of aspiration, and the result will be a demand for continued extension — the gradual extension of self-management produced by the mechanisms of individual psychology!

This assumption is naturally vulnerable to criticism. First, it must be remembered that there is a misapplication of the problem of 'level of aspiration,' as it is analyzed both theoretically and empirically. The discussion here concerns the individual's comparison of his own situation or achievement with that of other individuals,[5] not with an abstract objective of a social process. A more fundamental critique must be emphasized. Inferences cannot be made from such individual psychological mechanisms to the macro social processes we are concerned with. In the debate, however, there has been an argument for the expansive character of self-management with macro social reasoning, or, more precisely, a macro social allegory. In that allegory, the transformation, of feudalism into capitalism, and the function of the market in that transformation are referred to. The gradual expansion of the market meant that feudalism's conditions of existence were slowly eaten up from within, and finally there remained just the formal adjustment of the superstructure that happened in the bourgeois revolutions.

The problem with this allegory is, of course, that it does not analyze its premises. An analysis of two main questions is missing. First, is it fair to draw an analogy between the expansion of market mechanisms and the expansion of self-management? Do they have the same kind of relationship to technology and to the power structure throughout their development? Hardly! And with this, we touch on the second main question. Are the central processes, by which the decisive transformations in political power are produced, the same? Little by little, we have some rather good arguments that they are not.[6] Most of all, it must be remembered that the bourgeoisie could take over political power after a development of several hundred years that consolidated the economic basis for that takeover of power. The prerequisites for the overthrow of the capitalist social order are quite different from this — the working class, that must be the leading social force behind this overthrow, is without an economic basis for its political power.

Tenable arguments that there are inherent capacities in self-management that insure steady extension and development are thus lacking. On the contrary, there is no ground for supposing that the partial and limited allotment of self-management rights is a step on the way toward a self-governing socialist society. This is first and foremost due to the fact that the allotment of partial rights of self-management is essential in the integration strategies with respect to the working class, that are crucial for advanced capitalist societies.

We are in an historical phase just now, where it would be dangerous to simplify the problem in the revolutionary process. We would be doing that, though, if we assumed that the strategy of self-management had a snowball effect. We must substitute an analytical question for that supposition: under what conditions is the allotment of rights of self-management a step towards autonomy and socialism, and under what conditions is it a step towards integration on capitalist premises? This latter, in the wider perspective, diverts the working class from its course towards becoming an autonomous class in a socialist society.

The answer to this question cannot take the shape of a definitive specification of the terms by which different concrete situations can be evaluated. Varying from the one historical situation to the other, self-management strategies form part of widely different relationships, and influence and are influenced by far different areas of the total class struggle. Instead, we will attempt to emphasize some main features of the functional conditions of this strategy in the current phase of capitalism. Our hypothesis is that the vulnerable aspect of the self-management strategy lies in its functional relationships to strategies for the integration and harmonization of the working class with capitalism. Therefore, in the following, we will isolate these integration strategies and their connection to the social structural development of advanced capitalism. It is important to understand these integration strategies, because they constitute the most important functional condition for socialist oriented strategies of self-management.

II AUTONOMY AND INTEGRATION
IN THE PRESENT PHASE OF
CAPITALISM

From the vantage point of the working class, the decisive question as regards any development in society is, does it — in the long run — contribute to class autonomy? That is, does it further the possibilities of the working class for functioning as an independent social force? Or does it have subversive and retarding effects on class autonomy? Is there an undermining of autonomous organizations and collective learning processes, for the benefit of increasing integration on capitalist premises?

The decisive contradiction of the class struggle, therefore, consists of the relationship between integration and autonomy. However, we must not understand that contradiction on the basis of bourgeois ideology's voluntaristic ideas. That contradiction does not exist only by virtue of working class political will and intentions. It does not exist on a par with any other 'interest group's' desire to preserve its autonomous influence in the society. The working class position in that contradiction between autonomy and integration, unlike that of other interest groups, can be considered decisive for the continuation of the course of history. This is because it corresponds to the crucial socio-economic contradictions of capitalism itself.

What kind of connection is there, then, between these socio-economic contradictions of capitalism, and the position of the working class in the contradiction between autonomy and integration? Let us restate the main characteristics of capitalism. Just as in any other type of society, so too in the capitalist, there must be an ongoing production of goods, which should partly permit the present reproduction of society, and partly permit an expansion of the needs that are met. In other words, there must be an economic and technological basis for a continuous expansion of the production apparatus.

Throughout history, the changing technological basis of production has produced quite different principles of social organization as solutions to these fundamental economic demands, and the future will undoubtedly offer new variations. The dominant principle of organization in a large part of the world for the last 200-300 years has been capitalist. This means, primarily, that ownership of the means of production and products is private, and that the process of production, as a whole, therefore, is subject to the interests of the increasingly fewer members of society who own them. Whether or not it harmonizes with these owners' own personal inclinations, the system's economic logic forces them to maximize profit. Total social reproduction and growth have thereby been made subject to private improvement of profits.

There have been both progressive and regressive effects in the societies subject to this principle of organization. The economic survival of the capitalist depends on his continuous investment in, and exploitation of, technological progress. It is that compulsion and pressure on the technological level of production that Marx refers to in his sentence about 'capitalism's civilizing effects'. But it is this same development that necessitates a steady growth in the coordination of social production. The extreme division of labor and the reliance on an advanced technology increase interdependence and the need for coordination between society's different processes. Marx characterized this as rendering an intensifying interdependency (*Vergesellschaftung*).   The basis of the regressive effects of capitalist organization are given by this term. Instead of promoting society's development, the fact that production is subject to capitalist interest in profit now becomes an obstacle. Individual capitalists cannot establish the necessary coordination because they pursue their own objectives. And these objectives will often come into direct conflict with society's own well being. A discrepancy arises between the population's demand for goods and a suitable quality of life, and society's possibilities of meeting them with the given principle of organization.

Along with Lelio Basso, we can talk about two conflicting logics in capitalism.[7] According to the one, the production of profit subjugates the different areas of society. In this sense a kind of coherence is produced. According to the other, an advanced technology and division of labor produce a need for control and coordination which cannot be realized, and the result is economic and institutional crisis. These 'logics' interact — the more advanced the subjugation of society by the production of profit, the deeper the crises that are produced. When the principle of organization itself — 'the social order' — comes closer to a crisis, the first logic must be extended not only to elements of the economic circulation. The need arises to subordinate the formation of opinion and ideological currents. In this way, the system has become dependent on its ability to integrate the political appraisal of its members: as autonomous processes, their consciousness and self-organization become a potential challenge to the capitalist order.

The main contradiction of capitalist organization of society is between the few who possess the means of production and the many who do not. In the present phase of capitalism, that contradiction is expressed by the pressure for the loyalty and integration of the non-possessors into the capitalist order. Opposed to this is the struggle for their autonomy. The more inadequate capitalism is in producing a continued rational development of western society;[8] the more the objective foundation for the social forces that maintain autonomy is strengthened — and the more the pressure for integration will be intensified. The ability of the 'non-possessors' to avoid this pressure for integration and legitimacy has become decisive for the next great step in the history of societies. It will decide if such a step will be taken and the course of development of the new social order.

III THE STRATEGY OF INTEGRATION AND THE INSTITUTIONS OF SOCIETY: SELF-MANAGEMENT AND THE WELFARE STATE

Above, we discussed strategies aimed towards integrating the working class into the capitalist order. In this section we will look closer at how this kind of strategy is established and implemented.

First of all, it must be emphasized that we are not using the term 'strategy' in its usual sense. Normally, the word 'strategy' is used to designate a goal-directed action, with calculation of how difficulties can be overcome in order to reach that objective. Our use of the term preserves part of that definition. The intention is to keep the working class integrated in capitalist society, in spite of the disintegrative effects of its economic and institutional crisis. We do not, however, see rationally calculating subjects behind the execution of that strategy. Rather, the strategy is the result of actions from quite different groups, institutions and organizations in society. As long as we are discussing the more advanced parts of the west, there is no sense in attributing that strategy to any single conspiring elite in the capitalist class.

We should remember that almost all the institutions of society are established to create and maintain the existing social order. The demand to make the existing order function is felt, through daycare, courts, workers' parliamentary representatives, etc., and also in the growing crisis. Concrete individuals in these situations cannot be said to be conspiring to integrate the working class. But integration is the result of an extremely adaptable 'strategy' that consists of the sum total of many institutions' well meant attempts to 'solve the problems'. This should not make us forget that the bourgeoisie is always present in the political struggle. But this should help us remember that capitalism is neither maintained — nor destroyed — by conspiratorial endeavors.[9]

Thus, the question that was formulated in the beginning of this section, about how that strategy of integration is carried out, is an extremely broad and complex one. In a sense, it has been the main question in the tradition of Marxist analysis — and in a good part of non-Marxist sociology — since the classics of the 1800s.[10] In the last decade's breakthrough in Marxist analysis alone, we find abundant analyses of this question, in connection with critical investigations of family life, mass media, the educational system, legal system, state welfare politics, etc. Therefore, this article can discuss only two examples. These will be taken from the development of Danish society in the 1960s and 1970s. Both examples will illustrate capitalism's present difficulties in combining accumulation and growth with integration and loyalty to the system. The example from the 1960s will emphasize the development of the state's welfare institutions. We will attempt to show how these institutions developed as a consequence of both the reorganization of the production process, and of the changes in the social structure produced by growth. The state welfare institutions developed as a reaction to this reorganization. At the same time, new patterns of centralization of power emerged — and with them a loss of autonomy. While the section on the 1960s emphasizes the autonomy of the working class in the relationships among economic growth, costs of growth and the institutional answer in the form of the welfare state, the following section on the 1970s stresses the relationship between power changes in the enterprises and the economy itself.

With the beginning of the high conjuncture in the 1950s, conditions developed for the Danish Social Democratic Party to implement its reforms. Just after the war, a profound reform program was drawn up, but it had neither economic nor political possibilities of being implemented. A toned-down variation of this program began to be realized from the beginning of the 1960s. In this variation, the infringements on property rights had been removed. The reforms had two main dimensions. On the one hand, they were part of a program for increased equality. It was thought that this equality could be furthered only by redistributing incomes and social benefits. According to this program, the way ahead was by progressive taxation, state income transfers, social welfare programs, etc. Today, even within the Social Democratic Party, it is recognized that this program simply did not succeed — it did not produce social equality. But at that time it was the strategy, and together with other social and economic factors, combined to create a mushrooming state apparatus. The second dimension contained a policy for economic growth. It was a strategy for the acceleration and restructuring of capital accumulation in Denmark. This resulted in state stimulation and preferential treatment of investments, state pressure on demand, a liquidation of small units in agriculture to channel resources into industry, state expansion of infrastructure, etc. Extensive investments were undertaken throughout the 1960s, and rapid growth in the level of productivity was achieved. The assumption was that this economic growth was a precondition for the realization of the politics of equality and welfare.

However, it is difficult to combine growth and equality and welfare on the basis of capitalist accumulation. The rapid growth and restructuring in Denmark during the 1960s could not be achieved without costs. These costs appeared in many ways. For example, labor power was exposed to sharply increased attrition in the production process. During the course of the 1960s, several labor unions reached the point where only half of their members reached normal pension age. The other half was either dead or invalid — or pre-pensioned. The strain of the work process manifested itself both by an increased number of accidents at work, and increased psychological problems all due to shift work, speeded up and monotonous work.

The development of production also resulted in other problems that were just as serious, though less tangible. The family was restructured considerably in the 1960s. The demand for labor power exceeded what the traditional labor market — supplemented by the proletarianized small farmers — could supply. The result was an ample increase in female labor power. This presupposed, though, the building of institutions that could take care of children during working hours. The question of society's aged was added to the problem of the breakup of the family pattern. Modern industry cannot use them in production, they no longer have a function in the family, and the housing pattern makes a common life between generations impossible. The answer was the building of state institutons for the housing and care of the aged. This development during the 1960s dissolved several important social relations and functions that had been within the family, and placed them in institutions. From being a member of a family, the individual now became a client or a patient in a state institution.

Undoubtedly, for those exposed to these changes, there was a striking fall in the quality of life — a concept that, characteristically, arose in that period. Deterioriation of the quality of life proceeded in other ways too, as a by-product of economic growth. Industrial destruction of the environment became especially important. There was direct destruction of the natural environment. Housing and urban environment were also influenced, for instance in urban concentration, dominance of auto traffic in the city scene, air pollution in housing areas, etc. To these kind of deteriorations we can add the issue of the structural effects of an anarchistic principle of growth. This appears as regional imbalance in development, where the fringe areas have increasing problems with unemployment, and fewer possibilities of offering residents a reasonable share of the welfare.

These were some of the features in the development of Danish society under the leadership of the Social Democratic Party, which was committed to a program of equality and welfare. As we have seen, there is a fundamental contradiction between capitalist growth and ideals such as equality and welfare. The Social Democratic Party's 'solution' to that contradiction was to build a gigantic state apparatus that could attempt to maintain a reasonable level of welfare and equality and, at the same time, harmonize that objective with the demands for continued economic growth. Thus, another structural dislocation in Danish society arose during the 1960s. State expansion took place with amazing haste. Between 1960 and 1972, state expenses grew from 25 percent of the national income to 50 percent. The number of public employees doubled. The pressure of taxes became the highest in Europe. From 1966 until 1972, state investments increased by 150 percent. The expenditures for health and social services account for much of the growth of public expenses, though education is among the most expensive areas as well.[11]

What is really behind these statistics and reports of institutional expansions and displacements? If so desired, one can choose the ideological drapery the contents are clothed in. In the meantime, the contents cannot be denied. The state takes the responsibility of supplying compensation to members of society for the costs they have incurred in the economic growth. This is the essence of the remunerations of the social insurance system and also of the state financed health system. But these compensations have a specific purpose, to see to it that the client/patient/case becomes available for the labor market again as fast as possible. State expenses here are subject to the same rationale as outlays to infrastructure, investment subsidies, etc. Growth and integration form a synthesis! Financed by half the national income, this synthesis expresses itself in monolithic governmental institutions. And, in accordance with this logic, there was never a moment's consideration, in the formation of these state welfare institutions, of giving the users any control over them. The institutions are the instruments of the state as opposed to the users.

Whereas the users are cut off from any control of the institutions, different possibilities exist for their formal participation in the administration of them. This participation can take several forms, such as parent representation in day-care institutions' administration or in the 'public phases' of regional planning. We will not dwell on a critical examination of these arrangements, but just point out that Mandel's differentiation between participation and control has seldom been more relevant.[12]

Let us now focus our argument on the main theme of this chapter. Let us raise the question: what does the development of the Danish welfare state mean for the individual wage earner's autonomy? The construction of the welfare state is not just a story of economic growth that produces problems, which then find their

solution in state social policies. The construction of the welfare
state is also the story of a change in the margin of authority and
autonomy of the wage earner. It is the story of his loss of control
over a number of relationships in his life — relationships he is part
of and dependent upon.

This loss of control or de-authoritization appears in a two-fold
way:

1. The individual has no control over the growth he contributes
to. The Constitution's protection of property rights is the barrier
that makes it impossible for the individual citizen, even with his
political participation, to obtain any influence on the kind and content of growth. This decision-making authority is in the hands of
individual capitalists. (And, as we will see in the next section, reformism's dilemma about future development lies here. Even though
this decision-making authority can be undermined and collectivized
by law, the problem still remains that accumulation must take place
on capitalist premises.)

No Danish citizen has sanctioned, by his cross on the ballot, the
development of production that has resulted in the fundamental
problems we outlined above. Industrial accidents, family erosion,
and decay of urban and natural environments are the results of an
accumulation to which the worker has supplied only his labor
power — not his decision-making competence. This is really the
primary deprival of authority. This is not only a deprival of the
authority of the individual citizen, but also of parliamentary
democracy. As long as the social order upholds the separation of
economy and politics, the state will remain the element that supplies the corrections and compensations for the costs produced by
the 'development of society,' — a development whose essence lies
outside the decision-making area of politics.

2. This development is a loss of authority and control in another
sense. The state supplies the compensations, subsidies, treatments,
etc. A monolothic institutional apparatus has been constructed for
this purpose. The wage earners — the users of these institutions —
have not the least control over them. On the contrary, contact with
these institutions means that they will be reduced to 'a case,' 'a
client,' or be transformed in some other way into an object for professional treatment. On the one side, capitalist growth produces a
dissolution of daily life and reproduction. On the other, this

reproduction is reestablished via institutional solutions that lie outside the individual's control.

The powerlessness of the individual in this double development can be grasped even with the behaviorist definition of control that was rejected earlier. To a striking degree, the individual now has a reduced capacity for influence over fewer variables in his life.

This critique of the 1960s welfare state should not be considered a reactionary view — i.e., that it is not the obligation of the state to compensate and treat those who bear the burdens. Our critique tends in the opposite direction. We wish to point out that the history of the development of the welfare state does not deal just with social problems and their solution. This history also deals with the fact that these solutions became institutionalized in forms that increased the deprival of control — something that already lay in the principle of organization of society. In this sense, it could be said that the advanced Danish welfare state drained the autonomy and self-management of the individual.

This development must also be understood as the result of political pressure from the reformist bloc of the Social Democratic Party and labor movement. The demands of the wage earners from society have been formulated and channeled by this bloc, and these demands have often been realized via struggle against the bourgeois forces and parties. By supporting the social democratic bloc, the wage earner has gained, in return, the benefits of the welfare state. When demands are articulated, and the state reacts obligingly, an integrative effect is produced. The basic mechanisms in that effect is that the reformist center gives its political acceptance and support to the existing arrangements of society. In return, reformism gets the opportunity of realizing its demands with the aid of the state — provided that these demands do not challenge the principles of society's organization.[13] At the same time, reformism has a near monopoly over the formulation and channeling of wage earners' interests, and is dependent on that sustained support. Therefore, it uses its organizational and ideological resources to legitimize the results obtained in the political confrontation with the bourgeoisie. This integrative effect is produced as long as these connections function.

And this effect is amassed without any challenge to the capitalist order. The integrative effect is, in fact, the utmost consequence of the fact that that order functions unchallenged. These aspects of

the 1960s development can be summed up by the following
paradoxical tendencies:

1. The reformist bloc in the 1960s had better economic and
political conditions for realizing its program of growth, equality
and welfare.

2. The program was generally carried out during the 1960s. In
that respect there is evidence of increased political power for the
wage earner.[14]

3. In the meantime, the realization of the program intensified
the de-authoritization of the wage earners regarding the economic
development and regarding the build up of governmental institutionalization of reproduction and daily life.

4. The interaction between the citizen and the political system
has permitted the citizen's continued acceptance of the system. The
consequence has been an integrative effect.

The purpose of this analysis of the development in the 1960s has
been to show how complex the relationship between political power
and autonomy is. Political power is identical with parliamentary
power in the reformist strategy. And in that sense, the reformist
party had the power to carry out substantial parts of its program
throughout the 1960s. But as we can see, there is no simple relationship between receipt of political power and the development of
wage earners' autonomy. The example shows that political power,
exercised with flat acceptance of the capitalist society, leads to integration and loss of autonomy. If our objective and main strategy
is a dynamic, expanding interaction between self-management of
work and daily relationships, and the control of political power,
then we can conclude that the Danish welfare state of the 1960s did
not bring us closer to that goal. On the contrary, the period meant a
learning of integration amidst a loss of control.

IV A WAGE EARNERS' INVESTMENT
FUND. A STRATEGY FOR
WHAT? THE DANISH CASE
OF THE 1970s

In this section, we will discuss a Danish example from the 1970s,
the Social Democratic Party's proposal for 'economic democracy'.

This is really a complex of proposals. It is interesting in this connection because it gives a total impression of the way the class forces in Denmark function, which is decisive for working class autonomy. The proposal-complex attempts to solve the main, structurally conditioned problems of the capitalist economy in Denmark. It also supplies a blueprint for reprogramming the relationships between the institutions that administer society's main contradiction, i.e. the state, institutions for wage fixing, the labor movement's economic power, financial institutions, etc.

The proposal-complex was formulated in the beginning of the 1970s. It should be noted, first, that it was the child of the high conjuncture, and, second, that it could not be carried out in its entirety given the constellation of class forces in Denmark. We consider it a suitable point of departure for our analysis anyway, partly because the proposal gives an overall illustration of some central aspects of the integration strategy that is discussed in this chapter, and partly because the proposal still is — and in a certain sense must be — a cardinal point for the Social Democratic Party and, as such, can be expected to be carried out, step by step, when the political situation permits.

It should be evident that we must begin with the problems of Danish accumulation and class struggle that the proposal explicitly and implicitly refers to. A short sketch of the structural and historical conditions of its background is necessary.

The special feature of Denmark's economic development over the last century has been the central position of agriculture. The basis of Denmark's modernization from 1870 was intensive agriculture and the processing of agricultural products. Industrial development depended on these.[15]

The social organization of accumulation in agriculture in this modernization process was likewise significant. The widespread use of cooperative societies in slaughter houses, dairies, heavy goods, etc., was a conscious and successful strategy on the farmers' side to avoid the capitalization of agriculture (i.e. centralization and proletarianization). Up through this century, the country's principal industry remained in the hands of an agrarian petty bourgeoisie, and it was here that the Social Democratic Party found its primary alliance partners right from the beginning. It extended that alliance pattern to the petty bourgeoisie in the urban occupations.

It must be remembered that a real bourgeoisie was only weakly developed in Denmark. The lack of raw materials and thus basic heavy industries is one of the reasons for this. This basis of accumulation naturally gave Denmark severe problems with the rapid integration into the world market that set in after the second world war. At the end of the 1950s, entry into the EEC was under discussion. The difficulties that would arise for the Danish economy by the liquidation of protective tariffs illustrates the severity of the problem.

A second wave of industrialization in Denmark began with the high conjuncture in 1957, and the results of this in increased rate of growth and per capita income were impressive. However, the economy remained vulnerable because it was based on light industry. In some areas this industry was so advanced that it could assert itself on the world market with highly developed specialized products. But this industry as a whole was characterized by a low organic composition, a low degree of centralization and large sectors of capital and labor power bound in small artisan and retail enterprises.[16] The consequence of this vulnerability, until now, has been a large deficit in the balance of payments, and a relatively high rate of inflation. A high level of wage increases, state investment and consumption has augmented these difficulties. At the end of the 1960s and beginning of the 1970s, growing difficulties appeared in meeting the need for capital to continue this expansion. Private enterprises had a low level of savings.[17] At the same time, capital investors preferred to seek profits in the highly inflationary rise in land prices. In addition, capital sought the consumption sector's high profits and rapid turnover. Thus, the problems of low investment potential became even worse because a considerable part of the capital that was available was channeled away from industry.

When the crisis of the 1970s shocked the world economy, Denmark was relatively weak due to its internal structural crisis. This structural crisis is not just economic. It is also a crisis for the 'structure' of the class struggle. Throughout its 100 year history, the Social Democratic Party has been closely connected to the labor movement. Together, they have developed and administered the reformist program that has been able to maintain hegemony in the Danish working class, and find support in certain sectors of the middle classes and petty bourgeoisie. The Social Democratic Party identified itself with the expansion of the state sector in the 1960s as we discussed above. The crisis of the 1970s, and a bourgeoisie on the offensive, block a continuation of this policy, and instead demand a reduction of the state's welfare programs. A Social Democratic Party that must participate in a reduction of the level of welfare is obviously in an identity crisis, and in need of a supplement to the bulk of its political strategy.

The labor movement is in the same situation. The most important issue here is incomes policy. During the high conjuncture, it appeared that a free wage formation under full employment would contribute to an inflation the economy could not bear. The crisis in the 1970s has intensified the demand for political control of the wage level. In fact, since the crisis set in, there has been state regulation of the wage level. In this way, an important part of the labor movement's legitimacy has been undermined and essential parts of its basis of power removed.[18] For the labor movement, even more than for the Social Democratic Party, it is obvious that there is an inevitable need to restructure its functions and its power basis.

These are, in broad terms, the crisis in the economy and class struggle that must be understood as the background for the proposal-complex on 'economic democracy'. Let us look at the content of the proposal.[19]

1. A fund, owned by the wage earners, would be built up over a number of years. This fund would be created from a payment amounting to 5 percent of the annual wage sum that the employer will continually pay into it. The employers, however, do not have equal access to utilize the funds. The largest and most profitable enterprises would be in the best position; the considerable number of smaller enterprises would be in a bad position. This is partly because the proposed law insists that the fund's resources be used in growth areas of the Danish economy. When the fund is built up, it will have at its disposal a financing capacity that will be more than one-third of the total Danish share capital.[20] Therefore, we can conclude that the fund will have a central position in the allocation of capital in society, and that this influence will be used to restructure Danish industry. The proposal clearly aims at contributing to the solution of the fundamental structural problems of Danish capitalism.

2. Certificates as to the individual wage earner's share of the fund would be issued. This certificate can first be redeemed after

seven years. All wage earners receive the same share of the fund.

3. When the fund's resources are invested, it receives a block of shares in the enterprise corresponding to the investment. The fund's block of shares cannot be more than 50 percent of the total value of shares in a single enterprise. The shares give normal voting rights at the general meetings. The voting right is exercised by the wage earners in the said enterprise.

4. The fund is led by a council consisting of representatives from different interest groups and public officials. The wage earners' organizations have the real control over the fund's decisions. It is interesting, in this respect, that the individual holders of the fund's certificates do not elect or designate their representatives to the fund's leadership. Instead, these are designated by the officials of the Labor Organization and other wage earner organizations.

5. The construction of this wage earner fund has a definite relationship to incomes policy. Naturally, this does not appear literally in the text of the law proposal. But it is central in all the arguments in favor of the law. The labor movement's acceptance of this abrogation of its function of fixing wages — the crux in political determination of the wage level — forms part of a quid pro quo with the construction of a fund under its control. This is one of the points where the proposal's character as a child of the high conjuncture shines through. The high conjuncture's increased demand for labor power accelerated the development in wages — and put the labor movement in a strong position in negotiations about a regulation of wage increases by incomes policy. The economic crisis and unemployment have put the Social Democratic Party and the labor movement so much on the defensive that they have not been able to assert counter demands authoritatively in the last years' implementation of an incomes policy. This is undoubtedly one of the important reasons that the proposal has not become a reality.

Since this chapter has to be short, only the main features of this complex proposal can be described. We will be subject to this limitation in our analysis of the proposal below. The proposal raises a flood of questions. We will try to limit ourselves to those which directly relate to the problem of the present chapter. So let us look at the development of working class autonomy and its position in the power structure of society according to the proposal.

Institutionalization of corporative wage fixing is one of the most consequential aspects of the proposal. The wage struggle is the essence of the working class's laborious construction of industrial and trade organizations. The key instrument of power here is the strike, and the opponent is the capitalist who buys labor power. The state's fixing of the wage level removes this essential function from the labor organizations. Further, this is followed up by state sanctions against those sections of the working class that do not accept wage fixing. This will make it more difficult for the worker to localize the main contradiction in society amid the smoke of technocratic ideology, that it is even today.

No matter how you look at it, the main content of this development is the transference of autonomy and competence from working class organizations to the state. And at this level, the working class can only manifest itself as one among many interest groups. The counter-question is, does the working class receive anything in this transfer? It does, of course — and receives something that is a potential source of power: control over part of the society's capital. Not an unimportant strategic tool! The 'organization' of this power, though, is questionable, when seen from the main theme of this chapter — the division of power in relationship to the individual worker. We can raise two simple questions: 1. Who owns the fund? The individual wage earners by virtue of their certificates. 2. Who controls the fund and its decisions? The leaders of the wage earners' organizations. The right to designate the wage earners' representatives to the fund's leadership lies with these organizations. This right is not set up so that it can be exercised by the wage earner (for instance in one form of direct representation or another).

Does the wage earner, then, have no decision-making authority? He does have some, because the fund delegates its share-based voting rights to those employed in the individual enterprise. In principle, they can obtain parity in the management of the enterprise. A position on the company's management, though — even a position of parity — is a dubious prize for the workers. These arrangements of co-determination are already found in different forms and degrees in several countries. Parts of West German industry have already reached parity. The imposed secrecy over management's discussions is just one of the conditions that undermines the worker representatives' power. We will not dwell on the question, as it is well illustrated and analyzed in the literature about self-management.[21] A review of that literature shows that there is no real power in this form of representation. It is formal, and is easily undermined.

These developments in the division of power and its institutionalization can be read in the very words of the proposal. To these we must add developments that will arise as after-effects of the proposal, which cannot be seen in an analysis of the manifest institutions. This analysis is especially necessary because it touches on aspects that are perhaps most important in the long run.

First of all, the possibilities of producing contradictions and disorganization within the working class will be discussed. These possibilities appear as mechanisms that can function both in the enterprise and in the labor movement. This possibility lies in the underlying logic of the proposal. On the one hand, the labor movement attends to its traditional role of safeguarding the wage earners' interests. But, on the other hand, it is now subject to a community of interests with capital. In the labor movement's control of capital formation, the emphasis will be on the word 'capital'. The fund's fundamental interest would be to see optimal returns for its invested capital. Whether the labor representatives in the fund's management like it or not, they will have to administer these enormous resources on capitalist premises. This produces definite interests in such phenomena as wage sweating, rationalization, closing unprofitable enterprises in spite of unemployment problems, etc.

These interests are in direct contradiction with wage earners' interests. This contradiction has been transformed from being one between labor and capital to being one within the labor movement. The contradiction will appear also in the individual enterprise, where wage earner representatives in management may sanction decisions necessary for profit making, but which can also mean lay offs, speed ups, compromises about security and work environment, etc. On the national level, contradictions will appear when the proposal's structure-regulating intentions are to be realized. In certain branches, enterprises may be shut down, while other sectors' growth is accelerated — including improved wage conditions in these. There will always be some sort of regulation of the branch structure. But what is new is that the advantages and disadvantages of this regulation for the working class will be the result of decisions in this class's own organizations. The contradictions that will thus appear must be seen in light of the divisions that already exist in the Danish workers' movement, divisions that have regional, wage and political-ideological aspects. This is not an argument against working class usurpation of influence over the development of production. But it is an argument that there can be great risks in usurping that influence in forms that let capitalist premises go unchallenged.

We have had some experiences that pertain to this problem. Since the appearance of the crisis in Denmark, the Social Democratic Party has supported a political fixing of the wage level. The close relationship between the party and the labor movement has meant the latter's support for this policy. Though in a less refined form, we have the same situation here that will arise in the fund's decision-making. Decisions will have to be taken with the purpose of stabilizing capitalist accumulation, contrary to the wage earners' interests. The working class party and labor movement place themselves at the disposal of the forces that wish to realize this accumulation, and that, at the same time, wish to guarantee working class approval. Incomes policy has already produced a fall in real wages in some areas, and considerable opposition within the labor movement to accepting this kind of wages policy. The labor movement is forced to put down that opposition at times, and thus the conflict within its ranks is aggravated. The corporative tendencies show their consequences. The labor movement tries to put down those members who above all struggle for class interest, and who display some of the few attempts at self-organization, self-management, and adherence to rights of autonomy.

It is worth remembering, in this connection, that there is no movement within the working class behind the proposal for the fund. The proposal is the result of the leadership's attempt to find a strategy of development under altered conditions that necessitate incomes policy, structure regulation, and the like. There are no collective learning processes behind that strategy at the base of the labor movement; the proposal is not the result of a genuine democratically formulated strategy. This means, too, that if the proposal is realized, there will not be a movement in the working class that will allot to itself the institutions that will be created (the fund's management, representatives to the enterprise administration, etc.). Workers can be taught to handle these functions — in fact that is the intention, according to the proposal. But a social foundation as such for the institutions cannot be produced. They will be without a foundation, and will probably mean aggravation of the labor movement's present problems of passivity, bureaucracy, and only formally democratic decision-making processes. Despite appearances, the labor movement will be forced to combat the attempts at conscious self-organization that will come from the opposition, instead of building further on them.

Is this a one-sided critique? If we recall that the proposal was put forth by one party and one labor movement that support reformism, can it not be understood as one proposal among many that can produce the transformation to socialism by reforms? It is possible. The decisive thing is what is meant by socialism and how that socialism will be designed by the forces that precede it. The proposal implies profound changes. Accumulation will no longer be guided only by individual capitalist's interests. The fund will have considerable influence on the pattern of investment, and there will be a certain redistribution of the profits of production via the wage earners' ownership of fund certificates. There are important tendencies toward collectivization of both profit and investment.

But the real decision-making authority will be with the officials of the wage earners' organization. The essence of the proposal can be said to be that it moves a certain part of investment dispositions from the individual owners of capital to the leadership of the wage earners' organizations, who in the administration of the fund are supplemented by civil servants and representatives of other interest groups' administrations. There are no dynamic elements in the proposal that can initiate the development of a movement and self-organization at the basic level, which can control the centralization of power. This is cause of serious concern. One may be concerned about both the fact that the proposal is launched under the slogan of 'economic democracy', and about the division of power in the society that the proposal will reform us into. These concerns take on an added dimension when it is recalled that the proposal is a quid pro quo for the acceptance of corporative wage formation.

V SUMMARY AND CONCLUSION

We have discussed some of the features of Denmark in the 1960s and 1970s. For the 1960s, the development of the welfare state, and for the 1970s, the appearance of a Social Democratic Party strategy in which the labor unions receive increased power in controlling accumulation and in return subject themselves to corporative wage formation. This is a strategy that has still not been realized, but it reflects the nature of the contradictions in the Danish society of the 1970s.

Both examples — 1960s and 1970s — illustrate the theory of capitalism's present phase that was summed up in section II. Capitalism can no longer be administered by liberal principles. Technology, division of labor, and the system's dependence on its citizens' loyalty are all too advanced. So advanced that it is necessary to find solutions to the ruptures in the individual's reproduction that are produced by economic growth (solutions like the welfare state's compensations and planning). And so advanced that the pattern of investment can no longer be left at the disposal of individual capitalists, but must be adjusted by the wage earner funds' role in capitalist accumulation.

New institutions and power groups emerge from the crises in society's capitalist principle of organization (e.g., the state apparatus and investment funds). Our two examples point out the basic tendency towards centralization of control in these new institutions. The crises do not lead to a delegation of control but, in general, to a rendering of control in the state. At the same time, the development must appear as a decentralization of power to assure the integrative effect of these institutions. Can it be denied that one controls an increased portion of society with one's ballot, the larger and more regulative the state sector is? Does the wage earner not get new rights with his fund certificates and representation in the administration of corporations? Is this not an increase of individual power? Is it not increased 'self-management' of more aspects of life? No, it is not. It is a strategy for participation in a political system or enterprise but with no control over it. Thus it can be feared that the main tendencies in the present phase of capitalism are, on the one side, a de-authoritization and loss of control and, on the other, an integration and engagement in the system through strategies of participation.

The real cause of these tendencies is not just the crisis in capitalism. It is also the crisis of reformism. This latter crisis is brought about by the political logic of reformism as such: the basing of its own legitimacy on furnishing the legitimacy of an unchallenged capitalism. In the present period, reformism shows its

own weakness in a cumulative process. The more extensive the
crisis of capitalism becomes, the more extensively institutions
under state and quasi-state management must be constructed, and
the more reformist parties and organizations must actively combat
tendencies toward self-organization in the base, when that self-
organization is directed against the crisis and the de-authoritization
by institutions.

The logic in the present development in an advanced welfare
capitalist country like Denmark points in the direction of the appearance of a kind of state/labor union capitalism — in the space
of about one generation. This is naturally not an argument that the
struggle for self-organization and self-management, as essential
socialist objectives, should be given up. Rather, it is an argument
that specifies some of the conditions of that struggle.

NOTES

1. This criticism of behaviorism can only be in the form of a postulation at this
stage of the argument. The rest of the chapter can be read as the consideration that
changes this postulate to an argument. For a methodological development, see Th.
W. Adorno et al., *Der Positivismusstrit in der Deutschen Soziologie.* Neuwied and
Berlin, 1969. This tradition of philosophy of science is developed and specified in
relation to the analysis of capitalism in, for instance, H. Reichelt, *Zur Logischen
Struktur des Kapitalbegriffs bei Karl Marx.* Frankfurt a.M., 1970.
2. We will not talk about the discussion there has been about the kinds of relations of property and control in the transitional society. See, for instance, C. Bet-
telheim, *Economic Calculation and Forms of Property.* London and Henley, 1975.
3. For an elaboration of these basic issues in the strategical problematic, see, for
instance, L. Basso, 'Die Marxistische Staatsauffassung', in E. Altvater et al.,
Rahmenbedingungen und Schranken Staatlichen Handelns. Frankfurt a.M., 1976.
4. Cf. the criticism of J. Hirsch of social science's tendency to subject itself to
the 'departmentalization,' that corresponds to present ideology and practice around
the state and its relation to society. See J. Hirsh, *Staatsapparat und Reproduktion
des Kapitals.* Frankfurt a.M., 1974, especially chapter III.

5. See, for instance, J. Hansche and J. C. Gilchrist, 'Three Determinants of the Level of Aspiration,' *Journal of Abnormal Social Psychology*, 1956, 53; S. E. Asch, *Social Psychology*, New York, 1962, and D. V. Chapman and J. Volhman, 'A Social Determinant of the Level of Aspiration', *Journal of Abnormal Social Psychology*, 1939, 34.

6. See, for instance, Marxistische Aufbauorganisation, *Die Krise der kommunistischen Parteien*. Erlangen, 1973, chapter 2. And H-J. Krahl, *Konstitution und Klassenkampf, Zur historischen Dialektik von bürgerlicher Emanzipation und Proletarischer Revolution*. Frankfurt a.M., 1971.

7. Lelio Basso, 'Die Rolle der Legalität in der Phase des Ubergangs zum Sozialismus,' in L. Basso, *Gesellschaftsformation und Staatsform. Drie Aufsätze*. The article is also found in *Problemi del Socialismo*, 5/6, 1971, pp. 818-62.

8. For an elaboration, see Lucio Magri's contribution to the seminar on the crisis in Ariccia, 1975, translated to Danish, 'Krisens kvalitet go dynamik' in B. Amoroso and V. Sperling (eds.), *Arbejderbevægelsen og Krisen*, Århus, 1976.

9. In an ultra short form, we have here summarized some of the quite extensive discussions in Marxism on the relation between society and individual will, and relation between 'structure' and 'strategy'. In recent years, this discussion has been carried on in different relationships. See, for example, the debate between Miliband and Poulantzas in *New Left Review*, Nos. 58, 59, 82, and Ernesto Laclau, 'The Specificity of the Political: the Poulantzas-Miliband Debate,' *Economy and Society*, Vol. 4, No. 1. The topic has some points in common with the discussion over the past years between STAMOKAP theory and the so-called 'Berlin School'. See, for example, Margaret Wirth, 'Zur kritik der Theorie des staats-monopolistischen Kapitalismus,' *Probleme des Klassenkampfs*, 8/9, 1973, and Peter Hess' defense of STAMOKAP in a Marburg lecture, translated in *Spartakus*, 4, 1975, 'Statsmonopolistsk kapitalisme. Teoretiske sporgsmål.'

10. An interesting attempt to explicate this dimension in Marxist and non-Marxist theory is Curt Sørensen, *Marxismen og den sociale Orden*, GMT, Grenå, 1976.

11. A short review of the pattern of expansion of the public sector is found in the governmental report, PP II, part IV, Copenhagen, 1973.

12. E. Mandel, 'The Debate on Worker's Control,' *International Socialist Review*, May-June 1969.

13. Max Weber clearly saw that functional relationship, and he recommended the working class's integration into the state as a necessary means of stabilizing the capitalist state. (See, for example, 'Deutschlands künftige Staatsform' and 'Parlament und Regierung in Neugeordnete Deutschland' in *Politische Schriften*, Tübingen, 1958). An attempt to explain reformism's stabilizing effects with state theory in late capitalism is found in Sibylle von Flatow and Freerk Huisken, 'Zum Problem der Ableitung des Bürgerlichen Staates,' *PROKLA*, No. 7, 1973. A critique that is carried out by H. Reichelt in *Gesellschaft I*, Frankfurt a.M., 1974.

14. A review of Social Democracy's political results in these areas is found in H. Brender and Steen Scheuer, 'Socialdemokratiets krise i Danmark,' *Orientering fra KF*, 5, 1976.

15. See Sv.Aa. Hansen, *Early Industrialisation in Denmark*. Copenhagen, 1970. A development of this sketch of Denmark's economic history over the last 100 years is found in E. Olsen, *Danmarks Økonomisk Historie*. København, 1962, and Sv. Aa. Hansen, *Økonomisk Vækst i Danmark*, Vol. I-II. København, 1974.

16. An analysis of the Danish structure of production is found in, for instance, Bilag 3, of the report PP-II, Copenhagen, 1973.

17. Nils Groes, *Financieringsmønstre i industrien*. Copenhagen, 1973.

18. This development is partly parallel to the inflationary undermining of wages, and the problems this gives to the traditional relationship between labor and capital. See for instance, G. D. Garson, 'Beyond Collective Bargaining' and Daniel Bell, 'The Subversion of Collective Bargaining,' both in G. Hunnius et al., *Workers' Control*. New York, 1973.

19. *Forslag til Lov om lønmodtagernes medejendomsret*, and *Bemærkninger* and *Bilag*, in *Folketingstidende, 1972-73*, pp. 4694 ff.

20. The fund's central position in future investments and credit giving appears in the account made by the Economic Council in *Økonomisk demokrati i samfunds-økonomisk belysning*. Copenhagen, 1972.

21. A critique of the German arrangement is found in H. Schauer, 'Critique of Co-determination' in Hunnius et al., op. cit. The present Danish arrangement has been investigated, with the same general conclusion. See Ann Westenholz, *Employee Representation on Boards of Directors in Danish Companies*. Mimeographed paper. Copenhagen, 1976.

10

LIBERATION OF WORK AND THE ROLE OF SOCIAL RESEARCH

Bjørn Gustavsen,
Work Research Institute, Oslo

Liberation of work must be done by the workers themselves. The role of social research is to act as support and resource in such a process.

Liberated work is work where solidarity with other people around a joint cause, and mutual information between equal partners, provide the basis for what is to be done. Non-liberated work is work that takes place under social structures characterized by centralization and control. Centralization is usually argued for by the need to co-ordinate the efforts of many people; control is argued for by pointing out that the individual seldom knows enough to do the right thing by himself, nor is it always possible to trust him to do the right thing even if he actually knows what it is.

Liberation of work must emerge as a stepwise process where the workers bring more and more matters under their own control. Those elements of centralized decisions and control of people that might be necessary for real social or technological reasons must be

Author's note: I am indebted to a number of my colleagues for contributions to the ideas expressed in this paper; particularly to Bjørg Aase Sørensen and her study of the relationship between industrialization and community characteristics (Sørensen, 1977).

integrated with the primary jobs, and not be the objects of special roles filled with people who do nothing but make decisions about other people and control them.

Some will say that this is utopianism: we cannot hope to base the activities of a highly complex industrial society only on solidarity and communication between people. In this I do not agree; the organizational and technological issues that emerge cannot, however, be discussed in this paper. This is a shortcoming, but the topic is too big. On the other hand, I will argue for a stepwise strategy for change, where the main problem is to generate a liberating process. It is this issue that will be discussed here, not the structural problems emerging in a new type of society.

For a liberating process to emerge from the people themselves, they must gain confidence in their own ability to solve problems. Rather than focusing on the conditions for innovation and creativity among organization men, the utilization of experts, or getting politicians to perform 'planning for change,' we need to look at the way ordinary people approach problems outside such contexts as bureaucracies. These approaches, and the social systems emerging to support them — e.g., networks rather than bureaucracies — must be given status as legitimate and primary approaches.

The problem-solving ability of ordinary people outside the framework of formal organizations has been suppressed. And for this reason we clearly see a decline in this ability. People are to an increasing extent unable to approach problems constructively, and more and more turn to all sorts of authorities and experts who are as often as not equally unable to do anything really constructive. The difference is that the bureaucrats, experts and politicians believe that they can do something, because they have created a world around themselves where things seem to happen; an imaginary world where problems seem to be solved and progress seem to take place. To this imaginary world the social sciences have contributed; positively by providing constitutive elements, negatively by not holding forth the alternative world of people. This has been the tradition. Now we can see an emerging interest in the problem-solving approaches of workers, farmers, people as community inhabitants. Such research interest is, however, still relatively modest, and far from sufficient to give the backing research could give.

The purpose of this paper is to treat some of the tendencies within social research that have led the mainstream of such research to pass the issue of local problem-solving by, and to point out one possible set of characteristics for a research that can more adequately help to bring forth a liberating process from people themselves. This must be a decentralized research based on contact and complementarity with people on the local level through joint activity and action programs.

Views on social phenomena often emerge from a theory. Such theories can differ widely in specific content, but they are often characterized by some typical features. In traditional natural sciences one of the points of departure has been that it is possible to organize knowledge. The different 'bits' of knowledge generated through different research projects can be converted into part-theories, and the part-theories can be brought together in more comprehensive patterns. Such patterns actually mean that knowledge radiates from some sort of center in decreasing levels of generality. These central assumptions can be axioms; they can be general frameworks for picking out the important influencing factors behind human behavior like the much used norm- and value interpretations in sociology; they can be generalized characteristics of social systems (like in Parsonian functionalism); ideas about main generative factors behind a multiplicity of concrete social manifestations (like in marxism), or whatever. The point is the structuring as such — the belief that all knowledge in principle has a place in an all-over pattern.

Now, everybody with the slightest knowledge of the social sciences will know that such organizing principles do not function very well. Around us we see a multiplicity of theories, each competing with the other, and limited agreement on what the basic elements of a hierarchical structure should be. This, however, can not be taken as conclusive argument that the belief in the eventual possibilities of organization is not still there. It is, in fact, this belief that tends to make the picture chaotic, because it makes people seek for order and conciliation where no such criteria are fulfilled, rather than accepting the 'bits' as they are; elements of a much more lowly organized structure.

If we believe that knowledge can be fitted into larger, more comprehensive hierarchical structures in the form of general theory, then some consequences follow, particularly the belief in abstractions. If knowledge is to be brought into structures of grand, general theory, it must be taken out of the reality from which it emerges and given an autonomous existence. The knowledge must have meaning and existence outside the reality from which it emerges. But is it really true that knowledge from the social field can be abstracted and organized like this?

This is, of course, a very complex issue and no simple answer can be given. It is certainly so that some possibilities for organization and abstraction are present. The problem is rather how far these possibilities go. This issue cannot be analyzed here. Here, the point of view will be applied that such possibilities for abstraction and hierarchization are limited — much more limited than is usually assumed. Such a possibility has, in fact, been expressed by various social scientists through the years. One can, for example, find elements of such a view in Max Weber's works (cfr. the comments by Oaks to Weber, 1975).

One may have to accept that the knowledge we generate in the social sciences is:

— relatively bound by the time and place from which it emerges ('local');

— open and the object of continuous change, because the objects of study in themselves change in ways very different from the objects of the natural sciences;

— partial, in the sense that we rarely gain complete understanding of social phenomena through our research efforts — we clarify aspects, perspectives or whatever, but we rarely 'grasp' the social phenomenon in its totality of aspects, perspectives, meanings;

— not easily liable to organization, particularly not to large-scale hierarchical organization.

There are clearly exceptions to this. However, I do not argue that 'all' knowledge fits this paradigm, only that these characteristics might be the normal ones.

If one tries to generate general theories on the basis of knowledge that does not easily lend itself to such treatment, then the theorizing will clearly be problematic. The primary problem is the relationship between the theory and its correlating knowledge structure, on the one hand, and the surrounding social world, on the other. When difficulties emerge in this relationship, there are various possible ways out. One way is to make the theory sketchy and rudimentary, with relatively 'modest demands on reality'. This way is a minimum way that we all have to take; nobody — not even the most action oriented of researchers — can approach social phenomena completely free of some pre-given ideas.

Another way is to maintain a more elaborate general framework with a number of interacting elements and pre-given answers to a large array of possible questions, and base the defence of the theory on its ability to function not only as a 'model of reality' but also as a legal system. A legal system defines what projects are legitimate, and what projects are not, and it defines rules for the admission of evidence before the court. Projects defined as illegitimate can never produce any correction of the framework, simply because they are illegitimate. Neither can a case ever be won on the basis of inadmissible evidence. Some adherents of Marx seem to use marxism in this way — as a legal system — rather than as a somewhat more open framework for understanding the world.

A heavy weight on legitimation and illegitimation of projects and evidence is one way of ensuring the continued life of a general theory. Another way is to operate with a theory that can never under any reasonable circumstances, such as they happen to be in the social sciences, be brought into confrontation with reality. Parsonian functionalism is an example. Such a view on characteristics of social systems cannot be given a sufficiently concretized form to be brought into confrontation with the social world. And I do not talk about operationalization to meet the requirements of conventional empirism. Functionalism is equally untestable from much more liberal methodological positions. The decline of functionalism that has taken place in recent years is not owing to 'new evidence' as concerns its more specific theoretical points — as is often the case when theories in the natural sciences are modified or abandoned — but rather to an emergent feeling of inadequacy. Parsonian functionalism does not seem to provide the perspective that social scientists feel they need. But what we feel we need is clearly determined much more by general political developments than by what has happened in terms of social science research results (Gouldner, 1971).

Noting that Parsonian functionalism is no longer quite 'in' brings us to another perspective on the general theories. Knowledge is always attached to a system of bearers: social science knowledge to a system of social scientists. There are relationships between these scientists. As pointed out by Herbst (1974), there are interdependencies between the structure of knowledge and the social organization of the bearers of this knowledge. If we believe that knowledge can be ordered in terms of a hierarchical structure, we tend to think in terms of hierarchical structures also as concerns the social relationships between the bearers of the knowledge, with those providing the most general — or central — elements at the top of the hierarchy. As far as I can see, the belief in general theories and hierarchization of knowledge has led to quite a lot of centralization within the social science community. Not in formal terms, of course, but in a more informal sense. We do not only find 'grand theories', we also find 'grand theorists,' 'leading parts,' 'famous universities,' 'important men' (it is still usually men that are credited with importance in the social sciences) and so on and so forth. The diffusion of Parsonian functionalism from Parsons and Harvard to — if we are to believe Gouldner (1971) — practically every nook and cranny of American sociology (and large parts of European) is a particularly clear example of how a center is established (important man in important university) and then gains control over the rest. Establishment of figures of importance, definitions of 'ins,' 'trends' and 'styles' are important social mechanisms to maintain the belief in hierarchical and generalizable knowledge and constitute a very important part of the explanation of why the belief in knowledge hierarchies is as strong as it is.

The general theories, frameworks and abstractions determine what is seen and not seen when the researcher enters the world around him. The one who looks for shared values and joint norms to explain human behavior will certainly find them. That is: what he finds is concrete behavior — verbal responses to questions included — the values and norms enter the picture as interpretations or explanations. And, as pointed out by many — e.g., Barth (1966) — a normative coat can always be tailored to fit the behavior one might encounter. The one who wants to see the world in terms of exchanges (Homans) will certainly find that practically all behavior can be fitted into this framework. And so on.

The point is not whether these theoretically given conceptual grids are 'true' or 'untrue'. Such questions are almost devoid of meaning. There are certainly normative elements behind behavior, as there are aspects fitting a transactional model. Any social system can — very legitimately — be seen in terms of Parsons' social system characteristics. We can certainly — if we are so inclined —

see the evils of this world as concrete manifestations of certain basic characteristics of our societies like private ownership of the means of production and the specialization and commodity-character of work. The problem is that social phenomena are usually much more than this. And it is not necessarily so that these perspectives are the most relevant and interesting. If we look at social phenomena not from the point of view of contributing to theory, but rather from the point of view of contributing to actions under specific circumstances, very different aspects can be the most important. If the use of a general theory means that we look only for those aspects declared relevant by the theory, we will easily miss the most relevant aspects and not be able to make any contribution to the solution of people's problems. The use of general theories can, of course, be defended by saying that they provide a perspective — and not necessarily the whole truth. The perspective can be valid enough, and the theory for that reason something to bring along. In this I agree. But then we certainly devalue most general theories far beyond their actual claims. Because if something pretends to be a general theory, then it certainly cannot at the same time state that it is a partial framework that might, or might not, according to circumstances, be the intake to something of value. There are few, if any, 'grand theorists' who qualify their own thinking in this way.

When research interests are determined from 'the center and outwards' rather than from the people, the results include heavy focusing on other central bodies like big business, big government and anything else that seems important because it is big and has a center. If ordinary people are approached it is usually as elements in something big — e.g., as organization members — and from an interest external to those approached. To take my own field — industrial sociology — we see that when workers are approached by scientists from 'up there,' it is usually on the basis of one of the following interests:

— How to motivate them. This is linked to the productivity interest that for a long time dominated social research in working life. This has, though, changed quite a lot in recent years.

— How to satisfy them. Here we find the benevolent uncle interest, often found among social scientists.

— How to teach them. Here we find the public teacher interest — the belief that those who seem to know less than us must be developed or educated, partly because this is good in itself, but it is also common to hear that workers must be educated so as not to be manipulated by the managers and the experts. They have to meet managers and experts on their home ground. The problem is, of course, that the home ground of managers and experts is just the ground that produces a number of our societies' most critical problems.

— A fourth interest is to demonstrate the misery of workers. Here the researcher fulfils the requirements of 'critical' research.

I will not reject the importance of motivating, satisfying or teaching the workers, nor the need to demonstrate their misery. What is lost, however, is the *creativity* among workers: that they are in fact able to solve problems and develop social organization among themselves.

The basic importance of the workers' own ability to perceive problems and to work out solutions to them has emerged from various studies at the Work Research Institute. One of these studies was performed in collaboration with the Work Inspectorate Authority (Karlsen et al., 1975). Here we set out to study the accident prevention and health maintenance systems of a sample of companies. There is specific legislation as concerns this type of work, but these rules leave a lot of room for local variations. Not all companies are, furthermore, up to the requirements of the law. The point was to see if differences in these formal aspects of the health and safety work had effects on the results of this work. To some degree such a link could be found. But this link was not very strong, and did not constitute the most important explanation of observed differences in concrete work environments. The most important factor turned out to be something called workers' resources. Workers' resources are made up of two components: one relating to skills and the other to social organization. In brief: in enterprises where the workers had jobs that developed and maintained their skills, and had developed a social organization between them, the best results as concerns work environment were to be found. Correspondingly, in enterprises employing lowly skilled workers in jobs that had little or nothing to contribute to their skills, and where there was little or no social organization to link the workers to each other, the work environment the workers were confronting was also — relatively seen — the worst. This study highlighted the point that work environment improvement is dependent upon the workers themselves, their ability to see problems, raise issues, negotiate with management and work constructively with their own problems.

The social organization to emerge as important in this study is the network or system of horizontal informal links between the workers. It is certainly not the formal, hierarchical organization of the company. Nor is it always the local trade union. As concerns the trade union, though, there will usually be interdependence between the union and the resource network. At a workplace with problem-consciousness and a well developed social system among the workers, the workers are practically always organized, and the local trade union becomes a part of this social structure. Bringing the trade union movement into a workplace can also contribute in a positive way to the formation of workers' resources.

It is social systems like these that social research has to bring forth, to give status and legitimacy, and help to develop. Our ability to do this is dependent upon our ability to free ourselves from the problematic aspects of social research as it still is. Rather than concentrate on internal communications, social research must become outwardly directed. Rather than manipulating 'grand theories' and empty 'data', it is necessary to go out among people and see how they work with their problems. Today, ordinary people's ways of working with and solving problems are to be found in rather rudimentary forms and mostly on the local level — by 'local' can be meant a factory, local community, or even smaller units. We have to approach these parts of reality and enter into a collaborative relationship to the people we meet.

One way to set about this is to accept that the knowledge we generate in the social sciences has characteristics differing from those we usually assume, a point already mentioned. If we proceed from different assumptions as concerns this knowledge, such collaborative relationships to other people can emerge as the primary way of doing social research, and not as a secondary and problematic type of activity that take time from the 'real efforts,' namely to contribute to theories through writing 'scientific' books and articles; books and articles that are too difficult to be read by anyone but other social scientists, and will actually be read by very few of them because they are so busy writing their own books and articles.

Social research must be structured so as to reflect the fact that knowledge as a point of departure is:

— local;
— open and changing;
— partial;
— not liable to far reaching organization.

Basic organizational principles for such a research must — among others — include:
— The research must be decentralized;
— and based on collaboration with the people in the field;
— over time;
— where joint action is at the core.

Formal and real decentralization do not always accompany each other. Large, centrally located organizations, like big universities, can be decentralized in terms of some parts of the social structure among those working there. Still, the geographical 'heaping up' has consequences. It is, furthermore, a fairly sound principle to assume that real decentralization is supported by formal decentralization. Social research should be built up in relatively small, geographically spaced units.

As our knowledge is only partial, we can not 'work alone' with social phenomena. We have to establish collaborative relationships to the people in the field; go together with them in the approach to social issues and problems. This togetherness must be concrete and not only formal expressions of 'solidarity with the workers' put forth in contexts where it is highly unlikely that any worker will ever see it.

While administrators and other centrally located persons with access to bureaucratic resources can sometimes be interested in descriptions and analyses of situations — because they can now and then convert such descriptions into action programs — this rarely holds for ordinary people. Their burning question is usually what to do: how to set about attacking the problems they are confronting. Collaboration with people, then, must be collaboration that includes action; it has — to use that expression — to be action research.

Action research is often taken to mean the use of knowledge generated through 'ordinary' research, in special ways of application. The application implies that the researcher ventures out in the field and take responsiblity for working out concrete solutions to the problems. Compared to purely descriptive research, a willingness to enter the field and use knowledge is an important step in a right direction.

I prefer, however, to use the term 'applied research' for this situation, a situation that can sometimes occur also in the social sciences, but which is much more practical in the natural sciences. I would prefer to use the term 'action research' for situations where the action is an important part of the strategy for generation of knowledge. The action is not only application of knowledge, it is generation of knowledge. An example to illustrate the difference:

The issue of job satisfaction has played an important part in industrial sociology and psychology for various reasons. A distinction between 'purely descriptive' and 'applied' research would mean that a strategy for improvement of conditions in working life would consist of two main steps; firstly, descriptive studies to gather knowledge about the content of job satisfaction, and what conditions are favorable or unfavorable to such a phenomenon. Secondly, one would have to change conditions in a direction as indicated by the descriptive research. The problems attached to such an approach are, however, numerous. One of them is that when people are confronted with 'satisfaction questions' in, e.g., a questionnaire, a large majority usually declare themselves satisfied — the figure of 85 percent has emerged an astonishingly high number of times from the less sophisticated job satisfaction studies. The percentage of satisfied employees is made up of various groups; those who expect a reasonable job and have got it; those who do not expect much from their work and therefore do not react to not having got very much; those who really answer another question, e.g., about the instrumental value of work; those who will not admit to themselves that they are failures as far as work is concerned, and so on. Those using more sophisticated methods usually get somewhat lower satisfaction scores, but the figures are still highly problematic. And why? The reason is simply that people react to their working conditions on the basis of their life and job history and if this is a history of monotonous jobs and stressful life conditions, combined with low expectations, this will of course determine their answers, and answers determined in this way are of little value. Most of those who have argued for reform of working life have as one of their chief arguments that work shapes people's minds and outlooks and that this shaping is the problem. A more fruitful approach to the issue of job satisfaction is to change people's working conditions so as to enable them to gain varied experience. If this is done, a more valid reaction to the issue of job satisfaction will emerge, because the framework for evaluation will be expanded. And this, again, calls for action research because action will be necessary to generate the possibilities for different work experiences (Some will try to achieve the same results by using a cross-sectional method based on interviewing people who hold jobs that are believed to be different in terms of satisfaction potential. This approach, however, rarely works, because people with relatively different jobs rarely share the same life- and work history. It is possible to use this approach in some instances, e.g., when a factory has undergone changes affecting a part of a previously homogenous work force [or similar situations].)

In action research, action is used to generate knowledge. There are other schools that are in principle using the same approach, e.g., the enthnomethodologists. I would therefore like to underline that action research is not only action to generate knowledge, it is at the same time action together with other people to help them solve their problems. As concerns the ethnomethodologists, I would agree with Garfinkel (1967) on some points, e.g., the weight on everyday people and everyday situations; the interest in understanding the local and concrete rather than seeing everything in the light of 'contributions to grand theory' and the close similarities between social research and ordinary 'non-scientific' behavior and behavioral interpretations. Where I strongly disagree is in the use of action on the part of the researcher. By action I mean serious, open behavior and not camouflaged social tricks of the type that seem to be at the center of the contributions of the ethnomethodologists. Even when the ethical problems are looked away from, a social relationship based on ethnomethodological games from the researchers can never provide basis for joint, serious action. While we are onto the issue of research behavior, I will add that my fondness for semi-clinical psychological approaches is also very limited. I do not believe in change processes where the personal skills and characteristics of the researcher are to be the chief dynamic factors. In my opinion, the researcher has to be and to act like other people, sharing their shortcomings, also shortcomings in personal skills and dynamism. It is the cause that is to provide the dynamism; if there is no cause, then there is no need for social dynamism. (For some further comments on the characteristics of action research those who read Swedish can be referred to Gustavsen [1976].)

Collaboration with other people has a time perspective. Particularly where joint action is at the heart of the collaborative effort, it is necessary to be aware of all the social relationships and structures emerging between the researchers and the people in the field. This means that the researchers must guarantee presence as long as they are wanted. The researchers can not arbitrarily conclude the relationship and withdraw.

As the reader will easily agree, these were some rather sketchy remarks on difficult issues. As most researchers want to use a book (or more) to make clear their meta-scientific position, I can not claim ability to do it in 10 pages. The idea behind the paper is rather to point out some elements in a line of reasoning, where each element should of course be made the object of a more thorough discussion and analysis.

There is one possible objection to which I will dedicate a few concluding remarks: the relationship between the local and the central — between the structures emerging among workers, community members and other ordinary people in ordinary situations when they try to come to grips with their problems, and society in general. What I have done in this paper is to stress the need to focus on these local structures, and to help develop them. I do not argue that these structures are the only ones of importance — that they exist in a social vacuum. The reason why these structures are important is not least that the structures emerging from the social centers are not able to cope in a satisfactory way with the problems our societies are confronting; in addition they also generate problems because the centrally developed structures function through making ordinary people the objects of decisions and control by others. There is, of course, an interdependence between what happens at the grass roots and what happens centrally, e.g., in terms of development of large scale public and private organizations. What is argued for here is not that we should neglect these central institutions and trends, but that we should take the local and concrete approaches to problems as the point of departure for research and actions and emerge from there to the other types of structures. Approaching these structures from the grass roots and upwards will enable us to single out those aspects of the more general structures that are particularly important hindrances to the liberation of people and their work. It may be that these characteristics will be found to be some of those already pointed out by 'general theory' based social research — this is, in fact, highly likely — but approaching the center from the periphery enables us to single out the relevant dimensions on the basis of a much surer footing. Such a stepwise approach enables us, furthermore, to unite research and action — a combination that in my opinion is necessary. And action is bound in time and space in a way very different from 'pure thinking' or even thinking combined with hit and run empiricism. As long as no responsibility for action is taken by the researcher, he can freely move over the whole social field — a factory last year, a government agency this year, a country in Africa next year. If research is to be also a sequence of actions where one action is to build on the previous ones in a meaningful series of events towards an ultimate but distant goal, then the situation is very, very different. The researcher might choose basis one, two or maybe three times in his life, but that will be all.

At the Work Research Institute we have gained some experience in moving from the local to the central. In the 1960s and early 1970s the primary task of the institute was to generate and support changes in job design and work organization in a series of enterprises (some of these projects are described in Emery and Thorsrud, 1976). During these projects various problems and constraints were experienced. For example: outside a circle that was not in itself large enough to push a national development program it was difficult to gain an understanding of what new principles for design of jobs and work organization meant. Among those who could — intellectually — understand the meaning of the principles, not all would consider the alternatives legitimate. And among those who accepted the alternatives as legitimate, difficulties emerged with priorities if they felt the principles collided with other values, e.g., the right to decide on behalf of management.

To overcome some of these — and other — problems, the institute accepted an invitation from the Ministry of Labour to take part in the development of a new national Work Environment Act to replace the older Workers' Protection Act. During the last few years some of my colleagues as well as myself have had the work with this legislation and its various ramifications as our main task. The law is given a section on design of jobs and work organization — as far as we know this is the first law of its kind to do so; we know of no other country where this aspect of psycho-social work environment issues is actually treated in an act (In actual fact, most work environment laws in the industrialized world are fairly limited in scope in the sense that they treat accident prevention and some aspects of health maintenance but not, for example, psycho-social loads on the employees). (For a description of the psycho-social part of the Norwegian act see Gustavsen [1977].) Through this effort on the national level we hope to influence some of the values determining efforts and constraints in working life. We hope to overcome some of the obstacles as concerns the legitimacy and priority of alternative forms of work organization. Another thing gained — and which we find it right to utilize — is power. Through a law, national agencies like the Work Inspectorate and its central authority are brought to bear on the issue of design of jobs and work organization. The Work Environment Act also contains the usual criminal sanctions against those breaking law. Even though such sanctions obviously must be used with restraint, the issue of what jobs to offer people will in the future not be as dependent upon the goodwill of management as the case has been in the past.

I will not pursue these issues here. They are mentioned only to indicate that even though we give priority to local structures and problem-solving, this does not mean that we are blind to the issues of general social structures and the use of national power instruments — if this seems called for to support a development emerging from the grass roots.

REFERENCES

Barth, F., 'Models of Social Organisation.' Royal Anthropological Institute, Occasional Paper No. 23, 1966.

Emery, F. and E. Thorsrud, *Democracy at Work*: Leiden: Nijhoff, 1976.

Garfinkel, H., *Studies in Ethnomethodology*. Englewood Cliffs, NJ: Prentice-Hall, 1967.

Gouldner, A., *The Coming Crisis of Western Sociology*. London: Heinemann, 1971.

Gustavsen, B., 'Aksjonsforskning' (Action Research) Stockholm: Psykologiska Institutionen. *Rapporter*, No. 13, 1976.

Gustavsen, B., 'A Legislative Approach to Job Reform in Norway,' *International Labour Review*, Vol. 115, No. 3, May-June issue, 1977.

——, 'Work Reform and Social Research', in B. Gardell and G. Johansson (eds.), *Man and Working Life*. New York: Wiley, 1979.

Herbst, P. G., *Socio-technical Design. Strategies in Multi-Disciplinary Research*. London: Tavistock, 1974.

Karlsen, J. I., R. Naess, Ø. Ryste, S. Seierstad, and B. Aa. Sørensen, *Arbeidsmiljø og vernearbeid* (Work environment and its determinants). Oslo: Tanum, 1976.

McLennan, R. (ed.), *Proceedings of a University Staff Seminar on Organization Studies: Problems, Methods and Data*. Wellington: Industrial Relations Centre, Victoria University, 1977.

Seashore, S. E. and T. D. Taber, 'Job Satisfaction Indicators and their Correlates', in A. D. Biderman and T. F. Drury (eds.), *Measuring Work Quality for Social Reporting*. Beverly Hills, Calif. and London: Sage Publications, 1976.

Sørensen, B. Aa., *Industrien som levevei* (The making of an industrial community.) Oslo: Work Research Institute, 1977.

Thurmann, J. E., 'Job Satisfaction: An International Overview', *International Labour Review*, Vol. 117, No. 3, 1977.

Weber, M., *Roscher and Knies: The Logical Problems of Historical Economics* (with an introduction by Guy Oakes). New York: The Free Press, 1975.

11

THE POLITICAL ECONOMY OF THIRD SECTOR ENTERPRISES

Alasdair Clayre
Fellow of All Souls College, Oxford

Can a 'third sector' grow in the west between the forces of big business on the one hand and the state on the other, based on cooperation, in which people will have more control over their working lives through hiring their own managers rather than being hired and fired by them? Because of the title of this seminar certain questions have to be asked first about the concept of liberation in general before the problems of third-sector enterprises in a western economy are raised. Once these have been considered a positive example of a working system in a western economy will be examined.

What exactly does the 'liberation' of work mean? The phrase sounds attractive at first hearing: liberation of anything sounds attractive. But concretely what is involved? Liberation of work cannot be understood as something done once for all and complete in itself, like setting a prisoner free or opening the window for a butterfly. At best it can only be something partial: the comparative easing of constraints. For by its nature work always involves some constraints: it means, roughly, doing certain things helpful to other people, or making certain things more orderly or more productive or more beautiful, and carrying out the action well and reliably

The author is grateful to Professor J. E. Meade for kindly reading this paper before publication.

whether or not at every moment one wants to.

There are some constraints, outer or inner, from which people do not necessarily need to be liberated, such as the wish to produce work of quality, even if this is at cost to oneself. Most people derive their particular shape and character from the form this wish takes in them. Then as soon as one works with other people some disciplines of time-keeping and consistency of effort have to be accepted, though these may be made less onerous by 'flexible time' and by systems that entrust small groups of people with the responsibility for whole tasks and let them organize the schedule and the details of the task themselves. More broadly, market constraints of a kind have to remain in any large-scale economy if heaps of unwanted goods are not to be piled up everywhere, if local politicians are not to run all the new roads past their own farms and factories, and if most resources are to be used with a fair degree of efficiency; and such constraints are likely to continue to be more strongly felt, even under a co-operative system, by people working with highly expensive equipment in capital-intensive factories, since it must be a cost to someone somewhere if it is used exceptionally inefficiently.

As Eliot said of poetry: 'No *vers* is really *libre* for the man who wants to do a good job'; and completely free work, like completely free love, is a phrase with normal grammatical form, but not a practical meaning; at best it designates a theoretical limiting point on a scale, like the notion of infinity, which human begins do not experience in practice. So the wrong kind of solution to the problems involved is likely to be proposed if the wrong model (the butterfly and the window) is held fixedly in the mind.

Perhaps the best way of thinking of the 'liberation' of work is to ask how people with the worst jobs can have some of the choice and the interest, along with some of the disciplines and constraints, of those with the most satisfying work; and in areas where this is not possible, how hours can be cut. How does self-management fit into this context? Some improvements in the quality of work and in the balance between work and leisure may be expected to follow from self-management in so far as workers may require their hired managers to offer them a better 'mix' (from their own point of view) between good conditions, shorter hours and more pay than the hiring and firing managers choose to offer at the moment. Other, psychological benefits (as well as some costs) may be expected to follow simply from the freedom to choose the manager directly. And further benefits again — to productivity as well as to enjoyment — are likely to ensue from an increase in trust and commitment, although it cannot be lightly assumed that all self-managed enterprises will engender more trust or commitment than all other enterprises.

The question at the beginning can perhaps be rephrased, in an admittedly more cumbersome way (with some of the mud of the real world on its boots), in some such words as these: 'What are the possibilities for an easing of some of the constraints on work through an extension of third-sector enterprises, i.e., enterprises where those who perform the work — and only they — elect councils who appoint the top management and can recall them, or where in other ways the members of the enterprise hire their management expertise rather than being hired by management?'

Certain criticisms have recently been made of the likely viability of such third sector enterprises in the west from the point of view of economic theory and in particular 'property rights' theory (e.g., Chiplin and Coyne, 1977). The main arguments appear to be these:

(a) If workers do not own their enterprises, yet have control, it is argued that they will tend, instead of investing adequately, to push up their wages at the expense of whoever does own, or (if 'society' owns) at the public expense.

(b) If workers in all enterprises try to do this simultaneously, or if those in less productive firms, reasoning from arguments of fairness, call for the same wages as those in the most productive, they will tend to push down the value of the currency (inflation) at the expense of pensioners and those who have saved.

(c) If capital is (even initially) socially allocated, and if losses are subsequently met out of public funds, short-term political considerations (e.g., propping up unproductive local enterprises) and personal political influence will have strong and arbitrary effects on the allocation of resources, and everyone will be poorer than necessary.

(d) If individual workers own their own enterprises, different objections arise:

(i) The workers bear the risks as well as doing the labour and this is an unfair double burden.

(ii) Their risks are not spread like those of most shareholders in the west. If their firms go bankrupt their jobs and their savings vanish at the same moment.

(iii) They are also led to invest their savings in one particular enterprise (their own) rather than having the whole range of savings outlets to choose from freely. It is argued that (unless their firm happens to be the best in the market) they are not getting the best possible return on their savings and, therefore, that worker-owned firms are being subsidised economically at their own workers' expense.

(e) If co-operative enterprises rely wholly on internally raised finance, they will not have enough and will be producing below their most efficient level.

(f) If they rely on finance raised from outside, they will have difficulty in preventing outside control, by banks or the state.

(g) If all the equity is retained by the co-operative and a fixed rate of interest is offered on all borrowed money, the third sector enterprise is likely to suffer in competition with other firms in a western-style market economy, since it will be raising more of its external capital with heavy fixed interest burdens than its competitors, who can spread their finance between loans and equity shares.

(h) All these criticisms apart, it is often argued that the history of third sector enterprises or producer co-operatives in the west is not impressive; that few have been economically successful, or have even rivalled the ordinary achievement of average shareholder-owned firms in what they have done for the consumer and for their employees or members.

For all these reasons (it has been argued) it is misleading people to encourage them to put their savings or their working lives into such structures.

These objections raise questions about the relationship between 'economic' values and other human values; for some of the advantages that third sector enterprises may offer are hard or impossible to quantify and consist of possible improvements in the 'quality of working life' of those who take part in them. What is easily measurable is, of course, not for that reason alone more 'real'. However, if the economic objections to third sector enterprises can be discussed in economic terms, this is clearly more satisfactory than a general contention that the non-economic advantages are likely to outweigh any economic disadvantages; even though this is, for some people, almost certain to be true. The present paper can do no more than point to three ways — without following them to their conclusions — in which the economic case against self-management outlined here may perhaps be helpfully investigated in the future.

One is through further arguments, also from neo-classical principles, which may suggest major economic benefits likely to accrue to self-managed market economies, capable of outweighing the disadvantages suggested above. It has generally been assumed in theoretical discussions until recently that the introduction of self-management to any economy would result in a loss of efficiency. Thus self-management is often assumed to involve a net loss to production from expenditure of time in debating and voting, the avoidance of measures such as wage-restraint, unpopular in the short run though necessary for long-term expansion, and failure to deal severely with offenders against rules. It has not generally been argued until recently that there could be gains that might outweigh such factors in economic terms. However, the argument of Jaroslav Vanek (1970) is that, even in terms of neo-classical economic assumptions, the presupposition of greater inefficiency on the part of a system of workers' control does not have to be made. Firms in a labour-managed economy, according to Vanek's micro-analysis, would have a long-run general equilibrium at least as 'Pareto-optimal' as in a privately owned or Russian-style state-centralized system; and while, as in privately owned systems, firms could have reached equilibrium at less than optimal levels of output in the short-run, a labour-managed economy would tend to have more flexible prices and a more competitive market, with less need for advertising and product differentiation; and thus disequilibria would tend to be more readily corrected.

In terms of macro-analysis, Vanek argues that there would be less danger than in privately owned economies of trade cycles, and of long-run unemployment or long-run inflation. More dramatically, the gain from higher incentives, which Vanek believes would follow from the principles of labour-management, are suggested in his model as amounting to 'hundreds of per cent' of the national product.

There are problems in Vanek's theory, some of them mentioned in the well-known review article by James Meade (1972) which is, however, generally sympathetic to the main lines of the argument.

One problem may be mentioned here. Vanek sees capital assets as liable to be 'socially' owned or the property of the state, though his system is compatible with private or public owners and lenders, provided all are prepared to accept the relevant guarantees for the security of their investments, and fixed rates of interest. Control is exclusively in the hands of those who do the work. Some of the difficulties created by this assumption from the point of view of 'property rights' have been mentioned earlier and will undoubtedly require further examination.

A second way in which the case against self-managed enterprises may be questioned in the future, also at the level of theory, is through an examination of certain aspects of the behavioural foundations of neo-classical economics — particularly those dealing with the 'maximizing' behaviour of the individual — which may affect the weight that should be given to 'property rights' considerations against others. Sen (1977) has argued that there are valid alternatives to the traditional neo-classical assumption of the individual maximizing his personal gain (or it may be his personal utility, or expected life-time utility) which stop short of the assumption of total altruism which (Sen argues) has too often been presented as the one alternative. In particular, Sen shows that concepts such as 'commitment' can in principle be built into models as theoretically elegant as the traditional ones of neo-classical economic theory, and that models of man so constructed are not only more like real men in general, but represent more accurately the behaviour required by men in any productive system that actually works. From the point of view of industrial relations, Fox (1974) has stressed the importance of similar factors, especially of trust, in any functioning economic organization. These emphases contrast sharply with those of writers such as Alchian and Demsetz, who in an influential article (1972) stress the unique importance of supervision in the enforcement of contracts. Self-managed systems are likely to be poor at hierarchical supervision, but may well benefit unusually, not only through gains resulting from mutual supervision, but also from commitment and trust. It has only been an assumption, not a conclusion of empirical observation, that these last two factors can be largely neglected in calculating likely economic returns within organizations. The primacy given to individual mazimizing behaviour and to supervision (its corollary in organizational terms) has led quite naturally to this assumption. Of course, it cannot be assumed on the other side that self-managed enterprises will necessarily generate unusual degrees of trust and commitment. Nevertheless, these differences of emphasis, some of them at the roots of behavioural theory in economics, are likely to have a considerable impact on the way self-managed enterprises are considered in future theory.

The benefits from such features of self-managed enterprises as participation and profit-sharing (not only for 'job satisfaction' and motivation but also for productivity) have often been considered unquantifiable in economic terms, and this is no doubt one reason for their comparative neglect in economics. A long series of experiments by industrial psychologists up to the late 1960s has yielded the result that no correlation (or a very low correlation, sometimes positive and sometimes negative) could be established between 'satisfaction' and productivity in general (Argyle, 1972). However, the possibility remained that there were changes in the forms of work organization where gains in both these areas could independently be made, and an impressive list of examples was assembled by Blumberg (1968) where greater participation had been accompanied by increases in both. Felix R. Fitzroy and John R. Hiller (1978) have more recently developed a theoretical model for investigating quantitatively the effects on motivation, productivity and 'job-satisfaction' of workers' profit-sharing and participation and decision-making. The importance of work like this can only be guessed in advance, but an optimistic prediction would be that such studies could succeed in bringing these factors into the field of quantitative measurement and, therefore, of serious economic treatment alongside more readily measurable factors such as output and money income — for long the main concern of serious quantitative economics, yet (as all economists agree) only part of the total 'utility' which even the maximizing individual is supposed in neo-classical theory to be pursuing.

Finally, direct empirical evidence may be examined of self-managed enterprises that meet in practice some of the most forceful arguments from 'property-rights' theory by combining self-management with individual ownership and well-designed organization: for instance, cases where third-sector enterprises enjoy a considerable amount of internal (equity) finance through retained profit but do not rely on it exclusively; where there is a federation of like-minded enterprises supporting a co-operative bank that lends without seeking to control; where the federation has a good reputation locally so that outsiders are willing to lend to the co-operatives through the bank; and, finally, where workers build up deferred private ownership in their enterprises individually through the re-invested sharing of the profits. These conditions can be found in at least one highly successful group of third-sector enterprises — possibly the most successful co-operative system in the western world — Mondragón.

As is known from several recent descriptions in the literature (especially Campbell, Keen, Norman and Oakeshott, 1977) Mondragón is a group of over 70 mainly industrial co-operative enterprises in the Basque provinces of Spain which, in the generation since it was founded by a Catholic priest, José Maria Arizmendi, has expanded from a single firm with 23 workers to a federation of nearly 13,000, with a turnover of about £200m in 1976. There appear to be three fundamental reasons why Mondragón has succeeded: the fact that the individual workers (not the state or a collective) own the enterprise; the fact that it is a federation, not a single firm, and can respond to changing market conditions by asking workers to switch between trades and even between firms (a condition of the contract of employment); and the role of the co-operative bank, the *Caja Laboral Popular*, in providing finance, discipline and expert management advice.

The bank, founded in 1959, is owned by its staff and by the member firms. As with the individual co-operatives, an assembly of members elects a control board, which appoints the management. It lends money only to the co-operatives, and shares their interests (as a minor example, its staff receive the average profit-share of the federation). It has a management division which guides new co-operatives and monitors existing ones. If something goes wrong, instead of calling the loan (as a normal bank in the west would do) it investigates and helps put the problem right. In 20 years there has been only one commercial failure (a small fishing co-operative).

Workers put up an initial fee (currently £800) to enter, and receive a share in proportion to their pay of some 70 percent of the firm's annual profits. This is usually invested and drawn out only on retirement, so that 90 percent of all profit is ploughed back in a normal year. A worker's share can be transferred to other firms within the group, but 20 percent is lost if he leaves early except for compassionate reasons. Legal provisions and the standard contract between each firm and the bank require that 30 percent of profits go to a reserve fund and a social fund, with a higher proportion to reserves in years when profits are more than 50 percent of wages. The individual interests of Mondragón workers as sole owners coincide with those of the firm. They bear the losses as well as the profits. Thus they have an interest in hiring the most efficient management they can get. A general assembly of all members (one man one vote) elects the control board which meets monthly and can hire and fire top managers, while leaving them alone from day to day to appoint middle management and get on with their jobs. The highest paid manager gets 4½:1 differential from the lowest paid workers. The quality of the management attracted to Mondragón is said to be high.

The small size of each particular Mondragón enterprise is no doubt one of the reasons for the harmony and constructive enthusiasm that appear to impress all who visit the place. The only strike has been in the one large firm, ULGOR, which makes refrigerators, cookers and washing machines and now employs 3,462 workers.

Mondragón is devoted to education, and has recently been abolishing assembly lines and experimenting with group technology on the Volvo model. It stops short of creating a total co-operative environment like that of an Israeli kibbutz. Though it provides social security and health servies (denied by the state because co-operative workers are considered self-employed), workers live in their own homes, for example, rather than in any kind of collective housing.

There are special features of Mondragón that may make its success difficult to export wholesale: a local tradition of saving, strong Basque regional loyalty, benign neglect from central government and a tax structure which, in return for the 10 percent social fund and the absence of social security benefits, has since 1969 let cooperatives off lightly. But the essential features of Mondragón appear to be quite possibly exportable to other countries in the west. These are:

(a) the fact that those who work both control and own their enterprise through deferred individual shares;

(b) capital lent at low fixed interest rates by a co-operative bank sharing the interests of all the co-operative members and lending only to them;

(c) provisions to ensure that a sufficient proportion of profits is retained for investment;

(d) management expertise (in the case of Mondragón supplied also by the bank);

(e) a sufficient number of enterprises in a federation to provide varying employment for all members as demand inevitably fluctuates (such fluctuations being a function not of the particular economic system but of all large-scale economies, although central planning may exhibit them in different forms, e.g., as queues, gluts and unsatisfied or poorly satisfied consumers).

In Britain, interest in this whole range of ideas is growing. About 200 new co-operatives were started in Britain in 1976-8. In 1976 the Industrial Common Ownership Act defined a common-ownership enterprise in law for the first time, and in 1977 the Co-operative Productive Federation showed signs of establishing closer links with the common ownership movement and uniting to promote the growth of a 'third sector'. A Co-operative Development Agency — promised by the Labour Party since 1973 — started in 1978.

There is no suggestion here that the example of a single workable solution to the problems in Spain can override all the objections made by the pessimists and critics of the idea of self-management; still less is it suggested that argument at the level of pure economic theory or even of quantitative econometric measurement can settle matters conclusively in the real world. What happens in this 'third sector' will depend on chance and, no doubt, on creative misunderstanding as well as on wisdom and foresight. However, it is clear that both in practical and in theoretical terms the 'third sector' is at the moment particularly open to fresh developments in the west. It is also clear that there are formidable entrenched obstacles to its growth,and also reasoned objections that still require serious answers both in theory and in practice before it can be right to recommend such enterprises unreservedly to those who are considering investing their lives or their savings in them. However, some of the apparently most compelling reasoned objections rest on foundations that are themselves matters of a priori economic assumptions; and the validity of some of these assumptions is being questioned at the moment from within economic theory itself. Meanwhile, even if many of the objections still remain compelling, there may be ways of meeting them, practically, within the framework of self-managed enterprises; and these may turn out to be the most effective ways in such enterprises can in fact be organized.

REFERENCES

Alchian, Armen and Harold Demsetz (1972), 'Production, Information Costs, and Economic Organization', *American Economic Review*, 62, 27-52.

Argyle, Michael (1972), *The Social Psychology of Work*, London, Allen Lane, 1972.

Blumberg, Paul H. (1968), *Industrial Democracy: The Sociology of Participation*, London, Constable, 1968.

Campbell, Alastair, Charles Keen, Geraldine Norman and Robert Oakeshott (1977), *Worker-Owners: the Mondragón Achievement*, London, Anglo-German Foundation for the Study of Industrial Society, 1977.

Chiplin, Brian and John Coyne with Ljubo Sirc, *Can Workers Manage?* London, Institute of Economic Affairs, 1977.

FitzRoy, Felix R. and John R. Hiller (1978), *Efficiency and Motivation in Productive Organizations*, Berlin, International Institute of Management, Wissenschaftszentrum, Discussion paper 78-15.

Fox, Alan (1974), *Beyond Contract: Work, Power and Trust Relations*, London, Faber 1974.

Meade, J. E. (1972), 'The Theory of Labour-Managed Firms and Profit Sharing', *Economic Journal*, Special issue in honour of E. A. G. Robinson, March 1972,

402-28, reprinted in J. Vanek, *Self-Management: Economic Liberation of Man*, Harmondsworth, Penguin, 1975.

Sen, Amartya K. (1977), 'Rational Fools: A Critique of the Behavioural Foundations of Economic Theory', *Philosophy and Public Affairs*, 6, 317-44.

Vanek, Jaroslav (1970), *The General Theory of Labour Managed Economies*, Cornell, 1970.

12

SELF-MANAGEMENT AND COOPERATION AS THE VEHICLE OF THE NEW WORLD ECONOMIC ORDER

Jaroslav Vanek
Cornell University, USA

I INTRODUCTION

What is the relevance of self-management for the New International Economic Order? I have always felt that self-management, and in general control of their own environment and conditions emanating from those involved in the development process is the optimal course to follow. In the Preamble to the declaration on the establishment of a New International Economic Order of May 1974, we read:

> We, the members of the United Nations... solemnly proclaim our united determination to work urgently for the establishment of a New International Economic Order based on equity, sovereign equality, interdependence, common interest and cooperation among all states, irrespective of their economic and social system, which shall correct inequalities and address existing injustices, make it possible to eliminate the widening gap between the developed and the developing countries and insure steadily accelerating economic and social development and peace and justice for the present and future generations...

Clearly, the declaration is one of a humanistic conception of the New International Economic Order. Clearly, self-management, which by its very definition is based on the principles of participation and control on the basis of equality by those involved at various levels in the development process, is the most humanistic form of control of human affairs. Thus, without any doubt there is a deep philosophical consistency and harmony between the new economic order and self-management and economic self-determination.

But these statements of principle can serve us only as inspiration and points of departure for a much more careful and — in my view — much more useful and constructive analysis. Starting from the more general and moving towards the more specific, several broad notions must be grasped.

First of all, as is clearly implied by the above declaration, economic development and advancement of the less developed countries by no means should be equated to a never-ending process of economic growth and expansion irrespective of how the fruits of that growth are allocated among people, irrespective of how human dignity and fulfillment are affected thereby and irrespective of how the harmony among all peoples is enhanced or diminished. Once this conception of development is adopted, the case for self-management and economic self-determination is strengthened as against other forms of socio-economic organization. Especially in the context of the developing countries, a considerable edge becomes apparent over systems relying on private ownership of large enterprises and market forces, including those determining incomes. In Part II of our presentation below we will look more carefully into this broad economic significance of self-management and its comparative strength.

Another key issue that we must deal with in any meaningful discussion of the new economic order and world economic development is education. It is education that liberates human beings from their environment and from dependence. Again, it is education which allows people to work more efficiently and thus attain a higher degree of fulfillment and standard of living. And it is also education and dialogue that are at the heart of self-management and self-determination. And self-managed organization of work and the economy also becomes the most effective road towards a meaningful educational process. In Part III of our discussion we will delve into this important subject.

Probably the most important single reason for dependence associated with development today is the state and availability of and control over technology and organization of production. Again, as with education, self-management and self-determination implies control by people over technology and organization and development of their organic forms. These matters concerning technology, organization of work and self-management will concern us in Part IV.

Self-management, participatory education and what we may call organic technology are three key elements of an optimal structure defining a new world economic order. But these elements and this structure requires unity, requires to be put together. What will be the connecting forces? These forces as much as the structure must also be humanistic. These should not be markets which can blindly lead to immizeration of many and preserve opulence of some; they must be cooperative solutions arrived at freely by equals on principles of justice. Not that all markets and all market forces ought to be condemned, but only such can be accepted that are consistent with the over-riding rules of humanism. This cooperation, this uniting organic matter (not mortar or cement which are immutable without life) is also a form of self-management: it also reflects the spirit of the declaration of 1974. I will discuss these matters in more precise terms in the concluding part of this presentation.

II SELF-MANAGEMENT AS AN ECONOMIC SYSTEM

The New World Economic Order can be only as good as the economic orders of the countries which compose and which adhere to it. The member economies — and here I think in particular of the economies of the developing countries — must be as strong as possible and as healthy as possible. Only in this way will they become vigorous and truly independent partners in the order. We have advanced in our Introduction the proposition that self-management is the best guarantee of such economic health. And thus our first task is to substantiate our argument and show that in fact this is so. We will look in this part at the strictly economic aspects of this proposition, leaving other, broader considerations for other parts of our study.

It is true that theory without verification and without looking at real cases can never give full answers. But it is satisfying that the formal theory of self-management as an economic system gives that system a full bill of health on all accounts.[1] Not only will a decentralized self-managed economy grind out from given resources the maximum output but it will do so while guaranteeing the greatest satisfaction and fulfillment to the worker, with minimum alienation. The theory also tells us — and this is borne out by just about all experience of self-managed and cooperative workers' enterprises — that income distribution will tend to be equitable. It will be far more equitable than if determined strictly by forces of a market for labor, as in the capitalist economies.

But instead of dwelling on theory, let us look at actual facts. Yugoslavia offers us the most significant real example and its experience of self-management for over two decades is definitely most reassuring. The vitality of the economic system of Yugoslavia is such that it has not only been able to maintain itself in a world of very different economic organizations, but it has been able to progress and evolve to new and more democratic forms where working people can find an increasing degree of self-determination and self-management.

I will not dwell here on the many economic successes of the Yugoslav economy; there are many others who could do that better. But I would like to call attention to very recent work done in my Program on Participation and Labor-Managed Systems at Cornell University, piecing together several elements of analysis and evidence.[2] The results are based on some 70 countries, all the countries for which data were collected by the statisticians of the International Bank for Reconstruction and Development. In essence the analysis shows that self-management in itself (after the effects of structural inefficiency and other problems have been eliminated for the entire sample) is a system far superior in its productivity and overall economic performance as to other — what we may call — decentralized economies. This is not to say that Yugoslavia would not have structural and other problems, but these are not inherent in self-management.

Two brilliant doctoral theses, not yet published, were written in our Cornell Program. One is on the effects of participation in a sample of firms and industries during the Allende years in Chile and the other is on the performance of workers' cooperatives in England over the past 70 or 80 years.[3] Besides many other interesting results, both studies lead to a very clear conclusion that self-management and degree of participation is a positive factor of performance, innovative ability and job satisfaction.

There are a few self-managed enterprises in my own country, the United States. The fact that they are surviving and doing quite well in an entirely alien environment and that most of them sprung up from defunct capitalist firms through the efforts of their workers to me is the best testimony of viability of self-management.

Experience taken from many parts of the world teaches us that the problem of self-management is not the intrinsic efficacy of the economic organization (it is just the contrary); but self-management needs its own genuine environment, explicit recognition of interdependence, and a broad understanding by the whole society in which it is to be implanted. Thus isolated self-managed firms or cooperatives of workers in a capitalist environment are most unlikely to spread and eventually transform the whole economy. Self-management, to be successful, needs cooperation among many firms; it needs economic planning, specific to and organically related to self-management and it needs also some forms of national ownership and national control over capital formation. Without the latter, structural problems, distributional problems and deficiencies of the rate of capital accumulation will be inevitable.

All this points in the direction that a self-managed economy is scarcely possible without there being political will for it or at least a political openness which makes it possible to learn about the advantages of self-management. But this would bring me beyond the scope of my paper into areas where I do not consider myself expert and into areas that the New International Economic Order does not touch on explicitly.

The apologists of the capitalist system tell us that self-management is an impossibility in developing countries and that therefore a hierarchical, from top down, organization based on command is necessary because of the comparatively uneducated and undeveloped state of the worker. It would be naive not to recognize the significance of education; it would be even more naive to accept this fallacy, self-serving to those who enunciate it. The question of education and self-management is tremendously significant; we will devote to it Part III. But even here, to answer the above allegation, it should be noted that, while the workers in the developing country may be handicapped by their limited schooling, they may be tremendously advantaged because they and their ancestors may have been subjected for fewer generations, or not at all, to debilitating and oppressive forces. We have seen and have documented masterpieces of technical and organizational inventiveness in some parts of the world that my fellow American economists would call most undeveloped.[4] So much depends on the point of view: in a special issue of the French review, *Autogestion*, on the subject of self-management in North America, I argued that in fact my country is the most undeveloped country when it comes to self-management.[5] And yet no one has been able to refute the proposition that economic democracy and economic self-determination have as much right to be used as an indicator of development as aggregate output per capita.

III EDUCATION, SELF-MANAGEMENT AND THE NEW INTERNATIONAL ECONOMIC ORDER

The significance of learning and education for development and the New International Economic Order could hardly be over-emphasized. If we have had progress and evolution in the world economy, it has been first of all because we have learned how to master our environment, how to transform resources taken from nature to human advantage and because we have learned how to work together. Prior to capital and organization of production there had to be able, educated minds which made inventions and transformed and created that capital. Before there was any production there had to be skillful, human hands to carry it out.

But it is not only the historical logic that places learning and education in such an important position from our vantage point. Objective economic investigation leads to the same results. If we look at all the (44 or so) countries for which data are available, we find an incomparably higher contribution to development of income and output coming from resources allocated to education than to resources allocated to physical capital. It will be noted that these results obtained in our Program on Participation and Labor-Managed Systems at Cornell University measure the total social impact of resources allocated to education and not the so-called private or individual impact with which most western scholars are concerned.[6] Sometimes, it is also argued that income and development are the primary causes of education and not vice versa. But this proportion was subjected to an objective test both in my Program and by the experts of systems analysis at the New York University of Binghamton and has been strongly questioned and even if indeed some education were a consumption item[7] — as it may well be — the residual education which must be productive in our context would only have its productivity increased. This is so because a smaller expenditure on socially productive education would lead to the same increments in income and output and thus to a higher productivity.

But this is not the place to elaborate on technical details of an econometric investigation. What I would like to do now is to turn to the more specific question of self-management and education and do so referring to some further important results, also obtained in our Program. The case for self-management in the context of education is truly overwhelming.

First of all, it is well known that in the totality of the processes that we usually refer to as education a lot is a sheer waste from our point of view. It is education and learning which the student forgets, sooner or later, either because he never works with it or because he is not interested in it; or it is wasteful simply because it is untrue, or because it does not contribute to the burning problems of economic advancement and development. Because education is such a laborious and socially costly process, it is imperative to purify it (at least until humanity as a whole can afford it) of as much of this dead weight as possible. Education in the context of and through self-management in the place of work is most certainly the best method of doing this. Bringing the factory close to the school and the school to the factory and in most cases merging them together in a self-managed enterprise is the best guarantee (1) that priority will be given to things that are needed and relevant and (2) that the process will be one based on a cooperative dialogue and learning by doing (inherent in the very nature of self-management).[8]

Another one of our significant results — especially relevant for the developing countries — is that, in the sphere of education, very important time lags occur between the time resources are allocated to education and the time when the fruits of education are realized. Especially if generations of teachers must be educated as a precondition of general education of everyone, the time lags can be extreme. And this is also confirmed by our results.[9] Self-management — bringing together the educational and productive processes much more closely than other systems — can play an enormously important further role in enhancing the already significant effects of education. The time lags above noted between allocation of resources and reaping of fruits will be considerably shortened, and the need for a generation of school teachers can be reduced.

A further consideration is that a self-managed enterprise can internalize many benefits of education which in other systems and especially in profit-maximizing systems remain external and thus obstruct the education process. By this I mean that a workers' council of a self-managed enterprise often can vote an educational and training program even if costs are not fully recuperated in monetary terms. Indeed, some benefits to the community can arise in its direct satisfaction from improved knowledge and education. Especially in situations of considerable lack of development and education, this factor can be significant. An argument in the same direction is that democratic self-managed enterprises usually experience far greater stability of employment than profit-maximizing enterprises. And thus at least for this particular comparison there is the additional advantage that the fruits of an educational effort undertaken by the enterprise are likely to be enjoyed for a much longer period by the working community. And hence decisions to allocate resources to education will be taken much more easily.

Costs of the traditional type of education are so great these days that even in the richest countries they become prohibitive to large segments of the population. More modern, more effective and less costly methods must be sought everywhere, especially in the developing countries. Self-management, of course, provides directly an important portion of the answer. But there is also need for utilization of modern techniques of large scale electronic, television and radio communication media. But these methods, while efficient, carry within themselves the danger of misuse by some individuals (domestic and foreign) against others. Self-management and, more broadly, self-determination inherent in self-management are probably the best guarantees, for obvious reasons, against such misuse. More positively and constructively, the self-managed enterprise can provide the best and most objective source of information, at the base, about what educational programs are needed and desired in each particular area or industry.

My last point is general and relates directly to the New International Economic Order. The New Order cannot fully function until and unless all participating in it are imbued by its spirit — the spirit expressed in the quotation we have used in our Introduction. The many reservations of the developed countries to the Charter of the New Order is as much of a substantiation of what I am saying as the attitude of a typical American businessman or negotiator who believes that what the market decides is fundamentally just and desirable. And hence to have the New International Economic Order really implemented, all of us must be educated in its spirit and we must internalize it as a part of our outlook. But this cannot be done unless we also practise the principles of justice and cooperation in our immediate everyday life. And life and work in a self-managed environment become here the best instrument.

We will return to this subject in our last section. But even here the need for internal unity and logical consistency — call it organic harmony — becomes apparent. The elements are cooperation, self-management, education, justice and a New Economic Order and the emerging solutions must somehow all hang together. What must hold in the broad context must hold also in the narrow one; what is the heart of one domain must also be the heart of another; what is true in one context cannot be untrue in another.

IV TECHNOLOGY

Together with education, technology embodied in various concrete forms of capital is without any doubt the key factor of economic development and the strategy adopted by the developing countries with respect to it may play the decisive role in determining the success of the development process. But technology may also be a mix-ted blessing. Like a powerful drug, it can hurt or lead to dependence or, alternatively, it can help and be highly beneficial. Which alternative of the two will occur will depend precisely on the development strategy. Self-management, and, more generally, self-determination, as we will try to show in this section, is an important ingredient of the favorable outcome.

Most of the advanced technology reaching the developing countries, especially in the western orbit, and the manner in which it is transferred, is of the harmful 'inorganic' or 'alien' variety. It is developed in the advanced, richest countries of the world and heavily conditioned by (a) the availabilities and relative scarcities of productive factors in these countries; and (b) by the fundamentally capitalist organization of the advanced economies. Condition (a) tends to produce factor proportions, efficient scales of operation and forms of organization often very inappropriate for the developing countries. Very high capital to labor ratios, coupled with relative scarcity of capital, leads to minimal utilization of the labor force and the related phenomena of unemployment, underemployment and the dramatic maldistribution of income. What may be worse is that advanced technology indiscriminately applied, while related to creation of physical capital, may be destroying more traditional skills and 'human capital.'

The capitalist organization under (b) above, in its most pronounced form of multinational corporations reaching the developing countries, is likely to introduce a whole spectrum of undesirable effects ranging from economic to cultural and political. Extreme forms of dependence are being brought about. With or without the multinational corporation, an advanced complex technology coming from abroad most often is known only to those who produce it, that is, foreign engineers, technicians and organizers. Domestic people often play only a secondary role and acquisition of advanced skills and even partial mastery of the technology often requires extensive study in foreign countries. And this then often leads to uprooting and cultural expatriation. Those who go to study abroad often do not even return to their countries of origin and, if they do, they may become carriers of alien cultures, customs and outlooks which can be highly divisive from the point of view of the developing home countries.

What is probably the most irksome and economically conspicuous effect of such advanced technologies is that with the implicit very high capital-to-labor ratios there is very little hope that in any foreseeable future (even several generations) everyone in the world could be brought into the modern developmental sector. And thus if market forces were to remain the determinant of income distribution in the world, there would be very little hope for promotion of social welfare and truly improved material conditions for the majority in the developing countries. I do not expect that this will be the case in the long run and in fact I hope very much that this will not be so, but at least some residue of the pressures of relative market forces will always remain with us and thus the irksome effects of the inorganic advanced technology will always be with us as long as that technology prevails.

The corollary of income maldistribution under the inorganic technology is the de facto exploitation of those working under it by those possessing it. And this has unavoidable effects on class structures, power distribution and socio-political harmony whether within the developing countries or between them and the developed countries.

Obviously this is only a sketch of the problems inherent in modern technology which we have termed inorganic. And it is not our task here to transform the sketch into a complete treatise. [10] What we should do now is to turn to a more positive analysis of technology in its salutary form — the form which we have compared above to good and positive effects of a medication. We may refer to it as the organic technology.

By organic technology I mean modern technology based on the most advanced results of basic research, but technology subservient to the people of the developing countries rather than one oppressing them and making them dependent. It is that technology only over which the developing countries on the various levels of each country individually and of each firm using the technology — have full control. The developing countries also at all these levels must be able to control the main effects of technology and be in command of the processes by which technology is brought about, transferred and maintained. What is necessary for organic technology is self-management in its broadest sense, that is, economic and technological self-determination in the developing countries at all the three levels noted.

On the broadest level of the 77 there is considerable scope for cooperation in developing an organic technology for the developing countries. Ideally this ought to be done under the auspices of the United Nations, an effort which at least in part could be funded by the advanced countries. The effort would have to be quite considerable, delving into fairly concrete engineering studies in a continuing dialogue with those in the developing countries who would be using the new technology. Fruits of such extensive technological researches as much as other intermediate technologies adopted would have to become public goods to be used by all countries involved. The absurdity of present patent laws and other forms of monopolization of technological know-how is obvious. In a period when poverty and underdevelopment in the world are most critical issues, monopolization of technical know-how can lead to very bad effects, including loss of life. This is not to say that inventive efforts should not be stimulated in other ways.

In fact, self-management in enterprises, the third and most basic level of self-determination noted above, seems to be itself the best stimulus to innovation and adaptation of new technology. The growth of total productivity and overall efficiency, as shown in Yugoslavia, certainly indicates this.[11] Similar results were obtained for British workers' cooperatives in a doctoral dissertation by Derek Jones.[12]

Self-management can also play a further significant role in transferring technology — technology which automatically becomes organic because accepted by self-determining enterprises — from the advanced countries. Self-managed enterprises in the developing countries could attract technicians and organizational experts from the advanced countries not as members of multinational corporations but, so to speak, on a human and individual basis. Here I speak from direct experience. Many graduate students from the Cornell Business School (in fact the best among them) come into my courses on self-management frustrated by the outlook that the only jobs that they can get after ending school are jobs in capitalist corporations. I am sure that many would be happy to go to a developing country as individuals if they could participate in a democratic organization of work, even with incomes well below what the multinational corporations can offer.

A related argument is what I call in one of my other papers civilizing the multinational corporation.[12] This civilizing effect involves mandatory transformation of foreign corporations operating on the soil of the developing countries into self-managed enterprises where foreign technicians and organizers can stay on a personal basis as members of the democratic community together with domestic nationals of the developing countries, and not as wielders of power delegated to them by the corporate headquarters in New York. The human advantages of this are obvious. Of course the transformation necessitates re-negotiation of contracts on debt and patents and technology. The method also provides a significant safeguard against improper transfer pricing and tax avoidance so frequently encountered among multinational corporations. The effort of civilizing the multi-nationals would of course greatly depend on the ability of the developing countries to cooperate. In the absence of such cooperation, the leverage of individual developing countries might be too small to be effective.

The direct effect of self-management on the developing of an organic technology can be expected to be favorable for several reasons. First of all, no one knows as well as the working community in a particular place what are the many human, social and economic conditions. For example, introduction of a technology destroying or eliminating existing human skills, and thereby leading to massive unemployment, will be far less likely. A major problem today in some developing countries' agriculture is substitution of capital- and land-intensive exportable luxury crops for basic food crops produced with high labor intensity. Such changes destroy jobs as much as basic skills and result from the profit motive of absentee owners. They could never occur under self-management and self-determination. Technical knowledge concerns not only machines, equipment and technical processes, but also matters of organization, decentralization and hierarchical structures. Here, self-determination by those involved can lead to entirely different and far more desirable solutions than those offered by a capitalist organization. Moreover, because communication and dialogue is the very nature of self-management, minor everyday technical improvements heavily depending on such communication and dialogue are more likely to occur. And this is further strengthened by the collective self-interest in a democratic structure as compared to an oppressive exploiting organization.

Of paramount importance for the development of organic factor proportions in new technology which are adapted to factor availabilities in the developing countries is proper factor pricing. More specifically, capital must be relatively expensive so that as a resource it would not be misused by some while being unavailable to others. But here the self-management solution — especially a socialist self-management solution — offers an enormous advantage. Without going into details, let it just be noted that under capitalist conditions high capital prices — that is, rentals — imply exploitation of labor and extreme maldistribution of income towards the capital-owning classes. Under self-management, high prices of capital imply higher incomes for workers to the extent that workers' collectives are owners and, perhaps more realistically, higher national income and national accumulation for society if society is the owner.

V INTERNATIONAL COOPERATION AND PRICING

We now come to the fourth and last building block of our analysis involving the problem of pricing, transfer and income distribution between the rich and the poor countries. These arguments also are the oldest within the dialogue between the rich and the developing countries, most often associated with the name of Dr. Raul Prebisch, the originator of the United Nations Conference on Trade and Development. Early after the second world war it was realized that there was something wrong with the distribution of income inherent in the terms of trade between the developed and the developing nations and that something ought to be done to rectify the inherent injustice through an adjustment of one kind or another of the terms of trade relationships. The response of the western economists and hence of the politicians has become a masterpiece of distortion and hypocrisy. (Here I speak with a good deal of authority because I am also a western economist trained at MIT who, prior to a process of self-deschooling, was taught to believe these arguments.)

The arguments offered are that transfer through price rectification of whatever kind is sub-optimal (Pareto sub-optimal as economists like to call it) and that, instead, so-called lump-sum transfers, that is, transfers of purchasing power, ought to be utilized in correcting world-wide income maldistribution. But such transfers did not occur at all or remained minimal with respect to the size and volume of international trade between the developing and developed countries. There is no need to remind ourselves that it took many years before, through unilateral action on the part of the developing countries, some of the 'rents' of international exchange were returned — but returned, as in the case of oil, in a most haphazard and disorderly manner.

The truth of the matter is indeed that exploitation of the poor by the rich through international trade can attain fantastic dimensions. The model used by western trade economists in fact is incorrect and, using a theory which closely reflects conditions in the real world, it becomes apparent that at the heart of the process of exploitation are: (1) the enormous differences between wages in the rich and the poor countries (sometimes reaching 10,000 percent); (2) imperfections of the worldwide capital and labor markets; (3) the monopoly of ownership of technology and capital, and (even if in a sense justifiable) monopoly power of labor unions in the developed countries.[13] In a nutshell, what is at stake is that the values of developing countries' exports are pegged, so to speak, to the low subsistence wage prevailing in those countries, whereas values and prices of exports of the rich countries can climb, so to speak, without limit, buttressed by an interaction between technical progress, innovation and union demands for higher wages. Workers of the rich countries thus unwittingly become partners of the exploitative process of the developing nations, as much as the rich in some of the poor countries. Of course, what is to blame for all this in the final analysis are not the workers but the essentially capitalist market relationships ruling a good portion of the international exchanges in question.

It is not our task here to analyze in further detail all the complexities of the problem at hand. Perhaps we can return to them in our discussion. My main task in this section is to show how self-management could help us in the world to resolve these problems. Several arguments can be offered, ranging from very concrete economic to general and almost philosophical ones.

The first, while broader, is well illustrated by the situation which we have called in the preceding section civilizing the multinational corporations. If such a corporation is 'civilized' and its operations in a given developing country become a self-managed enterprise, then by definition the product produced in the country by the particular self-managed plant is appropriated by the working community. Only contractual payments must be made for borrowed capital, patents, all costs, taxes, etc. But the rent which normally accrues to the multinational corporation, represented by the differential between the value of the product and the labor cost (often reckoned at subsistence wages), now accrues to the working community. This does not mean that such rents, if very high, ought necessarily to be given to the workers in the community. But if it is deemed socially undesirable, the excesses can be taxed away or, even better, earmarked for further development and expansion of output and employment.

The members of the working community, while looking after their own interest, will also protect the interest of the developing country and the tax base from which the entire society benefits. This should be contrasted with the often impossible control over multinational corporations who, through transfer pricing and other devices, avoid taxes and in other ways pull down the very terms of trade that we spoke about above.

What we have pointed out in the example of civilizing the multinational corporations of course pertains to all firms operating in a developing country. The appropriation of the product by the working community and not by the owners of capital will always improve distribution of income between the rich and the poor, whether internationally or on the national plane of the developing country itself. After all, the objective of the New International Economic Order must be distributive justice and fairness everywhere and not only across national borders.

At the other end of the spectrum we have the more psychological and in fact philosophical fact that self-management fundamentally is a system based on justice and cooperation among those who work for their own living; whereas the moving force and raison d'être of the liberal market capitalism which so much influences our international relations is maximization of profit from trade in commodities and services produced by others than those for whom profits are maximized. As we have noted above, it is hard to expect a system based on this type of profit maximization to practise justice and fairness in determining prices for transactions. For is it not precisely by minimizing wages and maximizing selling prices to one's own advantage that the capitalist enterprise achieves its objective? To expect fair terms of trade from capitalist systems is like expecting flies to fly under the water.

By contrast, self-management's very purpose in a departure from a capitalist organization is distributive justice and humanization of relations of work. And distributive justive is precisely the objective of the New International Economic Order in general, and of fair exchange market values in particular. To this we must add the almost obvious — that the people living in a certain working relationship are also the same people as those determining, in international negotiations and elsewhere, the conditions of exchange.

This brings me to some further reflections with which I would like to conclude my discussion. Not only are the notions of justice and fairness inherent in self-management in an abstract and philosophical sense but in fact some necessary operating mechanisms of self-management very concretely call for distributive justice as a precondition of an efficient operation. To be concrete, suppose that in a factory one department supplies a semi-finished product to another. If the departments are to be at least partly autonomous for the purposes of democratic self-management, they must have an appropriate transfer price at which the semi-finished product is accounted for in such transactions. And the efficient or optimal price is the one which leads to equal incomes for workers in the two departments.

Of course, to transpose the essence of this example directly from transactions between two departments in a single factory to transactions between the developing and rich countries is not a simple matter. It is complex not only because of many unresolved economic, social and political questions, but also because many things in the real world cannot be accomplished overnight. Nevertheless, the situation ought to serve as a long range objective consistent with the spirit of the New International Economic Order. The role of transfer pricing in international income distribution and the many technical and factual questions related to it ought also to constitute a subject for research of high priority for those concerned with the issues at hand, whether the United Nations, the Organization of the '77' or others. it is my distinct feeling that the more recent experiences with social agreements (*drustveni dogovov*) in Yugoslavia, as regulatory devices of the economy based on dialogue and participation, are relevant here.

NOTES

1. J. Vanek, *General Theory of Labor-Managed Market Economies*. Ithaca, NY: Cornell University Press, 1970; *The Participatory Economy: An Evolutionary Hypothesis and a Strategy for Development*. Ithaca, NY: Cornell University Press, 1971; *Self-Management: Economic Liberation of Man* (ed.). Harmonsdworth, Mddx.: Penguin, 1975; *The Labor-Managed Economy: Essays*. Ithaca, NY; Cornell University Press, 1977.

2. J. Vanek, 'Workers' Management and Labour Management in Theory and Practice: A Comparative Study,' Cornell Department of Economics Discussion Paper No. 119; J. Vanek and J. Espinosa, 'The Subsistence Income, Effort and Development Potential of Labour Management and Other Economic Systems,' in *The Labor-Managed Economy: Essays*, op. cit.; B. Balassa and T. J. Bertrand, 'Growth Performance of Eastern European Economies and comparable Western European Countries,' in *Self-Management: Economic Liberation of Man*, op. cit.; S. K. Singh, *Development Economics: Some Findings*. Lexington, Mass.: D. C. Heath, 1975.

3. D. Jones, 'The Economics of British Producer Cooperatives,' Cornell PhD Dissertation, May 1974; J. Espinosa, 'The Experience of Worker Participation in the Management of Industrial Firms (The Case of the Social Ownership Area in Chile: 1970-1973,' Cornell PhD Dissertation, *PPLMS Series of Unpublished Studies*, No. 12, 1976.

4. For example, in Castle Bruce, a workers' agricultural cooperative in the Caribbean Island of Dominica an alternative to a one million dollar irrigation system was developed, based on indigenous bamboo pipes, by workers with no engineering training.

5. *Autogestion*, novembre 1975, No. 32.

6. Ante Lauc calculated that $Y = 73 + 2.63 \, X_1 + 0.11 \, X_2$ where Y is income per capital, X_1 is estimated cost of education per worker and X_2 is estimated value of capital per worker. Even accepting that the data and methods are crude, for 44 countries, it is clear that rate of return on education is larger by far than that on capital. Lauc's work on the subject was summarized in 'An Introduction to the Design of Social Development: An Attempt to Operationalize and Verify the Neglected Theory of Hegel' — a paper written for and available in the Program on Participation and Labor-Managed Systems of Cornell University. G. S. Becker and M. Blaug in their *Human Capital* and *Economics of Education* respectively, argue that investment in human capital has 2-3 times larger return than investment on physical capital. These two authors have used the monetary return (private benefits) while the social benefits as measured by Lauc suggest much larger returns.

7. Hugo Autenhove, an expert in Systems Theory at the State University of New York, Binghamton, has worked on the same subject as Dr. Lauc and, according to his results, the relation between these variables is in the order of human capital (i.e., education), efficiency and physical capital.

8. J. Vanek and T. Bayard, 'Education Toward Self-Management: An Alternative Development Strategy,' *International Development Review*, Vol. XVII, No. 4, 1975.

9. When Dr Lauc's sample is broken down into developed and less developed countries, we find a more significant impact of evaluation for the former. And this appears to be the reflection of the fact that the relatively poor countries did not yet have time enough to realize full fruits of their early educational efforts and of considerable neglect of education in just about all developing countries prior to their national or social liberation. The average impact of education on income in developed countries is 2.46 and for less developed countries is only 0.65.

10. J. Vanek, 'The Absurdity of the Rich Man's Trade Doctrine and Institutions for the Present Day World Economy and An Attempt to Reformulate,' Cornell University Department of Economics Discussion Paper No. 125. Also by J. Vanek, 'On Power, Oppression and Liberation in the World.' These two papers were presented for discussion at the International conference on Possibilities for the Liberation of Work and Political Power in Dubrovnik, January-February 1977.

11. J. Vanek, 'Self-Management, Workers' Management and Labor Management in Theory and Practice: A Comparative Study,' op. cit.

12. Jones, op. cit.

13. See the first article mentioned in Footnote 10 above.

NOTES ON CONTRIBUTORS

Peter Abell is Professor of Sociology at the University of Birmingham. His publications include *Organisations as Bargaining and Influence Systems* (ed., 1975), *On the General Theory of Social Class* (1980) and 'The Many Faces of Power and Liberty: Revealed Preferred Autonomy and Teleological Explanation,' *Sociology*, Vol. 13, 1977.

Eric Batstone is Senior Research Fellow at the SSRC Industrial Relations Research Unit, University of Warwick. His publications include *Industrial Democracy: European Experience* (with P. L. Davies, 1976) and *Shop Stewards in Action: The Organization of Workplace Conflict and Accommodation* (with I. Boraston and S. Frenkel, 1977).

Thomas Baumgartner holds a PhD from the University of New Hampshire. He is presently Research Fellow at the Université de Louvain and Senior Researcher at the Energy and Society Project, Institute of Sociology, University of Oslo. He is involved in policy research from the perspective of an actor-oriented systems theory in areas of development and the international order, energy and technology, planning and social accounting, as well as industrial democracy.

Tom Burns is Professor at the Universities of Oslo/Stockholm and Senior Researcher at the Scandinavian Institutes for Administrative Research (Stockholm). He has published articles on international and industrial conflict, political and economic sociology. He is currently conducting research on energy policy and institutions, industrial democracy, and community planning and development.

Alasdair Clayre is a television producer, author and scholar. His interests are in political science and from 1970-76 he was a producer of programmes for the Open University and in 1977 was Political Correspondent for the *Economist*. A Fellow of All Souls College,

Oxford, since 1959, he is author of *Work and Play* and editor of *Nature and Industrialization*.

Edmund Dahlström is Professor of Sociology at the University of Gothenburg. His areas of interest centre on social stratification, industrial relations and the sociology of knowledge. His publications include *Industri och arbetsorganisationer i Svensk samhällsstruktur i sociologisk belysning* (1965), *Fördjupad företagsdemokrati* (1969) and 'Produktion och jämlikhet' in G. Nordenstam, ed., *Värde, välfärd och jämlikhet* (1972).

Philippe DeVille holds a PhD in Economics from Stanford University and taught for several years at the University of New Hampshire. He is a former Professeur Invité at the University of Montreal and is currently at the Université de Louvain.

Bjorn Gustavsen is Director of the Institute of Work Psychology at the Work Research Institutes in Oslo. His background is in theoretical-descriptive as well as in action-oriented field research into working life. He has published a number of books and articles and took part in the preparation and execution of the new Norwegian Work Environment Act.

Branko Horvat trained in Economics, Sociology and Philosophy at Zagreb, Manchester, Harvard and MIT. He is Professor of Economics at the University of Zagreb and a Fellow of the Institute of Economic Sciences, Belgrade. He has taught at various Yugoslav universities and also at Ann Arbor, Washington, Santiago, Stockholm, Dar es Salaam, Notre Dame and Paris. He has published some 200 articles and 20 books, including *Economic Models, Interindustry Analysis, Towards a Theory of a Planned Economy, Business Cycles in Yugoslavia, The Yugoslav Economic System, Economic Analysis* and *Economics of Stabilization*.

Gerry Hunnius is an Associate Professor in the Social Science Department of Atkinson College, York University, Toronto. He is an author and co-editor of *Workers' Control: A Reader on Labor and Social Change* (1973).

Lars Erik Karlsson is Professor of Social Psychology of Working Life at the University of Luleå, Sweden. He has been active in the field of workers' self-management since 1969 and is the author of *Demokrati på arbetsplatsen* (Democracy at Work), among other books and articles on workers' participation and industrial democracy.

Veljko Rus is Senior Research Fellow at the Institute of Sociology, Ljubljana. His current research focuses on industrial democracy in Europe, decision-making in work organizations, and the meaning of work. He has published extensively in Yugoslavia and abroad, and is completing a book on the division of labour and alienation of work.

Dusko Sekulić is Assistant Professor of Sociology at the University of Zagreb. In 1977-78 he was Visiting Researcher at the University of South Carolina. He has published articles on planning, organizational theory, methodology and the development of Yugoslav society.

Finn Valentin is Associate Professor at the University of Copenhagen. His previous publications have centred on the relationship between state and class structure in countries with mixed economies, particularly Denmark.

Jaroslav Vanek is Professor of International Studies and Economics at Cornell University.